Personality, Social Skills, and Psychopathology

An Individual Differences Approach

PERSPECTIVES ON INDIVIDUAL DIFFERENCES

CECIL R. REYNOLDS, *Texas A&M University, College Station*
ROBERT T. BROWN, *University of North Carolina, Wilmington*

Current volumes in the series

Personality, Social Skills, and Psychopathology

An Individual Differences Approach

Edited by

David G. Gilbert

Department of Psychology
Southern Illinois University at Carbondale
Carbondale, Illinois

and

James J. Connolly

Private Practice
New London, Connecticut

PLENUM PRESS • NEW YORK AND LONDON

Library of Congress Cataloging-in-Publication Data

Personality, social skills, and psychopathology : an individual
  differences approach / edited by David G. Gilbert and James J.
  Connolly.
      p.   cm. -- (Perspectives on individual differences)
  Includes bibliographical references and index.
  ISBN 0-306-43793-7
      1. Psychology, Pathological. 2. Social skills--Psychological
  aspects. 3. Personality. 4. Individual differences.   I. Gilbert,
  David, G., 1947 Oct. 12- II. Connolly, James J., 1950-   .
  III. Series.
      [DNLM: 1. Interpersonal Relations. 2. Mental Disorders.
  3. Models, Psychological. 4. Personality. 5. Social Behavior.   WM
  100 P469]
  RC454.4.P464 1991
  155.2--dc20
  DNLM/DLC
  for Library of Congress   91-21360
                                                                 CIP

ISBN 0-306-43793-7

© 1991 Plenum Press, New York
A Division of Plenum Publishing Corporation
233 Spring Street, New York, N.Y. 10013

Printed in the United States of America

Contributors

Thomas N. Bradbury, Department of Psychology, University of California, Los Angeles, California 90024

David W. Brokaw, Azusa Pacific University, Azusa, California 91702

Ross Buck, Department of Communication Sciences, University of Connecticut, Storrs, Connecticut 06269–1085

Emil Chiauzzi, Northeast Psychiatric Associates, Brookside Hospital, Nashua, New Hampshire 03063

James J. Connolly, Private Practice, 400 Bayonet Street, New London, Connecticut 06320

Frank D. Fincham, Department of Psychology, University of Illinois at Urbana–Champaign, Champaign, Illinois 61820

Brenda O. Gilbert, Department of Psychology, Southern Illinois University at Carbondale, Carbondale, Illinois 62901–6502

David G. Gilbert, Department of Psychology, Southern Illinois University at Carbondale, Carbondale, Illinois 62901–6502

Stephen P. Hinshaw, Department of Psychology, University of California, Berkeley, California 94720

Joyce Hogan, Department of Psychology, University of Tulsa, Tulsa, Oklahoma 74104

Robert Hogan, Department of Psychology, University of Tulsa, Tulsa, Oklahoma 74104

Jack E. Hokanson, Department of Psychology, Florida State University, Tallahassee, Florida 32306

Michael A. McColloch, Private Practice, 3779 Vest Mill Road, Winston-Salem, North Carolina 27103

James P. McHale, Department of Psychology, University of California, Berkeley, California 94720

Clinton W. McLemore, Relational Dynamics Institute, Inc., P.O. Box 60725, Pasadena, California 91116

Mark P. Rubert, Department of Psychology, Florida State University, Tallahassee, Florida 32306

Preface

This book presents an introduction to the study of relationships among personality, social skills, and psychopathology. Although research findings during the last decade have made it clear that the relationships among these variables are almost always complex and multiply determined, many clinicians and theoreticians have not incorporated such complexities into their models of human behavior and therapeutic intervention. This discrepancy between clinical theory and research-based findings has been of special concern to us because we have been both empirically oriented academic researchers and practicing clinicians. It is our belief that clinical theory related to personality, social skills, and psychopathology can be enriched by research findings from a wide range of fields—from human genetics, temperament, and personality to family systems, affect, psychophysiology, and learning.

This book is divided into an introductory chapter and three sections. The introductory chapter provides an overview of the issues in the field, compares models, and provides suggestions for further integration and articulation of concepts related to personality, social skills, and psychopathology. The book's first section presents state-of-the-art general models of interactions among personality, social skills, and psychopathology. Connolly opens this section with a chapter that reviews longitudinal findings indicating that personality traits predict the onset of psychopathology and marital distress. The etiology of these and related findings is the subject of other chapters in this section. Brokaw and McLemore review interpersonal models of personality and psychopathology and provide an in-depth analysis of Benjamin-Smith's interpersonal model and its empirical support. Interpersonal models have not focused on what variables determine individuals' tendencies to adopt a particular social style. Thus Buck's chapter complements that of Brokaw and McLemore by addressing the important question of the development of individual differences in social and emotional skills. In this way, Buck provides a transition from the interpersonal domain to the more traditional individual focus on the relationship of personality to social behavior and psychopathology. Gilbert presents a model that builds on Buck's findings as it predicts social interaction as a function of the personalities of the interactants and the setting. The personality × personality × setting biosocial model developed by Gilbert relates individual differences in temperamental, personality, and psychophysiological processes to interpersonal processes, including emotional arousal and skill in interpersonal conflict resolution. In the final chapter of the first section, Robert and Joyce Hogan discuss relationships of personality and social behavior to social acceptance and status.

The book's second section provides excellent reviews of the relations of social skills to specific psychopathologies. Hokanson and Rubert assess interpersonal and social skill factors in the development and maintenance of depression. McColloch and Gilbert assess the development, maintenance, and stability of aggression in a review that pays close attention to the role of social skills in these processes. Chiauzzi assesses conceptual, methodological, and treatment issues in the social skill training for alcoholics. The effects of medication on social interactions have important implications for any model of interpersonal processes and social skill. The chapter by Hinshaw and McHale provides information that is a challenge for all models' interpersonal process. Stimulant medications have predictable effects on social interactions of hyperactive children. Such medication-induced effects can be viewed as pharmacologically induced changes of temperament and, thus, can be used to assess the role of the individual in social interactions.

In the book's final section, Bradbury and Fincham provide an excellent review of various state-of-the-art means of analyzing sequential social interactions. The techniques they review provide a means of operationalizing and assessing many of the social skills and processes that are the topic of this book.

We wish to thank all our authors for their cooperation and perseverance in producing this book. We believe that the final product is well worth their labors.

David Gilbert wishes to thank his family for their support, for their teaching so much about what can be good about social relationships: his wife Brenda for being the stable and supportive person he needed; his children Aline and Elizabeth, who contributed to this book with their love and wonderful—yet different—personalities; and his parents Naomi and Wyn Gilbert, who modeled how to have a successful family and marriage. James Connolly wants to thank his wife Roberta for her support. We both want to thank our colleagues at Plenum Press for their support and Robert T.

Brown, series editor, who encouraged us to make it the best book it could be.

David G. Gilbert
James J. Connolly

Carbondale and New London

Contents

Chapter 6 **Personality and Status** 137

Robert Hogan and Joyce Hogan

PART II. SOCIAL SKILLS AND SPECIFIC PSYCHOPATHOLOGIES

Chapter 7 **Interpersonal Factors in Depression** 157

Jack E. Hokanson and Mark P. Rubert

Chapter 8 **Development and Maintenance of Aggressive
    Behavioral Patterns** 185

Michael A. McColloch and Brenda O. Gilbert

PART III. STATISTICAL APPROACHES TO SOCIAL INTERACTION ANALYSIS

CHAPTER ONE

Personality, Social Skills, and Disturbed Behavior Patterns

An Introduction to the Issues

BRENDA O. GILBERT AND DAVID G. GILBERT

INTRODUCTION

The question of how psychopathology is related to social skills and to personality and temperament is important for a number of practical and theoretical reasons. Different clinical interventions make different assumptions concerning the causal relationships among personality, social skills, and psychopathology. Dissatisfaction among behaviorally oriented clinicians and researchers with personality-trait-based and nonempirically based (predominantly psychodynamic) conceptualizations of psychopathology and social behavior contributed to the rapid development and extensive use of social skills assessment and training (Phillips, 1985). During the last quarter of this century many social-skill-oriented writers (e.g., Gottman, 1979; Wine, 1981) and social systems theorists (e.g., Watzlawick, 1977; Watzlawick & Beavin, 1977) have criticized psychodynamic and other trait models that assume defects in development, biology, or personality cause psychopathology and interpersonal distress. Such criticism, in part, may be based on the misperception that for the social skills and learning orientations to be useful, productive, and valid, conceptualizations from trait and biological models of behavior must be useless, unproductive, and invalid.

BRENDA O. GILBERT AND DAVID G. GILBERT • Department of Psychology, Southern Illinois University at Carbondale, Carbondale, Illinois 62901-6502.

Personality, Social Skills, and Psychopathology: An Individual Differences Approach, edited by David G. Gilbert and James J. Connolly. Plenum Press, New York, 1991.

Because social skills training has been demonstrated to be highly effective in treating a number of different psychopathologies and behavioral disorders (L'Abate & Milan, 1985), social skills practitioners and theorists have tended to assume that the trait and biological views contain little of value. Social learning and skill theorists have also criticized trait and biological models of psychopathology and social behavior by noting that behavior of individuals is highly situation specific (Epstein, 1979, 1983), something not addressed by simplistic biological and trait models.

Criticism of biological and trait models has persisted in spite of the fact that biologically oriented researchers have developed effective psychotropic medications and have demonstrated important genetic and biological contributions to personality (Eysenck & Eysenck, 1985) and most of the major psychopathologies (Berger & Brodie, 1986). Furthermore, other developments during the last two decades have shown that although behavior is situation specific, it is also generalizable across time and situations (as personality theorists have argued) (Epstein, 1979, 1983). Thus, given the success of their models, proponents of biological and personality/temperament-based models of psychopathology may minimize, ignore, or reject the importance of learning and social skill factors in the development of psychopathology.

However, all three groups, the social skills researchers, personality theorists, and biological theorists, have clearly demonstrated the causal contributions of their variables to social behavior and psychopathology. This book approaches these three theoretical orientations from the view that now is the time to seriously address the importance of all three approaches and to strive for the integration and enrichment of concepts, rather than competition and hostile criticism. This book reflects our attempt to provide a balanced introduction to theoretical issues related to relationships between genetics, environment, temperament, personality, social skills, and psychopathology. In contrast to most previous works in this area, a number of possible mechanisms mediating relationships between genetics, personality, social skill, and psychopathology are discussed.

DEFINITIONAL AND CONCEPTUAL ISSUES

Psychologists vary in how they define personality, social skills, and psychopathology. It has been noted that there may be as many different meanings of the term *personality* as there are personality theorists; nonetheless, most definitions include the concept of individual differences in behavior, thoughts, and emotions that characterize an individual (Mischel, 1986, p. 4). Mischel also notes that the study of personality should examine how individuals interact with and influence their own life situations. Thus, it is believed by Mischel (as well as the editors and authors of this volume) that personality should be assessed in a social context, interacting with other "personalities" in different situations.

The concept of social skills is narrower, more situation specific, and learning based than is that of personality. In addition to differing degrees and types of social skills, the term *personality* implies a moderate degree of temporal and cross-situational stability (Epstein, 1979, 1983), as well as temperamental/genetic contributions that interact with the environmental setting (Gilbert, present volume; Eysenck & Eysenck, 1985). Another difference between personality and skill constructs is that of aims, goals, and preferences (see Hogan, present volume) versus skill in achieving these goals. Social skill is defined by Bellack and Hersen (1977, p. 145) as "an individual's ability to express both positive and negative feelings in the interpersonal context without suffering consequent loss of social reinforcement . . . in a large variety of interpersonal contexts . . . [involving] . . . the coordinated delivery of appropriate verbal and nonverbal responses." Although this broad and general definition of social skills seems to imply traitlike, cross-situational abilities, social skills research, unlike personality investigations, has focused on the specificity of social skills and the degree to which they do not generalize from one situation to another (Phillips, 1985). Thus a more recent definition by Schlundt and McFall (1985) defines social competence as the effectiveness of an individual's performance on a given task and social skills as the component processes that allow the individual to behave in a competent manner on a task. They note that "different tasks require different skills because the specific shape of competent behavior will vary from one task to the next."

What is the relationship of personality to social skills and social competence? Social skill has been shown to be related to extraversion and neuroticism, two well-researched, temperamentally/genetically based higher-order personality constructs (Gilbert, present volume). Additionally, it is reasonable to hypothesize that temperamentally based personality factors (behavioral dispositions) such as extraversion and neuroticism may play a more important role in individual differences in performance deficits (failure to implement an existing skill) than in skill deficits because these personality dimensions are related to the expression and inhibition of behavior. Emotional processes correlate with different temperamentally based traits and are involved in the inhibition of and timing of social-skill-based behavior (Gilbert, present volume). That is, one may have a specific skill but not exhibit it or show poor timing and execution due to propensities related to his/her personality. For example, one may know how to greet someone appropriately but, due to an emotional trait, either perform an awkward greeting (looking down, not smiling, looking uncomfortable) or fail to greet the other person at all. Furthermore, implementation of social skills is dependent not only on the capacity and knowledge of what to do but also when to display different skills, control and flexibility in displaying them, and motivation to do so (Michenbaum, Butler, & Gruson, 1981; Schwartz & Gottman, 1976). In their chapters, Buck and Gilbert argue that genetically based temperamental factors influence social skills and social environment, as well as the social expectations that an individual experiences by a series of complex feedback and feedforward systems.

Psychopathology, like personality and social skills, has been defined variously, and its etiology has undergone much speculation. Localization of psychopathology has been placed within the individual, within a social interaction, or within society. Whereas personality theorists tend to focus on internal individual resources and processes, environmental and skill-oriented theorists generally include the theme of poor behavioral adaptation or inadequate behavioral coping in one's environment as the essential portion of the definition (Phillips, 1985; Wine, 1981). Dohrenwend and Dohrenwend (1969) suggested that psychopathology is the outcome of severe stresses in otherwise normal individuals. Phillips (1985) similarly stated that pathology results from the interaction of deficient personal resources combined with stressful circumstances that the person cannot successfully resolve. Thus the focus is on an interaction of skill level and environmental stress level. Personality theorists such as Eysenck (1967) view psychopathology from a somewhat more complex diathesis (genetic plus learning predisposition) × environmental stress model. The diathesis–stress model is a significant conceptual advancement over pure social skills and simplistic personality trait models in that it combines social skill concepts with genetic dispositions to be skilled, as well as to be stress reactive. Furthermore, diathesis–stress models that include genetic–temperamental contributions suggest that certain environments will be more conducive to skillful performance by some personality types, whereas other environments will be conducive to skilled performance by other types. All of the models of personality presented by the authors of this volume use some form of a diathesis–stress model.

DIRECTIONS OF CAUSAL INFLUENCE

Genetics, environment, personality, social skill, and psychopathology may be interrelated through numerous possible and plausible direct and indirect causal paths. Some of these pathways have been seriously explored, whereas many equally plausible models have not been given adequate attention. It is clear that an extremely dysfunctional environment can lead directly to skill deficits, personality defects, and psychopathology. In the case of such extreme environmental dysfunction, it is unlikely that skill and personality deficits must mediate psychopathology. Trauma and classical conditioning may directly result in such cases, irrespective of any additional skill and personality deficits. A single environmental cause would result in correlations among personality, social skill, and psychopathology, independent of any causal interaction among the latter three variables.

In contrast to such simple and direct causal relationships, most theorists acknowledge that, in most cases, genetics/temperamental and environmental factors interact in the etiology of personality and psychopathology. However, few have considered the reasonable possibility that genetics influence an important percentage of social skills, learning, and environmental experiences and thus may account for relationships between social skills, personality, and psychopathology. Scarr and McCartney (1983) have outlined a number of likely means by which genetics influence these variables. Their model and evidence presented in their supportive review emphasize the much neglected effects of genotype in determining environmental effects. For example, they suggest that the individual with a genotype predisposition toward activity and social behavior is more likely to join social groups where social skills will be polished. Extrapolating this model to the development of psychopathology requires little imagination. Individuals who, for genetic reasons, have enhanced skills would be hypothesized by skills-deficits theoreticians to be less likely to suffer psychopathology in the face of stress. Similarly, a genetic disposition toward social expressivity may lead not only to the enhanced social skills hypothesized by Buck in the present volume but also to a broader set of social skills, goals, and preferences that one would be more inclined to label *personality*. Thus the strong evidence presented by Scarr and McCartney suggests that a third variable (genetics) mediates important associations between social skills, personality, and psychopathology.

Geneticists have been eager to call attention to genetic contributions to behavior and psychopathology (e.g., Pogue-Geile & Rose, 1987; Vandenberg, Singer, & Pauls, 1986), yet rarely speculate as to what biobehavioral mechanisms mediate these genetic contributions. However, in their chapters, Buck and Gilbert offer a number of examples of how genetics may interact with and determine environment and social skills. They review evidence suggesting genetically based psychobiological mechanisms and differential sensitivities to reward and punishment that may mediate important genetic contributions to certain forms of personality, social skill, and psychopathology.

There are simple, direct causal models with direct as well as complex multiway models of behavior, personality, and psychopathology (Loehlin, 1987; Schwartz, 1982). Given current knowledge, it seems unlikely that any of the theoretically simple, direct causal models accurately approximate relationships between genes, environment, personality, social skills, and most forms of psychopathologies. For example, it is clear that (with the possible exception of the simplest of social behaviors) environment does not "cause" social skill level or personality independent of genetics. In an extreme case, this can be demonstrated by individuals with genetic disorders in which the basic biologic capacity to understand language is absent. Instead, complex multiway models seem to provide a better accounting.

A discussion of the existence and degree of causal influence of each combination of influences is beyond the scope of the present chapter but is discussed or inferred to varying degrees by a number of the chapters of the present text. We hope that the reader will seriously consider the high complexity of the interrelated factors contributing to the development of specific social skills, general response dispositions (personality), and psychopathology. Although no one of this book's chapters nor the single chapter of any book can fully address the breadth and complexity of the causal relationships between these variables, we have the firm conviction that the reader will gain a great deal of conceptual enrichment from considering how the points made in one chapter augment and enrich points made in other chapters.

GENERAL MODELS OF RELATIONSHIPS BETWEEN PERSONALITY, SOCIAL SKILLS, AND PSYCHOPATHOLOGY

The five chapters of the present book's first section offer different conceptual frameworks for organizing relationships and interactions between personality, social skills, and psychopathology. Connolly's opening chapter traces personality over the life span by reviewing longitudinal studies of personality, psychopathology, and social behavior. He addresses major methodological and measurement issues associated with the study of consistency and variability of behavior over time. Studies demonstrate that early personality variables including extraversion, neuroticism, impulsiveness, and intelligence predict later emotional problems such as alcoholism, social behavior, and marital dissatisfaction. Connolly's review provides a clear set of relationships that call for explanation. Pathways that may mediate these associations are the topic of many of the following chapters.

The interpersonal nature of personality both in its development and expression is the focus of Brokaw and McLemore's chapter. For them, *personality* refers to behavioral regularities (probabilities) persisting over time. As part of our biological nature, individuals are social, entering social relationships to achieve the basic needs of satisfaction, security, and intimacy. Acknowledging that there are five or six basic personality dimensions including extraversion, neuroticism, and agreeableness that are reasonably sufficient to describe many aspects of personality, Brokaw and McLemore focus on the social interplay of these personality dimensions. Human behavior is explained within the context of circular causality and reciprocal influence. Complementarity is a basic premise where one type of behavior (e.g., dominant behavior) elicits another type of behavior from others (submissive behavior).

Brokaw and McLemore consider Benjamin's Structural Analysis of Social Behavior (SASB) to be the best example of their conceptualizations. They suggest that the SASB is "the most scientifically rigorous and clinically astute model published." The SASB views individuals as occupying a space representative of his/her intra- and interpersonal characteristics. The nature of the interaction with another is based on the complementarity these characteristics have with the other's characteristics. For example, social instability is predicted to occur if both interactants are highly dominant. The SASB model incorporates the basic personality traits, but personality is seen as meaningful only in the context of a social situation.

In this model, inherited temperament influences are minimally addressed, whereas early social experiences are highlighted. One of the key elements in the development of personality is early interpersonal experience with significant others. The individual develops a self based on the reflected appraisal of others that over time results in the perceptual mode of the individual. New information is viewed and interpreted in light of these perceptual modes; thus change is made difficult but not impossible.

Consistent with a social emphasis, psychopathology is the result of maladaptive social interactions. It is characterized by the following social events: (1) Someone is bothered. (2) Resulting from previous maladaptive interactions, the "ill" person has a restricted range of thoughts, feelings, and actions and, because the "ill" person utilizes this limited range of skills extensively, he/she is more "skilled" in these thoughts, feelings, and actions. As a result, "ill" individuals are more influential in a social relationship. (3) Thus the dysfunctional person trains others to complement his/her dysfunction instead of the "better functioning" person pulling the "dysfunctional" one into more normal interactions. The cure for psychopathology is corrective social interactions.

Buck's chapter complements that of Brokaw and McLemore by focusing on the contribution of biological inheritance to personality development, social skills, and psychopathology. Personality and social skills are seen as the outcome of inherited temperament and its interaction with the environment and changes over time. Individual differences in temperament (innate emotional disposition based on neural and hormonal mechanisms) are characterized by differences in expression versus inhibition of emotion. Such differences are particularly important in laying the groundwork for social behavior because individuals must "learn how to use" their temperamental characteristics in actual social situations. Because emotional communication is at the heart of this learning process, temperament determines in large part the nature of interpersonal social/emotional environment and thus influences the ease and nature of learning. In this way the expressive individual is hypothesized to create a socially and emotionally enriched environment.

According to Buck's model, we inherit two primary systems through which we relate to and interact with the environment. First, we inherit a general-purpose processing system made up of general learning and cognitive processes and, second, a specific-purpose processing system designed to serve specific emotional functions such as anger or sexual arousal. These two processes operate side by side. General-purpose processes involve intentional and symbolic communication. Specific-purpose processes are characterized by biologically structured sending/receiving communication that is unintentional, emotionally motivated, and always true (never false). This specific-purpose spontaneous communication system is the link between temperament and social and emotional competence.

Both social and emotional competence are delineated by Buck. *Social competence* refers to the ability to know about and deal with the social environment, whereas emotional competence is the ability to know about and deal with the internal, bodily environment of feelings and desires. Specifically, *social skills* refer to specific abilities to know about and deal effectively with relatively specific others, in relatively specific situations, involving relatively specific interpersonal and personal goals. Circumstances determine whether temperament or experience is more important in determining degree of competence in a given situation. For example, temperament would generally be relatively more important in novel situations.

Psychopathology, in Buck's model, results from either a social or emotional skills deficit or a situation where temperament is incompatible with the environment. The strength and quality of feelings and desires emanating from a special-purpose process system, such as aggressiveness, may be unmanageable in a given environment. The reverse may be true. Behavior problems result from environments that do not provide learning experiences promoting social and emotional competence. In another instance, the individual may have quite adequate social skills but maladaptive emotional skills. Thus, whereas McLemore and Brokaw focus more on the stimulus value of specific behaviors in eliciting certain other (complementary) behaviors, Buck focuses more on the individual's own emotional education and temperament influence on social and emotional tendencies and sensitivities.

Gilbert's chapter, complementing both Connolly's and Buck's work, explores personality, social skills, and psychopathology in a social interaction over the short run. He addresses issues of how and why Time 2 behavior can be predicted from Time 1 behavior. Gilbert's model, like Buck's, builds on evidence suggesting that individuals inherit temperaments that interact with the environment beginning in infancy and continuing through adulthood. The temperament of the person is seen as influencing environmental selection; that is, temperamental characteristics influence the places and people one chooses to interact with. Thus Gilbert's model is causal with the mutual interaction of individual personality, other's personality, verbal stimulus factors, and setting or task determining social behavior, affect, and psychophysiology. This model is relatively unique in its attempt to hypothesize mechanisms linking personality, temperament, and emotion to social skills and psychopathology.

The major tenets of Gilbert's model are:

1. Maximally effective communication occurs at intermediate levels of arousal.
2. Verbal stimulus parameters (i.e., rate and temporal pattern of speech, content, and affect of message) affect emotional arousal.
3. Sustained active attention and focusing on one's partner promotes decreased arousal and reduced negative affect.
4. Learning and temperament jointly determine social skill and behavior in social situations.
5. Personalities and social skills interact with situations to channel cognition, emotion, and motivation processes.

In the final of the five chapters presenting general models, Hogan views personality, social skills, and psychopathology from the perspective of personality and status. Personality is viewed from two perspectives, that of the observer (obtained from other ratings) and that of the actor (obtained from self-ratings). Based on descriptions by others, one's personality can be adequately described via three to seven basic personality dimensions including intelligence, adjustment, prudence or impulsiveness, sociability, ambitiousness, and likability. Observed personality significantly correlates with self-rated personality. Hogan's model focuses on the contribution of actor's perceived personality to the topic of personality, social skills, and psychopathology.

Like the book's other authors, Hogan views individuals as being born with different temperaments and experiencing different environments that interact to determine personality. All humans are hypothesized to be biologically programmed to seek attention, acceptance, approval, status, and power because these attributes have survival potential. Parents meet these basic needs for their children, but as children mature they must learn to fulfill these needs elsewhere in order to live and have families. Toward this end individuals adopt strategies by which to conduct their lives. As part of this strategy, an identity or self-presentational style is selected. This could be anything from a bank robber to a tough judge. Depending on the nature of the identity, interpersonal skills are more or less important for success in the role. Clearly those interpersonal or social skills helpful to a bank robber differ from those needed by a judge. Hogan's model is consistent with the notion that those of specific personalities select environments fitting their personality predispositions.

Focusing on occupation as an expression of personality, Hogan adopts Holland's type theory that classifies six generic patterns of personality leading to occupational choice based on interest, values, and motives (these can be biologically or environmentally derived). These patterns are realistic, investigative, artistic, social, enterprising, and conventional. Social skill, which entails the anticipation of who is affected, and how they would be affected, use of this information to guide actions, and self-control to use the plan, is particularly important for those in the social or enterprising occupations but less so for those in the other areas. Likewise, although psychopathology and poor adjustment are important inhibitors of success in most of the career areas, psychopathology apparently does not hinder those in the artistic field. In other areas, adjustment is important in that those less well adjusted do less well than their talent would suggest; similarly, the better adjusted do better than their talent would predict. Hogan suggests that the level of social skill may create more or less positive interactions between coworkers that add to or subtract from success in one's occupation.

MODELS OF SPECIFIC PSYCHOPATHOLOGIES IN LIGHT OF GENERAL MODELS

This book's second section is comprised of four chapters, each focusing on the role of personality and social skill in a specific psychopathology: depression, aggressivity, alcoholism, and hyperactivity. The placement of these specific pathology-focused chapters subsequent to the general models allows strengths and weaknesses of the specific models to be assessed from a broader context.

In the first of the four specific chapters, Hokanson and Rubert provide an excellent review of three major social learning theories of depression and how these theories fare in light of current empirical data. Lewinsohn's theory postulates that depression results from low rates of reinforcement or loss of previous reinforcement. Because of poor social skills, due to lack of training, ignorance, or inhibition, a higher level of reinforcers or new reinforcers is not easily obtained. This theory highlights the importance of social skills in the development and maintenance of depression. Lewinsohn's model pays little attention to possible environmental and biological pathways accounting for one's level of social skills.

Hokanson and Rubert then examine Coyne's theory. It provides an interpersonal perspective in which depressive symptomology elicits concern and support from others in a manner suggested by the SASB model reviewed by Brokaw and McLemore. However, the depressed individual does not know whether these responses are genuine and, thus, repeats the symptoms to help resolve the issue. Others tire of the aversiveness of the symptomatology and begin to give mixed messages (both supportive and negative) that promote even increased depressed symptoms. In Coyne's theory, the focus is on the interaction between persons. The persistent symptoms of the psychopathological person influence the behavior of others and elicit a mixed pattern of both supportive and nonsupportive responses. The focus on sensitivity to the feelings and thoughts of others (i.e., the inadequate sensitivity of the depressed person in detection of genuineness of other's concern and subsequent hypersensitivity to mixed messages) is similar in some respects to Buck's developmental–interactionist model.

Finally, Hokanson and Rubert consider Brown and Harris's theory, which proposes that depression results from three broadly defined factors. First, provoking agents (such as death or squalor) provide the fodder for the development of depression. However, without symptom formation factors such as a family history of depression and vulnerability, which is primarily determined by social support network, depression does not occur. This model allows several ways for social skills to influence level of depression. Social skills may contribute to vulnerability because of its relevance in building a support network. Likewise, social skills may be interfered with by symptom formation factors; for example, an individual may have learned to cope with stress by utilizing depressive symptomology (such as withdrawal) that interferes with the utilization of social (and emotional) skills. Additionally, a low level of emotional competence may interfere with the best use of one's resources to help deal with emotionally traumatic situations.

Whereas Brown and Harris stress family formation factors in the development of depression, Coyne focuses on interpersonal aspects, not specific to family history. Brown and Harris's model incorporates aspects of Lewinsohn's; that is, social support mitigates depression. All three of these behavioral models have primarily an environmental focus and enrich our conceptualization of environmental influences on depression. None of the models deals specifically with biological, temperamental, or personality contributions to depression. In this regard, the models might be enriched by consideration of temperamental and personality factors. For example, Gilbert (present volume) notes the work of Tiggermann, Winefield, and Brebner (1982) showing that introverts, like depressives, display more marked helplessness than do extraverts. This finding is consistent with work of Gray (1981) showing introverts to be exceptionally sensitive to punishing stimuli and with Gilbert's biosocial model. In addition, he calls attention to findings showing that introverts, like depressives, are viewed as less socially skilled than are extraverts and nondepressed individuals. Finally, Gilbert refers to Martin's (1985) work showing neuroticism to predict subsequent depression. Models of social skills and behavior of depressives might also benefit from Buck's formulations of interactions between temperament and the education of emotional and social skills.

In their chapter, McColloch and Gilbert evaluate the development and maintenance of aggression from perspectives common in the literature. Paradigms explaining the relationship of personality, social skills, and psychopathology are reviewed. To begin, aggressivity can be considered both a personality trait and a psychopathology. At some point along a continuum and in some situations, high levels of aggressivity are considered psycho-

pathological. Likewise, others would consider aggressivity a personality
dimension along which individuals can be placed. From this latter vantage
point, subsequent nonaggressive psychopathologies can be predicted (i.e.,
alcohol abuse, marital conflict).

Social skills, including emotional control skills, are key concepts in aggressivity. One approach suggests that aggressive behavior patterns persist
because other, more functional social skills fail to develop. The reverse has
also been suggested; that is, because an individual utilizes aggressive behavior patterns (and they work in the short run), other social skills are not
learned. Another possibility is that adequate social skills are present but
due to motivational factors or poor emotional control skills these adequate
social skills are not displayed. The highly significant roles that both cognitive factors such as perceptual mode and emotional factors such as anger
play in aggressivity are highlighted in this chapter. However, a comprehensive model has not yet materialized. Instead pieces of a larger pattern are
emerging in which genetic/temperament/personality factors (such as intelligence, difficulty as a baby, impulsiveness) and environmental factors (such
as parenting, peer group) have been demonstrated to be important. Emotional factors like anger and perceptual modes such as seeing the world as
hostile have been documented and associated with family and social life.

Chiauzzi evaluates social skills training in the treatment of alcohol
abuse. The social skills approach to alcohol treatment stresses the situational specificity of behavior, but the generalizability of drinking behavior
across similar situations is also assessed. However, the broader cross-situational and cross-temporal behavioral/personality traits associated with alcohol abuse are typically not addressed by researchers and therapists with a
social skills orientation. This sole focus on skills does not view personality as
central to the conceptualization of psychopathology or its treatment. Inadequate social skill in drinking situations, rather than an underlying personality trait or motivation, is viewed by the social skills theorists and practitioners as the psychopathology that must be changed. Social skills in
specified situations is the most relevant construct; indeed, perhaps the only
key concept. Chiauzzi provides a detailed and clinically insightful view of the
multiple components, complexities, and subtleties of social skills assessment
and treatment with alcoholics. He states that "it is time to eliminate theoretical struggles and find mechanisms to improve outcome."

Chiauzzi suggests that the great heterogeneity of the alcoholic population "is probably the major contributor to the lack of many definitive findings in the extant research." *Heterogeneity* is another word for individual
differences, a concept central to personality theory. Thus the social skills
approach to alcohol problems, like that noted to depression, would likely
benefit from an integration of personality and temperamental concepts outlined in the general models section of this book. Because genetic factors and

certain forms of affective disorder and psychopathology influence individual differences in the tendency to abuse alcohol, it would be useful to assess how these predispositional factors relate to social skills. Do the social skills deficits observed in depressed individuals (Hokanson and Rubert, present volume) predispose them to alcohol abuse? Do environmentally based social skill or performance deficits mediate dispositions toward alcohol abuse in some alcoholics, whereas heightened negative affect mediates genetic disposition toward social skill deficits, alcohol abuse, and social dysfunction in others?

Finally, Chiauzzi notes that the social skills approach typically considers both the drinking situation and interpersonal processes, with the alcohol-abusing person having inadequate social skills to deal appropriately or satisfactorily with others. Thus it might be useful for social skills researchers to consider the stimulus effects of alcohol-abuse-related behaviors on the behavior of significant others in a manner similar to that noted by Brokaw and McLemore in their chapter on interpersonal models of personality and psychopathology.

The chapter by Hinshaw and McHale showing the significant beneficial effects of stimulant medications on social interactions of hyperactive children is theoretically very important because such medications produce what is in effect a pharmacologically induced change in temperament that beneficially influences social behavior. This demonstration is important because many influential systems theorists have strongly argued that individual differences in temperament and personality are not important in interpersonal situations (Watzlawick, 1977). Thus changes in the individual can produce clinically important changes in the family system. The consistency of medication-induced effects is impressive, showing clear evidence of behavior change in the child, family members, and teachers. That is, the impact of the medication is seen not only in the child but also in those who are closest (and likely most influential) in his/her daily life. This change is analogous to a change in temperament or personality.

Yet, even with clear evidence of improved behavior (at least less negative behavior), Hinshaw and McHale show that these children do not become more popular with their peers. Indeed, changing popularity ratings of these children is very difficult even though they show less obnoxious interactions. One possible explanation for this is that these children have not yet acquired positive social skills. As with the aggressive child described by Patterson (reviewed in Chapter 8, present volume), their hyperactive behavior patterns may have prevented them from learning positive social skills. Thus, although they are no longer as aversive in their behavior, they are unable to make friends until new learning occurs. So Hinshaw and McHale's review illustrates the potential impact of both temperament (or personality) and social skills on one's adjustment in his/her environment.

SUMMARY AND CONCLUSIONS

Scientific progress is frequently stalled by failures to integrate apparently antithetical concepts (Rothenberg, 1979). Psychology needs to developed effective models of human social behavior that integrate a number of apparently antithetical concepts; for example, the idea that behavior is both generalizable and at the same time highly situation specific (Epstein, 1983). How can social skills be influenced by temperament, as well as by learning? This book will most assuredly contribute to the reader's understanding of the answers to these important questions. Although the authors stress different aspects of relations between personality, social skill, and psychopathology, there is an encouraging appreciation of certain findings. For example, all of the authors of the general models chapters acknowledge the importance of extraversion and neuroticism as two of the handful of fundamental personality descriptors. Similarly, there is growing appreciation of the fact that behavior is both highly situation specific and generalizable; that it is crucially dependent on interactive influences of environment, genes, and learning.

Personality, social skills, and psychopathology are important constructs that emphasize different aspects of and processes underlying behavior. The sophisticated psychology of the twenty-first century will need to further articulate the dimensions and processes that underlie and differentiate these three constructs. Efforts at integration and differentiation are certain to enrich theory and research within each of the areas.

REFERENCES

Bellack, A. S., & Hersen, M. (1977). *Behavior modification: An introductory textbook.* Baltimore: Williams & Wilkins.

Berger, P. A., & Brodie, H. K. H. (1986). *American handbook of psychiatry, Volume 8: Biological psychiatry.* New York: Basic Books.

Dohrenwend, B. R., & Dohrenwend, B. S. (1969). *Social status and psychological inquiry.* New York: Wiley.

Epstein, S. (1979). The stability of behavior I.: On predicting most of the people much of the time. *Journal of Personality and Social Psychology, 37,* 1097–1126.

Epstein, S. (1983). Aggregation and beyond. *Journal of Personality, 51,* 360–392.

Eysenck, H. J. (1967). *The biological basis of personality.* Springfield, IL: Charles C Thomas.

Eysenck, H. J., & Eysenck, M. W. (1985). *Personality and individual differences: A natural sciences approach.* New York: Plenum Press.

Gottman, J. M. (1979). *Marital interaction: Experimental investigations.* New York: Academic Press.

Gray, J. A. (1981). A critique of Eysenck's theory of personality. In H. J. Eysenck (Ed.), *A model for personality* (pp. 246–276). New York: Springer.

L'Abate, L., & Milan, M. A. (Eds.). (1985). *Handbook of social skills training and research.* New York: Wiley.

Loehlin, J. C. (1987). *Latent variable models: An introduction to factor, path, and structural analysis*. Hillsdale, NJ: Erlbaum.

Martin, M. (1985). Neuroticism as predisposition toward depression: A cognitive mechanism. *Personality and Individual Differences, 6*, 353–365.

Meichenbaum, D., Butler, L., & Gruson, L. (1981). Toward a conceptual model of social competence. In J. D. Wine & M. D. Smye (Eds.), *Social competence* (pp. 36–60). New York: Guilford Press.

Mischel, W. (1986). *Introduction to personality* (4th ed.). New York: Holt, Rinehart & Winston.

Phillips, E. L. (1985). Social skills: History and prospect. In L. L'Abate & M. A. Milan (Eds.), *Handbook of social skills training and research* (pp. 3–21). New York: Wiley.

Pogue-Geile, M. F., & Rose, R. J. (1987). Psychopathology: A behavior genetic perspective. In T. Jacob (Ed.), *Family interaction and psychopathology* (pp. 629–650). New York: Plenum Press.

Rothenberg, A. (1979). Einstein's creative thinking and the general theory of relativity: A documented report. *American Journal of Psychiatry, 136*, 38–43.

Scarr, S., & McCartney, K. (1983). How people make their own environments: A theory of genotype → environment effects. *Child Development, 54*, 424–435.

Schlundt, D. G., & McFall, R. M. (1985). New direction in the assessment of social competence and social skills. In L. L'Abate & M. A. Milan (Eds.), *Handbook of social skills training and research* (pp. 22–49). New York: Wiley.

Schwartz, G. E. (1982). Testing the biopsychosocial model: The ultimate challenge facing behavioral medicine? *Journal of Consulting and Clinical Psychology, 50*, 1040–1053.

Schwartz, R., & Gottman, J. (1976). Toward a task analysis of assertive behavior. *Journal of Consulting and Clinical Psychology, 44*, 910–920.

Tiggermann, M., Winefield, A., & Brebner, J. (1982). The role of extraversion in the development of learned helplessness. *Personality and Individual Differences, 3*, 27–34.

Vandenberg, S. G., Singer, S. M., & Pauls, D. L. (1986). *The heredity of behavior disorders in adults and children*. New York: Plenum Press.

Watzlawick, P. (1977). Introduction. In P. Watzlawick, & J. H. Weakland (Eds.), *The interactional view: Studies at the Mental Research Institute, Palo Alto 1965–74* (pp. xi–xv). New York: Norton.

Watzlawick, P., & Beavin, J. H. (1977). Some formal aspects of communication. In P. Watzlawick & Weakland (Eds.), *The interactional view: Studies at the Mental Research Institute, Palo Alto 1965–74* (pp. 56–70). New York: Norton.

Wine, J. D. (1981). From defect to competence models. In J. D. Wine & M. D. Smye (Eds.), *Social competence* (pp. 3–35). New York: Guilford Press.

PART ONE

GENERAL MODELS OF RELATIONSHIPS BETWEEN PERSONALITY, SOCIAL SKILLS, AND PSYCHOPATHOLOGY

CHAPTER TWO

Longitudinal Studies of Personality, Psychopathology, and Social Behavior

JAMES J. CONNOLLY

INTRODUCTION

Longitudinal studies of personality characteristics began in the early days of the scientific study of individual differences. The first empirical investigations of the longitudinal aspects of personality were begun in the 1920s and 1930s. Since that time, many other longitudinal studies have been initiated, so that a very extensive amount of information on the consistency and predictive power of personality characteristics is now available. The studies cover a wide variety of constructs, instruments, and populations. Unfortunately, this variety has combined with the long periods of time required to complete the studies to sometimes produce a lack of communication among longitudinal researchers and a literature that is often disjointed.

This chapter is an effort to organize and evaluate the longitudinal research on personality that has appeared in the last 20 to 30 years. The summary is restricted to studies involving adults or late adolescents at the initiation of data collection. The available studies will be evaluated in terms of five major issues.

1. Have major personality traits demonstrated an impressive degree of longitudinal consistency?

JAMES J. CONNOLLY • Private Practice, 400 Bayonet Street, New London, Connecticut 06320. Dr. Connolly legally changed the spelling of his name "Conley" to "Connolly" in 1989.

Personality, Social Skills, and Psychopathology: An Individual Differences Approach, edited by David G. Gilbert and James J. Connolly. Plenum Press, New York, 1991.

2. Is the longitudinal consistency found for personality traits best explained in terms of substantive consistency or as artifacts of measurement?
3. Is the longitudinal consistency of personality compatible with the fact that many personal characteristics change substantially over the lifespan?
4. Are personality traits predictive of the development of emotional and behavioral disorders?
5. Are personality traits predictive of important aspects of social behavior?

The treatment in this chapter of the available studies will not be exhaustive. In cases where adequate reviews or a portion of the literature are already available, the reader will be referred to them. In other cases, an adequate discussion of the issues at hand requires the presentation of new data, some of it not yet published. Most of this new data is derived from the Kelly Longitudinal Study, a study of 300 couples carried out over the years 1935–1981, which the writer is currently analyzing.

HAVE MAJOR PERSONALITY TRAITS DEMONSTRATED AN IMPRESSIVE DEGREE OF LONGITUDINAL CONSISTENCY?

As we watch our families, our friends, and our associates grow older, we notice the changes in their thinking and behavior, but we also notice the perseveration of certain characteristics that mark each person out from the others. These observations are often well summarized by the old French proverb, "The more things change, the more they stay the same."

But which are the more enduring characteristics that we think of as "personality"? Whose system of personality traits should be used? What are the *major* traits of personality? The question of structure has been a perennial problem in the study of human personality. A cursory examination reveals an almost endless variety of systems of traits and types. The disagreements among personality psychologists about structure have contributed to the general disrepute into which the concept has fallen and (more importantly) have reduced the ability of personality psychologists to communicate among themselves. In the absence of a consensus on basic structure, a vast corpus of tests and findings has accumulated. As this corpus has grown over the decades, the problem of personality structure has been transformed into an enormous empirical puzzle. The question of whether the original formulations of Allport or Cattell or Guilford or Eysenck were most accurate has receded into the background, and the issue has become whether a comprehensive structural theory can be brought to bear on the very complicated pattern of findings.

Fortunately, there is a growing consensus among personality psychologists on the issue of personality structure. Many researchers of personality ratings have reported 5-factor solutions that are highly similar to one another (Amelang & Borkenau, 1982; Borgatta, 1964; Digman & Inouye, 1986; Fiske, 1949; McCrae & Costa, 1987; Noller *et al.*, 1987; Norman, 1963; Norman & Goldberg, 1966; Passini & Norman, 1966; Smith, 1967; Tupes & Christal, 1961). In addition to Neuroticism ("emotional stability," "emotionality"), Social Extraversion ("sociability," "extraverson," "assertiveness"), Impulse Control ("conscientiousness," "dependability," "responsibility"), and Agreeableness ("likeeability"), these 5-factor solutions include a "culture" or "intellectual interests" trait.

There is even more impressive convergence on a 3-factor model including neuroticism, social extraversion, and impulse control. Royce and Powell (1983) have summarized much of the evidence pointing toward the 3-factor model, and the latest exchange between Guilford and Eysenck demonstrated their closeness on a 3-factor model (Eysenck, 1977; Guilford, 1975). Eysenck and Eysenck (1976) have separated the impulsivity components on their earlier trait of "extraversion" and included them in their psychoticism dimension. Goldberg (1981) and Hogan (1983) have noted the convergence of rating studies on a 3- to 5-factor model of personality traits similar to the "adequate" taxonomy of Norman (1963). Costa and McCrae (1977, 1980a) recognize neuroticism and extraversion as major traits and acknowledge the need for a "control" trait as well.

The traits of neuroticism, social extraversion, and impulse control (and, to some degree, agreeableness and "cultural interests") can safely be considered major traits for the purpose of investigating the longitudinal consistency of personality. Have these major traits demonstrated an impressive degree of consistency?

A substantial body of longitudinal studies of personality has accumulated over the years (Moss & Susman, 1980). The methods and constructs used have varied widely, but the general finding is a high degree of longitudinal stability for the major personality traits, even when the points of measurement are separated by a decade or more. Most longitudinal research on adult personality characteristics has relied on self-report measures. A review of the longitudinal findings for several standardized personality inventories concluded that self-reported anxiety and extraversion have 4-year to 10-year consistency coefficients of approximately .6 (Schuerger, Tait, & Tavernelli, 1982). Costa, McCrae, and Arenberg (1980) reported an average retest correlation of approximately .7 over a 12-year period for the 10 scales of the Guilford-Zimmerman Temperament Survey. Leon, Gillum, Gillum, and Gouze (1979) reported on the Minnesota Multiphasic Personality Inventory (MMPI) profiles of 71 adult male subjects studied over a 30-year period. The average of the retest correlations was higher than .4, and the Social Introversion Scale had a 30-year retest correlation of .74. Similar results have been reported by Finn (1986) for MMPI content scales. Woodruff and Birren (1971) carried out a 25-year follow-up on 85 subjects using the California Test of Personality. On the self-adjustment portion of the test, the correlation over a 25-year period was .58 for males and .65 for females.

Findings in the self-report data of the Kelly Longitudinal Study have corroborated that there is a substantial longitudinal consistency for the traits of neuroticism and social extraversion (Conley, 1984b). Measures of these personality traits correlated at .6 or higher over periods of 25 years and at .3 over periods of 45 years. Interestingly, the measures of neuroticism and social extraversion demonstrated convergent and discriminant validity. In other words, neuroticism measures at one time period were highly correlated with neuroticism measures at another time period but not with social extraversion measures of whatever time period. Social extraversion measures were likewise highly correlated over time with other measures of the same trait but were not correlated with measures of neuroticism (Conley, 1984b).

As noted, most studies of the longitudinal consistency of personality (as most personality studies generally) have been restricted to the self-report modality. In a much smaller number of adult longitudinal studies, researchers have used personality ratings by knowledgeable observers. The classic rating studies on the longitudinal stability of personality are those of the Berkeley Institute on Human Development (Eichorn, 1973). The time period reported by J. Block (1971) ran from senior high school to early adulthood. The median longitudinal stability for 100 personality descriptors (rated by different sets of observers, one set 18 years after the other) was just slightly below .3 (uncorrected Pearsonian correlations). In an offshoot of the Berkeley studies, Mussen, Eichorn, Honzik, Bieber, and Meredith (1980) extended the analysis of personality consistency into later adulthood. A group of the mothers of the subjects in the Institute of Human Development studies were rated at around age 30 and again at around age 70. Two personality factors were common to both ages: One related to neuroticism (worrisome, dissatisfied), the other to social extraversion (talkative, self-assured, energetic). The consistency correlations over 40 years were .34 for the neuroticism factor and .24 for the social extraversion factor. In other ratings studies of adults (Cox, 1970; Symonds & Jensen, 1961; Vaillant, 1974), researchers have used independent assessments by clinicians of the subjects' neuroticism over intervals varying from 10 to 29 years. The correlations obtained in these studies are in the neighborhood of .5.

In the data of the Kelly Longitudinal Study, the ratings of major personality traits were impressively consistent (Conley, 1985a). Over a period of two decades, peer ratings of the four traits of neuroticism, social extraversion, impulse control, and agreeableness generated consistency coefficients of .3 to .5. The greatest consistencies occurred when trait ratings were aggregated across several raters at a particular time period. Additional aggregative power came from the fact that the final measures for each of the major traits was a summation of several categories. Thus neuroticism was composed of ratings of "easily angered," "easily upset," and "impatient," and social extraversion was composed of ratings of "socially adaptable," "friendly," "popular," "not quiet," "energetic," and "optimistic."

The rather high levels of longitudinal consistency found for such major traits of personality as neuroticism, social extraversion, and impulse control should not be seen as an indication that other personality characteristics are not also longitudinally consistent. Indeed, what evidence is available indicates that other types of personality traits may also have substantial longitudinal consistencies. Mischel, Shoda, and Peake (1988) have found that "delay of gratification" has substantial consistency over time. (This trait should probably be considered a part (but only a part) of the larger trait of impulse control.) Huesmann et al. (1987) have reported impressive consistency of aggressive behavior over a 22-year period. Much the same can be said for a set of characteristics related to individuals' philosophical outlooks measured by the Study of Values devised by Allport and Vernon (1931). Reports of the longitudinal stability of the Study of Value scales are summarized in Table 1. The retest intervals vary from 2 to 25 years, and both men and women are represented in these studies. The stability coefficients at the shortest intervals have a mean of .58 and those at intervals of 19 or more years a mean of .40. The correlations from the 25-year interval in the study by Huntley and Davis (1983) are lower because the scales of the Study of Values are each being correlated with single-item measures of the values. The unreliability of the single-item measures places an artificial limit on the sizes of the correlations. Despite two anomalously low correlations for the social scale, and one for the political scale, the general picture is one of substantial longitudinal stability.

IS THE LONGITUDINAL CONSISTENCY FOUND FOR PERSONALITY TRAITS BEST EXPLAINED AS SUBSTANTIVE CONSISTENCY OR AS ARTIFACTS OF MEASUREMENT?

The longitudinal consistency found for measured personality characteristics could be either a reflection of a real consistency of personality over time or the result of methodological factors that produce an artificial correlation over time. Kagan (1988) has reiterated the difficulties of interpreting personality measures, particularly self-report measures. As noted, studies of the longitudinal consistency of personality have been (as studies of personality in general) largely self-report in nature. It is possible that people perceive a higher level of consistency in their personalities than is really there. We might, for instance, believe ourselves to be consistently

TABLE 1. Summary of Longitudinal Studies of the Allport-Vernon Study of Values

Study	Original population	Retest interval (in years)	Retest correlations						
			Theoretical	Economic	Aesthetic	Social	Political	Religious
Burgenmeister (1940)	164 College Women	2	76	63	74	67	61	74
Todd (1941)	90 Male High School Students	2	61	60	61	56	53	46
Plant and Telford (1966)	440 College Men	2	56	48	52	46	52	66
Plant and Telford (1966)	336 College Women	2	51	54	58	54	44	54
Whitley (1938)	84 College Men	3	56	56	45	38	65	66
Stewart (1964)	89 College Students (47 Men, 42 Women)	4	71	57	73	54	67	64
Arsenian (1970)	54 College Men	4	55	43	54	57	50	90
Huntley and Davis (1983)	532 College Men	4	54	59	45	42	48	57
Hoge and Bender (1974)	47 College Men	13	56	66	58	12	50	58
Hoge and Bender (1974)	60 College Men	15	44	53	64	-08	41	41
Kelly (1955)	214 Young Adult Men	19	52	53	55	33	53	59
Kelly (1955)	232 Young Adult Women	19	51	45	48	32	44	60
Arsenian (1970)	54 College Men	25	49	36	37	40	-03	43
Huntley and Davis (1983)	532 College Men	25	27	39	30	25	21	41

Note. The correlations for the 25-year interval of the Huntley and Davis (1983) study are between Study of Value scales (at the start of the interval) and single-item self reports corresponding to each of these scales (at the end of the interval).

socially extraverted when, in fact, our actual social habits had changed drastically over time. We are all comfortable with the idea that our perceptions of ourselves are often at least somewhat out of line with the way we are in actuality.

The studies of longitudinal consistency of personality characteristics are not exclusively self-report in nature, however, and the previous section noted several studies using personality ratings by other persons. In general, the peer ratings studies produce consistency coefficients that are somewhat lower than those in the self-report studies. Instead of correlations as high as .6 or .7 over periods of a couple of decades, the ratings studies are characterized by coefficients of around .35 to .50 over comparable periods of time. This would seem to indicate that self-report *inflates* the apparent level of longitudinal consistency, but by no means does it produce the entirety of the consistency. Note also that the peer ratings studies used different raters at each of the data collections so there is little likelihood that the observed consistency coefficients result from the consistency of a stereotype or perception in the mind of any single observer. If an observer in 1954 sees John Smith as more than the average on extraversion and another independent observer in 1980 concurs, the simplest explanation of the agreement in ratings is that John Smith has remained consistently extraverted.

Using the data of the Kelly Longitudinal Study, I attempted (Conley, 1985a) to produce a more formal analysis of the problem of substantive versus antifactual elements in the longitudinal consistency of personality. A new analytic method was developed to address the problems of constructs and methods in longitudinal studies of personality. The logic of Campbell and Fiske's (1959) multitrait–multimethod matrix is applied fully to the longitudinal context. The result is a multitrait–multimethod–multioccasion matrix. In extending the logic of Campbell and Fiske's (1959) multitrait–multimethod matrix, I found it necessary to simplify the terminology to avoid confusion. The use of the prefixes *hetero* and *mono* has been replaced by the subscripts s (for same or "mono") and d (for different or "hetero"). Variations of traits, methods, and occasions are abbreviated as T, M, and O, respectively. Thus $T_s M_d O_s$ coefficients are comparisons of the same trait in which one uses different methods of assessment but at a single occasion of measurement. As another example, $T_d M_s O_s$ coefficients are comparisons across different traits but with the same method and at the same occasion. Convergent validity involves contrasting M_s elements with M_d elements while holding the values of T and O constant. Discriminant validity involves contrasting T_s elements with T_d elements while holding the values of M and O constant. Longitudinal stability involves contrasting O_s elements with O_d elements while holding the values of T and M constant. A discriminantly and convergently valid trait that is longitudinally stable would demonstrate a maximum of T_s versus T_d differences and a minimum of both M_s and M_d and O_s versus O_d differences.

A summary of the multitrait–multimethod–multioccasion relations is presented in Table 2. The first row contains estimates of the interrater reliability of each trait. There are four traits, two occasions (1935–1938 and 1954–1955), and three methods (self-rating, spouse rating, and the average of ratings by five acquaintances). One may determine the discriminant validity of the four personality traits by comparing each set of T_s coefficients with the corresponding set of T_d coefficients. In these comparisons, the T_s coefficients of neuroticism, social extraversion, and impulse control are uniformly much higher than the corresponding T_d coefficients. The discriminant validity of the trait agreeableness does not appear to be as strong as that of the other three traits, particularly in the comparison of the $T_s M_d O_d$ and $T_d M_d O_d$ coefficients. From this analysis of discriminant validity, one can conclude that neuroticism, social extraversion, and impulse control are distinct traits. The measures of each of these traits correlate much more strongly with other sorts of measures of the same trait than with the measures of other traits.

Campbell and Fiske (1959) suggested that one may determine convergent validity by comparing the validity coefficients to various standards, including statistical significance, absolute magnitude, and magnitude relative to the heterotrait–monomethod ($T_d M_s O_s$) coefficients. In this analysis, these comparisons must be undertaken for both the synchronic validity coefficients ($T_s M_d O_s$) and the diachronic validity coefficients ($T_s M_d O_d$). All of the synchronic and diachronic validity coefficients in Table 2 are significant at the .01 level, and the great majority have absolute magnitudes in excess of .3. The average synchronic validites of neuroticism, social extraversion, impulse control, and agreeableness (given in Table 2) were .48, .52, .36, and .27, respectively, for men and .39, .48, .38, and .25 for women. Clearly the trait agreeableness has the weakest synchronic validity for both sexes. When compared with any of the T_d rows, however, the synchronic validity of even agreeableness appears substantial. The pattern of diachronic validity is similar to that of synchronic validity. The average diachronic validity coefficients for men are .43, .36, .30, and .16, and for women they are .30, .41, .29, and .17 (for neuroticism, social extraversion, impulse control, and agreeableness, respectively). In other words, individual differences on the traits *neuroticism, social extraversion,* and *impulse control* are rather stable even when measured via different methods at occasions separated by a gap of almost 20 years. With *agreeableness,* on the other hand, there appears to be serious problems of diachronic validity.

Longitudinal stability may be assessed within methods ($T_s M_s O_d$) or across methods ($T_s M_d O_d$) because the diachronic validity coefficients are also longitudinal measures. By both standards, neuroticism, sociability, and impulse control show reasonable levels of stability. For men, the average longitudinal stability coefficients of these three traits are .50, .47, and .32, respectively, whereas the diachronic validities are somewhat lower at .43,

TABLE 2. Summary of Multitrait–Multimethod–Multioccasion Relationships for the Factor Scores of the Personality Ratings

Coefficient	Males				Females			
	Neuroticism	Social extraversion	Impulse control	Agreeableness	Neuroticism	Social extraversion	Impulse control	Agreeableness
$T_sM_sO_s$ [a]	76	70	59	64	77	66	67	50
$T_dM_sO_s$	07	06	07	07	05	06	07	08
$T_sM_dO_s$	48	52	36	27	39	48	38	25
$T_dM_dO_s$	07	11	08	08	11	11	10	11
$T_sM_sO_d$	50	47	32	33	39	52	43	46
$T_dM_sO_d$	08	08	10	10	07	12	15	08
$T_sM_dO_d$	43	36	30	16	30	41	29	17
$T_dM_dO_d$	08	11	09	09	10	11	11	09

[a] Estimated from interrater agreement of acquaintance ratings for highest loading rating categories on each recurrent factor.
Note: N = 189 males and 189 females.

.36, and .30. For women the comparable correlations are .39, .50, and .43 for the longitudinal stability coefficients and .30, .41, and .29 for the diachronic validity coefficients. The figures indicate that neuroticism may have somewhat greater longitudinal consistency among men than among women and that the reverse may hold true for social extraversion. The longitudinal stability of agreeableness appears moderately high when measured via the same method, but (as noted earlier) it is reduced to a minimal level when assessed via different methods at different occasions.

The results of this multitrait–multimethod–multioccasion analyses were encouraging. A set of four traits was present in each of three methods of assessment and in both of two developmental periods. Three of these traits (neuroticism, social extraversion, and impulse control) were longitudinally stable for both sexes. The coefficients of stability range from .3 to .5 for a period of 19 years and were resilient across three assessment methods (self-rating, spouse rating, and acquaintance rating). These three traits had substantial convergent and discriminant validity.

IS THE LONGITUDINAL CONSISTENCY OF PERSONALITY COMPATIBLE WITH THE FACT THAT MANY PERSONAL CHARACTERISTICS CHANGE SUBSTANTIALLY OVER THE LIFE SPAN?

A major stumbling block of personality research has been the tendency to regard personality traits as either illusory or absolutely fixed. The previous section leads to the conclusion that the longitudinal consistency of personality is almost certainly not an artifact or an illusion. We must now fend off the opposite error of enshrining personality traits as absolutely fixed characteristics. This requires a shift of perspective in personality research. Personality should be seen as *relatively* rather than absolutely fixed. Classical psychometric theory was based on the assumption of the absolute permanence of personality. Differences between two administrations of a personality test (in the form of correlations falling short of 1.0) were attributed to measurement error. This has been the primary manifestation of the rigid form of the stability assumption underlying conventional theories of personality. It is now necessary to abandon this assumption. As Helson and Moane (1987) have argued: "If personality interacts with situations in any meaningful manner, it hardly makes sense to claim that personality does not change over time" (p. 185).

To illustrate some of the implications of this view of personality characteristics as relatively rather than absolutely consistent entities, a simple mathematical model may be used to account for the observed data on longitudinal consistency and relate it to the probable underlying level of substantive consistency (Conley, 1984a). Converse and Markus (1979) had demonstrated the utility of considering the observed retest coefficient as equal to the product of instrument reliability and annual stability or

$$C = Rs^n$$

where C is the observed retest coefficient, R the internal consistency or period-free reliability of the measuring instrument, s the annual stability, and n the interval (in years) over which the coefficient was calculated. This equation is useful as a model for personality consistency.

The crucial element in this equation is the idea of an underlying annual stability. According to the model, the greater the length of time, the less the actual consistency of personality. Thus personality consistency is subject to a decay function. A wide array of inventory and rating studies converge on an estimate of .98 as the real annual stability of personality traits (see Conley, 1984a). This estimate is derived by separating the internal reliability of the measuring instruments from the temporal stability of the constructs, a crucial clarification of two issues previously confounded under the heading of *reliability* (Conley, 1984a). Although in the conventional atemporal personality psychology, annual stabilities of .98 would be interpreted as evidence of almost absolute permanence, an analysis across several decades of adulthood leads to a very different conclusion. An annual stability of .98 implies a stability of .45 over a span of 40 years. The proportion of the variance that may be regarded as permanent over such a 40-year period is 20%. Thus the individual differences that we refer to as personality tend to reorder themselves through the years of adulthood. This accommodates the personality perspective to the very realistic insistence of critics that structures cannot remain wholly unchanged.

Using an annual stability of .98 for personality traits and the published period-free reliabilities of the various instruments (which in the personality domain run from .90 for some self-report inventories to about .50 for some types of ratings), it was possible to provide a tight fit between observed and expected coefficients of stability (Conley, 1984a). Annual stability of .98 and period-free reliability of .70 result in predicted longitudinal consistencies of about .45 over 20 years and about .30 over 40 years. These are roughly the average levels of the observed coefficients discussed in the first section of this chapter.

Seeing personality as a decay function allows psychologists to accommodate both consistency and change within the same perspective. Personality is seen as consistent only in a relative sense. Table 3 presents estimates of the underlying (as opposed to measured) consistency of intelligence, personality, and self-opinion (the latter refers to variables such as self-esteem, morale, alienation). The underlying annual stability of intelligence is approximately .99, that of personality around .98, and that of self-opinion approximately .94 (Conley, 1984a). Note that intelligence has a reasonable percentage of variance due to temporal consistency even over periods of as

TABLE 3. Estimated Longitudinally Consistent Correlations and Percentages of
Variance for Intelligence, Personality Traits, and Self-Opinion
(assuming perfect period-free reliability)

	1	5	10	20	30	40	50	60	70
Correlations									
Intelligence	99	95	90	82	74	67	60	54	49
Personality traits	98	90	82	67	55	45	36	30	24
Self-opinion	94	73	54	29	16	08	05	02	01
Percentages of variance									
Intelligence	98	90	82	67	55	45	36	29	24
Personality traits	96	82	67	45	30	21	13	09	06
Self-opinion	88	54	29	09	03	01	00	00	00

long as 70 years, whereas personality's consistency over such a period has
faded to only approximately 6% of the variance. Self-opinion's consistency,
on the other hand, reaches negligible portions of variance after only a little
over 20 years.

Personality thus appears to be very different from the doggedly, absolutely consistent entity presumed by conventional psychometric theory.
Personality is merely a relatively consistent entity that gains part of its
apparent consistency from the fact that we usually observe it over very
limited periods of time. When viewed over very long periods of time (say,
several decades), there appears to be a very substantial reordering of the
individual differences we call *personality traits*. This reordering is not
merely due to measurement problem but is inherent in the temporal nature
of the underlying personality traits themselves.

Despite having its constancy decaying over time, personality has a
degree of underlying consistency that gives it a reasonable amount of order
and predictability over the period of 20 to 50 years of adulthood that most of
us will experience. Self-esteem, opinions on particular political issues, and
satisfaction with work or spouse will change much more rapidly than personality characteristics just as basic intelligence will change more slowly.

A comprehensive personality theory must address both the change and
the constancy within human psychological phenomena. The personality psychology needs to incorporate the concept of personality change and consider
the relation of personality variables to other psychological characteristics.
Personality is, after all, only important insofar as it acts to structure other
aspects of human life. It is necessary to demonstrate that personality structures influence more superficial and/or transient psychological phenomena,
especially in the areas of psychopathology and social behavior.

ARE PERSONALITY TRAITS PREDICTIVE OF THE
DEVELOPMENT OF EMOTIONAL
AND BEHAVIORAL DISORDERS?

Personality characteristics have played a central role in many psychological theories of the etiology of behavioral disorders. This has been true for both "temperament" theorists, such as Eysenck and Meehl, and for psychoanalytic theorists. In both cases, personality characteristics have been assumed to be mediators of more primary causes of behavioral disorders. Temperament theorists have emphasized the heritable component of behavior as the primary cause, and psychoanalytic theorists have usually made the early social environment the primary cause. Meehl assumes that the genetic predisposition for schizophrenia manifests itself in a "schizotypal personality" that develops in predisposed individuals "regardless of their particular social reinforcement histories" (Golden & Meehl, 1979). Eysenck has argued that the principal heritable personality traits (neuroticism, extraversion, and psychoticism) represent predispositions to particular psychological disorders. In one version of Eysenck's theory, dysthymic (anxious and depressive) disorders stem from high levels of neuroticism and low levels of extraversion, whereas psychopathic disorders stem from high levels of neuroticism and high levels of extraversion. Psychoanalytic theorists have described several patterns of parent–child interaction that are presumed to result in personality formations predisposing for hysteria, obsessive-compulsive neurosis, depression, schizophrenia, and alcoholism (Knight, 1942; Stern, 1964).

Given the importance of personality constructs in etiological theories, it is surprising and somewhat unsettling to realize that the empirical case for a predictive relationship between personality and psychological disorders has seldom been set forth in an organized and compelling way. In large part, this is due to the difficulties of conducting prospective studies of behavioral disorders. Many of these difficulties extend to reconstructive longitudinal studies where already existing records (usually school records) are found on the past behavior of persons who have succumbed to serious behavioral disorders (usually schizophrenia). First of all, most of the predictive studies have been carried out over limited segments of the adult life span, so there is no assurance that their results represent all the forms of a disorder that may develop. The majority of studies are restricted to early adulthood and thus miss the opportunity of detecting later-developing psychopathology.

A second problem is the unrepresentative character of the groups under study. Among the more extensive psychological longitudinal studies, the Grant study is restricted to Harvard graduates, the McCord study to working- to lower-class urbanites, and the Terman study to persons with IQs above 130. Other studies are based on groups "at risk" for various psychological disorders, usually the children of disturbed parents. Although such studies have great potential for revealing the genetic–environmental interactions that may lead to behavioral discrepancies, these "at risk" populations are not even representative of all persons succumbing to the particular pathology under study. As Gottesman and Shields (1982) point out, most persons who become schizophrenics do not have schizophrenic parents, and most children of schizophrenics do not develop the disorder themselves.

A third problem with existing prospective studies of behavioral disorders is the forms of available personality assessment devices. In many cases these are of a self-report, ad hoc, or subjective character. Reconstructive longitudinal studies are restricted to surviving data usually gathered by nonpsychologists for purposes vastly different from prospective psychological analysis. These present serious problems of validity and comparability of findings across the various studies, and it is sometimes difficult to relate the measures used in these studies to the refined factorial systems of personality descriptions developed by Eysenck (1968), Norman and Goldberg (1966), and others.

This review of the findings of the personality predictors of psychopathology is divided by sex of the subjects and by alcoholism versus nonalcoholic emotional disorders. The prospective studies of alcohol abuse in males have yielded fairly clear results. Several studies (Jones, 1968; Loper, Kammier, & Hoffman, 1973; McCord & McCord, 1960; Robins, Bates, & O'Neal, 1962; Vaillant, 1980; Vaillant & Milofsky, 1982) converge on the finding that prealcoholic adolescent males when compared with their peers who do not develop alcohol problems exhibit a pattern of impulsiveness, uncontrollability, and rebelliousness. Vaillant has used two longitudinal data sets to argue that many personality differences between alcoholics and alcoholics are a result of the condition itself. His own data, however, are consonant with the findings of the earlier studies. In his 1980 study, prealcoholic adolescents exhibited greater impulsivity than their peers. In the 1982 study, "premorbid antisocial personality" (evidenced by truancy and school behavior problems) was a major predictor (along with ethnicity and familial alcoholism) of the development of alcoholism. A longitudinal study of drug abuse (Stein, Newcomb, & Bentler, 1987) had results similar to the alcoholism studies. A trait of "rebelliousness" was a strong predictor of drug abuse during late adolescence and early adulthood. It is important to note that all of these prospective studies of substance abuse deal only with early adulthood. Conley and Prioleau (1983) have suggested that these alcoholics may represent only an early developing "essential" form of alcoholism characterized by psychopathic behavioral trends. A second "reactive" type of alcoholic with neurotiform behavior may develop later (mainly after age 40).

Longitudinal studies of nonalcoholic emotional disorders in males have varied widely in the populations studied and the methods employed. The results of both the Grant Study (Vaillant, 1974) and the Precursors Study

(Thomas & McCabe, 1980) indicate that measures of level of emotional stability taken on males in very early adulthood are reasonable predictors of the presence or absence of mental illness two or three decades in the future. Reconstructive and at-risk studies of schizophrenics indicate that some combination of emotional instability (neuroticism) and social withdrawal substantially antedates the full onset of the disorder (Johns et al., 1982; Lewine et al., 1980; Watt, 1972; Watt et al., 1982). These findings indicate that high levels of neuroticism (emotional lability) and low levels of social extraversion may be the most powerful personality antecedents of some nonalcoholic emotional disorders.

In addition to suggesting the probable personality antecedents of emotional disorders and alcohol abuse, earlier studies have suggested several environmental events that may have an influence on the occurrence of psychological disorders. These include early environmental events such as parental absence or death, ordinal position, and various aspects of the quality of parent–child interaction (McCrarie & Bass, 1983; Schwarz & Zuroff, 1979; Talovic et al., 1980; Walker et al., 1981) as well as stressful social events in adulthood (Gurwitz, 1981; Monroe et al., 1983; Murphy, 1982; Myers et al., 1972). Although these environmental factors may have some influence on the development of psychological disorders, several other studies indicate that this influence is very limited both for childhood environment (Crook & Eliot, 1980; Vaillant, 1974) and for stressful life events during adulthood (Harder, Strauss, Kokes, Ritzler, & Gift, 1980; Rabkin, 1980). Description of the causal pathways among the various antecedents of psychological disorders is an area of research that has hardly begun.

There is a general dearth of information on the long-term antecedents of psychological disorders in women. Less longitudinal information is available for women than for men. For instance, there are six longitudinal studies of alcohol abuse in males but only one longitudinal study of alcohol abuse in women (Jones, 1971). Many of the major psychological longitudinal studies have included only men. This is true of the Grant Study (Vaillant, 1977), the Cambridge-Somerville Study (McCord & McCord, 1960), and the Baltimore Longitudinal Study (Costa, McCrae, & Arenberg, 1980). The numbers of women participating in the Precursors Study (Thomas & McCabe, 1980), the Student Council Study (Cox, 1970), and the Adolescent Fantasy Study (Symonds & Jensen, 1961) were small, and most of their data on women have not been analyzed separately. Of the classic longitudinal studies only those of the Berkeley Institute of Human Development (Block, 1971; Eichorn, 1973), the Study of the Gifted (Oden, 1968; Terman, 1926), and the Kelly Longitudinal Study (Conley, 1984b, 1985a; Kelly, 1955) contained large numbers of women. These studies provide a large portion of our basic knowledge about the etiology of women's psychological disorders.

Several studies have reported neuroticism-related antecedents of women's psychological disorders. Stewart (1962) reported on the adolescent precursors of the psychosomatic disorders and behavioral maladjustment that the women in the Oakland Growth Study had developed by their mid-30s. Both conditions were predicted by higher than normal levels on adolescent self-reports of nervous tension. Jones (1971) reported on problem drinking in the same group. As adolescents, the women who later developed drinking problems were characterized by trained observers as more guilt ridden, oversensitive, anxious, and irritable than their female peers. Dealing with a combined sample of the Oakland Growth Study and the Berkeley Guidance Study, Gurwitz (1981) found that self-reports and observer ratings of women in their 30s indicating an "anxious–neurotic" personality profile were highly predictive of entrance into psychotherapy over the next 12 years. A report on the women of the Berkeley Guidance Study (Livson & Peskin, 1967) found that a "tension-free" orientation at preadolescence predicted good psychological health at age 31. In the Terman Study of the Gifted, parent ratings of female adolescents as high in self-confidence and low in feelings of inferiority predicted general life satisfaction of the gifted women when they were in their 60s (Sears & Barbee, 1977). Two short-term studies of the test scores of college women who later sought psychological counseling found higher than average levels on the "neurotic tetrad" of the MMPI and the Alienation and Discomfort Scales of the Psychological Screening Inventory (Bruch, 1977; Cooke & Kiesler, 1967).

In addition to the negative effect of neuroticism, a positive effect of early social extraversion has been reported in several studies. Among the women in the Berkeley Guidance Study, preadolescent behavior that was "independent" and "active" predicted good psychological health in the 30s (Brooks & Elliott, 1971; Livson & Peskin, 1967). Bruch's short-term study found a positive effect of social extraversion and social expressiveness on adjustment. In a reconstructive longitudinal study of women who became schizophrenic, the principal adolescent predictors (judged on the basis of teacher's comments in school records) were "compliance," "shyness," and "introversion" (Watt, 1972). Further research has raised the possibility that this predictive relationship may be specific to schizophrenia (Lewine, Watt, Prentky, & Fryer, 1980).

The predictive relationships of impulse control and agreeableness to the psychological health of women have received little attention in the various longitudinal studies. In fact, no findings bearing directly on the trait of agreeableness have been reported. Mixed results have been found for impulse control. Low levels of adolescent impulse control were predictive of the development of problem drinking (Jones, 1971), and low levels of adolescent "perseverance" predicted lessened general life satisfaction of older women (Sears & Barbee, 1977), but other studies have reported that the dimension of impulse control may have less predictive significance for women than it does for men (Gurwitz, 1981; Livson & Peskin, 1967; Watt, 1972).

Both retrospective and longitudinal studies have found that such aspects of the early social environment as conflict with parents and inconsistent treatment by parents are related to the occurrence of psychological problems in adult women (McCranie & Bass, 1984; Schwarz & Zuroff, 1979; Seigelman et al., 1970). A large amount of theoretical work (e.g., Parsons & Bales, 1955) and empirical work by Gilligan (1982) suggests that women are more immersed in and influenced by the familial social environment than are men, and this may hold true for environmental influences during adulthood as well as the preadult environment. One longitudinal study of women found that stressful life events within the families of adult women are predictive of symptoms of depression over a 14-year-period (Stewart & Salt, 1981).

Research based on the Kelly Longitudinal Study (KLS) has gone at least some distance toward addressing the methodological inadequacies of earlier studies on the relationship between personality and psychopathology. Although it is not large enough to permit a detailed analysis of the various psychodiagnostic groups, it began in 1935 with a group of 300 engaged couples drawn from the general population of young adults. Although most were somewhat higher in social class, educational attainment, and intelligence than the average of the general population, the KLS subjects are much less atypical in these matters than the subjects of most of the other major longitudinal studies. The follow-up studies in 1954–1955 and 1980–1981 were successful in obtaining information on alcohol abuse and emotional disorders from 78% of the original panel of 600. Because they cover a period from the early 20s until near or after retirement, these data approximate lifetime incidence information. The first data collection is firmly based in standardized personality assessment devices. Although some of the tests employed are rather dated, the data set allows a multitrait–multimethod assessment of personality and provides a linkage of prospective psychiatric research with refined factorial systems of personality description. Predictive measures of personality were obtained from the ratings of acquaintances in the 1935 KLS data collection. The criterion information on emotional disorders and alcoholism was drawn from detailed responses by the participants and their spouses in the 1954 and 1980 data collections. The great majority of these disorders became serious for the first time 10 or more years after the acquaintance ratings were made. The fact that the predictor variables were assessed by acquaintances and the criterion variables by self- and spouse report removes the most serious problems of methodological contamination.

The 76 participants who later developed emotional disorders or alcoholism had substantially higher neuroticism ratings in 1935; the differences between the disturbed groups and the normal group ranged between half and three-quarters of a standard deviation (see Figure 1). The alcoholics of both sexes had significantly lower impulse control ratings than normals or the emotionally disturbed, but these differences varied widely in magnitude (from .2 to .6 of a standard deviation). These differences demonstrate the

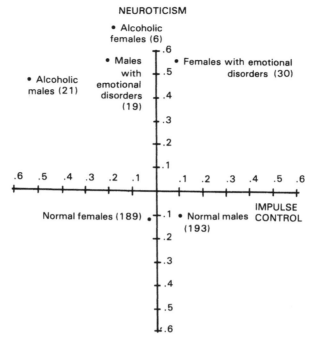

FIGURE 1. Scores of KLS participants on 1935–38 acquaintance ratings factors of neuroticism and impulse control (in standard deviation units) in relation to psychological health outcome. Numbers in parentheses are the *N*s of each group.

formative influence of personality traits on behavioral disorders. The social environmental component of the causation of behavioral disorders was measured by an index of stressful life events incurred from 1935 to 1954. The differences between the disturbed groups and normals on this index averaged about half of a standard deviation, and the interpretation of this finding must take into account that the time periods separating the life stresses and the onset of the disorders is shorter than that separating the personality ratings and onset. Thus it appears that personality exerts an influence on the etiology of behavioral disorders that is at least as large as environmental stress (Conley, 1985b).

There are indications in the KLS data that the time of onset of psychological disorders is associated with different patterns of personality antecedents. For instance, alcoholic males whose conditions became severe in early adulthood had 1935 personality ratings as highly impulsive, but this was less true of alcoholics whose conditions became severe in later adulthood. Earlier longitudinal studies of the personality antecedents of alcoholism were restricted to early adulthood and thus appear to have identified only the early developing "impulsive" type of alcoholic, leaving undetected a late developing "neurotic" alcoholic.

ARE PERSONALITY TRAITS PREDICTIVE OF IMPORTANT ASPECTS OF SOCIAL BEHAVIOR?

Because psychopathology and personality have important longitudinal relationships, it might also be expected that personality would also have predictive relationships with social behavior. The most frequently studied social behavior in longitudinal research is marital compatibility. Another area of inquiry is the relation of personality to important personal choices (for instance, occupational choice and childbearing). Recently some researchers have begun to investigate the relationship of personality and life satisfaction.

There are several longitudinal studies of martial compatibility. These studies have rather consistently supported a neuroticism hypothesis of marital distress. Adams (1946) reported on the personality inventory scores of the members of 100 married couples. The personality inventories were administered before marriage, and self-report measures of marital adjustment were taken 2 to 3 years after marriage. Emotional instability and irritability before marriage were predictive of low marital adjustment scores. Terman and Oden (1947) found that a self-report measure of emotional stability administered to their gifted subjects when they were 7 to 14 years of age was related to marital happiness 18 years later. The relationship was statistically significant for both sexes and the combined biserial correlation was .25. In 1940, Terman administered a "marital aptitude" test to his gifted subjects that consisted mainly of neuroticism items but also included material on social and family backgrounds. The concurrent correlation of marital aptitude with marital happiness was .62, and the great bulk of this relationship was accounted for by the neuroticism items ("The effects of childhood and family background are nearly all contained in the personality items themselves," concluded Terman and Oden, p. 258). The members of couples that divorced between 1940 and 1946 had 1940 marital aptitude scores that were a full standard deviation lower than the members of couples that remained married. Sears (1977) related the 1940 marital aptitude test scores with marital outcome as of 1972 (when the average age of the subjects was 62). The marital aptitude score of both sexes significantly differentiated broken marriages from unbroken marriages (the point-biserial correlation for the wives was .28 and for the husbands .12).

Burgess and Wallin (1953) reported correlations of .25 for men and .18 for women between scores on the Thurstone Neurotic Inventory before marriage and low marital adjustment scores after 3 to 5 years of marriage. Uhr (1957) analyzed a portion of the data of the Kelly Longitudinal Study.

Neuroticism scores on the Bernreuter Personality Inventory taken before marriage was significantly related to men's (but not women's) marital happiness 18 years after marriage. Vaillant (1978) found a strong relationship between psychopathology and poor social adjustment, on the one hand, and low levels of marital adjustment, on the other hand. Antecedents of poor marital adjustment included poor social adjustment and "fearfulness" in college. Bentler and Newcomb (1978) followed 77 newlywed couples for a period of 4 years. The emotional stability and objectivity of women and the deliberateness and introversion of men were predictive of a composite marital adjustment score that was administered to both couples that were still married and those who had divorced. Markman (1979, 1981) followed a small group of couples from before marriage through the fifth year of marriage. Unrewarding communication patterns during the premarital period were predictive of low levels of marital satisfaction.

All of the longitudinal studies of marital compatibility described found some predictive role of neuroticism or disturbed communication patterns. The findings of Bentler and Newcomb indicate that an additional predictive factor may be the impulse control or conscientiousness of the male member of the couple. This is consistent with nonlongitudinal studies by Terman *et al.* (1938) and Johnson and Harris (1980) that found divorced males were characterized by more impulsive behavior than males with stable marriages. Terman *et al.* (1938) and Burgess and Wallin reported the following impulse-related characteristics to be associated with marital instability in males: irregular employment, aggressive and domineering social demeanor, and high levels of premarital sexual activity. Thus the set of personality predictors of negative marital outcome appears to include low impulse control of the husband as well as high neuroticism of both members of the couple.

Although the longitudinal studies discussed thus far indicate that personality characteristics are predictive of marital compatibility, there are serious methodological problems both on the side of the predictors and on the side of the criterion. The two major problems involving the predictor variables are the use of self-report measures of personality characteristics and the embedding of personality measures in composite predictive indexes. Self-report methods of assessing personality characteristics are a serious problem when the criterion is marital happiness or marital satisfaction, which invariably is also assessed by way of self-reports. The correlation of self-reported neuroticism and marital satisfaction may be attributable to social desirability or other biases of self-presentation. When personality variables are only analyzed as part of composite predictive indexes, it is difficult to determine the contribution of antecedent personality variables relative to social background and other components of the indexes. This is a serious problem in Terman's Study of the Gifted and also affects most of the analyses of Burgess and Wallin. Terman initiated the practice of constructing predictive indexes for their use in applied settings, especially marriage counseling, but this tends to obscure the very interesting theoretical problem of whether personality characteristics or social experience has the greater predictive relationship with marital compatibility.

The criterion of marital compatibility is also beset by two major methodological problems. The first is whether to use marital stability (whether the marriage continued or resulted in divorce) or marital satisfaction (typically restricted to those who remain married) as the measure of marital compatibility. Both stability and satisfaction are useful measures of marital compatibility, and ideally longitudinal studies would use both of them. This has, unfortunately, not been the case for earlier studies. Adams, Burgess and Wallin, Uhr, and Markman used only marital satisfaction and restricted their analyses to intact marriages. In his analysis of the data of the Terman Study of the Gifted, Sears made the opposite choice, employing only marital stability as the criterion of marital compatibility. Obviously, either of these two approaches applied in isolation is likely to underestimate the relationship of personality and marital compatibility, because personality is likely to operate both on the relative compatibility of intact marriages and as a contributing cause of marital dissolution.

The second methodological problem in measuring marital compatibility is the restriction to relatively brief intervals after marriage. Most of the longitudinal studies examine only the first 5 or fewer years after marriage. The Vaillant study, Terman's Study of the Gifted, and the Kelly Longitudinal Study are the exceptions in this regard. These studies gathered data on marital outcome over two or more decades. Most divorces occur after the first 5 years of marriage, and it is quite possible that the causal factors of instability and dissatisfaction are different in early and in mature marriages. Interestingly enough, these differences have seldom been explored by the authors of the various longitudinal studies of marital compatibility.

The antecedents of marital stability (divorce or remaining married) and marital satisfaction (within the group that remains married) were investigated using the KLS panel of 300 couples who have been followed from their engagements in the 1930s until 1980 (Kelly & Conley, 1987). Twenty-two of the couples broke their engagements, and of the 278 couples who married, 50 got divorced at some time between 1935 and 1980. Personality characteristics (measured by acquaintance ratings made in the 1930s) were important predicators of both marital stability and marital satisfaction. The three aspects of personality most strongly related to marital breakup were the neuroticism of the husband, the neuroticism of the wife, and the impulse control of the husband. In combination, the 17 major antecedent variables were moderately predictive of a criterion variable composed of both marital stability and marital satisfaction (multiple $R = .49$). The three major aspects of personality (extraversion, neuroticism, and impulsivity) accounted for more than half of the predictable variance. The remaining variance was accounted for by attitudinal, social, environmental, and sexual history variables.

The Kelly Longitudinal Study used a more comprehensive criterion and a longer follow-up period than the other studies, the former difference probably increasing and the latter decreasing the size of the multiple correlation obtained between predictors and criterion. The KLS figure of approximately .5 represents the best available estimate of the predictability of marital compatibility with premarital characteristics of the couple. This level of predictability is by no means negligible, but as Ellis (1950) pointed out, it permits little accuracy at the level of individual predictions, and thus the use of such predictive schemes in premarital counseling is limited.

The most striking finding of the marriage data of the Kelly Longitudinal Study is the relatively strong predictive relationship of personality traits and marital compatibility. The traits were measured by acquaintance ratings and were not contaminated by self-report biases. The personality traits were the strongest predictors of the composite measure of compatibility, accounting for more than half of the predictable variance. The neuroticism of both spouses and the husband's impulsiveness are very potent predictors of negative marital outcome. High neuroticism of both spouses was common to both the divorced group and the stably married but dissatisfied group. The stably married but dissatisfied group differed from the divorced group in the low social extraversion and agreeableness of the husbands (Kelly & Conley, 1987).

Other longitudinal studies have examined the formative influences of personality in a life cycle context and focused on personal choices. These studies were undertaken by Huntley and Davis (1983), Himmelweit and Swift (1976), Livson (1976), Elder and MacInnis (1983), and Helson, Mitchell and Meane (1984). Huntley and Davis examined the predictive correlations of the Allport-Vernon Study of Values and occupational choice over a period of 25 years in an original population of college males. Occupational groups such as physicians, engineers, businessmen, and college professors had characteristic interest profiles many years before they actually settled on their final occupational choices. Himmelweit and Swift followed the patterns of media usage and taste in a group of English males from adolescence through middle adulthood. After social class and other background factors were taken into account, variables related to personality and personal outlook (in particular, authoritarianism, "forward looking," and achievement motivation) had significant predictive relationships with the media tastes the men developed. Both Livson and Elder and MacInnis used data on the women in the Oakland Growth Study. These two studies followed the females from adolescence into middle adulthood and contrasted the emerging lifestyles of those with conventional and unconventional sociocultural orientations. Women with conventional orientations tend to marry and have children early in life and pass smoothly into middle age. Women with unconventional orientations tended to marry and have children later and often experienced the decade of their 40s as a time of personal crisis. Helson *et al.* followed a group of college women over a period of 23 years and found evidence of reciprocal relations between personality and aging and environmental changes. Patterns of sociocultural values predicted the timing and occurrence of major life events (marriage, having children, starting a career, divorce). Factors such as self-assurance, unconventionality, and intellectual independence influenced the ways in which the women structured their lives and were in turn influenced by the occurrence of major life events. For instance, the women who later divorced appeared to be especially independent during their college years, and in the aftermath of their divorces, they showed a marked increase in psychological mindedness.

Personality traits have recently been related to levels of life satisfaction. Some concomitants of the life satisfaction of the aged are quite well established. Life satisfaction is associated with good physical health, sound financial position, and high levels of social activity (Larsen, 1978; Palmore & Kivett, 1977). Other factors that have been shown to be correlated with satisfaction are age, race, and frequency of sexual intercourse. These factors may be referred to as the manifest correlates of life satisfaction. The influence of these variables on feelings of satisfaction is hardly surprising, and the ways in which they exert their influence appear to be relatively straightforward.

The study of life satisfaction has now moved on to more complicated matters. Until recently, almost all research on life satisfaction proceeded as if directed at a universal aged person, ignoring important individual difference within the aged population. The individual's personality characteristics appear to influence the level of life satisfaction in old age. A number of other studies (Costa & McCrae, 1980a; Costa, McCrae, & Norris, 1981; George, 1978; Mussen *et al.*, 1982) have shown that temperamental characteristics such as neuroticism, extraversion, and intelligence are related to life satisfaction.

Conley (1985b) showed that the personality traits of neuroticism and social extraversion have a long-term influence on life satisfaction. This influence operates over intervals as long as 45 years. The negative effect of neuroticism and the positive effect of social extraversion operate both directly and indirectly on life satisfaction in late adulthood. The indirect effects are mediated by physical health and by social relationships. Costa and McCrae (1980b) and Costa *et al.* (1981) found that neuroticism and extraversion had a predictive influence on life satisfaction of men over periods of 5 to 13 years. In the KLS, these relationships were confirmed in a study covering a much larger segment of the adult life span. Personality characteristics in early and middle adulthood have an effect on the life satisfaction of aged men and aged women.

CONCLUSION

Longitudinal studies of personality have made a great deal of progress, and this is clear when the studies are examined in the aggregate. The cases for both the consistency of major personality traits and their predictive relationships to psychopathology and social behavior now rest on rather firm empirical foundations. Several major methodological limitations in this field have been discussed, but there has been substantial progress toward sounder methodology. Multimethod assessment is especially promising in a longitudinal context.

In coming years, longitudinal personality research may begin to make good on its promise of providing a firm basis for theories of personality development and the etiology of mental and psychophysiological disorders. White (1966) was fundamentally correct when he referred to "a gap at the center of our knowledge about personality. The neglected area can be identified as continuous development over periods of time amid natural circumstances" (p. 22). As longitudinal studies mature, this gap is slowly but surely being filled.

REFERENCES

Adams, C. R. (1946). The prediction of adjustment in marriage. *Educational and Psychological Measurement, 6*, 185–193.

Allport, G. W., & Vernon, P. E. (1931). A test for personal values. *Journal of Abnormal and Social Psychology, 26*, 231–248.

Amelang, M., & Borkenau, P. (1982). Uber die factorielle Struktur und externe Validitat einiger Fragebogen-Skalen zur Erfassung von Dimensionen der Extraversion und emotional Labilitat. [Concerning the factor structure and external validity of certain questionnaire scales conceptually related to the dimensions of extraversion and emotion lability.] *Zeitschrift fur Differentielle und Diagnostische Psychologie, 3*, 119–146.

Arsenian, S. (1970). Change in evaluative attitudes during 25 years. *Journal of Applied Psychology, 54*, 302–304.

Bentler, P. M., & Newcomb, M. D. (1978). Longitudinal study of marital success and failure. *Journal of Consulting and Clinical Psychology, 46*, 1053–1070.

Block, J. (1971). *Lives through time.* Berkeley: Bancroft.

Borgatta, E. F. (1964). The structure of personality characteristics. *Behavioral Science, 9*, 8–17.

Brooks, J. B., & Elliott, D. M. (1971). Prediction of psychological adjustment at age thirty from leisure time activities and satisfactions in childhood. *Human Development, 14*, 51–61.

Bruch, M. A. (1977). Psychological Screening Inventory as a predictor of college student adjustment. *Journal of Consulting and Clinical Psychology, 45,* 237–244.

Burgenmeister, B. B. (1940). The permanence of interests of women college students: A study in personality development. *Archives of Psychology* (No. 255), 1–59.

Burgess, E. W., & Wallin, P. (1953). *Engagement and marriage.* New York: J. B. Lippincott.

Campbell, D. T., & Fiske, D. W. (1959). Convergent and discriminant validation by the multi-trait-multimethod matrix. *Psychological Bulletin, 56,* 81–105.

Conley, J. J. (1984a). The hierarchy of consistency: A review and model of longitudinal findings on adult individual differences in intelligence, personality, and self opinion. *Personality and Individual Differences, 5,* 11–26.

Conley, J. J. (1984b). Longitudinal consistency of adult personality: Self-reported psychological characteristics across 45 years. *Journal of Personality and Social Psychology, 47,* 1325–1333.

Conley, J. J. (1985a). Longitudinal stability of personality traits: A multitrait-multimethod-multioccasion analysis. *Journal of Personality and Social Psychology, 49,* 1266–1282.

Conley, J. J. (1985b). A personality theory of adulthood and aging. In R. Hogan (Ed.), *Perspectives in personality* (Vol. 1, pp. 81–115). Greenwich, CT: JAI Press.

Conley, J. J., & Prioleau, L. A. (1983). Personality typology of men and women alcoholics in relation to etiology and prognosis. *Journal of Studies on Alcohol, 44,* 996–1010.

Converse, P. E., & Markus, G. B. (1979). Plus a change . . . : The new CPS Election Study panel. *American Political Science Review, 73,* 32–49.

Cooke, M. K., & Kiesler, D. J. (1967). Prediction of college students who later require personal counseling. *Journal of Counseling Psychology, 14,* 346–349.

Costa, P. T., Jr., & McCrae, R. R. (1977). Age differences in personality structure revisited: Studies in validity, stability, and change. *Aging and Human Development, 8,* 261–275.

Costa, P. T., Jr., & McCrae, R. R. (1980a). Still stable after all these years: Personality as a key to some issues in adulthood and old age. In P. B. Baltes & O. G. Biran, Jr. (Eds.), *Life-span development and behavior* (pp. 185–203). New York: Academic Press.

Costa, P. T., & McCrae, R. R. (1980b). Influence of extraversion and neuroticism on subjective well-being: Happy and unhappy people. *Journal of Personality and Social Psychology, 38,* 668–678.

Costa, P. T., McCrae, R. R., & Arenberg, D. (1980). Enduring dispositions in adult males. *Journal of Personality and Social Psychology, 38,* 793–800.

Costa, P. T., McCrae, R. R., & Norris, A. H. (1981). Personal adjustment to aging: Longitudinal prediction from neuroticism and extraversion. *Journal of Gerontology, 36,* 78–85.

Cox, R. D. (1970). *Youth into maturity,* New York: Mental Health Materials Center.

Crook, T., & Eliot, J. (1980). Parental death during childhood and adult depression. *Psychological Bulletin, 87,* 252–259.

Digman, J. M., & Inouye, J. (1986). Further specification of the five robust factors of personality. *Journal of Personality and Social Psychology, 50,* 116–123.

Eichorn, D. H. (1973). The Berkeley longitudinal studies: Continuities and correlates of behavior. *Canadian Journal of Behavioral Science, 5,* 297–320.

Elder, G. H., & MacInnes, D. J. (1983). Achievement imagery in women's lives from adolescence to adulthood. *Journal of Personality and Social Psychology, 43,* 394–404.

Ellis, A. (1950). Discussion of papers by Terman, Burgess, and Adams. *Marriage and Family Living, 12,* 51–55.

Eysenck, H. J. (1969). *The biological basis of personality.* Springfield, IL: Charles C Thomas.

Eysenck, H. J. (1977). Personality and factor analysis: A reply to Guilford. *Psychological Bulletin, 84,* 405–411.

Eysenck, H. J., & Eysenck, S. B. G. (1976). *Psychoticism as a dimension of personality.* London: Hodder & Stoughton.

Finn, S. E. (1986). Stability of personality ratings over 30 years: Evidence for an age/cohort interaction. *Journal of Personality and Social Psychology, 50,* 813–818.

Fiske, D. W. (1949). Consistency of the factorial structures of personality ratings from different sources. *Journal of Abnormal and Social Psychology, 44,* 329–344.

George, L. K. (1978). The impact of personality and social status factors upon levels of activity and psychological well-being. *Journal of Gerontology, 33,* 840–847.

Gilligan, C. (1982). *In a different voice: Psychological theory and women's development.* Cambridge: Harvard University Press.

Goldberg, L. R. (1981). Language and individual differences: The search for universals in personality lexicons. In L. Wheeler (Ed.), *Review of personality and social psychology* (Vol. 2, pp. 318–359). Beverly Hills, CA: Sage Publications.

Golden, R. R., & Meehl, P. E. (1979). Detection of the schizoid taxon with MMPI indicators. *Journal of Abnormal Psychology, 88,* 217–233.

Gottesman, I., & Shields, J. (1982). *Schizophrenia: The epigenetic puzzle.* Cambridge, United Kingdom: Cambridge University Press.

Guilford, J. P. (1975). Factors and factors of personality. *Psychology Bulletin, 82,* 802–814.

Guilford, J. P. (1977). Will the real factor of extraversion-introversion please stand up? A reply to Eysenck. *Psychological Bulletin, 84,* 412–416.

Gurwitz, P. M. (1981). Paths to psychotherapy in the middle years: A longitudinal study. *Social Science and Medicine, 15E,* 67–76.

Harder, D. W., Strauss, J. S., Kokes, R. F., Ritzler, B. A., & Gift, T. E. (1980). Life events and psychopathology severity among first psychiatric admissions. *Journal of Abnormal Psychology, 89,* 165–180.

Helson, R., & Moane, G. (1987). Personality change in women from college to midlife. *Journal of Personality and Social Psychology, 53,* 176–186.

Helson, R., Mitchell, U., & Meane, G. (1984). Personality and patterns of adolescence and nonadherence to the social clock. *Journal of Personality and Social Psychology, 46,* 1079–1096.

Himmelweit, H., & Swift, B. (1976). Continuities and discontinuities in media usage and task: A longitudinal study. *Journal of Social Issues, 32,* 133–156.

Hogan, R. (1983). A socioanalytic theory of personality. In M. Page (Ed.), *Nebraska Symposium on Motivation* (pp. 418–452). Lincoln, Nebraska: University of Nebraska Press.

Hoge, D. R., & Bender, I. E. (1974). Technical appendix to "Factors influencing values change among college graduates in adult life" (NAPS-01959).

Huesmann, L. R., Evon, L. D., & Yarmel, P. W. (1987). Intellectual functioning and aggression. *Journal of Personality and Social Psychology, 52,* 232–240.

Huntley, C. W., & Davis, F. (1983). Undergraduate Study of Values scores as predictors of occupation twenty-five years later. *Journal of Personality and Social Psychology, 45,* 1148–1155.

Johns, R. S., Mednick, S. A., & Shulsinger, F. (1982). Teacher reports as a prediction of schizophrenia and borderline schizophrenia: A Bayesian decision analysis. *Journal of Abnormal Psychology, 91,* 399–413.

Johnson, H. H., & Harris, W. G. (1980). Personality and behavioral characteristics related to divorce in a population of male applicants for psychiatry evaluation. *Journal of Abnormal Psychology, 89,* 510–513.

Jones, M. C. (1968). Personality correlates and antecedents of drinking patterns in adult males. *Journal of Consulting and Clinical Psychology, 32,* 2–12.

Jones, M. C. (1971). Personality antecedents and correlates of drinking patterns in women. *Journal of Consulting and Clinical Psychology, 36,* 61–69.

Kagan, J. (1988). The meanings of personality predicates. *American Psychologist, 43,* 614–620.

Kelly, E. L. (1955). Consistency of the adult personality. *American Psychologist, 10,* 659–681.

Kelly, E. L., & Conley, J. J. (1987). Personality and compatibility: A prospective analysis of marital stability and marital satisfaction. *Journal of Personality and Social Psychology,* *52,* 27–40.

Knight, R. P. (1942). The dynamics and treatment of chronic alcohol addiction. *Bulletin of the Menninger Clinic, 1,* 223–250.

Larson, R. (1978). Thirty years of research on the subjective well-being of older Americans. *Journal of Gerontology, 33,* 109–125.

Leon, G. R., Gillum, B., Gillum, R., & Gouze, M. (1979). Personality stability and change over a 30-year period—Middle to old age. *Journal of Consulting and Clinical Psychology, 47,* 517–524.

Lewine, R. R. J., Watt, N. F., Prentky, R. A., & Fryer, J. H. (1980). Childhood social competence in functionally disordered psychiatric patients and in normals. *Journal of Abnormal Psychology, 89,* 132–138.

Livson, F. B. (1976). Patterns of personality development in middle-aged women: A longitudinal study. *International Journal on Aging and Human Development, 7,* 107–115.

Livson, N., & Peskin, H. (1967). Prediction of adult psychological health in a longitudinal study. *Journal of Abnormal Psychology, 72,* 509–518.

Loper, R. G., Kammier, M. L., & Hoffman, H. (1973). MMPI characteristics of college freshman males who later became alcoholics. *Journal of Abnormal Psychology, 82,* 159–162.

Markman, H. J. (1979). Application of a behavioral model of marriage in predicting relationship satisfaction of couples planning marriage. *Journal of Consulting and Clinical Psychology, 47,* 743–749.

Markman, H. J. (1981). Prediction of marital distress: A 5-year follow-up. *Journal of Consulting and Clinical Psychology, 49,* 760–762.

McCrae, R. R., & Costa, P. T., Jr. (1987). Validation of the five-factor model of personality across instruments and observers. *Journal of Personality and Social Psychology, 52,* 81–90.

McCord, W., & McCord, J. (1960). *Origins of alcoholism.* Stanford, CA: Stanford University Press.

McCrarie, E. W., & Bass, J. D. (1984). Childhood family antecedents of dependency and self-criticism: Implications for depression. *Journal of Abnormal Psychology, 93,* 3–8.

Mischel, W., Shoda, Y., & Peake, P. K. (1988). The nature of adolescent competencies predicted by preschool delay of gratification. *Journal of Personality and Social Psychology, 54,* 687–696.

Monroe, S. M., Imhoff, D. F., Wise, B. D., & Harris, J. E. (1983). Prediction of psychological symptoms under high-risk psychosocial circumstances: Life events, social support, and symptom specificity. *Journal of Abnormal Psychology, 92,* 338–350.

Moss, H. A., & Susman, E. J. (1980). Longitudinal study of personality development. In O. G. Brim and J. Kagan (Eds.), *Constancy and change in human development* (pp. 530–595). Cambridge: Harvard University Press.

Murphy, E. (1982). Social origins of depression in old age. *British Journal of Psychiatry, 141,* 135–142.

Mussen, P., Eichorn, D. H., Honzik, M. P., Bieber, S. L., & Meredith, W. (1980). Continuity and change in women's characteristics over four decades. *International Journal of Behavioral Development, 3,* 333–347.

Mussen, P., Honzik, M. P., & Eichorn, D. H. (1982). Early adult antecedents of life satisfaction at age 70. *Journal of Gerontology, 37,* 316–322.

Myers, J. K., Lindenthal, J. J., Pepper, M. P., & Ostander, D. R. (1972). Life events and mental status: A longitudinal study. *Journal of Health and Social Behavior, 13,* 398–406.

Noller, P., Law, H., & Comrey, A. L. (1987). Cattel, Comrey and Eysenck personality factors compared: More evidence for the five robust factors? *Journal of Personality and Social Psychology, 53,* 775–782.

Norman, W. T. (1963). Toward an adequate taxonomy of personality attributes: Replicated factor structure in peer nomination personality ratings. *Journal of Abnormal and Social Psychology, 66,* 574–583.

Norman, W. T., & Goldberg, L. R. (1966). Raters, ratees, and randomness in personality structure. *Journal of Personality and Social Psychology, 4,* 681–691.

Oden, M. H. (1968). The fulfillment of promise: Forty-year followup of the Terman gifted group. *Genetic Psychology Monographs, 77,* 3–93.

Palmore, E., & Kivett, U. (1977). Change in life satisfaction: A longitudinal study of persons aged 46–70. *Journal of Gerontology, 32,* 311–316.

Parsons, T., & Bales, R. F. (1955). *Family socialization and process.* New York: Free Press.

Passini, F. T., & Norman, W. T. (1966). A universal conception of personality structure? *Journal of Personality and Social Psychology, 4,* 44–49.

Plant, W. T., & Telford, C. W. (1966). Changes in personality for groups completing different amounts of college over two years. *Genetic Psychology Monographs, 74,* 3–36.

Rabkin, J. G. (1980). Stressful life events and schizophrenia: A review of the literature. *Psychological Bulletin, 87,* 408–425.

Robins, L. N., Bates, W. N., & O'Neal, P. (1962). Adult drinking patterns of former problem children. In D. J. Pittman & C. R. Snyder (Eds.), *Society, culture and drinking patterns* (pp. 395–412). New York: Wiley.

Royce, J. R., & Powell, A. (1983). *Theory of personality and individual differences: Factors, systems, and processes.* Englewood Cliffs, NJ: Prentice-Hall.

Schuerger, J. M., Tait, E., & Tavernelli, M. (1982). Temporal stability of personality by questionaire. *Journal of Personality and Social Psychology, 43,* 176–182.

Schwarz, J. C., & Zuroff, D. C. (1979). Family structure and depression in female college students: Effects of parental conflict, decision-making power, and inconsistency of love. *Journal of Abnormal Psychology, 88,* 398–406.

Sears, P. S., & Barbee, A. H. (1977). Career and life satisfaction among Terman's gifted women. In J. Stanley, W. C. George, & C. Sdano (Eds.), *The gifted and the creative: A fifty year perspective* (pp. 78–94). Baltimore: Johns Hopkins University Press.

Sears, R. R. (1977). Sources of life satisfactions of the Terman gifted men. *American Psychologist, 32,* 119–128.

Seigelman, E., Block, J., Block, J., & von der Lippe, A. (1970). Antecedents of optimal psychological adjustment. *Journal of Consulting and Clinical Psychology, 35,* 283–289.

Smith, G. E. (1967). Usefulness of peer ratings on personality in educational research. *Educational and Psychological Measurement, 27,* 967–984.

Stein, J. A., Newcomb, M. D., & Bentler, P. M. (1987). An 8-year study of multiple influences on drug use and drug use consequences. *Journal of Personality and Social Psychology, 53,* 1094–1105.

Stern, P. J. (1964). *The abnormal person and his world.* Princeton, NJ: Van Nostrand.

Stewart, A. J., & Salt, P. (1981). Life stress, life-styles, depression, and illness in adult women. *Journal of Personality and Social Psychology, 40,* 1063–1069.

Stewart, L. H. (1962). Social and emotional adjustment during adolescence as related to the development of psychosomatic illness in adulthood. *Genetic Psychology Monographs, 65,* 175–215.

Stewart, L. H. (1964). Change in personality test scores during college. *Journal of Counseling Psychology, 11,* 211–220.

Symonds, P. M., & Jensen, A. R. (1961). *From adolescent to adult.* New York: Columbia University Press.

Talovic, S. A., Mednick, S. A., Schulsinger, F., & Falloon, I. R. H. (1980). Schizophrenia in high risk subjects: Prognostic maternal characteristics. *Journal of Abnormal Psychology, 89,* 501–504.

Terman, L. M. (1926). *Genetic studies of genius. Volume I: Mental and physical traits of a thousand gifted children.* Stanford: Stanford University Press.

Terman, L. M. (1950). Predicting marriage failure from test scores. *Marriage and Family Living, 12*, 51–55.

Terman, L. M., & Buttenwieser, P. (1935). Personality factors in marital compatibility. *Journal of Social Psychology, 6*, 143–171.

Terman, L. M., & Oden, M. H. (1947). *The gifted child grows up: Twenty-five year followup of a superior group.* Stanford: Stanford University Press.

Terman, L. M., Buttenwieser, P., Ferguson, L. W., Johnson, W. B., & Wilson, D. P. (1938). *Psychological factors in marital happiness.* New York: McGraw-Hill.

Thomas, C. B., & McCabe, O. L. (1980). Precursors of premature disease and death: Habits of nervous tension. *Johns Hopkins Medical Journal, 147*, 137–145.

Todd, J. E. (1941). Social norms and the behavior of college students. *Columbia University Contributions to Education*, No. 833. New York: Teachers College, Columbia University Bureau of Publications.

Tupes, E. C., & Christal, R. E. (1961). Recurrent personality factors based on trait ratings. *United States Air Force ASD Technical Reports*, Nos. 61–97.

Uhr, L. M. (1957). *Personality changes during marriage.* Unpublished manuscript dissertation, University of Michigan.

Vaillant, G. E. (1974). Natural history of male psychological health—II. Some antecedents of healthy adult adjustment. *Archives of General Psychiatry, 31*, 15–22.

Vaillant, G. E. (1977). *Adaptation to life.* Boston: Little, Brown.

Vaillant, G. E. (1978). Natural history of male psychological health: VI. Correlates of successful marriage and fatherhood. *American Journal of Psychiatry, 135*, 653–659.

Vaillant, G. E. (1980). Natural history of male psychological health: VIII. Antecedents of alcoholism and "orality." *American Journal of Psychiatry, 137*, 181–186.

Vaillant, G. E., & Milofsky, E. S. (1982). The etiology of alcoholism: A prospective viewpoint. *American Psychologist, 37*, 499–503.

Walker, E., Hoppes, E., Emory, E., Medniak, S., & Schulsinger, F. (1981). Environmental factors related to schizophrenia in psychophysiologically labile high-risk males. *Journal of Abnormal Psychology, 90*, 313–320.

Watt, N. F. (1972). Longitudinal changes in the social behavior of children hospitalized for schizophrenia as adults. *Journal of Nervous and Mental Disease, 155*, 42–54.

Watt, N. F., Grubb, T. W., & Erlenmeyer-Kimlin, L. (1982). Social, emotional, and intellectual behavior at school among children at high risk for schizophrenia. *Journal of Consulting and Clinical Psychology, 50*, 171–181.

White, R. W. (1966). *Lives in progress: A study of the natural growth of personality.* New York: Holt, Rinehart & Winston.

Whitely, P. L. (1938). The constancy of personal values. *Journal of Abnormal and Social Psychology, 33*, 405–408.

Woodruff, D. S., & Birren, J. E. (1971). *Age and personality: A twenty-five year followup.* Unpublished manuscript, University of Southern California.

CHAPTER THREE

Interpersonal Models of Personality and Psychopathology

DAVID W. BROKAW AND CLINTON W. MCLEMORE

INTRODUCTION

Few intellectual achievements *truly* qualify as "paradigm shifts." However, as argued by the eminent Hans Strupp (1982) in his foreword to the *Handbook of Interpersonal Psychotherapy*, the new emphasis on *interpersonal transactions*—between patient and therapist, patient and family members, and patient and other significant persons—*and their intrapsychic consequences*, perhaps does so qualify.

Interpersonal psychology grew out of the rich theoretical writings of the neo-Freudians—Karen Horney, Frieda Fromm-Reichmann, Erich Fromm—but most notably from the systematized lecture notes of the great teaching psychiatrist, Harry Stack Sullivan (1953a,b, 1954, 1956, 1962, 1964). Sullivan was the first clinician to focus the searchlight of therapeutic scrutiny on what actually happened between patient and therapist in the consulting room, viewing this as symptomatic of how the patient structured his or her "interpersonal world." He was forever asking the simple but heuristic question, "What is this person trying to do with or toward me in this situation?" Naturally, Sullivan also attended carefully to what the patient did in relation to other people, as described either by the patient or third-party observers. Perhaps the most famous of all Sullivanian theses is

DAVID W. BROKAW • Azusa Pacific University, Azusa, California 91702.   CLINTON W. MCLEMORE • Relational Dynamics Institute, Inc., P.O. Box 60725, Pasadena, California 91116.

Personality, Social Skills, and Psychopathology: An Individual Differences Approach, edited by David G. Gilbert and James J. Connolly. Plenum Press, New York, 1991.

the suggestion that "it takes people to make people sick, and it takes people to make people better."

It was left to the infamous Timothy Leary (1957) to set the lyrics of Sullivan to the music of empiricism—specifically, to melodies built around two independent themes: dominance/submission and love/hate. Whatever may have been Leary's personal failings or professional shortcomings, the work he did at the Kaiser Hospital in Oakland was brilliant enough to earn him an appointment to the Harvard faculty. Before extending his interests into such esoterica as the chemical expansion of consciousness, he articulated the fundamental building blocks of interpersonal transactions.

The primary applications of interpersonal theory have thus far been to personality and psychotherapy. Anchin and Kiesler's *Handbook of Interpersonal Psychotherapy* (1982) provides an excellent introduction to how leading interpersonalists view personality and how they go about the business of helping people change. The "interpersonal school" prepared the grounds for a number of fruitful offshoots, including family systems theory, communication theory, and the study of nonverbal behavior.

GENERAL ASSUMPTIONS ABOUT PERSONALITY

We cannot pretend to offer a precise definition of *personality*. Indeed, this highly abstract term encompasses a continuum of meanings, from the more peripheral attributes used to distinguish between people (sometimes referred to as "traits") to that which is at the core of a person (sometimes referred to as "character"). A classic personality text (Hall & Lindzey, 1978) asserts that it is not possible to apply any *substantive* definition of personality with any generality—when all arguments and counterarguments have been balanced out, the answer to "What is personality?" is ultimately determined by one's theoretical preference. Nevertheless, we will venture to suggest a common starting point by reviewing some, by now, generally accepted assumptions about personality, based on well-established clinical and research literature.

1. *Personality has to do with sameness and differentness.* We now know that there *are* regularities in behavior that persist over time (Block, 1981; Costa & McCrae, 1986; Epstein, 1979). For example, aggressive youngsters are likely to become aggressive adults, whereas prosocial behavior during youth predicts prosocial behavior 22 years later (Eron, 1987; Huesmann, Eron, Lefkowitz, & Walder, 1984). The "sameness" of personality thus has to do with stability, with what is consistent and predictable about a person over time. "Differentness" refers to that which distinguishes one person from another, with what makes each person unique and distinct.

Formal *theories* of personality tend to emphasize commonalities among many people, whereas single case studies (e.g., in the psychoanalytic tradition) deal more with the unique patterns found within a particular individual. A proposal by Duke (1986) argues that further progress in "personality *science*" will require a greater emphasis on the "softer" methodologies— methodologies (e.g., personal narratives, subjective observations, introspection, N-of-1 case studies) more finely attuned to individual differences.

2. *Personality is inferred.* "Personality" is a hypothetical construct, a kind of mental synthesis, a way of giving meaning to our observations. Personality is no more subject to direct observation than Freud's "id" or the tooth fairy. Its nature, both nomothetically and ideographically, is inferred from consistencies in our "thought, feeling, and action patterns" (TFAPs) [see below]. In many theories, personality is viewed as the unseen *cause* behind behavior.

3. *Statements about personality are properly statements of probability.* Although individuals often act consistently in different circumstances, no one is *totally* predictable. Any statement about personality is implicitly qualified by its placement on the normal curve.

For example, we might say, "Harry has a friendly, outgoing personality." Our general comment about Harry's personality represents a prediction, implicitly cross-situational, based on our experiences with him. However, if we were to videotape and code all of Harry's behavior on a given day, we might find, more precisely, that Harry has an 80% probability of being friendly and outgoing in social group situations but a 20% probability of enacting various other behaviors (e.g., sulking, withdrawing, competing, and so on). We might also find that, when alone with his wife, Harry is more likely to enact tender but passive behaviors.

Consider, as a further example, the prediction of dangerousness. We might conclude, on the basis of his or her personal history and formal test results, that an individual is likely to be dangerous to others. We might even be able to predict the types of triggering events associated with a high probability of dangerous behavior. Despite multiple assessment procedures, however, we are *not* able to determine the day that this person will harm another, who will be harmed, or even whether this individual will ever "act out" at all.

In contrast to medicine, where at least some laboratory tests can confirm or rule out the presence of certain pathogens, behavioral science is rarely exact. People are just too complex and, therefore, "personality" will probably never be totally objectified or measured.

4. *Behavior is "determined" by multiple causes.* Despite the fact that empirical research can draw an association between certain environmental "causes" and certain personality "effects," such research explains only a *portion* of the variance in behavior. Linkages between causes and effect are rarely straightforward. Thus, although a given cause may predict a certain effect in a particular group of people, this "cause" is not necessarily linked to the same effect in a different group of people, nor need it result in the

same effect in the same group of people at a different point in time. Conversely, a given cause may be found in some persons apart from the predicted effect or in association with different behavioral effects. This is because behavior is an end product that reflects multiple, interacting causal forces.

For example, male children who observe their fathers abuse their mothers, or are themselves abused, are much more likely than are children from nonviolent homes to subsequently batter their own wives. One study (Roy, 1982) indicates that 81% of wife beaters come from such a home. Yet, not all male children from a violent home will beat their wives, nor are all wife beaters from violent homes. Other causal variables enter into the final behavioral equation.

5. *Five, at the most six, personality factors are both necessary and reasonably sufficient to describe the major dimensions of personality.* Although this assumption would be challenged by those who doubt that personality traits even exist, factor analytic studies of personality have consistently yielded five similar dimensions (first described by Tupes & Cristal in 1961; see also Digman & Inouye, 1986; Goldberg 1981; McCrae & Costa, 1986; Norman, 1963). Some researchers have described this multiply replicated finding as "practically a law" of human personality (Digman & Inouye, 1986).

Using McCrae and Costa's (1986) labels, the five consistent dimensions of personality are as follows:

1. *Neuroticism,* described variously as emotional stability, anxiety, or "ego strength versus emotional disorganization"
2. *Extraversion (versus introversion),* a factor closely associated with Jung's personality theory, also portrayed as "sociable versus retiring" or "fun-loving versus sober"
3. *Openness (to experience),* described also as intellect, reflects such attributes as "imaginative versus down-to-earth" or "independent versus conforming"
4. *Agreeableness,* described in other studies as consideration, "friendly compliance versus hostile noncompliance," or "soft-hearted versus ruthless"; this factor seems to identify one's capacity for friendly relationships
5. *Conscientousness,* a factor that includes such qualities as persistence and goal directedness, also defined by such adjectives as "self-disciplined versus weak-willed"

Although some studies have identified *creativity* as a sixth independent factor, it does not emerge with the same degree of consistency as the prior five factors and, therefore, is not considered reliable.

The theoretical position represented in this chapter argues that social interactions reflect the most vital dimensions of personality and, consequently, we will follow other interpersonal theorists in focusing on two of the five primary factors: Extraversion/Introversion and Agreeableness/Disagreeableness. These dimensions are also designated as Control and Affiliation, respectively, and are represented by the dominance/submission and love/hate axes of the Interpersonal Circle described later.

INTERPERSONAL ASSUMPTIONS ABOUT PERSONALITY

We now turn to a more distinctly "interpersonal" treatment of personality. Just as we could not offer a generally accepted definition of personality, neither are we able to provide a definitive statement of the interpersonal *approach* to personality. An "interpersonal orientation" is more a *perspective* on personality than a formal theory. Therefore, we will simply offer some foundational assumptions with which most interpersonal theorists would agree. The reader who would like to delve deeper into this area is referred to the excellent summaries by Kiesler (1982, 1983).

1. *Personality is manifested only in interpersonal situations.* In contrast to individualistic approaches, which tend to focus on the person as an isolated entity, interpersonalists insist that personality is best understood *within the context of social transactions.* Sullivan went so far as to argue that the word *personality* has no meaning *apart from* one's characteristic interaction with others. This is *not* to say that personality disappears when no one is present. Indeed, we interact both with those who are physically present and with those whom we carry about in our heads (described by Freud as "introjects"). Even the marooned sailor interacts with "others," specifically with imagined "actors" based on his memories of significant others (otherwise known as "personifications").

We now offer an oft-cited interpersonal definition of personality: "Personality is nothing more . . . than the patterned regularities that may be observed in an individual's relations with other persons, who may be real in the sense of actually being present, [or] real but absent and hence 'personified,' or illusory" (Carson, 1969, p. 26).

2. *Our "self" develops out of early interpersonal experiences.* Consistent with this definition of personality, Sullivan taught that one's "self-concept" (patterns of self-perception) as well as one's "self-system" (patterns of defense against anxiety) develop out of one's interpersonal transactions with "significant others." Drawing upon the social psychology of Cooley (1956) and Mead (1934), he explained that the content of one's "self" is based upon the "reflected appraisals" of others. For instance, we begin to view ourselves psychologically in the same way that we sense important other persons to view and respond to us. Our self-concepts tend to mirror what we believe they "see" in us. Once a "sense of self" has been established, new "appraisals" are likely to be internalized only to the extent that they are

consistent with our existing appraisals. Discrepant appraisals, even if more positive than existing appraisals, arouse anxiety and, thus, are subject to selective inattention (Kiesler, 1982; Sullivan, 1953a,b, 1956).

Relatedly, the interpersonal view suggests that the two *primary* determinants of social behavior are (1) personal predispositions, based upon one's self-definition, and (2) the environment *as perceived by the individual* (Kiesler, 1982). Thus avoidant persons will enact behaviors based both on fears that they are not likely to be accepted (self-definition) and their personal interpretations ("filtering") of environmental experiences ("I believe that Joe canceled because he really doesn't like me, not just because his car broke down").

3. *Behavior is motivated to achieve satisfaction, security, and intimacy.* Although our theoretical viewpoint emphasizes the interpersonal aspects of personality, it is clear that people are biological creatures. Ultimately, all thoughts, feelings, and behaviors have physical correlates. The interpersonal perspective recognizes that behavior is often motivated by a *need for satisfaction* of such biological tensions as hunger, thirst, sex, and so on.

Interpersonal clinicians, however, focus primarily on the individual's *needs for security and intimacy.* Security is maintained by avoiding or minimizing anxiety, whereas intimacy is achieved through emotional closeness with others.

As Sullivan (1953a,b) pointed out, anxiety is among our most unpleasant experiences. Although people may actually pursue some unpleasant experiences now and then (e.g., the fear that is intertwined with the excitement of parachuting out of an airplane), presumably no one seeks anxiety. Thus, Sullivan—as well as Horney and Fromm—posited an "antianxiety" system in the human personality, asserting that anxiety avoidance is one of the core organizational principles underlying the operations of the self.

Our initial experiences of anxiety are believed to involve "empathic contagion," wherein the mother transmits anxiety to her infant (Sullivan, 1953a,b). The infant's experience of anxiety is extremely unpleasant, characterized by a major loss in his or her sense of well-being. As the child grows older, anxiety comes to be associated with situations involving the disapproval of significant others, most notably the parents. Subsequent experiences of anxiety typically involve another person (again, whether *in vivo* or in imagination) and most often have to do with the other's disapproval. In Sullivan's schema, anxiety is triggered by threats to self-esteem. Horney (1945) suggests that anxiety is associated with helplessness and danger, whereas Fromm (1947) relates anxiety to isolation and weakness. Despite their differences as to the source of anxiety, all three view anxiety as a distinctly interpersonal phenomena.

Anxiety is presumably kept within manageable limits by eliciting a predictable or "complementary" response from others—responses that confirm our self-perceptions and self-presentations. In fact, some interpersonalists have gone so far as to argue that the raison d'être of interpersonal behavior is to elicit complementary behaviors from others. Carson (1969), for example, suggests that "the adoption of a particular interpersonal stance in large part serves the function of producing a particular stance in the other person" (p. 143), that is, a complementary response. Although self-confirming or complementary responses are believed to enhance self-esteem and security, noncomplementary responses tend to disconfirm our definition of self, thereby creating anxiety. In general, interpersonal models predict that *complementarity* occurs on the basis of correspondance with respect to affiliation (love elicits love and hate elicits hate) and on the basis of reciprocity with respect to control (dominance elicits submission and vice versa).

As we have indicated, after satisfaction and security, a third motivator is the *need for intimacy*. Interpersonalists assume that *people are relational by nature* and that intimacy reflects "that quality of interpersonal relationships that is most conducive to happiness, fulfillment, and meaning in human life" (McLemore & Hart, 1982, p. 227). Supporting this assumption are findings that infants deprived of intimacy seem to be at greater risk for illness and, ultimately, death (Spitz, 1945).

Just as the need for security is associated with the avoidance of anxiety, the need for intimacy is associated with the avoidance of loneliness. Or, put another way, loneliness drives us toward intimacy. This motivator is so great that we are often willing to pay a high emotional price in order to purchase some approximation to intimacy: "We need to be involved with other people and we will go to great lengths to bring this about; we prefer the involvement of love, but if that escapes us, hate will do" (Beier & Valens, 1975, pp. 16–17).

Parenthetically, there is often an inherent conflict between intimacy and security: Intimacy requires self-disclosure (you cannot be intimate with someone who does not know you), and self-disclosure invariable involves threat to self-esteem and consequent anxiety ("He/she wouldn't like me if he/she knew *that* about me"). Thus persons are faced with the choice between remaining secure but unknown ("securely lonely") or enduring short-term anxiety in the hope of developing longer term intimacy. Our clinical bias is to encourage people, within prudent limits, to risk experiencing the anxiety in order to achieve intimacy. Unfortunately, in the ordinary course of human affairs, the need for present security often supercedes the need for future intimacy. Of course, the clinical extreme of this pattern is seen in the avoidant personality.

4. *Human behavior is best explained within the context of circular causality and reciprocal influence.* Circular causality refers to the notion that human interaction does not lend itself to a linear understanding of cause and effect, that is, that Person A's behavior is an independent cause of

Person B's behavior. Rather, Persons A and B are in positions of mutual influence, where the behavior of each represents both a *response* and a *stimulus* to the other's behavior (Staats, 1975). Sullivan (1953b, 1954) recognized this when he rejected the notion that a psychoanalyst could truly be a "blank screen." He asserted that therapists and clients make up a two-person field in which the therapist cannot help but be a "participant observer," one who inevitably influences—and is influenced by—the patient's presentation, simply by virtue of being present (i.e., you cannot *not* communicate).

Assume, for example, that Sue's self-definition incorporates a strong caretaking theme; perhaps because, at an early age, she was responsible for her ailing mother. Consistent with this definition of self, Sue will most likely "train" others to be dependent on her (submission is complementary to dominance). As she so interacts, a "circular" effect will occur such that her caretaking behaviors will elicit "needy" responses from others that, in turn, will further elicit and reinforce her caretaking, and so on, in an ongoing cycle. Her successful negotiation of this caretaking/dependency cycle confirms her self-definition, thereby minimizing anxiety and maintaining her sense of security because her interpersonal world is predictable. Should someone rebuff her attempts to define herself as a caretaker in the relationship ("Quit mothering me!"), Sue is likely to become anxious. At this point, she will either redouble her efforts to take care of the other or withdraw from the relationship.

We have diagrammed a second example, more clinical in nature, having to do with what we have come to call the "Withdrawal-Deprivation Cycle" (see Figure 1). In the diagram, diamonds depict reported internal states, boxes portray observable behaviors, and circles show hypothesized internal (mediating) processes. Before we describe, in words, what Figure 1 communicates graphically, note that we are presenting the most rudimentary version of what is, in reality, a set of transactions of mind-boggling complexity. It is not difficult, with a little effort, to expand such a "transactional diagnosis" so that it covers a large wall. Theoretically, we presume that the intricacy of such a sequential analysis is limited only by the nuances of human psychology coupled with our inability to understand them.

In the Withdrawal–Deprivation Cycle, Person A feels needy, lonely, and essentially depressed, which quite expectedly leads to fantasies of moving closer to people, perhaps of asking for nurturance from at least one other human being. Unfortunately, because of previous interpersonal trauma and frustration, such affiliative idea wishes are quickly supplanted by expectations of rejection, turbocharged by toxic "self-statements" (e.g., "If you open up, you'll only get hurt"). Person A, instead of moving toward people, avoids them, further withdrawing from the only *real* and lasting source of emotional gratification available to homo sapiens. Parenthetically, such withdrawal is more or less self-perpetuating, in that it leads to a

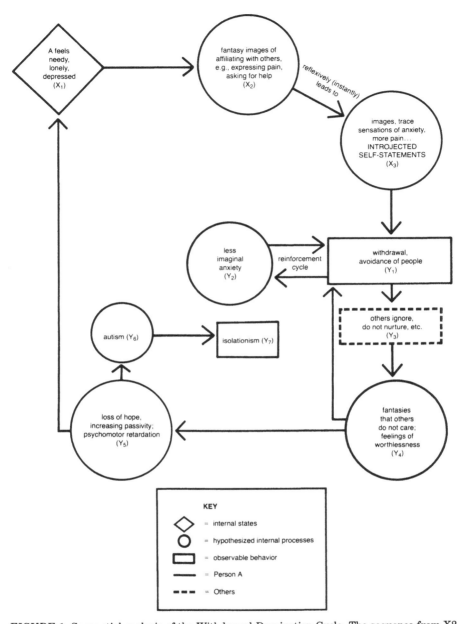

FIGURE 1. Sequential analysis of the Withdrawal-Deprivation Cycle. The sequence from X2 to X3 is perhaps originally learned in interactions with "significant others" but is perhaps maintained by the sequences found from Y1 to Y4. The sequence from Y5 to Y7 represents the potential end point to this vicious circle, after having moved directly from Y5 to X1 and through the cycle enough times that hope for a meaningful relationship with others has been completely lost. Copyright © 1988 by Relational Dynamics Institute, Inc. Reprinted by permission.

decrease in anxiety, which of course "reinforces" what immediately preceded it (withdrawal).

Person B predictably ignores Person A, failing to meet a need, in the latter, which has never been evident—because Person A, out of uneasiness, never took the risk of communicating this need. All of this serves only to fuel his or her fantasies of being unloved and worthless, which in turn leads to a loss of hope, further passivity, and perhaps a retarded depression. Once again, Person A may report to us in treatment feelings of neediness, loneliness, and general despondency. Along the way, as he or she repeats the cycle with seemingly endless persistence, Person A's perceptions may become increasingly autistic, which may eventually lead to termination of the cycle by a kind of exile of the self: Person A retreats forever to the illusory safety of "schizoid never-never land."

5. *Statements about personality must be anchored to level(s)*. Leary (1957) argued that unilevel statements of personality are meaningless because it is unclear whether they refer to overt behavior, self-description, or underlying motivations.

Leary suggested five levels of personality: (1) public communication, having to do with the social impact of the individual's behavior (their *real* behavior); (2) conscious descriptions, having to do with the individual's subjective, verbal description of his or her own and others' behaviors (this level is highly vulnerable to perceptual distortions); (3) private symbolization, representing preconscious, autistic aspects of personality; (4) unexpressed unconscious, defined to include interpersonal themes that are consistently avoided through selective inattention and "forgetting"; and, (5) ego ideal, having to do with the individual's consciously reported values and his or her conceptions of good and evil.

Interpersonal theorists have attended primarily to the first two levels.

INTERPERSONAL ASSESSMENT AND MODELS OF BEHAVIOR

Given the assumption that personality has little meaning apart from social transactions, it is not surprising that interpersonal theorists would attempt to build social models of behavior in order to "chart" personality styles.

As noted, Leary (1957) was the first to construct such a model, which he called the "Interpersonal Circle" (see Figure 2 for the most recent descendent of his model). It has since come to be known as the Leary Circle. Leary's genius was in constructing a simple, yet sophisticated method of graphing the major types of behaviors that people enact toward one another.

Built around a vertical "Control" axis—ranging from dominance to submission—and a horizontal "Affiliation" axis—ranging from love to hate,

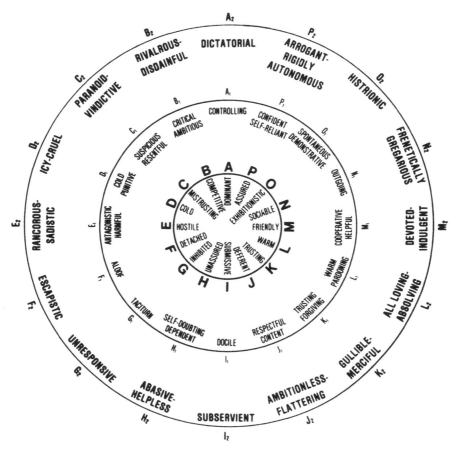

FIGURE 2. Kiesler's 1982 Interpersonal Circle. From "The 1982 Interpersonal Circle: A taxonomy for complementarity in human transactions," by D. J. Kiesler, 1983, *Psychological Review, 90*, p. 189. Copyright © 1983 by the American Psychological Association. Reprinted by permission of the author.

the Leary Circle is based on the assumption that any social behavior involves a certain "weighting" along these two orthogonal dimensions. In other words, the research of Leary and his colleagues suggested that each action can be plotted along a dimension ranging from love to hate, and a second dimension, ranging from dominance to submission. Further, the two "plottings" are presumed to be completely independent of each other. Thus, as later simplified by Rausch, Dittman, and Taylor (1959) and Carson (1969), any behavior could be mapped within one of four quadrants, *friendly dominance* (the northeast quadrant of Figure 2), *hostile dominance* (northwest quadrant), *hostile submission* (southwest quadrant), or *friendly submission* (southeast quadrant).

In addition to plotting behaviors along these two dimensions, the Interpersonal Circle incorporates several other important characteristics of social behavior.

First, the model builds in an *intensity* dimension, having to do with the "strength" of a behavior. For example, though controlling and dictatorial behaviors are both "dominant" (represented in segment A of Figure 2), the latter is a more intense expression of the former.

Second, the model presents a "circumplicial" ordering of behavior. In other words, the behavioral descriptors are ordered around the circle (more technically, the "circumplex") so that the most opposite (least correlated) behaviors are 180 degrees apart (e.g., competitive behaviors, segment B, versus deferent behaviors, segment J). Behaviors with more in common (more highly correlated) are more spatially close (e.g., acting competitively and acting dominantly are found in segments B and A, respectively).

Third, and perhaps most impressively, this model predicts behavioral sequences—what behaviors will prompt, pull, elicit (and reinforce) what other behaviors. In interpersonal terms, behaviors that are statistically likely to follow certain other behaviors are termed *complementary* behaviors. Using Carson's (1969) simplification, the model predicts that hostile dominance (HD) prompts and reinforces hostile submission (HS), and vice versa, and that friendly dominance (FD) prompts and reinforces friendly submission (FS), and vice versa (Brokaw & McLemore, 1983).

A few examples may clarify these predictions. If Jim says to his basketball coach, "Could you give me a little help with my foul shooting technique?" (a respectful expression of dependence, coded "FS"), the coach is predicted to respond with something along the lines of, "Sure, maybe we should start with how you're placing your feet" (strong helpful direction, coded "FD").

If, on the other hand, Jim whines to his coach, "How come you never help me with my foul shooting, I don't think you really want me on the team" (a distrusting, hostile complaint, coded "HS"), the coach is more likely to respond with something along the lines of, "No, I don't want you on the team if all you're going to do is complain" (a stern and rejecting response, coded "HD").

Note that circumplicial interpersonal models presuppose that dyadic interactions reflect a process of negotiating both who, in the relationship, is going to exercise more control (who will be dominant and who will be submissive) as well as how affiliative (hostile or friendly) the relationship will be (Kiesler, 1986).

The assessment instrument used in conjunction with the Leary Circle is the Interpersonal Check List (ICL; LaForge & Suczek, 1955; Leary, 1957). The ICL consists of 128 adjectival phrases or items, 8 items for each of the 16 categories represented on the Interpersonal Circle. The rater simply indicates ("checks off") the items that are believed to describe the person being evaluated. Dominance, Submission, and Intensity scores are derived from the completed ICL. With appropriate norms available (Lees-Haley, 1981; Pepe, 1985), the ICL allows one to map a person's behavior ("personality style") onto the Leary Circle. The ICL and Interpersonal Circle remain popular among modern-day researchers and clinicians.

Since Leary first published his model, it has undergone progressive refinements by various researchers. We will comment on several of these.

Lorr and his colleagues (Lorr, Bishop, & McNair, 1965; Lorr & McNair, 1963, 1965, 1967) developed the Interpersonal Behavior Inventory (IBI), reflecting a translation of adjectives from Leary's ICL into more overt interpersonal behaviors. Scores derived from the IBI enable the charting of social behaviors on their version of the interpersonal behavior circle, which includes some modifications of Leary's categories and their placements.

Wiggins's refinement of the interpersonal circle (1979, 1982) boasts of an improved circumplex structure and bipolar dimensions that, unlike the Leary circle, reflect true semantic opposites (e.g., ambitious-dominant vs. lazy-submissive, gregarious-extraverted vs. aloof-introverted). Without truly opposite poles, "it is impossible to derive precise and consistent predictions of interpersonal complementarity" (Kiesler, 1983, p. 186). Interpersonal behavior can be mapped onto this circle with the Interpersonal Adjective Scales (IAS; Wiggins, 1979).

Kiesler and his colleagues (Kiesler, Anchin, Perkins, Chirico, Kyle, & Federman, 1976; Perkins, Kiesler, Anchin, Chirico, Kyle, & Federman, 1979), drawing upon the work of Leary, Lorr, and Wiggins, offer what appears to be the most sophisticated reconstruction of Leary's model to date: the "1982 Interpersonal Circle" (Kiesler, 1983, see Figure 2).

In addition to the characteristics delineated in describing Leary's circle, Kiesler (1983) indicates that the 1982 Interpersonal Circle provides a more comprehensive measurement of behaviors located in the northeast (FD) and southwest (HS) quadrants, greater polarities between behaviors located at opposite positions on the circle, and more accurate placement of some "misplaced" behavioral segments.

The assessment instrument used in conjunction with the 1982 Interpersonal Circle is the Impact Message Inventory (IMI), available from Consulting Psychologists Press. The IMI is designed to measure the affective, cognitive, and behavioral impact that Person A has on Person B, as rated by Person B. Scores derived from the IMI may be used to locate the characteristic interpersonal style of Person A on the 1982 Circle.

Orford (1986), in his significant review of 14 empirical studies of complementarity, indicates that theoretical predictions of complementarity (which generally have been well accepted) are oversimplified and still quite imperfect (also note Wright & Ingraham, 1986). In reviewing these studies of complementarity, Orford found that predictions of complementarity generally worked well for behaviors on the friendly side of the circle: friendly-dominant and friendly-submissive behaviors were frequently and consistently observed to operate in complementary ways. On the other hand, predictions of complementarity on the hostile side of the circle seem not to be dependable (see also Kiesler & Goldston, 1988).

For example, the research cited repeatedly found that hostile dominance is *most likely* to elicit further hostile dominance by the other (not the predicted hostile submission!), *particularly when the interchange occurs between two equals* (such as a husband and wife; Orford, 1986). The predicted response of hostile submission to hostile dominance appears more likely to occur when the expression of HD is considered legitimate, or when the respondent, because of limited resources or status, has little choice but to "absorb" the hostile dominance (e.g., as seen in the response of a son to his mother).

Relatedly, although hostile submission in one person was sometimes followed by hostile dominance in the other (as predicted), it appeared equally likely that HS would be followed by further HS—and most likely that HS would be followed by friendly dominance (Orford, 1986).

Thus, although the general concept of complementarity appears sound, Orford (1986) suggests that interpersonal circle models of social behavior may be oversimplified, particularly in their attempts to predict hostile behavior. He concludes that future models must take into account such intervening variables as status, role, and setting.

Looking, for example, at status, current interpersonal models do not appear to incorporate the principle that persons are highly likely to defend against threats to their personal status. Hostile-dominant acts, representing a major threat to one's status, are often "defended against" with like behavior (Orford, 1986). On the other hand, the frequently observed friendly-dominant response to hostile submission (described by Orford) may well reflect the respondent's desire to restore an appropriate status balance to the relationship. Among other variations from classic rules of complementarity is this: "The prediction that can be made with most confidence . . . [is] that relatively high status (however it is achieved or ascribed) makes friendly-dominance a more likely response than it would otherwise be, whatever the antecedent" (Orford, 1986, p. 376).

Kiesler (1987) challenges Orford's (1986) critique of the interpersonal circle on a number of grounds. He argues, for example, that Orford's conclusions are based on research that used an outdated model—13 of the 14 studies cited made use of Leary's (1957) Interpersonal Circle, rather than more advanced interpersonal circles, such as those constructed by Kiesler (1983) or Wiggins (1982).

Kiesler (1987) further points out, in responding to Orford (1986), that all studies of complementarity to date have analyzed overt action/reaction chains of behavior. Kiesler suggests that the principles of complementarity may apply more accurately to interactional sequences involving the link between Person A's overt action and Person B's covert-impact response. He argues that "contextual and other intervening factors govern whether person B's covert impacts lead to automatic [complementary] reactions, or are altered in overt expression" (Kiesler, 1987, p. 2).

Another area addressed by Kiesler (1987) has to do with a common misunderstanding of interpersonal theory. Contrary to the implication of Orford's (1986) review, interpersonal theory does *not* postulate that any two interactants will show complementary behavior patterns or even that one should expect to find complementary pairings in most social sequences. Rather, specific behaviors are predicted to *pull* for complementary responses from the other. Whether or not complementarity actually occurs "depends crucially on what *the other person* concurrently wants, seeks, and is most comfortable with" (Kiesler, 1987, p. 2).

The final interpersonal model that we will review—Benjamin's Structural Analysis of Social Behavior (SASB; 1974, 1979a)—has been described as "the most detailed, clinically rich, ambitious, and conceptually demanding of all contemporary models" (Wiggins, 1982, p. 193). It is perhaps "the most scientifically rigorous and clinically astute model published" (McLemore & Hart, 1982, p. 233).

As seen in Figure 3, the SASB replaces the single interpersonal circle with two interpersonal surfaces (the top and middle circumplicial diamonds) and adds a third surface (the bottom diamond) that has to do with intrapsychic experiences. The top surface of the SASB ("Focus on Other") describes *actions directed toward* another person, whereas the middle surface ("Focus on Self") has to do with one's *reactions* to others. Although Benjamin has tended recently to shy away from this terminology, these two surfaces are sometimes known, respectively, as "parent" and "child," in that "prototypically speaking, focus on others (doing something to, for, or about the other person) is characteristic of parents, whereas focus on self (being in a reactive state) is characteristic of children" (Benjamin, 1984, p. 128). Thus, in contrast to classic interpersonal circles that deal primarily with "adult" behaviors, the SASB also incorporates the more self-focused or "childlike" behaviors classified by circumplicial models such as Schaefer's (1965).

Whereas the Leary models have described submission as the opposite of dominance, the SASB describes submission as the *complement* of dominance, in that these two styles form a stable combination. With Schaefer (1965), Benjamin defines emancipation as the *opposite* of dominance: the former involving a "letting go" of control, the latter involving a high degree of control. Further, the SASB offers a high degree of specificity, describing 108 social behaviors as compared to the 16 nodal interactional styles incorporated by most interpersonal circles. A simplified version of the SASB divides each of the three surfaces into octants (see Figure 4). Most research and clinical applications of the SASB have used this octant version. The popularity of the octant version appears to stem from its greater simplicity

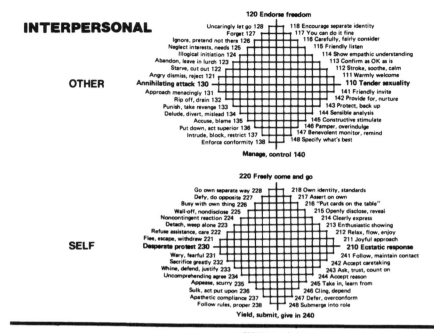

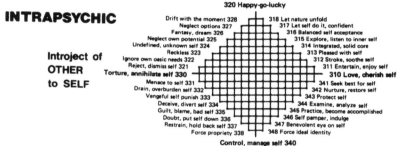

FIGURE 3. Model for Structural Analysis of Social Behavior (SASB), full version. From "Structural analysis of differentiation failure," by L. S. Benjamin, 1979a, *Psychiatry*, *42*, p. 6. Copyright © 1979 by William Alanson White Psychiatric Foundation. Reprinted by permission of the author.

(only 24 as opposed to 108 reference points), which better lends itself to memorization and is associated with higher interrater reliability when applied to research.

Looking, for a moment, at the interpersonal surfaces only (the top and middle diamonds), the SASB is constructed around three (as opposed to two) dimensions of interpersonal behavior: affiliation, interdependence, and focus. As with the two-dimensional models, the horizontal axes have to do with affiliation, ranging from hostility on the left to love on the right. The

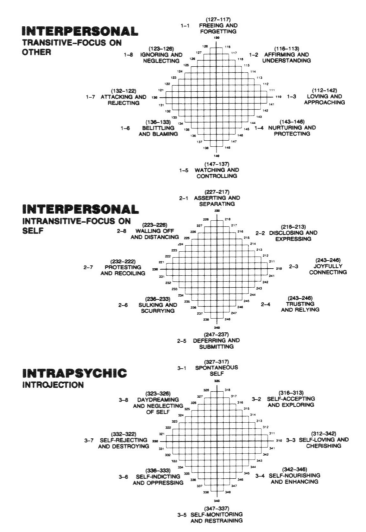

FIGURE 4. Model for Structural Analysis of Social Behavior (SASB), 1986 cluster version. From "Use of the SASB dimensional model to develop treatment plans for personality disorders. I: Narcissism," by L. S. Benjamin, 1987, *Journal of Personality Disorders, 1*, p. 53. Copyright © 1987 by Guilford Publications. Reprinted by permission of the author.

vertical axes have to do with interdependence, ranging from independent or differentiated behavior (the top half of the diamond) to interdependent or enmeshed behavior (the bottom half of the diamond).

The vertical axis of the "Focus on Other" diamond represents independent behavior as autonomy giving and interdependent behavior as power. Autonomy and power are considered opposites. The vertical axis of the

"Focus on Self" diamond ranges between the opposites of individualism (top) and submission (bottom).

The bottom diamond—"Intrapsychic"—has to do with introjects, or what occurs when one treats oneself as important others have in the past. The behaviors toward self described on this surface represent the likely introjects of the parental behaviors located at identical locations on the *top* surface. Thus if a young man were to be diagnosed as guilty and self-blaming (see Figure 3, Introject surface, point 335), it implies that he perceived important others as accusing and blaming (Other surface, point 135).

Benjamin (1979b) suggests that the SASB incorporates four quadrants, having to do with autonomy, which "interpersonal circles" ignore. These are the *upper* halves of the Self and Other surfaces of the SASB (see Figures 3 and 4). For example, examination of the two quadrants making up the upper half of the "Focus on Other" surface reveals behaviors described to invoke hostile autonomy and to encourage friendly autonomy. According to Benjamin, there are no corresponding behaviors located on the Interpersonal Circle (see Figure 2).

Turning to Benjamin's (1979b) view of the commonalities between the SASB and the interpersonal circles, she notes a rough correspondence between the *lower* half of the SASB *Focus on Other* diamond (see Figure 3) and the *top* half of the interpersonal circle (see Figure 2). Also approximately corresponding are the *lower* half of the SASB *Focus on Self* diamond and the *lower* half of the interpersonal circle.

PRINCIPLES OF SASB

We will now define some specific behavioral relationships that are based on SASB theory (please refer to Figure 3).

Opposite behaviors are located 180 degrees apart in terms of affiliation and interdependence but reside on the same surface. So, for example, to cling and depend upon another (point 246) is defined as the opposite of being busy with one's own thing (point 226).

Complementary behaviors are located at corresponding points on the Other and Self diamonds. For example, if a husband protects and backs up his wife (point 143), she is predicted to "complement" him by trusting and counting on him (point 243). Using SASB terminology, complementary SASB behaviors are characterized by the same degree of affiliation and interdependence, with one of the interactants focusing on the "other," whereas the "other" is focusing on his or her self.

A state of *maximal instability* is created when two persons attempt to act out of the same region of interpersonal space, indicated by identical locations on the SASB model (Benjamin, 1984). Thus, although it may be apparent that two persons who mutually attack and reject one another (point 1-7, "Focus on Other" surface, Figure 4) are creating a highly unstable relationship, it is also true that two caretakers, two blamers, two whiners, two wallflowers, or two controllers are creating an equally unstable relationship. As Benjamin puts it, "If both people have the same, rather than complementary focus, there is no 'connection.' If I focus on you and you focus on me, we're not talking about the same thing and we're not going to have a stable transaction" (1984, p. 134).

A major advantage of the SASB model is its utility in predicting how best to *change* another's behavior. *Antithetical* behaviors are applied, in treatment, in order to get another to behave in a manner opposite to how he or she is currently behaving. Antitheses are defined as opposites of complements (or complements of opposites). For example, looking at Figure 3, the antithesis of 236, "sulk, act put upon" is 116, "carefully, fairly consider." The principle of antithesis predicts that the sulky, sullen patient will, over time, respond to careful and fair consideration by others and will eventually "put [his or her] cards on the table." Of course, one would not immediately move to an antithetical position and expect a complementary change in the other. Rather, the person attempting to effect change would move through some intermediary transactions on the way to an antithetical stance.

Although the SASB may be applied on the basis of clinical impressions, a sophisticated psychometric package is also available. SASB assessment is based on a series of questionnaires completed by either the subject or third-party observers. Completed ratings are used to analyze self-concept and significant interpersonal relationships. Among other options, computer analysis of the questionnaires provides an SASB "map" of how the subject interacts with important others as well as a computer-generated interpretive narrative. Scores may also be generated that measure whether the patient's style is perceived to revolve around control, submission, withdrawal, conflict, or friendliness. The most recent addition to the SASB assessment battery is the WISPI (Wisconsin Personality Inventory), a measure of Axis II personality disorders (Benjamin, 1987). Further information on these psychometrics may be obtained from the INTREX Interpersonal Institute, Inc., c/o Lorna Benjamin, Ph.D., 677 Cortez Street, Salt Lake City, Utah 84103.

OTHER USEFUL RATING SYSTEMS

Although not interpersonal circles or their direct descendants, several other interpersonal assessment instruments deserve mention.

First, there is the Interpersonal Style Inventory (ISI), developed by Maurice Lorr and colleagues (Lorr, 1986; Lorr & Manning, 1978; Lorr, O'Conner, & Seifert, 1977). The ISI provides scores on 15 bipolar scales having to do with five primary dimensions of personality (interpersonal

involvement, socialization, autonomy, self-control, and stability). A short
form is also available (Lorr & DeJong, 1986). The ISI yields a computer-
generated report and is published by Western Psychological Services.

William Schutz (1960) developed the Fundamental Interpersonal Relations Orientation–Behavior (FIRO-B), designed to measure the subject's
characteristic interpersonal behavior, in terms of expressed and wanted
inclusion, control and affection. The FIRO-B can be completed in 10 to 15
minutes. Among other instruments based on the FIRO scales are measures
of (a) characteristic feelings toward others (the FIRO-F), (b) relationships
between parent and child (Life InterPersonal History Enquiry, "LIPHE"),
and (c) marital satisfaction (Marital Attitudes Evaluation, "MATE"). The
FIRO scales are available from Consulting Psychologists Press.

Leonard Horowitz (1979) filled a major gap in interpersonal assessment
with his Inventory of Interpersonal Problems (IIP). The IIP provides an
efficient means for clients to indicate what they perceive to be their primary
areas of interpersonal difficulty. They simply select, from a list, the problem
areas that apply.

In an attempt to assess clients' less accessible interpersonal percepts,
we have also been experimenting with 20 Interpersonal Inkblots (IIB).
These inkblots are specifically designed to elicit "people responses"
(McLemore & Hart, 1982), which most Rorschach experts agree are of
central diagnostic importance.

INTERPERSONAL DIMENSIONS OF ADJUSTMENT

Interpersonalists, like many other personality theorists, view normal
and abnormal behavior along a continuum. This perspective is reflected in
Sullivan's (1953a) One Genus Postulate, "We are all more simply human than
otherwise, be we happy and successful, contended and detached, miserable
and mentally disordered or whatever" (p. 16). Thus we would expect that
every human being's personality, whether adaptive or maladaptive, could be
described and measured along common dimensions. The following represent
dimensions of healthy adjustment that are of particular interest to
interpersonalists.

1. *Emotional health and well-being are dependent upon the ability to
communicate clearly.* Clear communication is the bedrock of satisfactory
interpersonal relations. Although good communication, like "mental
health," is often defined by what it is not—for example, not double binding,
confusing, indirect, contradictory, or self-defeating—we might generally
say that clear communication is characterized by congruence between verbal and nonverbal channels. If someone says that they are angry or in love
with you, their gestures, facial expressions, and tonal qualities should be
consistent with that. Healthy communication allows for "an open, direct and

clear relationship with other persons" (Kiesler, 1982, p. 14). Further, healthy communication is expressed from a clear field, in reaction to the real behaviors of the other, as opposed to being "parataxic distortions" based on earlier interpersonal experiences.

On the other hand, *maladjustment is characterized by duplicitous or disturbed communication.* Duplicitous communication consists of "indirect, confusing, ambigous, incongruous, and self-defeating messages" (Kiesler, 1988, p. 17). Through the action of extreme and intense behaviors, the maladjusted person consistently elicits a constricted range of aversive responses from others but does not take responsibility for the other's response and is unaware of the self-defeating aspects of his or her communicational style. Kiesler (1988) describes the relationship between disturbed communication and maladjustment as follows:

> Individuals are said to experience emotional problems when as a relatively consistent consequence of their interpersonal communication (a) they experience enduring and unaccountable aversive feelings or negative self-evaluations and/or (b) when over time their communication leads to consistent and unaccountable aversive communication from significant others in their lives. . . . The results are unintended, unwanted, unaccountable, and aversive consequences. (p. 16)

An example of the interrelationship between disturbed communication and disordered behavior is found in research on the role of "expressed emotion" in schizophrenia. In brief, this research, begun by British researchers (Vaughn & Leff, 1976a,b) over a decade ago, suggests that certain kinds of expressed emotion (EE) in families is related to the course of schizophrenia spectrum disorders. Among other findings, family environments in which there are high levels of expressed negative emotion (those which involve a great deal of criticism, hostility, and overinvolvement) have been associated with higher relapse rates among schizophrenics who return home, as well as with the onset of schizophrenia spectrum disorders among disturbed (but not yet psychotic) teens. This research has been replicated and extended in the United States, through such ambitious undertakings as Goldstein's UCLA Family Project study of schizophrenia (Doane, Falloon, Goldstein, & Mintz, 1985; Goldstein, 1988; Goldstein, Judd, Rodnick, Alkire, & Gould, 1968; Goldstein, Rodnick, Jones, McPherson, & West, 1978; Miklowitz, Strachan, Goldstein, Doane, & Snyder, 1986).

2. *Healthy personality is manifested in an ability to successfully negotiate reciprocal roles with others.* Central to adaptive social relations is an ongoing process of negotiation between the participants in order to meet complementary needs. Successful negotiation implies a mutually acceptable definition of roles as well as mutually rewarding experiences. In the work setting, for example, this may mean that both individuals in a relationship agree that one of them has the role of "boss" and will therefore be dominant, whereas the other will take the more submissive "employee" role. A less healthy personality (e.g., the passive–aggressive) may experience difficul-

ties with authority and, therefore, be completely unable to successfully sustain an employee role that, in turn, will eventually lead to the termination of the relationship.

3. *Adaptive relationships are based on equitable interpersonal exchanges.* With Thibaut and Kelley (1959), we believe that "every individual voluntarily enters and stays in any relationship only as long as it is adequately satisfactory in terms of his rewards and costs" (p. 37). Persons are likely to remain in relationships that enhance security (and other needs) but to terminate relationships that frustrate them. True social "reinforcers" are most accurately conceptualized as complementary behaviors (Brokaw & McLemore, 1983; Wachtel, 1977; see Carson, 1969, for a detailed discussion of exchange theory).

"Pathological" interpersonal transactions are marked by the attempt of one party to bind the other into an *inequitable* social exchange. Cashdan (1973, 1982) has described four exploitative interpersonal strategies—dependency, martyr, sexuality, and power—commonly used in "hooking" others into inequitable relationships. Such relationships may persist over long periods of time. However, once the "victim" becomes aware of the inequity, he or she is likely to react with either rage or withdrawal and to refuse to continue in the relationship under those conditions (Cashdan, 1973).

4. *The healthy personality is characterized by flexibility, moderation, and balance.* As first described by Leary (1957), "Adjustment in terms of the over-all personality organization consists in flexible, balanced, appropriate, accurate interpersonal behavior. In terms of the subdivisions of personality—the levels of public interaction, perception, and private symbolism—it consists of appropriate, accurate, and balanced interpersonal behavior respectively" (p. 31).

Defining this in terms of the Interpersonal Circle (Figure 2), better adjusted persons enjoy a *flexible* repertoire of behaviors, a variety of response options for interacting with others. Ideally, *moderate* expressions from any portion of the circle can be enacted when appropriate, for example, taking charge on some occasions (segment A), following another's lead on others (segment I). He or she may sometimes be oppositional and rude (segment E) but other times courteous and pleasant (segment M). As implied by flexibility, the well-adapted personality enacts a *balanced blend* of interpersonal behaviors. The person is *not* rigidly loving, suspicious, or managing, though all three types of interaction might be observed in the course of his or her day.

The maladjusted person "tends to overdevelop a narrow range of one or two interpersonal responses. They are expressed intensely and often, whether appropriate to the situation or not" (Leary, 1957, p. 126). Although maladjusted persons may not respond appropriately to the interpersonal bids of others, they will be highly skilled in the expression of their limited repertoire of behaviors. Or, put another way, they only play one note, but they play it very well.

Contrary to what one might expect, when two persons interact, it is typically the least healthy person who, through *greater* skill and intensity, will often determine the nature of the relationship. Recalling the principle of interpersonal complementarity, the maladjusted person maintains his or her maladaptive interactional stance by eliciting restricted, complementary responses from the other (Carson, 1969; Kiesler, 1988; Leary, 1957).

Turning to Figure 2, it can be seen that paranoid individuals take an active role in maintaining their disturbance by rigidly enacting behaviors out of segments C, D, and E (paranoid/suspicious, punitive, antagonistic behaviors). These elicit complementary behaviors in segments G, F, and E, respectively (inhibited, detached, and antagonistic behaviors). Although the other might initially attempt to negotiate a more friendly relationship (e.g., moderate expressions of warmth and friendliness, coded in segments L and M), the paranoid's refusal to even acknowledge such bids and his or her tendency to react consistently with hostility will eventually make it exceedingly difficult for the other not to react with reciprocal hostility or withdrawal. The paranoid thus confirms his or her suspicions that others are, after all, undependable or "out to get you" through an identifiable self-defeating interactional cycle.

5. *Emotional health is characterized by an ability to establish and maintain intimate relationships.* As noted, we assume that people, by nature, are relational. We *need* intimacy with others. Those who are *able* to achieve intimacy with others will do so. Thus we regard the ability to achieve intimacy as "a pivotal criterion of psychological integrity" (McLemore & Hart, 1982, p. 229). That is to say, the ability to establish and maintain an emotionally close relationship with another is a prime indicator of "mental health."

Correlatively, *maladjustment will be characterized by difficulties in sustaining intimacy.* In general, we can understand healthful emotional closeness (intimacy) to include both a balance between dependence and independence and equality of overt power (Beavers, 1985). Relatedly, Benjamin (1984) characterizes the healthy intimate relationship as a relationship in which "one attends to one's own needs, reactions, and states about as often as one focuses on those of the other person" (p. 128). Difficulties with intimacy are reflected in interpersonal patterns involving either *extreme dependence* (symbiosis, enmeshment, weak ego boundaries), *extreme independence* (detachment, schizoid, disengagement), *significant imbalances in power* (expressed through intimidation, guilt induction, and angry attack or, from the "weaker" position, becoming suicidal, nonfunctional, or childlike), *extreme ambivalence* (difficulties with commitment), and/or *confused or disordered communication* (loose associations, double binds, incongruence, word salad, and so on; Beavers, 1985; Kiesler, 1982; McLemore & Hart, 1982; Sullivan, 1956).

6. *Adaptive behaviors generally conform to social norms.* Carson (1969) suggests that adjustment and maladjustment are differentiated according to

the criteria of social convention. Those who so break basic cultural "rules" that others can no longer ignore or find a "normal" reason for the rule breaking are showing "disturbed" behavior.

Benjamin (1974) takes a compatible position, defining socially desirable behavior to involve affiliation without undue power or autonomy. Deviations from this standard are defined as pathological. Healthful behaviors are classified on the right side of the SASB model, located at points ending in 01 to 20 and 41 to 44 of Figure 3. SASB definitions of adaptive functioning emphasize friendly affect, the giving and receiving of autonomy, and selected expressions of either friendly influence or acceptance of that influence. Less healthy behaviors are classified in the remaining areas.

Benjamin's (1974) notions of emotional health and maladjustment are supported by findings emerging from McLemore's Interaction Research Project in Pasadena, California (e.g., McLemore & Brokaw, 1987). Strong associations have been obtained between positive mental health and interactional styles located in friendly autonomous SASB areas (Boghosian, 1982) and also between psychopathology and submissive, disaffiliative social styles (Cerling, 1980).

INTERPERSONAL DIAGNOSIS AND DYSFUNCTIONAL INTERPERSONAL BEHAVIOR

Interpersonalists have long argued that "the rigorous and systematic description of *social behavior* is uniquely critical to effective definition and treatment of the problems that bring most individuals for psychiatric or psychological consultation" (McLemore & Benjamin, 1979, p. 18, italics added; also see Adams, 1964; Carson, 1969; Leary, 1957). Rather than referring to the various psychiatric conditions as "mental illness," interpersonalists are more likely to emphasize the social context of the disturbance, using such terms as *problems in living*, or as *disordered, dysfunctional*, or "maladaptive" *interpersonal* behavior.

Ironically, current psychiatric practice defines *mental disorder* in terms of symptomatology but, in a broad sense, carries out interpersonal treatment (Horowitz & Vitkus, 1986). Almost invariably, therapists of all orientations set *interpersonal* treatment goals (e.g., to get along better with others, to become more assertive), address interpersonal situations and conflicts (e.g., grieving over a major loss or rejection, changing recurrent self-defeating behavior sequences), and conduct therapy through a process involving an interpersonal relationship.

Recognizing this, McLemore and Benjamin (1979) recommend an interpersonal behavior taxonomy, a diagnostic system that focuses on characteristic interpersonal transactions and sequences. Interpersonal diagnosis would not only support a better understanding of abnormal behavior but, in conjunction with interpersonal models now available, would imply treatment goals and strategies for achieving those goals. Psychosocial diagnosis may even help to identify the various factors associated with healthful human development, thus promoting preventative mental health efforts.

We now turn to a brief review of three general principles involved in disordered behavior.

First, to label someone as *disturbed* is perhaps no different than to indicate that the individual has disturbed someone else. The diagnosis of a mental disturbance is based on the individual's noxious social impact. This is not to say that the disturbed (or disturbing!) person does not experience dysfunctional thoughts or feelings, in addition to and perhaps underlying dysfunctional behaviors. Rather, "we would argue that disordered personality, by nature, involves the enactment of disordered thought-feeling-action patterns (TFAPs) *in relation to* significant other people" (McLemore & Brokaw, 1987, p. 271).

A second principle is that dysfunctional behavior is typically enacted in a highly skilled manner. As noted, "disordered" persons tend to manifest only a limited repertoire of behaviors, expressed in an extreme and rigid manner. Their interactions tend to be more intense and inflexible than those of the "average" person. Thus, when a poorly adjusted individual interacts with someone who is "healthier," it is generally the former who determines the nature of the relationship by virtue of his or her greater intensity and resistance to change.

A third principle is that disturbed persons take an active role in maintaining their interpersonal difficulties. For example, the highly dependent person, through ongoing messages of weakness and helplessness, is constantly training others to help him or her reman dependent: "The overly dependent individual may elicit behavior from others in which they assume what should be his responsibilities and thereby do not allow him to develop his own resources sufficiently so that his dependency can begin to diminish" (Wachtel, 1977, p. 216).

PERSONALITY DISORDERS

We will now comment, from an interpersonal perspective, on four selected personality disorders (see McLemore & Brokaw, 1987, for a more extended treatment of "Axis II disorders").

The *paranoid* person demonstrates a characteristic perceptual distortion based on the belief (cognition) that others will be threatening and unfriendly. Because of this parataxia, the paranoid is likely to experience certain feelings (fear and anxiety) that result in characteristic actions (withdrawal or attack). Note the intimate interconnection between thoughts, feelings, and actions. This "thought–feeling–action pattern" results in a self-fulfilling prophecy: What was originally a perceptual distortion becomes, through the "mechanism" of paranoid social behavior, a relatively accurate description of how others are feeling and behaving, thus adding one more confirmation to the paranoid's distorted world view (see Cameron, 1943).

Milder forms (perhaps more characteristic of an Axis II disorder) are reflected in a diagnosis that emphasizes protest and withdrawal (points 221, 230, and 231 of Figure 3). This diagnosis predicts the characteristic self-defeating cycle: Others are likely to respond to hostile withdrawal with such *complementary* behaviors as hostile rejection or attack (points 121, 130, and 131) that serve simply to reinforce further hostile withdrawal. More "disturbing" forms of paranoia (characteristic of an Axis I disorder) emphasize overt attack and aggression toward others (SASB points 121 and 130–133) that, of course, are likely to elicit reciprocal aggression.

The *histrionic* (or hysteric) is a "pleasing person," characterized by affiliative, overconventional, and "love-seeking" social behaviors (Andrews, 1984). As described by Andrews, the hysteric's rigid commitment to being a pleasing person comes at the cost of appropriate expressions of hostility or assertiveness. As a consequence, the hysteric is likely to communicate with double messages: solicitous, pleasing, seductive messages, in combination with "leakages" of suppressed hostility (e.g., inconsiderate demanding-ness). As with any double message, others find it difficult to negotiate a successful relationship under these conditions. A like response to the seduction will be rebuffed, whereas withdrawal or confrontation, in reaction to the (unacknowledged) hostility, will be seen as rejecting or attacking (Kiesler, 1986).

In addition, the hysteric's "safety oriented" style, which does not allow for much directness or assertiveness, forces a strong reliance on *indirect* strategies to meet personal needs (e.g., conversion symptoms, social manipulation).

As others react negatively to the hysteric's double binds, "sick" role, or manipulation, the histrionic person experiences threat, resulting in a re-newed commitment to overconventional, socially pleasing behaviors (Andrews, 1984).

Turning to the interpersonal circle (Figure 2), Kiesler (1986) suggests an interpersonal diagnosis of the hysteric as in the more intense regions of segments N and O, which emphasize social and flamboyant interpersonal characteristics. Descriptions of behaviors classified in this region include "driven to seek others' company," "always talking to someone," "constantly takes extreme stands," and "can't stop dramatizing." According to the rules of interpersonal complementarity, a stable relationship with the hysterical requires the other to enact such gullible, oversympathetic behaviors as "indulges others with lenience," "seems capable of excusing anything," and "unbelievably gullible and an easy 'mark'."

Because few persons are willing to sustain such an inequitable relationship, the hysteric needs an additional "hook." In Cashdan's terms (1973, 1982), the hysteric is a "sexual strategist." Rather than building relationships on the basis of an equitable exchange, others are hooked through the manipulative use of sexuality: double entendres, flirtatiousness, and other forms of seduction.

Narcissistic disorders have been characterized as involving self-inflated expectations for admiration (Horney, 1939) and an overly competitive social orientation (Leary, 1957). These individuals support fragile self-esteem by "triumphing" over others, by demonstrating their superior intellect, beauty, or accomplishments.

Narcissism is self-defeating. A basic incompatibility exists between the individual's need for admiration and success, and the hostile competitive social style that is used to achieve them. The inherent conflict between goal and social style sets up a self-defeating cycle: The more the narcissist attempts to gain admiration in competitive, exploitative ways, the more likely others are to disrespect him or her; the more others show disrespect, the more compulsively the narcissist is driven toward doing "more of the same," and the cycle continues.

Benjamin (1987) has demonstrated how the various diagnostic criteria for narcissism can be translated into social behaviors. She finds it helpful to divide SASB diagnoses of the narcissist into four states, for example, a baseline position, the state when criticized or ignored, and so on. Using the cluster version of the SASB (see Figure 4), the narcissist's baseline position is "diagnosed" to include "absolute control (1-5) combined with utter uninfluenceability (2-1), contempt for others (1-6), and unrealistic (3-8) self-love (3-3)" (p. 56). The SASB diagnosis changes when the person is criticized: "The narcissist feels guilty (3-6) and empty (3-8), and is likely to attack for control (1-7) or withdraw for distance (2-7)" (p. 56).

On the basis of SASB analysis, Benjamin (1987) suggests that the narcissist demands absolute control in order to force others' admiration and nurturance. When others do not provide the desired support, the narcissist may become enraged. Rather than seeing this rage as an unmanageable instinct, Benjamin views it as a means of regaining control of others, particularly in the service of acquiring support and nurturance. Etiologically, SASB analysis suggests that the prenarcissistic child was idealized by parents, thus leading to the introjection of unrealistic expectations that others will do so as well.

As with histrionic and narcissistic individuals, the *antisocial* person is profoundly self-absorbed and is thus completely unconcerned with the rights or well-being of others. Leary (1957) describes these persons as attaining "adjustment though aggression," a notion supported by research demonstrating a strong association between this diagnosis and aggressive–sadistic interpersonal styles (Morey, 1985). Given these deficiencies, it is not surprising that such persons seem quite unable to sustain intimate or affectionate relationships (recall our assertion that one's capacity for intimacy represents a primary criterion of mental health).

Both Leary (1957) and Kiesler (1986) locate the antisocial personality in the most hostile regions of the interpersonal circle (see Figure 2, segment E). This segment encompasses behaviors ranging from "oppositional and rude" to those described as "rebellious, vicious, and vulger." Consistent with clinical lore that psychopaths cannot love, the interpersonal diagnosis of this personality is located exactly opposite to the friendly and loving behaviors at segment M. In this case, the self-defeating cycle is quite obvious: Hostility elicits reciprocal hostility.

The corresponding SASB diagnosis of the antisocial personality includes cluster 1-7 ("attacking and rejecting," see Figure 4), the SASB's most hostile, other-directed position. Such a location is consistent with research suggesting that the antisocial personality expresses behaviors that replicate an early home environment characterized by severe parental rejection and deficiencies in affection (McCord & McCord, 1964).

The SASB model predicts that antisocial behaviors tend to result in reactions from others that include fear, desperate protest, and attempts to escape (see points 221, 230, and 231 of Figure 3). The self-perpetuating aspect of antisocial behavior is evident: Fearful reactions by others may serve not only to reinforce the antisocial individual's sense of aggressive power but also to make it exceedingly difficult for the antisocial person to benefit from a "corrective emotional experience" (e.g., the healing power of intimacy)!

DEPRESSION

We conclude our discussion with a brief review of three interpersonal perspectives on depression.

The first perspective is represented by Coyne's (1976a,b) seminal research on the interpersonal consequences of depression. Coyne has argued that the manner in which depressed persons interact with others—how they solicit support or communicate their distress—serves actively to perpetuate a depressive social cycle. This theory emerged out of research findings that subjects who had a phone conversation with a depressed outpatient were likely not only to reject and devalue the depressed person but to feel more depressed, anxious, and hostile themselves! A number of published studies during the past decade have confirmed his findings, particularly as they relate to the role of the other in rejecting and devaluing the depressive. Less clear is the consistency with which the "other" (nondepressive) also experiences depression and hostility. The research to date suggests that the other's reaction to a depressed person is best characterized as a "diffuse negative mood state" (Gurtman, 1986).

These findings suggest a self-defeating cycle wherein the depressed person's aversive communication patterns (e.g., dwelling on personal difficulties and failures) tend to generate rejection and avoidance from others, thus "spoiling" his or her social support system. With each such experience, this individual's sense of insecurity and victimization is reinforced, thereby stoking the fires of the "vicious circle."

A second interpersonal viewpoint has emphasized the contribution of specific interpersonal deficits to depression. For example, one study found that depressed persons are more likely than comparison groups to experience difficulties in such interpersonal areas as socializing, assertiveness, and intimacy (Youngren & Lewinsohn, 1980).

Horowitz and his colleagues (Horowitz, French, Lapid, & Weckler, 1982; Horowitz & Vitkus, 1986) suggest that depression, just as any clinical syndrome, represents a network of interrelated cognitive, affective, and interpersonal elements (recall that behavior is multiply determined). Although the ingredients making up the depressive syndrome may vary significantly between persons, some ingredients emerge more frequently than others. These researchers have placed a particular emphasis on identifying the interpersonal elements that most commonly occur in the theoretical "prototypic" depressed person.

Depression is a broad prototype, one that includes multiple subtypes. It appears that different subtypes of depression may incorporate different interpersonal problem areas. Thus within a group of depressed persons, one may suffer from social skills deficits leading to loneliness; another may experience particular difficulties allowing for intimacy; while a third person, just as depressed, may feel completely unable to take an aggressive stand when necessary (Horowitz *et al.*, 1982; Horowitz & Vitkus, 1986). Differentiating the specific interpersonal problems undergirding the various subtypes of depression may often facilitate a more thorough understanding of the interpersonal patterns sustaining the depression.

For example, Horowitz and Vitkus (1986) describe the self-defeating cycle sustained between "helpful" others (O) and depressed persons (D) who are characterized by difficulties with assertiveness:

> The depressed person's submissiveness leads O to dominate D. That dominance in turn (according to the principle of complementarity) invites D to continue feeling incompetent and helpless, which invites O to continue taking charge, and so on. Thus, we see a vicious circle develop in which both participants are doomed by their own methods. The depressed person, by openly displaying discomfort, makes an inadvertent bid for O to take charge; and O, by trying to cheer, support, or coerce D into improvement, elicits more submissive behavior, thereby sustaining D's depression. (p. 456)

Consistent with Coyne's (1976a,b) findings, the logical conclusion to such a cycle is that the "other" will move from a posture of helpfulness to a state of frustration and eventually to irritation and rejection.

A third interpersonal perspective has emphasized intervention. This "strand" is well represented by a short-term treatment approach developed by Klerman and his colleagues (Klerman, Weissman, Rounsaville, & Chevron, 1984), termed Interpersonal Psychotherapy of Depression (IPT).

IPT focuses on the interrelationship between depression and its social context. The initial clinical assessment incorporates a careful review of the patient's important current and past relationships in an attempt to identify one of four common problem areas for intervention. The first problem area has to do with abnormal grief reactions. These are typically based on a failure to proceed through the mourning process after a significant loss. The second area concerns disputes over nonreciprocal role expectations. For example, a mother and daughter who "always used to be close" might disagree on how much the daughter should disclose about her personal life. Difficulties with life-role transitions make up a third potential problem area, for example, adjusting to retirement or a divorce. The final area relates to interpersonal deficits (e.g., an ineffectual communication style) that might result in social isolation and loneliness.

Intervention is based on a problem-solving approach: identification of the problem area associated with the onset of the depression, exploration of the various options for dealing with the problem area, and the development of new behavior. Of course, this is a very "streamlined" description of IPT.

Despite the fact that IPT is tailored toward only four potential interpersonal problem areas, it has fared extremely well in rigorous outcome studies. Results from a 6-year, $10-million NIMH study of depression indicate that, over a 16-week period, IPT, cognitive therapy, and antidepressant pharmacotherapy were equally effective in reducing depressive symptomatology (Mervis, 1986).

SUMMARY

We have described an approach to personality and psychopathology that revolves around the interconnection of the individual with his or her social environment. This "new" emphasis on interpersonal transactions has been described as a true "paradigm shift." Despite such a favorable assessment, however, interpersonal psychology is not yet a highly formalized theory but simply a perspective on human behavior. It is a theoretical orientation that specifies what is important—social behavior—and, therefore, to what the clinician should ordinarily focus most of his or her attention.

The interpersonal point of view is rooted in the work of the neo-Freudians—particularly the teachings of Harry Stack Sullivan. Over the past several decades, this approach has been operationalized through the development of several models of social behavior, most notably increasingly sophisticated versions of the Interpersonal Circle and the innovative Structural Analysis of Social Behavior.

These models have generally emphasized two of the five "primary" personality factors: Extraversion-Introversion (Control) and Agreeableness-Disagreeableness (Affiliation). As we have demonstrated, the interpersonal models can be applied in multiple ways. They can, for example, be used to classify characteristic interpersonal styles, "map out" recurring patterns of social behavior, and generate treatment plans of considerable precision. Relatedly, a number of relevant assessment instruments have been constructed and validated.

Within the context of reviewing these developments, we articulated the primary theoretical assumptions undergirding most interpersonal approaches. In addition to the presuppositions of almost any personality theory—for example, that personality is inferred and that behavior is multiply determined—certain assumptions are distinctly interpersonal: Personality is pivotally rooted in the social environment, desires for security and intimacy are critical motivators, certain types of behavior are highly likely to "draw out" certain other types of behaviors in another person, and social transactions are best explained through the specification and prediction of repetitive "interactional cycles" under particular circumstances. Not only does Person A's behavior lead to predictable behaviors by Person B, but all of this may be moderated by "situational variables," such as which of the two is higher in "status."

A number of common dimensions underlie adaptive and maladaptive adjustment. Some critical dimensions reviewed have to do with how the individual communicates, whether clearly or ambiguously; the individual's ability to negotiate mutually satisfying relationships; the person's interpersonal flexibility (rigidity) and moderation (intensity); the individual's capacity for intimacy; and, the match between the person's behavior and extant social norms.

We have argued for the merits of interpersonal diagnosis, suggesting that an accurate understanding of the client's self-defeating patterns of social behavior ("pathological cycles") is more useful for clinical intervention than most traditional psychiatric diagnosis. Although emotional disturbances typically involve disordered thought–feeling–action patterns, interpersonal behavior is almost always the fulcrum that sustains functional symptomatology.

Near the end of the chapter, we demonstrated the application of interpersonal principles to four common personality disorders and to the often baffling problem of depression.

REFERENCES

Adams, H. B. (1964). "Mental illness" or interpersonal behavior? *American Psychologist, 19*, 191–197.
Anchin, J. C., & Kiesler, D. J. (Eds). (1982). *Handbook of interpersonal psychotherapy.* Elmsford, NY: Pergamon.

Andrews, J. D. W. (1984). Psychotherapy with the hysterical personality: An interpersonal approach. *Psychiatry, 47,* 211–232.

Beavers, W. R. (1985). *Successful marriage.* New York: Norton.

Beier, E. G., & Valens, E. G. (1975). *People reading.* New York: Warner.

Benjamin, L. S. (1974). Structural analysis of social behavior. *Psychological Review, 81,* 392–425.

Benjamin, L. S. (1979a). Structural analysis of differentiation failure. *Psychiatry, 42,* 1–23.

Benjamin, L. S. (1979b). Use of structural analysis of social behavior (SASB) and Markov chains to study dyadic interactions. *Journal of Abnormal Psychology, 88,* 303–319.

Benjamin, L. S. (1984). Principles of prediction using Structural Analysis of Social Behavior. In R. A. Zucker, J. Aronoff, & A. I. Rabin (Eds.), *Personality and the prediction of behavior* (pp. 121–174). New York: Academic Press.

Benjamin, L. S. (1987). Use of the SASB dimensional model to develop treatment plans for personality disorders. I: Narcissism. *Journal of Personality Disorders, 1,* 43–70.

Block, J. (1981). Some enduring and consequential structures of personality. In A. I. Rabin, J. Aronoff, A. M. Barclay, & R. A. Zucker, (Eds.), *Further explorations in personality* (pp. 27–43). New York: Wiley.

Boghosian, J. (1982). Interpersonal dimensions of mental health (Doctoral dissertation, Fuller Theological Seminary, School of Psychology). *Dissertation Abstracts International, 43,* 397A.

Brokaw, D. W., & McLemore, C. W. (1983). Toward a more rigorous definition of social reinforcement: Some interpersonal clarifications. *Journal of Personality and Social Psychology, 44,* 1014–1020.

Cameron, N. (1943). The paranoid pseudo-community. *American Journal of Sociology, 49,* 32–38.

Carson, R. C. (1969). *Interaction concepts of personality.* Chicago: Aldine.

Cashdan, S. (1973). *Interactional psychotherapy: Stages and strategies in behavioral change.* New York: Grune & Stratton.

Cashdan, S. (1982). Interactional psychotherapy: Using the relationship. In J. C. Anchin & D. J. Kiesler (Eds.), *Handbook of interpersonal psychotherapy* (pp. 215–226). New York: Pergamon.

Cerling, D. (1980). Interpersonal dimensions of psychopathology (Doctoral dissertation, Fuller Theological Seminary, Graduate School of Psychology, 1979). *Dissertation Abstracts International, 40,* 5804B.

Cooley, C. H. (1956). *Human nature and the social order.* Glencoe, IL: Free Press.

Costa, P. T., Jr., & McCrae, R. R. (1986). Personality stability and its implications for clinical psychology. *Clinical Psychology Review, 6,* 407–423.

Coyne, J. C. (1976a). Depression and the response of others. *Journal of Abnormal Psychology, 85,* 186–193.

Coyne, J. C. (1976b). Toward an interactional description of depression. *Psychiatry, 39,* 28–40.

Digman, J. M., & Inouye, J. (1986). Further specification of the five robust factors of personality. *Journal of Personality and Social Psychology, 50,* 116–123.

Doane, J. A., Falloon, I. R. H., Goldstein, M. J., & Mintz, J. (1985). Parental affective style and the treatment of schizophrenia: Predicting course of illness and social functioning. *Archives of General Psychiatry, 42,* 34–42.

Duke, M. P. (1986). Personality science: A proposal. *Journal of Personality and Social Psychology, 50,* 382–385.

Epstein, S. (1979). The stability of behavior: I. On predicting most of the people much of the time. *Journal of Personality and Social Psychology, 37,* 1097–1126.

Eron, L. D. (1987). The development of aggressive behavior from the perspective of a developing behaviorism. *American Psychologist, 42,* 435–442.

Fromm, E. (1947). *Escape from freedom.* New York: Rinehart.

Goldberg, L. R. (1981). Language and individual differences: The search for universals in personality lexicons. In L. Wheeler (Ed.), *Personality and social psychology review* (Vol. 2, pp. 141–165). Beverly Hills, CA: Sage.

Goldstein, M. J. (1988). The family and psychopathology. *Annual Review of Psychology, 39,* 283–299.

Goldstein, M. J., Judd, L. L., Rodnick, E. H., Alkire, A., & Gould, E. (1968). A method for studying social influence and coping patterns within families of disturbed adolescents. *Journal of Nervous and Mental Disease, 47,* 233–251.

Goldstein, M. J., Rodnick, E. H., Jones, J. E., McPherson, S. R., & West, K. L. (1978). Familial precursors of schizophrenia spectrum disorders. In L. C. Wynne, R. L. Cromwell, & S. Matthysse (Eds.) *The nature of schizophrenia: New approaches to research and treatment* (pp. 489–498). New York: Wiley.

Gurtman, M. B. (1986). Depression and the response of others: Reevaluating the reevaluation. *Journal of Abnormal Psychology, 95,* 99–101.

Hall, C. S., & Lindzey, G. (1978). *Theories of personality* (3rd ed.). New York: Wiley.

Horney, K. (1939). *New ways in psychoanalysis.* New York: Norton.

Horney, K. (1945). *Our inner conflicts.* New York: Norton.

Horowitz, L. (1979). On the cognitive structure of interpersonal problems treated in psychotherapy. *Journal of Consulting and Clinical Psychology, 47,* 5–15.

Horowitz, L., & Vitkus, J. (1986). The interpersonal basis of psychiatric symptoms. *Clinical Psychology Review, 6,* 443–469.

Horowitz, L., French, R. S., Lapid, J. S., & Weckler, D. A. (1982). Symptoms and interpersonal problems: The prototype as an integrating concept. In J. C. Anchin & D. J. Kiesler (Eds.), *Handbook of interpersonal psychotherapy* (pp. 168–189). New York: Pergamon.

Huesmann, L. R., Eron, L. D., Lefkowirtz, M. M., & Walder, L. O. (1984). The stability of aggression over time and generations. *Developmental Psychology, 20,* 1120–1134.

Kiesler, D. J. (1982). Interpersonal theory for personality and psychotherapy. In J. C. Anchin & D. J. Kiesler (Eds.), *Handbook of interpersonal psychotherapy* (pp. 3–24). New York: Pergamon.

Kiesler, D. J. (1983). The 1982 Interpersonal Circle: A taxonomy for complementarity in human transactions. *Psychological Review, 90,* 185–214.

Kiesler, D. J. (1986). Interpersonal methods of diagnosis and treatment. In R. Michels & J. O. Cavenar (Eds.), *Psychiatry* (pp. 1–24). Philadelphia: Lippincott.

Kiesler, D. J. (1987, October). Complementarity? Between whom and under what conditions? *Clinician's Research Digest* (Supplemental bulletin). (Available from Clinical Information Services, P.O. Box 61725, Pasadena, CA 91116-7025.)

Kiesler, D. J. (1988). *Therapeutic metacommunication.* Palo Alto, CA: Consulting Psychologists Press.

Kiesler, D. J., & Goldston, C. S. (1988). Client-therapist complementarity: An analysis of the Gloria films. *Journal of Counseling Psychology, 35,* 127–133.

Kiesler, D. J., Anchin, J. C., Perkins, M. J., Chirico, B., Kyle, E. M., & Federman, E. J. (1976). *The Impact Message Inventory* (Form II). Richmond: Virginia Commonwealth University.

Klerman, G. L., Weissman, M. M., Rounsaville, B. J., & Chevron, E. S. (1984). *Interpersonal psychotherapy of depression.* New York: Basic Books.

LaForge, R., & Suczek, R. F. (1955). The interpersonal dimensions of personality: III. An interpersonal check list. *Journal of Personality, 24,* 94–112.

Leary, T. (1957). *Interpersonal diagnosis of personality.* New York: Wiley.

Lees-Haley, P. R. (1981). College norms for the Leary Interpersonal Checklist. *Journal of Consulting and Clinical Psychology, 49,* 302–303.

Lorr, M. (1986). *Interpersonal Style Inventory [ISI] Manual.* Los Angeles: Western Psychological Services.

Lorr, M., & De Jong, J. (1986). A short form of the interpersonal style inventory (ISI). *Journal of Clinical Psychology, 42*, 466–468.

Lorr, M., & Manning, T. T. (1978). Higher order personality factors of the ISI. *Multivariate Behavioral Research, 13*, 3–7.

Lorr, M., & McNair, D. M. (1963). An interpersonal behavior circle. *Journal of Abnormal and Social Psychology, 67*, 68–75.

Lorr, M., & McNair, D. M. (1965). Expansion of the interpersonal behavior circle. *Journal of Personality and Social Psychology, 2*, 823–830.

Lorr, M., & McNair, D. M. (1967). *The Interpersonal Behavior Inventory, Form 4*. Washington, DC: Catholic University of America.

Lorr, M., Bishop, P. F., & McNair, D. M. (1965). Interpersonal types among psychiatric patients. *Journal of Abnormal Psychology, 70*, 468–472.

Lorr, M., O'Conner, J. P., & Seifert, R. F. (1977). A comparison of four personality inventories. *Journal of Personality Assessment, 41*, 520–526.

McCord, W., & McCord, J. (1964). *The psychopath: An essay on the criminal mind*. New York: Van Nostrand Reinhold.

McCrae, R. R., & Costa, P. T., Jr. (1986). Clinical assessment can benefit from recent advances in personality psychology. *American Psychologist, 41*, 1001–1003.

McLemore, C. W., & Benjamin, L. S. (1979). Whatever happened to interpersonal diagnosis? A psychosocial alternative to DSM-III. *American Psychologist, 34*, 17–34.

McLemore, C. W., & Brokaw, D. W. (1987). Personality disorders as dysfunctional interpersonal behavior. *Journal of Personality Disorders, 1*, 270–285.

McLemore, C. W., & Hart, P. P. (1982). Relational psychotherapy: The clinical facilitation of intimacy. In J. C. Anchin & D. J. Kiesler (Eds.), *Handbook of interpersonal psychotherapy* (pp. 227–247). New York: Pergamon.

Mead, G. H. (1934). *Mind, self and society*. Chicago: University of Chicago Press.

Mervis, J. (1986, July). NIMH data points way to effective treatment. *APA Monitor*, pp. 1, 13.

Miklowitz, D. J., Strachan, A. M., Goldstein, M. J., Doane, J. A., & Snyder, K. S. (1986). Expressed emotion and communication deviance in families of schizophrenics. *Journal of Abnormal Psychology, 95*, 60–66.

Morey, L. C. (1985). An empirical comparison of interpersonal and DSM-III approaches to classification of personality disorders. *Psychiatry, 48*, 348–364.

Norman, W. T. (1963). Toward an adequate taxonomy of personality attributes. *Journal of Abnormal and Social Psychology, 66*, 574–583.

Orford, J. (1986). The rules of interpersonal complementarity: Does hostility beget hostility and dominance, submission? *Psychological Review, 93*, 365–377.

Pepe, D. (1985). Factor structure of an interpersonal assessment battery (Doctoral dissertation, Fuller Theological Seminary, School of Psychology, 1984). *Dissertation Abstracts International, 45*, 3955B.

Perkins, M. J., Kiesler, D. J., Anchin, J. C., Chirico, B. M., Kyle, E. M., & Federman, E. J. (1979). The Impact Message Inventory: A new measure of relationship in counseling/psychotherapy and other dyads. *Journal of Counseling Psychology, 26*, 263–367.

Rausch, H. L., Dittman, A. T., & Taylor, T. J. (1959). The interpersonal behavior of children in residential treatment. *Journal of Abnormal and Social Psychology, 58*, 9–26.

Roy, M. (1982). Four thousand partners in violence: A trend analysis. In M. Roy (Ed.), *The abusive partner: An analysis of domestic battering* (pp. 17–35). New York: Van Nostrand Reinhold.

Schaefer, E. S. (1965). Configurational analysis of children's reports of parent behavior. *Journal of Consulting Psychology, 29*, 552–557.

Schutz, W. C. (1960). *FIRO: A three-dimensional theory of interpersonal behavior*. New York: Holt, Rinehart & Winston.

Spitz, R. (1945). Hospitalism: Genesis of psychiatric conditions in early childhood. *Psychoanalytic Study of the Child, 1,* 53–74.

Staats, A. W. (1975). *Social behaviorism.* Homewood, IL: Dorsey.

Strupp, H. H. (1982). Foreword. In J. C. Anchin & D. J. Kiesler (Eds.), *Handbook of interpersonal psychotherapy* (pp. ix–xi). New York: Pergamon.

Sullivan, H. S. (1953a). *Conceptions of modern psychiatry.* New York: Norton.

Sullivan, H. S. (1953b). *The interpersonal theory of psychiatry.* New York: Norton.

Sullivan, H. S. (1954). *The psychiatric interview.* New York: Norton.

Sullivan, H. S. (1956). *Clinical studies in psychiatry.* New York: Norton.

Sullivan, H. S. (1962). *Schizophrenia as a human process.* New York: Norton.

Sullivan, H. S. (1964). *The fusion of psychiatry and social science.* New York: Norton.

Thibaut, J. W., & Kelley, H. H. (1959). *The social psychology of groups.* New York: Wiley.

Tupes, E. C., & Cristal, R. E. (1961). *Recurrent personality factors based on trait ratings* (USAF ASD Technical Report No. 61-97). Lackland Air Force Base, TX: U.S. Air Force.

Vaughn, C. E., & Leff, J. P. (1976a). The influence of family and social factors on the course of psychiatric illness. *British Journal of Psychiatry, 129,* 125–137.

Vaughn, C. E., & Leff, J. P. (1976b). The measurement of expressed emotion in the families of psychiatric patients. *British Journal of Psychiatry, 129,* 157–165.

Wachtel, P. L. (1977). *Psychoanalysis and behavior therapy: Toward an integration.* New York: Basic Books.

Wiggins, J. S. (1979). A psychological taxonomy of trait-descriptive terms: The interpersonal domain. *Journal of Personality and Social Psychology, 37,* 395–412.

Wiggins, J. S. (1982). Circumplex models of interpersonal behavior in clinical psychology. In P. C. Kendall & J. N. Butcher (Eds.), *Handbook of research methods in clinical psychology* (pp. 183–221). New York: Wiley.

Wright, T. L., & Ingraham, L. J. (1986). A social relations model test of the Interpersonal Circle. *Journal of Personality and Social Psychology, 50,* 1285–1290.

Youngren, M. A., & Lewinsohn, P. M. (1980). The functional relation between depression and problematic interpersonal behavior. *Journal of Abnormal Psychology, 89,* 333–341.

CHAPTER FOUR

Temperament, Social Skills, and the Communication of Emotion

A Developmental–Interactionist View

Ross Buck

Social skills have been found to be important in the determination of mental health over the life span of the individual, and there is growing evidence of their importance in physical health as well. However, little has been done in the analysis of the origins and causation of social skills. In particular, although it seems clear that temperament and social experience interact in the determination of social skills, there is little coherent theory about the specific aspects of temperament that are important, exactly how they interact with social experience, or the differential importance of the roles that they play in specific circumstances. Also, although it is clear that notions of emotional expression and communication are important to social skills—to the extent that social skills are sometimes measured in terms of emotion communication abilities—there is no detailed theoretical rationale explaining *why* this is the case.

This chapter considers the nature of the interaction between temperament and social skills from the point of view of a developmental–interactionist theory of emotion (see Buck, 1976, 1984, 1985, 1988). It argues that temperamental characteristics involving the expression or inhibition of emotion are particularly important in setting the groundwork for social behavior. The individual must, of course, "learn how to use" these temperamental

Ross Buck • Department of Communication Sciences, University of Connecticut, Storrs, Connecticut 06269–1085.

Personality, Social Skills, and Psychopathology: An Individual Differences Approach, edited by David G. Gilbert and James J. Connolly. Plenum Press, New York, 1991.

characteristics in actual social situations, but because emotional communication is itself at the heart of this learning process, temperament determines the nature of the interpersonal socioemotional *environment* in many respects and thus determines the ease of learning. Therefore, all else being equal, the expressive individual tends to *create for him- or herself* a socially and emotionally enriched environment. In addition, this chapter suggests that a consideration of the overall adaptive success of the individual must take into account "emotional competence," which is related to, yet distinct from, "social competence."

The first section of the chapter considers the definition of *temperament* and *social skills*. The second discusses the similarities and differences between social and motor skills, relating these to the roles of temperament and social experience in the determination of socially skilled behavior. The third section presents the developmental–interactionist theory of emotion; the fourth considers the evidence relating social skills and emotional expression/communication; and the final section outlines the specific implications of developmental–interactionist theory to the analysis of relationships between temperament, social competence, and emotional competence.

DEFINITIONS

TEMPERAMENT

Temperament is defined as an innate emotional disposition, based upon neural and/or hormonal mechanisms (Thomas, Chess, & Burch, 1970). The particular disposition that is emphasized in this chapter is spontaneous emotional expressiveness.

The relationship between temperament and social behavior is very close: Indeed, some have argued that the variability in temperament within a given species is related to the complexity of its social behavior. Thus Fox (1974) has differentiated three kinds of canids based upon their social behavior. One type, exemplified by the red fox, lives alone except during the breeding season. A second type, exemplified by the coyote, forms permanent male–female pairs. The third type, exemplified by the wolf, lives in complex, organized packs consisting of a number of individuals. Fox suggests that the complexity of the social behavior in these species is matched by their degree of heterogeneity in temperament. The red fox shows little temperamental variation from individual to individual, the coyote considerably more. The wolf, in contrast, manifests an impressive range of individual differences ranging from confident and dominant animals to the shy, insecure, and anxious. Fox argues that this variation in temperament between individuals may be necessary for complex, organized social behavior:

> In the wolf litter, the constellation of temperaments represents a nuclear pack
> structure with one or two leaders, a number of middle-ranking supporters, and a

few low-ranking followers. . . . These early differences in temperament may lead
to further social differentiation and role formation in later life. (pp. 33–34)

It might be noted here that each of the temperamental "types" makes a
positive contribution to the adaptation of the group as a whole. For example, the less dominant individuals, being shy and fearful, may be more
sensitive to danger and give prompt warning of threats to the others in the
pack.

SOCIAL SKILLS/COMPETENCE

Skills are often viewed as part of a broader construct known as *competence* (Gresham, 1986). Competence has been defined generally as the ability
to know about and deal effectively and adaptively with the environment.
White (1957) suggested that the organism has an intrinsic need to explore,
manipulate, and generally to *have an effect* on the physical environment. He
termed this need *effectance motivation*. The result of the application of
effectance motivation, given (it should be stressed) a supportive environment, is *competence* in that environment. Competence is made up of more or
less specific *skills*, which refer to particular areas of knowledge and
application.

This chapter defines social and emotional "competence" in an analogous
way, where social competence refers to the ability to know about and deal
with the social environment and emotional competence to the ability to
know about and deal with the internal, bodily environment of feelings and
desires. In both social and emotional competence, there is assumed to be
intrinsic motivation underlying the exploratory behaviors that lead to competence[1]; in both cases this exploratory process can be sidetracked or enhanced by a deprived or enriched environment, and in both cases competence can be seen as composed of more or less specific skills. In the case of
social competence, the latter are "social skills" (see Gresham, 1986).

SOCIAL SKILLS

Social skills, then, refer to relatively specific abilities to know about and
deal effectively with relatively specific others in relatively specific situations
involving relatively specific interpersonal and personal goals. The notion of
social skills has proved to be remarkably useful in many ways: It is a flexible
concept that can be applied to a wide variety of situations; it has both

[1]The motivation underlying social competence may involve the endogenous opiates. Panksepp
(1986; Panksepp & Sahley, 1987) has suggested that social behavior and motivation are elabo-
rated by brain opioid activity and that a dysfunction of this activity is involved in early
childhood autism. If this is correct, it would suggest that the lack of social skills seen in autism
is due to a basic lack of motivation for social contact and communication.

theoretical and practical implications; it has led to a great volume of research in recent years, and there is evidence that social skills training is effective for the pursuit of a variety of treatment outcomes (see, for example, Schneider & Byrne, 1985).

Despite this encouraging picture, there is little consensus on the specific definition of social skills: Indeed, Dodge (1985) has suggested that the number of definitions in the developmental literature approaches the number of investigators in the field. Dodge suggests that part of the problem of definition is due to the fact that different investigators are interested in different facets or aspects of social interaction in their approach to social skills. Some emphasize specific behaviors (assertive behavior, nonverbal behaviors such as smiling and gaze, frequency of interaction, etc.); others emphasize sociometric status, cognitive abilities, or the self-concept (see Gresham, 1986).

Social and Motor Skills: Similarities

There is one aspect of the notion of social skills that seems implicit in the concept, and that may explain much of its flexibility and usefulness. Argyle (1981a; 1988) has emphasized the analogy between social and motor skills. That is, he suggests that the notion of social skills implies an analogy with a variety of other kinds of skills, such as motor skills like typing or driving a car (Argyle, 1981a). Furthermore, it is implied that just as one can develop a motor skill with the proper training, one can develop a social skill. Carried further, it is implied that techniques that are useful in the development of motor skills should be similarly useful for the development of social skills: for example, identifying specific behaviors that are important and focusing upon them for training.

The analogy with motor skills is also useful in that it implies that social skills may vary with the other person involved and with the task at hand. One's skill at driving does not necessarily predict one's skill at typing. Because of this specificity of "skills," the notion of social skill does not carry a necessary implication of "traitlikeness," and it can easily handle situational differences.

Social and Motor Skills: Differences

Judging the Other

On the other hand, there are clear differences between social skills and motor skills. One of the most important differences is that social skills involve interaction with another person or persons. Typewriters and cars passively accept the application of skilled motor performance; people do not. Specifically, people follow psychological, rather than physical laws; they have their own goals that they pursue on their own initiative (Argyle, 1981b). Argyle (1981b, 1988) suggests that the ability to judge accurately the reactions of others during the course of social behavior is an aspect of social skill that does not have an analog in motor skill. Such an ability has often been treated as if it has a transsituational, "traitlike" quality, as in the notions of a general "accuracy in person perception," "nonverbal receiving ability," or "empathy" (see Morrison & Bellack, 1981).

The ability to judge accurately the reactions of another has two major aspects. One is the knowledge of, and ability to follow, the *rules* that specify the behavior that is appropriate in a given relationship or situation (Argyle, Henderson, & Furnam, 1985). For example, a person visiting a culture different from his or her own is well advised to learn as much as possible about the particular pattern of rules that govern interpersonal behavior in that culture. These include rules about spacing, gaze, politeness, deference, and the like. The failure to follow such rules makes it difficult on both sides to judge the reactions of the other interactant, and this can make social interaction distinctly unrewarding.

The other aspect of the ability to judge the other involves the "on-line" interaction, and includes the ability to "read" and respond appropriately to the subtle cues that have been found to organize the informal social transaction. This "metacommunication" process includes cues about the construction and dissolution of the interaction, the turn-taking process within the interaction, and many aspects of the quality of the interaction (intimacy, affective content, friendliness, dominance/submission, etc.). This is the process that is perhaps most closely related to "empathy."

It should be noted that the ability of a given person to "read" the implicit thoughts and feeling of the other is based not only on his or her skills as a receiver (i.e., attending and responding appropriately to the other's cues) but also his or her skills as a *sender*, (i.e., by being expressive, encouraging the other to express those cues). Indeed, the most *controllable* way to be a good receiver is to (a) be a good sender, encouraging the other to be expressive, (b) attend to the expressive cues in the other, and (c) respond appropriately to those cues (Buck, 1983, 1984). This is at its essence a process of emotional communication.

Emotional Communication

Another difference between social skills and motor skills is that the former arguably involve, at their very essence, emotional expression and communication. Emotional factors of course influence motor performance: The usual notion is that motor performance varies with general emotional arousal in an inverted-U fashion, with the best performance associated with moderate levels of arousal. In the case of social skills, however, I suggest that both the *object* of the application of skill, and the *tools* by which the skill is applied, are emotional in nature. Specifically, I am arguing that the sensitivity to, and manipulation of, the feelings of others via emotionally expressive behavior is at the essence of social skills.

Conclusions

The area of commonality between social and motor skills may define the domain in which social skills are person- and situation-specific, whereas the differences between social and motor skills may suggest the domain in which temperament plays a role. That is, viewing social skills as similar to motor skills tends to diminish the importance of the qualities of the individual. There are, of course, individual differences in motor skills, but these are not usually emphasized in motor skill training. Instead, attention is typically paid to creating a training program that will efficiently teach a given skill regardless of the individual qualities of the "student."

On the other hand, it is undoubtedly the case that some students will be more successful in a given training program than are others and that a different training program may produce a different pattern of results. It is here that the analysis of temperament becomes important, and I suggest that spontaneous emotional expressiveness is a critical, if not *the* critical, temperamental factor that must be considered in the analysis of social skills and social competence.

The next section outlines a developmental–interactionist theory of emotion that is meant to provide a theoretical and conceptual basis for the analysis of the relationship between temperament, social skills, and emotional communication. Following it, I review relevant data on the relationship of emotional expressiveness and social skills and examine the implications and predictions derived from this point of view.

DEVELOPMENTAL–INTERACTIONIST THEORY

Developmental–interactionist theory is an approach to the study of emotion from the point of view of an interaction between biologically based special-purpose processing systems structured by evolution and general-purpose processing systems structured by experience. In this it is similar in some respects to the Schachter and Singer (1962) self-attribution theory, which regarded emotion to be a product of physiological arousal and cognitive labels, explanations, or "attributions" associated with that state of arousal. The present view differs from that of Schachter and Singer by, first, considering the physiological side of the interaction to involve structured information derived from the functioning of highly differentiated special-purpose processing systems, and, second, by emphasizing that this interaction has a developmental history unique to each individual (see Buck,

1976, 1988). In other words, the physiological systems contribute highly differentiated information, in that the subjective experience of anger differs from that of fear, or hunger, or cold, or sexual arousal. Also, the individual learns about these subjective experiences—what they are and how to deal with them—in a developmental context in a process of *emotional education* that is a major determinant of emotional competence.

SPECIAL-PURPOSE PROCESSING SYSTEMS

The special-purpose processing systems that constitute the physiological side of the interaction have evolved to serve particular functions: That is, they constitute phylogenetic adaptations that involve a kind of knowledge that is conferred by inheritance (LeDoux, 1986). In other (simpler) words, they are innate and "hard-wired."

The special-purpose processing systems include primary motivational-emotional systems, or *Primes*, which are hierarchically organized in the brain (see Buck, 1985, for an elaboration of this view). At the lower end of the hierarchy are reflexes; and instincts, drives, primary affects, and effectance motivation appear at progressively higher levels. All of these have evolved as phylogenetic adaptations that serve specific functions related to the survival of the species. As one goes up the hierarchy from reflexes to effectance motivation, these special-purpose processing systems interact increasingly with general-purpose processing systems.

GENERAL-PURPOSE PROCESSING SYSTEMS

The general-purpose processing systems include classical conditioning, instrumental learning, and more or less complex information processing, depending upon the particular capabilities of the species in question. They are structured by the organism's experience during ontogeny, that is, during the development of the individual. In other words, these are systems that have evolved to be sensitive to the organism's experience with reality: Their content is structured by that experience. The motivational force behind the structuring of the general-purpose processing systems involves curiosity and exploratory drives, or effectance motivation.

In humans, the importance of the general-purpose processing systems are greatly increased by linguistic competence. Linguistic competence gives human beings a formal means by which to process information. It allows the use of a few elements, such as the phonemes of language or the numerals of mathematics, to be combined according to rules into an infinite variety of statements that can be comprehended by anyone who knows the elements and their rules of combination. The result is a flexible system that allows communication about events that have never been, and indeed never could be, experienced. For example, human beings can reason about, and have in the past argued heatedly about, the number of angels who can stand on the head of a pin. We can also imagine entering a black hole or standing on the surface of the sun.

EMOTIONAL EDUCATION

Definition

Gibsonian perceptual theory has described how perceptual systems evolve that give the organism access to certain information in the external environment (see Gibson, 1966; 1979). The organism has evolved to "pick up" directly certain information in the external environment that is relevant to survival. Developmental–interactionist theory extends this reasoning to events in the internal, bodily environment. The subjective experience of motives and emotions—feelings and desires—occurs because organisms have evolved to be sensitive to, or directly acquainted with, certain important events in the internal, bodily environment.

These events constitute a source of structured information internal to the organism that the individual must learn to deal with—to label, understand, and act upon—just as the individual must learn to deal with events in the external environment. For example, a child must learn about feelings of hunger and cold, fear and anger: what they are called, what they mean, and what to do about them when they occur. This involves first learning whether to *attend* to such events or to ignore them in the process of the *education of attention*. In Gibsonian perceptual theory, "skilled" perceivers differ from "unskilled" perceivers in that the former have learned to be more efficient at attending to the most important events in the perceptual field.

Assuming that the child learns to attend to certain feelings and desires, he or she must next learn what they are, why they occur, whether other people have such experiences, and what to do about them. In other words, the child must become educated about feelings and desires just as he or she must become educated about events in the external world. This is the process of emotional education.

Harlow demonstrated that social animals like the rhesus monkey require social experience in early life, as the special-purpose processing systems involving feelings and desires are just coming "on line" (Harlow & Mears, 1983). Perhaps this allows the animal to form basic emotional attachments with other monkeys before feelings such as fear or anger become fully salient. In human beings, an additional level of complexity is present because of language: The child must learn how to label feelings with words and to relate them to other feelings also identified with words. Of course, these words differ from culture to culture, and there are cultural differences in the expectations about how one emotional *word* is related to another. In other words, cultures have somewhat different expectations about how feelings and desires are related to events in the world, and to one another. This gives the study of human motivation and emotion a unique linguistic component (Harre, 1979; Harre, Clarke, & DeCarlo, 1985).

How Emotional Education Occurs

The process by which the child learns about his or her feelings and desires should be analogous in many respects to the process of perceptual learning in Gibson's theory, but with a major difference. In normal perceptual learning, the object of perception is similarly and simultaneously accessible to both the child and the socialization agent, so that little disagreement develops about what is "red" and what is "blue." However, as Skinner discussed in his analysis of "private events," the subjective experience associated with the arousal of the special-purpose processing systems is directly accessible to the child, but not the socialization agent (see Skinner, 1953). The latter has access, instead, to the child's *expressive behavior* associated with the arousal of the special-purpose processing systems.

Let us consider this process in some detail, with a child (C) experiencing a feeling and/or desire and a socialization agent (S) observing the child. We shall assume that, for one reason or another, C's brain has been aroused in the neurochemical Prime system associated with what we in our culture call *anger* or *rage*, and that C expresses this by screaming, showing a characteristic facial display similar to that described by Ekman and Friesen (1975) as associated with the primary affect of anger; and by throwing a block at S.

Developmental–interactionist theory suggests that the arousal in the neurochemical system has three separate consequences or *readouts* (see Buck, 1985). First, the arousal causes changes in peripheral adaptive/homeostatic systems, including the autonomic nervous system, endocrine system, and immune system (Emotion I). Often this pattern of changes is similar to the fight-or-flight response described by Cannon (1915). Second, the arousal causes tendencies to display the state in posture, facial expression, tone of voice, and overt behavior (Emotion II). Third, the arousal causes subjective experience: The child is directly aware of a particular experiential state (Emotion III). In other words, the state associated with the arousal of this particular special-purpose processing systems is manifested or "read out" in these three ways. The external display and internal subjective experience are assumed to be qualitatively distinct from the displays and experiential states associated with other Primes.

These three consequences are differentially *accessible* to C and S. The subjective experience is accessible only to C, and I have suggested that C's display is more accessible to S than to C (see Buck, 1984). Moveover, of the different expressive behaviors S is more likely to *notice* some than others. It is likely that S will notice the block being thrown, but S may not notice C's tone of voice. Finally, the peripheral adaptive/homeostatic responses are normally unaccessible to either C or S.

S will respond to C's expressive behavior, particularly those aspects that are most salient, or noticed, by S. S's response constitutes feedback to C that is crucial for C's emerging understanding of his or her own subjective experience. For example, S might say: "You're angry. You must be frustrated. Everybody gets frustrated sometimes, but you shouldn't throw blocks at people." In this simple response, C gains a rich store of information by which to label and understand the subjective experience: learning that it is called anger, that other people get angry too, that frustration is a common cause of anger, and that throwing blocks is not an acceptable response. On the other hand, if S shouts "You're a bad girl" and smacks C, a very different lesson occurs. C may learn that the *subjective experience* of anger is associated with being a bad person and be less able to deal with such feelings in the future. In particular, the overt expression of such feelings may be suppressed or inhibited, such inhibition possibly being associated with increases in the autonomic/endocrine "fight-or-flight" response and with decreases in immune system functioning (Buck, 1980, 1984).

SOCIAL BIOFEEDBACK

S's response to C is analogous to the process of biofeedback, in which a physiological response that is normally inaccessible to the subject is associated with a highly accessible and salient feedback signal. Through this association, the subject becomes able to control the physiological response. In effect, the physiological response is rendered more accessible because of its association with the feedback signal.

The interchange between C and S constitutes an example of *social biofeedback* in which the other person—S in this example—is the feedback device. Just as the feedback device is constructed to respond to a certain physiological signal, S responds to certain salient aspects of C's expressive display. S's response is thus associated with these salient aspects of the display and also with the subjective experience that is associated with the episode.

EMOTIONAL ALIMENTS

I suggest that the child is intrinsically motivated to explore the internal environment of feelings and desires just as he or she is intrinsically motivated to explore the external environment. Piaget (1971) suggested that the process of acquiring an internal cognitive representation of external reality is associated with an assimilation–accomodation process, in which events that are slightly beyond the child's current level of understanding evoke particular interest. Through effectance motivation, the child is intrinsically motivated to explore such events and eventually masters them or accomodates his or her understanding so that the new information fits in. The child then loses most interest in those particular events. Such assimilable, but not yet accomodated events constitute food for cognitive growth which Piaget terms *aliments*.

The same sort of process may apply with respect to emotional education: the exploration of the internal, bodily environment. Events that evoke feelings and desires that are assimilable, but not yet accomodated, may create a powerful sense of interest and, indeed, fascination. Once accomodated, the same events may be ignored.

A possible example of this process concerns the fascination among some persons for the sorts of sex-related information that in our culture is called "pornography." The biological situation that naturally occurs at puberty, when the sexual systems become activated by changes in the levels of sex hormones, creates an altered pattern of bodily information that the young person must come to deal with. There is some evidence that adolescents have a heightened interest in sex-related materials of various sorts, including pornography (Abelson, Cohen, Heaton, & Suder, 1970). This heightened interest normally declines, perhaps as the young adult accommodates the feelings and desires associated with his or her new sexuality. However, there is evidence that among adult male "habitual users" of pornography, the exposure to sex-related materials during adolescence was relatively low (Goldstein, Kant, Judd, Rice, & Green, 1971; Nawy, 1970). Nawy and Goldstein *et al.* suggest that a strong adult interest in pornography, and also sex-related crimes such as rape and pedophilia, may in males be related to a lack of exposure to such material in adolescence: "It appears that sex deviates and (habitual) users are noticeably lacking in experience, during their adolescent years, with stimuli representing our culture's definition of 'the normal sex act'" (Goldstein *et al.*, 1971, pp. 7–8).

In terms of the present view, it may be that sex-related materials normally become aliments during adolescence and that they may aid in the normal accommodation of sexual feelings and desires. If this accommodation does not occur in good time for one reason or another, it may have lasting effects that command the interest of the adult individual in an immature and perhaps inappropriate manner.

SOURCES OF EMOTIONAL EDUCATION

The foregoing has considered two major sources of emotional education: the social biofeedback process and social models. The individual learns about his or her feelings and desires both through direct face-to-face interaction, in which others respond to the individual's expressive behavior, and from the observation of other persons giving expression to their own feelings and desires. The latter can occur by observing models in the arts: in drama, literature, music, mass media. Such sources of information are perhaps particularly important in dealing with feelings and desires that are difficult to express in face-to-face encounters: for example, sexual and aggressive feelings and desires. The importance of social models as aliments for the understanding of one's sexual, aggressive, and other feelings and desires is perhaps a reason why human beings have always been so strongly motivated to expose themselves to such materials (Buck, 1988).

SPONTANEOUS COMMUNICATION

Whether emotional education is based upon social biofeedback or the observation of social models, *spontaneous communication* plays an essential role. Spontaneous communication is viewed by developmental–interactionist theory as a communication process that exists side-by-side with the process of intentional, symbolic communication (Buck, 1984; Buck & Duffy, 1980).

The characteristics of spontaneous communication are as follows. First, spontaneous communication is *biologically structured* in both its sending and receiving aspects: The organism is phylogenetically prepared both to display emotion and to respond appropriately to such displays when they are noticed in others. In effect, we know *directly* the state associated with the display in the other, and this knowledge is conferred by inheritance.

Second, as implied, spontaneous communication is *in no way intentional*. It is an automatic process, although the display can be, and often is, intentionally altered by "display rules." Third, spontaneous communication is based upon *signs* that have a natural, biologically based relationship with their referent. Fourth, spontaneous communication cannot be false, for if the sign is present, the referent must be present by definition. Therefore, spontaneous communication is *nonpropositional*. Fifth, the content of spontaneous communication consists of *motivational–emotional states*.

In contrast, symbolic communication is learned and culturally patterned, it is at some level intentional, it is composed of symbols with arbitrary relationships to their referents, and it is composed of propositions (see Buck, 1984).

TEMPERAMENT, SPONTANEOUS COMMUNICATION, AND SOCIAL AND EMOTIONAL COMPETENCE

THE ROLE OF SPONTANEOUS COMMUNICATION

Perhaps the central claim of developmental–interactionist theory in the analysis of social and emotional competence is that *spontaneous communication is the link between temperament on the one hand and social and emotional competence on the other.* Suggestions of differences in temperament along an "externalizing–internalizing," "extraversion–introversion," or "expressive–inhibited" dimension have a long history in psychology. Also, there is recent evidence from a wide variety of sources—from studies of animal learning to studies of right versus left hemisphere damage in humans—that support the reality of such a dimension (see Buck, 1984).

Temperament, then, arguably determines the overall expressiveness of the individual, at least initially, and the level of expressiveness has important social and emotional implications. The more expressive child provides more information to others regarding the child's motivational/emotional states. Through their response, others provide richer social biofeedback to the expressive child, presumably enhancing the process of emotional education and encouraging emotional competence.

The expressive child will not only have more feedback about his or her *own* emotional state; he or she will also have more information about the other person. By being expressive, the child presumably encourages expression on the part of the other and therefore has a better basis for making accurate "empathic" judgments about them. This will in turn enhance the development of social skills and encourage social competence. In effect, the expressive child creates *for him- or herself* an "enriched" socioemotional environment.

EVIDENCE

The General Expressiveness Factor

There is much evidence that spontaneous expressiveness is in fact related to social skills and competence: Emotional competence has been less studied. Argyle (1988) has reviewed evidence for a "general expressiveness factor" in social skills. Socially skilled persons show moderately high levels of smiling, gaze, proximity, nodding, and leaning forward during interaction. These behaviors appear to signal positive social approach within the rules of our culture. Furthermore, manipulations of these behaviors have powerful albeit often "unconscious" effects upon others: Others regard persons exhibiting these behaviors in positive terms, and vice versa, but often cannot explain the reasons for these evaluations. For example, Sabatelli and Rubin (1986) showed that spontaneously expressive persons are rated as more warm and likeable, independent of their physical attractiveness.

Spontaneous versus Posed Expressiveness

It is essential to distinguish spontaneous expressiveness from the ability to intentionally pose emotion. Studies that have correlated the two generally find modest positive correlations (e.g., Buck, 1977; Cunningham,

1977; Zuckerman, Hall, DeFrank, & Rosenthal, 1976). However, there is evidence that spontaneous and posed expressiveness are distinct and associated with different social behaviors.

Briggs, Cheek, and Buss (1980), in a factor analysis of Snyder's (1979) Self-Monitoring (SM) scale, found three factors: (a) *Extraversion*, which as we have seen is closely related to temperament; (b) *Acting*, which seems to be associated with the ability to control, or pose, emotional displays; and (c) *Other Directedness*, which seems related to one's willingness to change one's behavior to suit others. The first two factors appear to be related to spontaneous sending accuracy and posed sending ability, respectively (Argyle, 1988; Riggio & Friedman, 1983). Riggio (1986) subsequently developed the Social Skills Inventory (SSI), which has subscales for Emotional Expressivity and Emotional Control that were explicitly designed to measure spontaneous and posed expressiveness, respectively. It is noteworthy that, on the SSI, social skills are *defined* in terms of expressiveness.

The scales assessing spontaneous and posed expression have been found to be related rather differently to other personality measures. The Extraversion subscale of the SM scale has been positively related to measures of self-esteem, sociability, and extraversion, and negatively related to shyness. The Acting subscale is most strongly correlated with acting ability, dominance, and the desire to entertain and put on a show. The Other Directedness subscale, in contrast, is positively related to shyness, anxiety, and neuroticism, and is negatively related to self-esteem (Argyle, 1988; Briggs *et al.*, 1980; Riggio & Friedman, 1983). Further research on the behavioral correlates of these scales will be of great interest (see Darius, 1988).

Persuasiveness

Another line of evidence relating expressiveness to social skills involves persuasiveness: the ability of an individual to influence the thoughts, feelings, and behaviors of others. This is closely related to the definition of social skill as the ability to achieve one's goals in interaction with others (Argyle, 1981a).

A number of studies have indicated that persuasiveness is related to the judicious and appropriate use of expressive behavior (see Argyle, 1988, for a review). This may be in part because the effective persuader evokes emotional responses and serves emotional needs in the receiver. A leader who can effectively articulate and express emotion may establish a *charismatic* relationship with persons in whom certain emotional needs are unmet: needs for a satisfying self-defining relationship with other persons, for example (Buck, 1988). They may become, in effect, an emotional aliment to persons whose emotional education is incomplete or has been challenged. Such a leader may exert a powerful influence, particularly because it appears that this process of emotional communication between leader and follower can take place via mass media.

Studies of American politicians have shown that the emotional response to a leader can be a powerful determinant of support (Abelson, Kinder, Peters, & Fiske, 1982). Other studies suggest that the leader's expressive displays may be critical in generating such a response. Televised displays of happiness–reassurance, anger–threat, and fear–evasion on the part of President Ronald Reagan elicited similar microexpressions on the faces of viewers, as assessed by facial EMG recordings, *regardless of the viewer's attitude toward the president* (McHugo, Lanzetta, Sullivan, Masters, & Englis, 1985). Significantly, the unsuccessful 1984 Democratic nominee, Walter Mondale, was relatively ineffective in influencing the facial EMG responding of viewers.

Political leaders may be more "charismatic" on one affective channel than another. The major leaders of the 1930s—Churchill, Roosevelt, Hitler—had powerful voices and were very effective in expressing emotion over the radio. Television altered, among other things, the sorts of emotional displays that are effective. In the 1960 Kennedy–Nixon debates, persons watching television regarded Kennedy as the "winner," whereas those listening on radio preferred Nixon. Although neither candidate appeared to influence political attitudes through rational argument, the percentage of voters saying that they would vote for Kennedy jumped from 44% to 50% (Comstock, Chaffee, Katzman, McCombs, & Roberts, 1978).

It appears that a charismatic leader can get away with transgressions that, if viewed from a "rational" or "logical" viewpoint, seem significant, and yet not lose his persuasive appeal. The ability of President Reagan to maintain his popularity despite his repeatedly showing a lack of knowledge, making major factual errors and presiding over the Iran-Contra scandal became known as the "Teflon factor": Nothing negative seemed to stick to him. Similarly, many followers of "charismatic" Christian television evangelists in the United States seemed prepared to overlook in their ministers behaviors—adultery, consorting with prostitutes, homosexuality—which in other persons would tend to be judged rather harshly as sinful transgressions.

IMPLICATIONS OF DEVELOPMENTAL–INTERACTIONIST THEORY

The preceding section has summarized the evidence for the importance of spontaneous expressiveness in the link between temperament on the one hand, and social and emotional competence on the other. The present section considers from the point of view of developmental–interactionist theory how this link is actually formed in the development of the individual, and it specifies testable hypotheses and suggests research directions that can be derived from this position.

THE RELATIONSHIP OF TEMPERAMENT AND SOCIAL SKILLS

Developmental–interactionist theory emphasizes the interaction between special-purpose processing systems and general-purpose processing systems in a developmental context. It can be argued from the foregoing that temperament (e.g., spontaneous expressiveness) is based upon special-purpose processing systems, whereas the aspects of social skills that are similar to those of motor skills involve general-purpose processing systems that are structured by social experience. This experience may occur in the context of a "deficient" or "enriched" social–emotional environment, although, as we have seen, the expressive child may create his or her own "enriched" environment to a certain extent.

In any event, developmental–interactionist theory suggests that the end result, the eventual adult pattern of social and emotional competence, will be related to both temperamental factors and to experience in a given social situation and so will vary from situation to situation. The extent to which temperament will be related to this "end result" will depend upon how much experience the person has had in the given situation: The more experience, the more the individual's social behavior will be based upon what the individual has learned to do in that situation and the less the apparent contribution of temperament. In other words, if the person has a great deal of experience in a given situation, temperament will not be very predictive of his or her response. On the other hand, if a person is new to a situation and has not learned much about it, temperament should be a more important predictor.

It follows that, all else being equal, temperament should be more predictive of social behavior in children than in adults because children have had fewer relevant learning experiences. It also follows that temperament should be more predictive of social behavior in a new situation than in a familiar situation. In other words, spontaneous expressiveness should be closely related to measures of social skills in young children but not necessarily in adults.[2] However, spontaneous expressiveness should in adults be related to their ability to adapt to new situations: to *cope* with the novel and unexpected (Reardon & Buck, 1989).

A dramatic example of a new situation that requires coping by the

---

[2]The results of Buck (1977) and observations in an unpublished study using sociometric measures by J. Goldman, A. Dreyer, and myself suggest a close correspondence between spontaneous expressiveness and social skills in preschoolers. Darius (1988), studying adults, found little evidence for such a correspondence. The latter studies are now being replicated and/or subjected to further analysis.

individual is in the case of the development of a serious, chronic illness. This alters the life of the individual in major ways and renders less relevant the patterns of response learned earlier in life: the expectations or rules governing one's actions, social behaviors, feelings, desires. At such points of challenge, it may be that the temperamental characteristics of the individual—particularly his or her spontaneous expressiveness—again become important. There is in fact much evidence that persons with strong social networks are better able to cope with disease (Sarason, Sarason, Hacker, & Basham, 1985), and it may be that more expressive persons are better able to maintain their social support networks, or if necessary to build new ones.

EMOTIONAL COMPETENCE

Whereas there has been a great deal of research on social skills and competence, comparatively little has been done in the area of emotional competence. Nevertheless, the nature of emotional competence and its relationship with social competence is a question of considerable theoretical and practical interest.

The concept of emotional education carries with it the implication that children differ in its results. Some children are undoubtedly "better educated" emotionally than are others, in that they may have the same sorts of labels and expectations about emotional responding as do others in the culture, and they may know what to do when certain feelings and desires occur. This could come about because of their temperament: We have seen how expressive children should have an advantage. In addition, the strength and quality of the feelings and desires engendered by the particular set of special-purpose processing systems possessed by a given child may or may not be within normal community experience, so that it may or may not be easy for that child to follow community expectations. For example, some children may possess biologically based tendencies to be unusually aggressive, depressed, or fearful.

Differences in emotional education could also come about because of differences in experience: Some children may be raised in "emotionally enriched" environments, in which feelings and what to do with them are expressed and discussed freely. In any event, the end result of the process of emotional education is a certain level of *emotional competence* that is analogous to competence in dealing with events in the external environment. One need not, however, go with the other: Emotional competence does not necessarily imply competence with the external environment, and vice-versa.

The relationship of emotional and social competence is also a matter for conjecture. On the one hand, we have seen that a spontaneously expressive temperament may enhance both social and emotional competence, and in general it may be that the two are positively related. However, it is easy to imagine a person who is socially competent but not emotionally competent.

The "Type C personality pattern" that has been associated with cancer may be an example: Such persons are said to be conforming, compliant, unassertive, and patient; they are submissive, passive, and anxious to please (Baltrusch & Waltz, 1985; Greer & Watson, 1985). However, they do not express negative emotions, particularly anger, and this lack of emotional expression may be associated with immunosuppression and other physiological responses that encourage the development of cancer. Thus the "pathological niceness" that may lead to apparently competent social behavior may at the same time promote physiological disregulation (Renneker, 1981).

The example of the Type C personality illustrates a certain tension between being true to oneself versus responding to the needs and wishes of others. There is some danger in being so entrained to the social environment that one's own feelings and desires go unfulfilled, and perhaps even unrecognized. This tension was caricatured in the motion picture *Zelig*, by Woody Allen, in which the main character is so obsessed with being liked that he becomes similar to whomever he is with. He becomes a psychiatrist, a rabbi, a fat person, a musician. Eventually, he becomes a Nazi. Allen's "chamelion" character gently reminds us of the tension between being ourselves and satisfying others and of the disaster that can ensue when the self is surrendered. It suggests the possibility that emotional competence—our ability to effectively deal with our own feelings and desires—may be a necessary condition for truly authentic social competence.

Although we have seen that social competence and emotional competence should be positively related to each other, in the end social competence is based upon social rules and expectations, and emotional competence is based upon the biological reality of feelings and desires. Social rules and expectations tend to encourage certain patterns of emotional education, and this phenomenon may have important sociocultural effects. McClelland (1961), for example, argues that cultures that encourage achievement motivation tend to show later economic growth. The pattern of emotional education encouraged by a culture may also have biological effects: For example, the tendency in our culture to discourage emotional expression in males and anger expression in females could conceivably have deleterious effects upon health. In general, it may be that social expectations can be incompatible with biological reality, and when they are, social and emotional competence tend to become separated. It then becomes difficult for a person to be competent socially and at the same time be able to deal competently with his or her own feelings and desires.

CONCLUSIONS

In summary, this chapter has argued that:

1. The similarities between social skills and motor skills define the domain in which social skills are person- and situation-specific,

whereas their differences define the domain in which social skills are based upon temperament.

2. Spontaneous emotional expressiveness is a critial temperamental factor in the development of social skills.

3. Spontaneous expressiveness tends to determine the efficiency of the social biofeedback process and thus the degree to which the socioemotional environment is "deprived" or "enriched." For this reason, spontaneous expressiveness is an important link between temperament and both social and emotional competence.

4. The strength of the link between temperament (i.e., spontaneous expressiveness) and social and emotional competence will be negatively related to the amount of learning that an individual has had in a given situation. Thus this link will be stronger in children and in new kinds of situations.

5. Emotional competence—the ability of the individual to know about and deal with the internal bodily environment of feelings and desires—is positively related to social competence but is a distinct concept.

6. Cultural expectations and rules that are at variance with biological reality may tend to produce a split between social and emotional competence, possibly having negative consequences for the individual and for society.

ACKNOWLEDGMENTS

This chapter was written while the author was a Visiting Fellow, Wolfson College, Oxford University. The author thanks Michael Argyle and Barry Schneider for their assistance in the preparation of this chapter and their valuable comments and suggestions. He also thanks Franklin A. Darius, whose research on social skills and nonverbal communication will make a significant contribution to this literature.

REFERENCES

Abelson, H., Cohen, R., Heaton, E., & Suder, C. (1970). National survey of public attitudes toward and experience with erotic materials. In *Technical reports of the Commission of Obscenity and Pornography* (Vol 6). Washington, DC: U.S. Government Printing Office.

Abelson, R. P., Kinder, D. R., Peters, M. D., & Fiske, S. T. (1982). Affective and semantic components in political person perception. *Journal of Personality and Social Psychology, 42*, 619–630.

Argyle, M. (1981a). Introduction. In M. Argyle (Ed.), *Social skills and health*. New York: Methuen.

Argyle, M. (1981b). The nature of social skill. In M. Argyle (Ed.), *Social skills and health*. New York: Methuen.

Argyle, M. (1988). *Bodily communication* (2nd ed.). New York: Methuen.

Argyle, M., Henderson, M., & Furnam, A. (1985). The rules of social relationships. *British Journal of Social Psychology, 24,* 125–139.

Baltrusch, H. J., & Waltz, M. (1985). Cancer from a biobehavioral and social epidemiological perspective. *Social Science Medicine, 20,* 789–794.

Briggs, S. R., Cheek, J. M., & Buss, A. H. (1980). An analysis of the Self-Monitoring Scale. *Journal of Personality and Social Psychology, 38,* 679–686.

Buck, R. (1976). *Human motivation and emotion* (1st ed.). New York: Wiley.

Buck, R. (1977). Nonverbal communication accuracy in preschool children: Relationships with personality and skin conductance. *Journal of Personality and Social Psychology, 33,* 225–236.

Buck, R. (1980). Nonverbal behavior and the theory of emotion: The facial feedback hypothesis. *Journal of Personality and Social Psychology, 38,* 811–824.

Buck, R. (1983). Nonverbal receiving ability. In J. Weimann & R. Harrison (Eds.), *Nonverbal interaction* (pp. 209–242). Beverly Hills, CA: Sage.

Buck, R. (1984). *The communication of emotion.* New York: Guilford Press.

Buck, R. (1985). Prime theory: An integrated approach to motivation and emotion. *Psychological Review, 92,* 389–413.

Buck, R. (1988). *Human motivation and emotion* (2nd ed.). New York: Wiley.

Buck, R., & Duffy, R. (1980). Nonverbal communication of affect in brain-damaged patients. *Cortex, 16,* 351–362.

Cannon, W. B. (1915). *Bodily changes in pain, hunger, fear, and rage.* New York: Appleton.

Comstock, G., Chaffee, S., Katzman, N., McCombs, M., & Roberts, D. (1978). *Television and human behavior.* New York: Columbia University Press.

Cunningham, M. R. (1977). Personality and the structure of the nonverbal communication of emotion. *Journal of Personality, 45,* 564–584.

Darius, F. A. (1988). *Communicative competence and nonverbal communication: A developmental study of resident assistants.* Unpublished Master of Arts thesis, University of Connecticut.

Dodge, K. A. (1985). Facets of social interaction and the assessment of social competence in children. In B. H. Schneider, K. H. Rubin, & J. E. Ledingham (Eds.), *Children's peer relations: Issues in assessment and intervention.* New York: Springer.

Ekman, P., & Friesen, W. V. (1975). *Unmasking the face.* Englewood Cliffs, NJ: Prentice-Hall.

Fox, M. W. (1974). *Concepts in ethology: Animal and human behavior.* Minneapolis: University of Minnesota Press.

Gibson, J. J. (1966). *The senses considered as perceptual systems.* Boston: Houghton-Mifflin.

Gibson, J. J. (1979). *The ecological approach to visual perception.* Boston: Houghton-Mifflin.

Goldstein, M. J., Kant, H. S., Judd, L. L., Rice, C. J., & Green, R. (1971). Experience with pornography: Rapists, pedophiles, homosexuals, transexuals, and controls. *Archives of Sexual Behavior, 1,* 1-15.

Greer, S., & Watson, M. (1985). Towards a psychobiological model of cancer: Psychological considerations. *Social Science Medicine, 20,* 773–777.

Gresham, F. M. (1986). Conceptual issues in the assessment of social competence in children. In P. S. Strain, M. J. Guralnick, & H. M. Walker (Eds.), *Children's social behavior: Development, assessment, and modification* (pp. 143–180). New York: Academic Press.

Harlow, H. F., & Mears, C. E. (1983). Emotional sequences and consequences. In R. Plutchik & H. Kellerman (Eds.), *Emotion: Theory, research, and experience. Vol. 2. Emotions in early development* (pp. 171–198). New York: Academic Press.

Harre, R. (1979). *Social being.* Oxford: Blackwell.

Harre, R., Clarke, D. D., & DeCarlo, N. (1985). *Motives and mechanisms.* London: Methuen.

LeDoux, J. (1986). A neurobiological view of the psychology of emotion. In J. LeDoux & W. Hirst (Eds.), *Mind and brain: Dialogues between cognitive psychology and neuroscience* (pp. 301–354). New York: Cambridge University Press.

McClelland, D. C. (1961). *The achieving society*. Princeton, NJ: Van Nostrand.

McHugo, G. J., Lanzetta, J. T., Sullivan, D. J., Masters, R. D., & Englis, B. G. (1985). Emotional reactions to a political leader's expressive displays. *Journal of Personality and Social Psychology, 49*, 1513–1529.

Morrison, R. L., & Bellack, A. S. (1981). The role of social perception in social skill. *Behavior Therapy, 12*, 69–79.

Nawy, H. (1970). The San Francisco erotic marketplace. *Technical Report of the Commission on Obscenity and Pornography* (Vol. 4). Washington, DC: U.S. Government Printing Office.

Panksepp, J. (1986). The psychobiology of prosocial behaviors: Separation distress, play, and altruism. In C. Zahn-Waxler (Ed.), *Social and biological origins of altruism and aggression*. New York: Cambridge University Press.

Panksepp, J., & Sahley, T. L. (1987). Possible brain opioid involvement in disrupted social intent and language development of autism. In E. Schopler & G. B. Mesibov (Eds.), *Neurobiological issues in autism* (pp. 357–372). New York: Plenum Press.

Piaget, J. (1971). Piaget's theory. In P. Mussen (Ed.), *Handbook of child development* (Vol. 1). New York: Wiley.

Reardon, K. R., & Buck, R. (1989). Emotion, reason, and communication in coping with cancer. *Health Communication, 1*, 41–54.

Renneker, R. (1981). Cancer and psychotherapy. In C. G. Goldberg (Ed.), *Psychotherapeutic treatment of cancer patients*. New York: Free Press.

Riggio, R. E. (1986). Assessment of basic social skills. *Journal of Personality and Social Psychology, 51*, 649–660.

Riggio, R. E., & Friedman, H. S. (1983). Individual differences and cues to deception. *Journal of Personality and Social Psychology, 45*, 899–915.

Sabatelli, R., & Rubin, M. (1986). Nonverbal expressiveness and physical attractiveness as mediators of interpersonal perceptions. *Journal of Non-Verbal Behavior, 10*, 120–133.

Sarason, B., Sarason, I. G., Hacker, A., & Besham, R. B. (1985). Concomitants of social support: Social skills, physical attractiveness, and gender. *Journal of Personality and Social Psychology, 49*, 469–480.

Schachter, S., & Singer, J. E. (1962). Cognitive, social, and physiological determinants of emotional state. *Psychological Review, 69*, 379–399.

Schneider, B. H., & Byrne, B. M. (1985). Children's social skills training: A meta-analysis. In B. H. Schneider, K. H. Rubin, & J. E. Ledingham (Eds.), *Children's peer relations: Issues in assessment and intervention* (pp. 175–192). New York: Springer.

Skinner, B. F. (1953). *Science and human behavior*. New York: Macmillan.

Snyder, M. (1979). Self-monitoring processes. *Advances in Experimental Social Psychology, 12*, 85–128.

Thomas, A., Chess, S., & Burch, H. G. (1970). The origin of personality. *Scientific American, 223*, 102–109.

White, R. W. (1957). Motivation reconsidered: The concept of competence. *Psychological Review, 66*, 297–333.

Zuckerman, M., Hall, J. A., DeFrank, R., & Rosenthal, R. (1976). Encoding and decoding of spontaneous and posed facial expression. *Journal of Personality and Social Psychology, 15*, 966–977.

CHAPTER FIVE

A Personality × Personality × Setting Biosocial Model of Interpersonal Affect and Communication

DAVID G. GILBERT

INTRODUCTION

Social behavior, affect, and psychophysiological activity are highly depen-
dent on the interaction of one's personality, the personality of the person
with whom one interacts, and the task or setting (Abbott, Sutherland, &
Watt, 1987; Birchler, Weiss, & Vincent, 1975; Buss, 1981; Thorne, 1987).
For example, task performance and heart rate are a function of one's personality (Type A versus Type B), partner's personality (Type A versus
Type B), and degree of task control (Abbott, Sutherland, & Watt, 1987).
This evidence showing multiple determination of social behavior is consistent with the observations made by Bowers (1973) in his reanalysis of 11
studies evaluating the influence of person, setting, and the interaction of
person and setting. In these studies 13% of the variance was attributable to
the person, 10% to the situation, and 21% to the person by situation interaction. Bower's findings suggest that much of the variance in behavior is a
function of the interaction of personality with situation. For interpersonal
behavior, the most influential part of the situation is usually another person,

DAVID G. GILBERT • Department of Psychology, Southern Illinois University at Carbondale, Carbondale, Illinois 62901-6502.

Personality, Social Skills, and Psychopathology: An Individual Differences Approach, edited
by David G. Gilbert and James J. Connolly. Plenum Press, New York, 1991.

a person that can be characterized by personality and other individual difference variables. The second part of the situation is the setting—the components of the situation other than the other person.

In spite of the previously noted evidence, there are no well-developed models of interpersonal behavior as a function of the setting and personalities of the interactants. Although numerous studies have evaluated relationships between personality, interpersonal behavior, and social skills, little is known about how personalities and setting interact to determine style of communication and patterns of physiological and emotional activity. The main purpose of the present chapter is to provide a tentative personality × personality × setting (PPS) model of interpersonal affect and communication that integrates principles and findings from a number of relevant fields. Prior to more fully describing the PPS model, a review is provided of findings pertaining to the relationship of personality to social behavior, genetics, and biology. Determinants of social behavior include important main effects of personality, as well as personality by personality by setting interactions.

INDIVIDUAL DIFFERENCES AND SOCIAL INTERACTION

PERSONALITY, SOCIAL SKILLS, AND CONSTITUTIONAL FACTORS

Relationships between social skill and genetically based temperamental factors are likely to develop from the first months of an infant's life through adulthood. The smiling, active, and socially extraverted infant elicits a different environment than the quiet infant (Lytton, 1980). Later in life, the individual with a genetically based social and active disposition is more likely to join social groups where social skills will become more highly polished and differentiated (Scarr & McCartney, 1983). Unattractive and intellectually dull individuals may experience high rates of rejection from the earliest days of schooling and may become not only socially unskilled but socially anxious and withdrawn. Emotionally labile and irritable infants and children are likely to elicit negative reactions from family and rejection by and isolation from peers. Isolation, in turn, precludes the learning of important social and emotional skills, including appropriate responses to emotions in others, as well as the modulation of one's own emotions (reviewed by McColloch & Gilbert, present volume). Genetic factors are major determinants of the environment an individual experiences (Scarr & McCartney, 1983), and the interaction of the experienced environment and genetic factors determines social skill development and degree of social and emotional competence (Buck, present volume).

Extraversion and neuroticism are important, interpersonally relevant, genetically influenced personality dimensions. These two dimensions are typically the first two higher-order factors in personality questionnaires and generally account for more variance than other higher-order factors (Kline & Barrett, 1983). Extraversion and neuroticism usually account for a high percentage of the variability in lower-order factors such as dominance, sociability, anxiety, and depression. Extraversion and neuroticism, as well as their lower-order-component factors are related to a wide range of social behavior and psychopathology. Thus extraversion and neuroticism are two of the three personality dimensions considered in detail in this chapter. The third dimension addressed is the Type A personality/behavior pattern. Type A behavior is a trait of special interest. This construct relates to interpersonal, affective, and cognitive styles, as well as to coronary heart disease and cardiovascular hyperreactivity (Matthews, 1982).

The extraversion–introversion personality dimension (hereafter referred to simply as "extraversion") has received a great deal of attention for at least three reasons (Graziano, Rahe, & Feldesman, 1985). First, the dimension is related to clearly evident, common behaviors that are inherently interesting to many people. These include the degree of sociability, dominance, assertiveness, impulsivity, and activity (Eysenck & Eysenck, 1985). Extraverts are sociable, assertive, active, and generally prefer high levels of environmental stimulation. On the other hand, introverts prefer nonsocial situations, do not like excitement, and prefer to avoid arousal and tension-producing conditions (Eysenck & Eysenck, 1985). Second, extraversion is related to a wide variety of psychological and behavioral constructs ranging from individual differences in sensitivity to rewards and punishments (Gray, 1981) to individual differences in psychophysiological responses to drugs (Gilbert, 1987; Smith, Wilson, & Jones, 1983). Finally, evidence suggests that about half of the variance in extraversion is genetically determined (Martin & Jardine, 1986), and there are significant physiological differences between extraverts and introverts (Eysenck & Eysenck, 1985; Gale, 1983). Thus extraversion suggests a biopsychological framework that relates biological factors to psychological and social processes.

Neuroticism is the higher-order personality factor indicated by the high intercorrelations of primary emotional traits such as anxiety, depression, anger, moodiness, and emotional lability (Eysenck & Eysenck, 1985). Studies demonstrate a genetic basis to the higher-order neuroticism factor as well as to its constituent primary factors (Martin & Jardine, 1986; Vandenberg, Singer, & Pauls, 1986). We now turn our attention to fuller description of these genetic and biological factors.

GENETICS, TEMPERAMENT, AND THE BIOLOGICAL
BASIS OF PERSONALITY

Biological mechanisms that may mediate genetic influences on temperament, affect, and behavior have received growing attention during the last two decades. Eysenck (1967) hypothesized that a genetically determined tendency of the central nervous system (CNS) toward a relatively low level of arousal is the biological factor promoting extraversion, whereas a tendency toward high CNS arousal promotes introversion. That is, he proposed that introverts have a more chronically aroused and arousable cerebral cortex and reticular activating system than do extraverts. Assuming that the optimal level of arousal is a moderate one, introverts would be expected to spend more time and energy trying to control their cortical arousal by seeking to reduce external stimulation. On the other hand, in order to elevate their arousal from its inherent low level to a more ideal level, extraverts would be expected to spend more time trying to increase the intensity of external stimulation. There is some support for these arousal-related hypotheses (reviewed by Claridge, 1986; Eysenck & Eysenck, 1985; and by Gale, 1983).

Gray (1981) has provided evidence that the biological basis of extraversion is related to the septohippocampal "stop" and hypothalamic "go" systems of the brain. He argues that extraverts are highly sensitive to potential rewards but are relatively insensitive to potential punishments. Extraverts are thus seen as impulsive and low in anxiety. Conversely, introverts are less impulsive and more anxious because they are sensitive to potential punishments and less influenced by potential rewards. Of special relevance to our concern with social interaction are the findings by Gupta (1984) that support Gray's formulations by showing extraverts and introverts to be differentially influenced by reinforcement and punishment during a verbal conditioning paradigm. The theorizing of Gray and Eysenck suggests that many differences should be found between the social behavior of introverts and extraverts, as well as between neurotic and stable individuals.

The genetically determined biological bases of the various neurotic processes may be located in the brain's limbic system and associated outputs to the sympathetic nervous system. Specifically, individuals with low thresholds for limbic system activation are often assumed to be predisposed toward more frequent, prolonged, and intense emotional reactions that manifest themselves in overly intense and prolonged activation of the pituitary–adrenal cortical system and the sympathetic nervous system (SNS) and its end organs so as to produce increases in heart rate, blood pressure, skin conductance, as well as increased outputs of cortisol, epinephrine, and related hormones (Eysenck, 1967; Kaplan, 1987; Mandler, 1984).

Pathologically anxious individuals seen during acute episodes of distress in clinical settings often are characterized by heightened levels of many indexes of SNS activation (reviewed by Naveteur & Baque, 1987). On the other hand, clinically depressed individuals and those prone to depression tend to have abnormally low levels of skin conductance (reviewed by Ward & Doerr, 1986) but tend to have elevated plasma cortisol concentrations (a measure of stress-related hormonal activity) (Henry, 1986). In contrast to clinical settings, in nonclinical settings individuals scoring high on self-report measures of neuroticism and anxiety are typically characterized by abnormally low, rather than high, levels of SNS activity (Naveteur & Baque, 1987; Netter, 1985; Roessler, 1973). Nonclinical individuals high in trait neuroticism and anxiety have reduced plasma catecholamine concentrations in nonstress conditions and low plasma epinephrine concentrations in certain stressful situations (Forsman, 1980; Netter, 1985). Thus, although some clinically neurotic individuals exhibit exaggeration of SNS and pituitary–adrenal–cortical axis overactivity, nonclinical populations scoring high on neuroticism tend to be under, rather than over, reactive in these respects in at least some situations.

Very few studies have assessed the physiological correlates of neuroticism in social situations. Neuroticism did not correlate significantly with heart rate or skin conductance levels or reactivity during the presentation of a speech in a past study (Gilbert, 1985). Yet heart rate and electrodermal responses to one's spouse presenting his or her major marital complaint have been found to correlate positively with neuroticism (Gilbert, Hermecz, & Davis, 1982).

Because a number of different primary factors contribute to the higher-order neuroticism factor, it is not surprising that neuroticism is not consistently related to either over- or underactivation of the SNS. The frequently made assumption that neurotic individuals are characterized by limbic and SNS overactivation appears to hold for only those individuals scoring high on certain of the primary factors of neuroticism and then only when these individuals are in specific types of situations. Whether or not individuals scoring high on neuroticism demonstrate high SNS activation in a particular setting is likely to be a function of a variety of factors, including degree of setting pull for active versus passive coping. Such person-by-situation specificity is seen in interactions of Type A and Type B individuals, where cardiovascular response magnitude is a function of task control, as well as the personalities of each of the interactants (Abbott et al., 1987). Unfortunately, studies to date have generally not used stimulus conditions typical of those that are likely to be especially stressful to neurotics or are likely to differentiate neurotics from stables. Researchers have not considered how types of neuroticism interact with different types of situations.

An additional consideration when assessing relationships between neuroticism and SNS activation is that there is no reason that neuroticism's various components should have identical or even similar associations with physiological measures. In this regard, Claridge (1986) has noted that there is no reason why the existance of neuroticism as a descriptive factor implies that it must have a unitary biological basis.

It is reasonable to hypothesize that many neurotic individuals are characterized by bimodal response dispositions. Neurotics and others suffering from psychopathology are frequently preoccupied with internal stimuli and/or engaged in passive coping. Thus it should not be surprising that, when in such states, they are less aroused by external stimuli than most individuals (Roessler, 1973). However, when stimuli are highly personal, psychologically disturbed individuals may no longer be able to cope by avoidance (Bernstein, Schneider, Juni, & Pope, 1980). In such situations, many neurotics and other individuals high in psychopathology are likely to become aroused to a normal or above-normal degree. In support of this hypothesis, schizophrenic individuals have been found to be electrodermally underreactive when word stimuli are irrelevant and easily ignored but to be normally responsive when the task makes the words personally relevant (Bernstein *et al.*, 1980). One can take Bernstein's findings a step further and suggest that some individuals suffer catastrophic reactions when they become actively engaged with environmental factors that are highly personally involving, yet over which they feel little ability to control (Abramson, Seligman & Teasdale, 1978). They may thus be conditioned to psychologically and behaviorally avoid personally stressful situations. However, when they cannot avoid stressful engagements they may become hyperaroused and thus conform to the characterization of neuroticism so common in the literature. Consistent with this reasoning, Singer (1974) argued that engagement–involvement is the critical factor determining degree of psychophysiological responsivity. Thus neurotics, including depressives and others with chronic interpersonal problems, may be characterized by alterations between avoidance-motivated underengagement and catastrophic overengagement with associated heightened activation. In the underengaged state the neurotic would be, relative to stables, characterized by underactivation of emotion-related physiological systems. In contrast, catastrophic overengaged states are associated with heightened physiological activity.

Further support for a coping-strategy-specific model of neurotic arousal level is provided by the fact that cardiovascular arousal is a function of motor-related processes associated with active coping (Obrist, 1981), whereas pituitary–adrenal hormones are related to passive coping, learned helplessness, and depression (Henry, 1986). Effects of perceived control on cardiovascular, hormonal, and emotional responses to stressful situations may be understood in terms of perceived control over a stressor and the strategy used to cope with the stressor (Henry, 1986).

Cognitive processes, including a low degree of perceived control, may make neurotic individual vulnerable to clinical depression (Abramson, Seligman, & Teasdale, 1978). Cognitive biases associated with neuroticism include a tendency to recall negative memories more frequently and more rapidly than positive memories (Martin, 1985). The biological mechanisms underlying these information-processing biases appear to be associated with underactivation of the left and/or overactivation of the right frontal cortex (Davidson, 1984; Lolas, 1987). The left hemisphere is associated with active coping, whereas the right hemisphere appears less related to such processes and more associated with negative affect and passive coping (Tucker & Williamson, 1984). Lateralized neuroprocessing of information may contribute to individual differences in active versus passive coping styles and thus to personality and social interaction. Neurophysiological-processing biases may increase the probability of seeing oneself as being helpless in a given situation and thus may promote a lack of coping that in turn further promotes feelings of helplessness. It is not yet clear how biological and experiential factors combine to produce a disposition towards right-hemisphere-based depressive information processing.

EXTRAVERSION AND SOCIAL INTERACTION

Consistent with Gray's (1981) hypothesis that extraverts are relatively more sensitive to rewards, whereas introverts are relatively sensitive to punishments, extraverts remember rewarding and positive characteristics about interactions and the people with whom they interact, whereas introverts remember more of the negative aspects (Graziano et al., 1985; Thorne, 1987). Evidence of a relative sensitivity to punishment in introverts is also provided by studies showing introverts to anticipate more disagreement between themselves and others (Cooper & Scalise, 1974), to report such disagreement more aversive (Norman & Waston, 1976), and to rate others more negatively than extraverts (Lishman, 1972). Consistent with their greater sensitivity to reward and/or a diminished sensitivity to punishment, extraverts tend to date frequently and to engage in sex at an earlier age and with more partners (Eysenck & Wilson, 1979), whereas those who date rarely are more often introverted and/or neurotic (Himadi, Arkowitz, Hinton, & Perl, 1980).

Also consistent with a relatively lessened sensitivity to punishment and a greater preoccupation with potential reward are findings showing extraverts to be more assertive and dominant than introverts (Infante, 1987), to talk more, talk first and talk more rapidly and loudly, and to be more persuasive and less persuadable than introverts (Carment & Miles, 1971; Markel, Phillis, Vargas, & Harvard, 1972). This active, assertive and reward-oriented behavior is also seen in stressful situations, where extraverts are more likely to experience anger, whereas introverts are more likely to experience anxiety and communication apprehension (Bell & Daly, 1985; Sipprelle, Ascough, Detrio, & Horst, 1977).

Although Gray (1981) has hypothesized that the differences in sensitivity of extraverts and introverts to rewards and punishments are genetically based, it may be that these negative cognitive assessments of introverts result from environmental factors such as a high rate of negative social feedback resulting from poor social skills. Extraverts tend to be rated by both introverts and extraverts as being more interesting at parties, having the ideal personality, and being the preferred leader (Hendrick & Brown, 1971). Although high rates of negative social feedback may contribute to the introvert's negative evaluation of social situations, introverts have a selective attentional bias and recall for negative aspects of social situations (Graziano *et al.*, 1985). This selective recall could be based on biological dispositions and/or a history of negative social experiences. It is reasonable to hypothesize that some introverts may be introverted solely because of learning histories and poor social skills. On the other hand, it is likely that complex temperament by environment interactions produce differences in both punishment versus reward sensitivities (Gray, 1981) and in social skills (Scarr & McCartney, 1983).

NEUROTICISM AND SOCIAL INTERACTION

Although introverts may be less socially skilled and enjoyable to interact with than are extraverts, unlike depressed individuals, they are not prone to cause social partners to experience negative affect (Graziano *et al.*, 1985). Depressed persons induce negative affect in those with whom they interact, apparently because they display fewer friendly, pleasant, appropriate, and skilled behaviors and more negative ones (reviewed by Hokanson & Rubert, present volume). Responsiveness and attentiveness are also inversely related to neuroticism and loneliness (Cegala, Savage, Brunner, & Conrad, 1982). Thus it is not surprising that depressed individuals and their spouses have more stressed marriages and lower marital satisfaction than nondepressed individuals (Lewinsohn, Steinmetz, Larson, & Franklin, 1981). Because neuroticism is associated with repeated acute bouts of depression (Martin, 1985), neuroticism may be largely a function of a cognitive–affective–behavioral disposition to act in an unskilled and/or cognitively and emotionally defeating manner. Such self-defeating behavior would account for the heightened frequency of social frustrations and negative affect in individuals high in neuroticism. Although a significant amount is known about depression and social interaction (Hokanson & Rupert, this volume), much more needs to be learned about the relationship of social skill and performance to nondepressive components of neuroticism and about how neurotic processes (including depression) differ from and are similar to those associated with introversion.

TYPE A BEHAVIOR, ACTIVITY LEVEL, AND SOCIAL INTERACTION

The Type A behavior pattern (TABP) is an interpersonally relevant construct that may be a risk factor for heart disease (Mathews, 1982). This behavioral pattern includes extreme achievement striving, time urgency, impatience, and hostility, whereas the Type B individual is characterized by a relative lack of these traits. The TABP is defined in terms of interpersonal stylistics that are typically assessed during a standardized social interaction—the Structured Interview (Chesney, Eagelston, & Rosenman, 1980). Heightened psychophysiological responsivity and strenuous active coping are associated with the TABP (Matthews, 1982). Although questionnaire-assessed Type A behavior and its component factors consistently correlate with extraversion and neuroticism (Byrne, Rosenman, Schiller, & Chesney, 1985; Chesney, Black, Chadwick, & Rosenman, 1981), neuroticism and extraversion correlate minimally with behavioral observations of Type A behavior during the Structured Interview (Byrne *et al.*, 1985; Chesney *et al.*, 1981). This substantial independence of the TABP from questionnaire-defined measures suggests that the TABP is more than just a combination of questionnaire-defined extraversion and neuroticism.

Consistent with the person × person × setting (PPS) model, the nature of social interactions and cardiovascular activities of A's and B's are a function of one's personality, the personality of one's partner (Type A versus Type B) and the task (Abbott *et al.*, 1987; Van Egeren, 1979; Watkins & Eisler, 1988). Further support for the PPT model is provided by the finding that although level of marital satisfaction is not related to degree of Type A versus B behavior of either partner when considered alone, it is related to one of four possible husband–wife pairings. Type A husbands married to Type B wives have a substantially lower degree of marital satisfaction than the other three possible pairings of A's and B's (Blaney, Brown, & Blaney, 1986).

TABP and heightened physiological arousal characterize Type A individuals only in situations where there are moderate external incentives to be achieved by active coping (Houston, 1983). Type A's react to threats of loss of control with high degrees of active coping compared to type B's (Rhodewalt & Davison, 1983). Given this concern with maintaining control by active coping, it is not surprising that Type A's generally demonstrate greater hostility and physiological arousal when interpersonally challenged or harassed (Houston, 1983). Relative to Type B's, Type A individuals are competitive (Byrne *et al.*, 1985), experience reactance when they perceive reduced behavioral freedom (Rhodewalt & Davison, 1983), and experience elevated cardiovascular activity when in challenging interpersonal situations where they have an opportunity to exert some control (Abbott *et al.*, 1987).

Because much negative affect in interpersonal relationships is a result of interpersonally frustrated goals (Berscheid, Gangestad, & Kulakowski, 1984), one might expect Type A's to experience more intense negative affect related to interpersonal conflict than B's. Consistent with this prediction, Watkins and Eisler (1988) found Type A's to express anger less appropri-

ately during challenging situations but to display greater overall social skill
and to be more interesting than B's. Trait hostility also was a moderator
variable of this affect–behavior relationship. Hostile Type A's dominated
conversations and responded aggressively to interpersonal challenges. Hostile Type B's were the least skilled of all groups and were passive or sarcastic in response to interpersonal challenges.

COMPETENCE AND SKILL IN SOCIAL INTERACTIONS

Distressed marriages and families are characterized by what have been
viewed as low levels of social skills, for example, higher frequencies of
dysfunctional communications, than are happy marriages and families
(Bradbury & Fincham, 1987a; Gottman, 1979; Patterson, 1982). It is frequently asserted that such faulty communications are a primary cause of
marital and family distress and that these faulty patterns of communication
are the result of communication skill deficits (Gottman, Notarius, Gonso, &
Markman, 1976; Jacobson & Margolin, 1979). Distressed couples tend to
communicate in a highly rigid and predictable manner that includes excessive blaming statements, repetition of views, and disagreement, combined
with rare expression of agreement and infrequent reaching of mutually
agreed upon solutions (Gottman, 1979).

Although males in distressed marriages may be less skilled in reading
nonverbal messages than males in happy marriages (Gottman & Porterfield,
1981; Noller, 1984), there are reasons to question the validity of a simple
communication–skills-deficit formulation of the dysfunctional interpersonal
patterns and of marital and family distress. One reason is that although
communication training has been shown to be more effective than control
conditions in the treatment of marital distress (Jacobson, Follette, & Elwood, 1984), only about half of the couples who receive behavioral marital
therapy that includes communication training increase in their level of marital satisfaction to the level typical of nondistressed couples (Jacobson et al.,
1984). A second reason to question a simple communication skills model is
based on observations that whereas distressed spouses communicate in a
negative and apparently poorly skilled manner with their spouses, they
interact with strangers of the opposite sex in a "skilled" manner (Birchler,
Weiss & Vincent, 1975; Winter, Ferreira, & Bowers, 1973). A third reason is
based on the observation that the degree to which skillful communication
occurs is highly emotional state and motivational state dependent. For example, individuals report that even though they know how to communicate
using all of the techniques taught them by their communication skills therapist/trainer, when they get angry they do not feel like using or want to use
these skills (Jacobson & Holtzworth-Monroe, 1986). The model outlined

next contributes to the understanding of such state-dependent motivation and "skill."

PERSONALITY × PERSONALITY × SETTING (PPS) MODEL OF INTERPERSONAL AFFECT AND COMMUNICATION

The PPS model outlined here is based on evidence reviewed before showing that there are a large number of systematic relationships between personality, situation, psychophysiology, affect, and social behavior. Earlier versions of the model are described in Gilbert (1981, 1986).

PROPOSITION 1

Maximally effective communication and conflict resolution is most likely to occur when group members are at intermediate levels of arousal. High levels of arousal tend to potentiate anger, defensiveness, reactance, and rigid, overlearned, and overly constricted problem-solving strategies, whereas very low levels of arousal and interpersonal engagement are associated with inefficient problem solving and poor interpersonal attention.

This proposition is based on the observation that performance on a wide variety of cognitive and behavioral tasks is maximal when arousal is at an intermediate level (reviewed by Eysenck, 1982). Zillmann (1979) suggests that annoyance-motivated behavior is largely controlled by cognitive processes when excitation is at intermediate levels, but that at supra- or suboptimal levels of excitation, annoyance-motivated behavior is impulsive. High levels of physiological arousal reduce the efficiency with which environmental cues are processed. Anxiety and other forms of emotional arousal reduce the ability to concentrate on external stimuli because worry, self-concern, and other emotion-related cognitions are powerful internal distractors (Eysenck & Eysenck, 1985). In addition, high arousal may reduce the range of cues to which an organism responds (Easterbrook, 1959). At extremely high and at low levels of arousal, the individual is unable to process complex response alternatives and is preoccupied with avoiding potential annoyances or with eliminating annoying stimuli (Zillmann, 1979). At these extreme levels of arousal, behavioral responses are aimed at immediate relief, irrespective of their long-term implications. Zillmann argued that at high levels of excitation, the capacity to anticipate reward and punishment and overall cost are reduced and that at extremely high levels of arousal, nonimmediate consequences of behavior are ignored completely. During states of high arousal, high habit strength behaviors dominate and motor behavior is extreme and roughly proportionate to the level of sympathetic nervous system arousal (Zillmann, 1979).

Consistent with these formulations, changes in cue utilization have been described since the earliest work in the field of emotion and stress (reviewed by Froelich, 1978). Increasing environmental stressor level and emotion have been seen as decreasing the ability to discriminate between objective and subjective aspects of situations, as if shifting attention from external to internal messages or cues (Sarason, 1972).

For maximally flexible and creative conflict resolution to occur, parties must appropriately attend to multidimensional aspects of the other communicator's messages as well as to their own complex experiences (Watzlawick, Beavin, & Jackson, 1967). Competent communication has been defined as the degree to which individuals perceive they have achieved goals in a situation without jeopardizing their chances of achieving subjectively more important goals (Parks, 1985). Achieving such a balance requires flexible monitoring of a wide variety of processes, long-, and short-term personal goals as well as the goals of the person with whom one is interacting. An accurate integration and understanding of the other's goals, as well as one's own desires, requires attention to and the integration of information about the other's goals and emotions. An intermediate level of arousal is expected to facilitate the complex, multidimensional, information processing needed in such situations.

PROPOSITION 2

Verbal stimulus parameters affect listener emotional arousal. These parameters include rate and temporal patterning of the message, message content and affect, degree to which the message interferes with ongoing cognitive and/or behavioral sequences, and the degree to which interactional cues elicit previously conditioned cognitive-affective responses.

Parameters influencing physiological arousal to repeated stimulation include intensity, rate, and temporal patterning of stimulation (Zillmann, 1979). Residual physiological arousal, left over from an event or activity as much as 20 minutes or more earlier, can combine with the physiological response to a present threat in a manner that increases the net physiological and emotional arousal in proportion to the magnitude of the residual physiological arousal (Zillmann, 1979). Arousal and the period of time over which it can be transferred are a function of the magnitude of the initial arousal response and the rate at which preceding arousal dissipates (Zillmann, 1979). Thus an individual's capacity for transfer of arousal is a direct function of SNS arousal responsivity and inversely proportional to the capacity to dissipate excitation (Zillmann, 1979). Individuals with heightened SNS arousal responsivity and slowed dissipation capacity are expected to experience heightened emotionality in situations involving continued emotional stimulation. Type A individuals, certain neurotics, and hypertensives (Houston, 1983; Lynch, Long, Thomas, Malinow, & Katcher, 1981) fall into this category of heightened and prolonged SNS activation. Duckworth's (1975) findings showing experimentally induced stress to decrease the ability of neurotic introverts, relative to stable introverts, in identifying their spouse's feelings from tone-of-voice cues is consistent with this proposition.

Arousal from a variety of sources (sexual, aggressive, and aggressive stimuli, as well as physical activity) can be transferred in such a manner as to increase subsequent hostility and aggression (Zillmann, 1979, 1983). Studies have frequently involved an instigation to anger (insult, etc.), subsequent manipulation of arousal (low or high), and finally, the opportunity to retaliate against the instigator. Figure 1 depicts the arousal summation and transfer that occurs over time from the sequential presentation of arousal-producing stimuli. Arousal from the instigation to anger (A) combines with the arousal from subsequent arousing situation (B) to form a heightened summated total of SNS arousal (C). This summated arousal contributes to heightened aggression if the aroused individual attributes his/her arousal to the first stimulus, the initial instigation of anger/annoyance.

Figure 2 depicts two different physiological and emotional arousal level patterns over time. It emphasizes the ongoing nature of human interactions by generalizing Zillmann's two stimulus model (depicted in Figure 1) to multiple sequential stimulus–response reactions that will or will not summate (escalate) depending on the nature of the stimulus, interstimulus interval, and the personality (physiological/emotional lability and coping pattern) of the individual. Moderate-sized arousal responses (M) paced over time can fully dissipate so there is no residual suprabaseline arousal from the preceding stimulus available to summate with subsequent stimuli. In this situa-

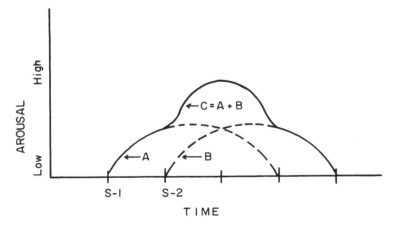

FIGURE 1. Zillman's model of arousal summation over two stimuli. A = arousal component elicited by the initial stimulus (S-1); B = arousal component contributed by a subsequent stimulus (S-2); C = total organismic arousal resulting from the summation of arousal from stimuli S-1 plus S-2.

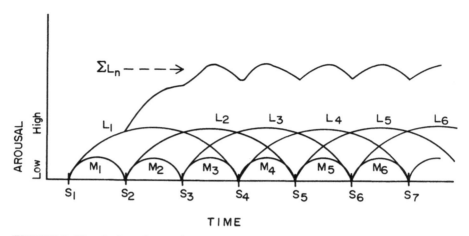

FIGURE 2. Magnitude and rate of successive arousal responses to sequential stimuli determine arousal level. Moderate arousal responses (Mn) can fully dissipate between stimuli so
there is no summation of arousal. On the other hand, residual arousal from large amplitude
responses and/or rapidly occuring stimuli summate (Σ Ln) so as to produce arousal escalation.

tion, the individual's arousal varies periodically within the moderate arousal
range that corresponds to most efficient cognitive processing and interpersonal cue utilization.

The large amplitude–duration (L) arousal responses depicted in Figure
2 represent responses by the average individual to highly provoking stimuli
or responses by an individual who tends to overreact to stimuli and who
recovers to baseline arousal levels slowly. Whatever the cause, large-ampli-
tude responses occurring rapidly will result in an escalation of arousal (Σ L)
due to progressive summation of residual arousal from preceding stimuli.
Such escalations quickly result in high levels of arousal. Thus it is hypothesized that rate of message presentation is a crucial determinant of emotional and physiological arousal levels. Rapidly repeated interruptions, challenges of control, and/or affect-eliciting verbal or nonverbal messages are
predicted to escalate physiological arousal to high levels that reduce the
efficiency of cognitive functioning and potentiate emotional processes.

Message-response relationships have received relatively little systematic attention in the experimental literature. Gottman (1979) is one of the
few investigators to carefully evaluate the effects of different message parameters on listener response. His studies have evaluated the conditional
probabilities of different responses given different message types during
marital-conflict-resolution tasks. Distressed couples are characterized by
greater reciprocity of negative affect and have more rigid and predictable
communicational action sequences than satisfied couples. Distressed couples' communications are characterized by contents that are defensogenic
(i.e., promote defensive responses). In contrast, satisfied couples' commu-

nications are characterized by attentionogenic messages (i.e., contents that tend to elicit listening and nondefensive behavior). Gilbert, Hermecz, and Davis (1982) supported Gottman's correlational findings by showing both message content and message affect to be important determinants of physiological arousal level (heart rate and skin resistance) in individuals listening to their spouse comment on their major marital problem. Frustration and insult are relatively reliable elicitors of physiological arousal, anger, and aggression (Gentry, 1970; Hokanson, Willers, & Koropsak, 1968; Rule & Hewitt, 1971; Schill, 1972).

A number of theoreticians have presented evidence favoring the view that frustration leads to aggression and/or to a variety of emotional states (Berscheid *et al.*, 1984; Dollard *et al.*, 1939; Mandler, 1984). Berscheid (1982) hypothesizes that emotion in close relationships occurs when one person interrupts or interferes with the partner's plans and/or ongoing action sequences. She bases her model of social affect on that proposed by Mandler (1984) in which interrupted cognitive plans are hypothesized to cause increases in SNS arousal, which is then labeled as a particular type of emotional experience, depending on what cognitive label is attached. The closer the relationship between interactants, the greater the number of interdependent action sequences and the greater the probability that frustration of action sequences will occur. Thus close interpersonal relationships have a very high potential for interruptions, arousal, and emotion. However, although frustrated plans are likely to cause many occurrences of affect in close relationships, processes not included in Berscheid's model are also important in the development of emotional states (Bradbury & Fincham, 1987a,b). Increased physiological arousal accompanies the presence of others (Gale, Lucas, Nissim, & Harpham, 1972; Patterson, 1976; Zajonc, 1965), the simple act of speaking (Gilbert & Spielberger, 1987; Lynch *et al.*, 1981), and conditioned emotional responses (Tursky, Lodge, & Reeder, 1979).

Findings in the field of nonconscious social information processing (Lewicki, 1986) support the contention that subtle nonverbal cues, even those of which the listener is not consciously aware, can have important effects on listener affective and evaluative states. Emotion-related coping tendencies and affective–perceptual biases can be primed by very subtle experiences that occur out of the awareness of the listener (Lewicki, 1986; Zajonc, 1984). The present model hypothesizes that nonverbal stimuli that are not consciously processed or cognitively linked to one's motivational and emotional state frequently influence the nature and outcome of information-intensive social interactions by evoking affective, perceptual, and related information-processing biases that tend to promote arousal and the escalation of either positive or negative affective states. It seems likely that such nonconscious social information in some cases elicits SNS arousal summation. In addition it is probable that localized and lateralized central nervous system (CNS) emotion-related neurobiological processors exhibit arousal summation and contribute to states of heightened emotionality in a manner analogous to those proposed for SNS arousal. Thus, unlike Zillman's model, the present one suggests that emotion-specific CNS activation as well as nonspecific CNS and SNS arousal contribute to the momentum of emotional states.

Corollaries of the proposition that verbal stimulus parameters affect emotional arousal in the manners described above include (a) relationships in which both partners interrupt, speak rapidly, and/or with little censoring of defensogenic contents will tend to be characterized by an escalation of negative affect and associated physiological arousal and (b) interventions aimed at slowing the rate of speaking and defensogenic content will be effective in lowering interactant arousal and negative affect and will increase the probability of effective problem solving.

PROPOSITION 3

Sustained active attention and focusing on one's partner promotes a reduction in arousal and negative affect in the listener as well as the speaker and decreases negative mood-state-dependent associations.

Attention to external stimuli can produce decreased arousal (Lacey, 1967; Tecce, 1972). Based on these findings, Gilbert, Hermecz, and Davis (1982) hypothesized that attentionogenic messages would produce cardiac deceleration, whereas defensogenic messages would produce cardiac acceleration. The apparent arousal-decreasing effects of externally focused attention may be a partial psychophysiological explanation of why it is widely assumed by marital therapists that actively listening and attending to one's partner tends to promote effective communication and conflict resolution. In addition, active listening decreases interruptions of the speaker's plans and thereby helps maintain the speaker's arousal within ideal limits.

PROPOSITION 4

Learning history and temperament jointly determine social skills, affect, and behavior in social situations.

This proposition follows naturally from the preceding three propositions and from evidence reviewed earlier in this chapter supporting the importance and interactions of genetic–temperamental and environmental–learning factors in determining social behavior. The importance of social learning processes in determining the nature and magnitude of behavioral response, as well as the rate of SNS recovery from social threats, has been clearly demonstrated (Hokanson et al., 1968). Social responses to threat are frequently a result of being conditioned to escape an aversive social situation.

Escape conditioning models have been developed by Patterson (1982) and Gottman and Levenson (1986) in attempts to explain the development and maintenance of high levels of negative affect in distressed families and marriages. The escape conditioning model developed by Gottman and Levenson extends Patterson's model by relating reductions in physiological arousal to the reinforcement of sequences of negative-affect-ladden communication. Escape moments during interpersonal communication are defined as occurring when both interactants move from high levels to low levels of SNS arousal; that is, from tension to calmness. Gottman and Levenson (1986) hypothesized that the behavioral patterns that immediately precede such reductions in SNS arousal will be reinforced and thus increase in unconditional probability and in probability conditional on high levels of physiological arousal. In support of their escape-conditioning hypothesis, Gottman and Levenson (1986) provided an example of a wife who was rarely angry in nonescape moments (less than 7%) but was angry in 53% of the escape moments. The wife's anger was correlated with subsequent reductions of SNS arousal. The wife's expression of negative affect apparently reduced the level of physiological and affective tension in the short term but may have reinforced the pattern of escalation and anger in the long run. Gottman and Levenson suggest that rigid patterns of negative affect and related communications are developed by the reinforcing effects of such escape conditioning. Gottman's escape-conditioning model implies that individual differences in personality and temperament should contribute to individual differences in social learning to the degree that these variables are related to lability of the SNS. It is reasonable to hypothesize that escape conditioning also increases the probability of negative-affect-related cognitive processes concerning the one from whom one is escaping.

Interest in the contributions and interactions of affect and cognition in relationship satisfaction and distress has grown tremendously in the last decade (Berscheid, 1982; Bradbury & Fincham, 1987a; Jacobsen & Holtzworth-Monroe, 1986). Much of this interest has been fostered by the inadequacies of purely skill-based marital therapy approaches that do not consider the complex manner in which cognition and affect influence interpersonal conflict resolution and marital satisfaction. Bradbury and Fincham (1987a) have presented an excellent in-depth analysis of the manner in which cognition and affect might be expected to interact in close relationships.

PROPOSITION 5

The personalities and social skills of the participants interact with each other and the situation so as to channel cognitive, emotional, and motivational processes.

This proposition follows from the preceding four propositions and from evidence reviewed earlier. The remainder of this chapter elaborates on this proposition as predictions are made based on the PPS model.

PPS-BASED PREDICTIONS OF AFFECT AND
COMMUNICATIONAL STYLES

The five propositions listed combine to predict social interactions as a function of personalities of interactants and the setting. The hypothesized ideal style of communication and conflict resolution as well as three conflict styles that have been described in the literature are presented in the following paragraphs.

IDEAL STYLE

Heart rates associated with the ideal conflict resolution and communication process are depicted in Figure 3. Interactants are identified as "S" and "O." Individual S initiates a verbal transaction, and O listens attentively in a nondefensive, open manner. The message is formulated so as to maximize O's nondefensive attentiveness and to increase the likelihood that O is in or moving toward an intermediate level of arousal (as reflected in heart rate) that facilitates maximal cognitive control and flexibility. During this time O listens attentively, without interfering cognitions. This pattern of attentional focus is hypothesized to be consistent with the open sharing of information, tolerance for the other's feelings, and successful short- and long-term problem resolution.

This ideal style is expected to occur more frequently in dyads consisting of two individuals who both stand at the stable end of the neuroticism–stability dimension and the Type B end of the A/B continuum. This is because the autonomic arousal of Type B's and stable individuals tends to be

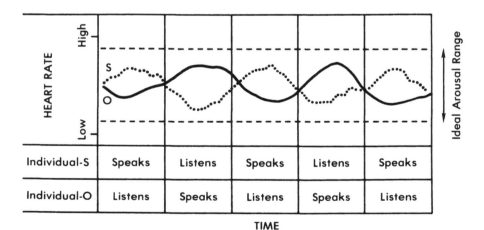

FIGURE 3. Heart rates/arousal of Person S and Person O across speaking and listening turns during ideal interpersonal transactions.

lower and to dissipate relatively rapidly, thus minimizing tendencies for residual arousal to summate after repeated stimulus inputs. Also, Type A's and neurotics are expected to interpret a given message as more threatening than are individuals with more stable personalities and thus are expected to react in a more defensive and less attentive manner.

Heart rates of interactants during an ideal conflict resolution transaction are thought to reflect both attentional and emotional-arousal factors. Lacey (1967) and others have shown that a variety of situations involving action and/or emotional processes (including thinking and problem solving) result in heart rate increases, whereas empathic listening and open attentiveness to the external environment lead to heart rate decreases. Based on these observations, Gilbert (1981) hypothesized that heart rate decreases frequently mirror nondefensive, attentive listening, whereas heart rate increases reflect defensive and internal preoccupations on the part of the listener. The physical act of speaking and associated ideational processes increase the heart rate of the speaker, even during ideal interpersonal communications (Gilbert & Spielberger, 1987). Thus the phasic heart activity of individuals during an ideal situation would be expected to be 180 degrees out of phase, reflecting the alternation of speaking and listening roles. Confirmation of this pattern of rises and falls of heart rate to form interlocking sine waves has been found in a majority of dyads in which partner's alternated speaker and listener roles at 1 minute intervals (Gilbert & Spielberger, 1987). A number of studies have demonstrated speaking to produce significant increases in heart rate and blood pressure (Long *et al.*, 1982; Lynch *et al.*, 1981). Individuals who are effective in resolving their interpersonal conflicts may use listening periods as opportunities to lower their arousal levels by means of attentive, nondefensive listening and a minimum of internal preoccupation.

DEFENSIVE ESCALATION STYLE

Among the least satisfied group of marriages is that characterized by high levels of confrontation combined with negative affect (Davis, Haymaker, Hermecz, & Gilbert, 1988; Rands, Levinger, & Mellinger, 1981; Rausch, Barry, Hertel, & Swain, 1974). Gilbert (1981) suggested that such interactions are especially probable in distressed couples composed of two extraverted neurotics because extraverts, relative to introverts, are less likely to avoid high stimulus intensity situations (Eysenck & Eysenck, 1985) and are more likely to deal with stressors via anger than anxiety (Sipprelli *et al.*, 1977). Lansky (1986) labeled couples characterized by such interactions as "blaming couples". Research and clinical findings suggest that impulsivity (a component of extraversion) is also strongly related to this pattern (Kelly & Conley, 1987).

Hypothesized physiological correlates of the defensive conflict escala-

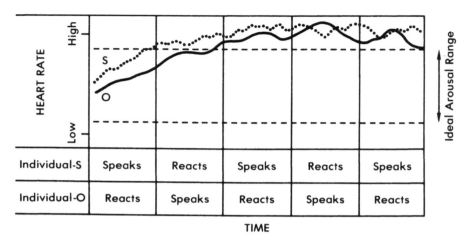

FIGURE 4. Heart rates/arousal of Person S and Person O across speaking and listening turns during an interpersonal transaction characterized by mutual defensive escalation.

tion style are depicted in Figure 4. A verbal transaction is initiated by S in such a manner as to create a defensive response in O, and O's defensive and attacking response in turn contributes to an attacking defensive response from S. Such patterns of negative-affect escalation take place much more often in distressed than in nondistressed couples and families (Gottman, 1979; Patterson, 1982). S's defensogenic message interacting with O's cognitive/affective system produces heightened arousal by means of conditioned emotional responses and defensive cognitive coping techniques such as self-verbalizations (Ellis, 1962; May & Johnson, 1973; Rimm & Litvak, 1969). These attempts at defensive coping and attack and their associated heightened physiological arousal occupy a large portion of O's cognitive and attentional capacities. O actively generates covert counterarguments and is largely internally preoccupied with counteracting the perceived threat posed by S. Breadth of attention is narrowed due to heightened arousal and a defensive focus. This narrowed focus excludes attention to the details of S's message and to the long-term functioning of the relationship.

Preoccupations with the generation of defensive responses frequently lead to their overt expression. When this overt expression occurs, S is likely to feel that his/her message has not been heard, leading to frustration, arousal, and internal preoccupations similar to those experienced initially by O. Thus, O's nonlistening defensive behavior and subsequent response elicit the same nonattentive, preoccupied behavior on the part of S that S's message originally elicited in O. An escalating cycle of nonlistening, highly emotional, defensive, and attacking transactions ensues. The more overtly expressive, Type A and neurotic the members of the dyad, the more likely this pattern of conflict will be seen. This is partly because of the increased tendency for escalation of physiological arousal caused by the high physiological responsivity and slow dissipation of physiological arousal seen in these individuals and partly because Type A's and neurotics tend to interpret disagreement as threatening.

The mutual progressive and sustained heart rate increases seen in Figure 4 are also hypothesized to characterize the attentional and arousal characteristics of such a nonlistening conflict escalation because cognitive work, active coping, and most forms of emotional arousal are associated with increased SNS and CNS arousal that are not allowed to dissipate during periods of open attentiveness to and acceptance of the partner's message. Defensive counterargument generation closes off the listener from potentially important interpersonal cues and eliminates opportunities for arousal decay that could occur during open-attentive listening.

Consistent with these predictions, studies monitoring autonomic nervous system arousal (cardiovascular and electrodermal activity) have shown greater autonomic activation in distressed than nondistressed couples (Gottman & Levenson, 1986) and in individuals who dislike the person with whom they are interacting (Kaplan, Burch, & Bloom, 1964). Furthermore, in comparison with satisfied couples, distressed couples exhibit higher degrees of physiological covariance or linkage when trying to solve marital problems (Gottman & Levenson, 1986). Physiological arousal is expected to be higher in this style of interaction than in others proposed. This should be especially true of cardiovascular activation because active coping and motor activity are potent contributors to cardiovascular arousal (Lynch *et al.*, 1981; Obrist, 1981).

ENGAGED/DISENGAGED STYLE

This interpersonal style has been referred to as the distancer and pursuer (Satir, 1975) and the detached versus the demanding spouse (Strean, 1985). One individual is emotionally detached whereas the other demands emotional involvement and problem resolution. Gilbert (1981) predicted that the disengaged individual would more likely be an introverted neurotic, whereas the overengaged individual would be an extraverted neurotic. Evidence suggests that men are apparently more likely to be disengaged, whereas women are more likely to be overengaged. For example, Hawkins, Weisberg, and Ray (1980) reported that a very common complaint of wives about their husbands is that their husbands avoid emotional engagement with them and do not listen often or well enough for them to feel understood.

Gottman and Levenson (1986) found that marriages in which the husband withdraws during conflict while the wife escalates are characterized by decreases in marital satisfaction over time. This supports the view that little resolution of conflicts is expected to occur during such interactions.

These results are consistent with the finding that marriages composed of relatively more extraverted wives and introverted husbands tend to be less satisfying than those where the husband is more or equally extraverted (Carlson & Williams, 1984; Eysenck & Wakefield, 1981). It is likely that the characteristic tendency of males to be emotionally disengaged is exaggerated in male introverts but counteracted by higher degrees of extraversion.

As depicted in Figure 5, it is hypothesized that the overengaged individual, S, initiates the communication while in a higher state of emotional arousal than O, the disengaged individual. The longer the overengaged individual talks, the higher his/her physiological arousal is likely to become. The lack of a significant response on the part of the disengaged individual not only engenders frustration-induced arousal and emotion in the overly engaged partner, but it denies the engaged partner the opportunity to disengage and return to a less emotional and more efficient level of arousal. Thus the disengaged individual unwittingly promotes the very emotional arousal in the engaged spouse that he/she is trying to avoid. Similarly, the overengaged individual's intensity contributes to the disengagement of the partner by producing a level of intensity that the disengaged partner prefers to avoid. The literature reviewed earlier suggests that the overly engaged partners are likely to be extraverts, whereas the disengaged spouse are likely to be introverts and/or men. Consistent with this view, Gottman and Levenson (1984) have noted evidence (Gottman & Porterfield, 1981; Noller, 1984) supporting the view that husbands in distressed marriages are less emotionally responsive to their wives than the wives are to their husbands. They suggest that the husband's lack of emotional responsiveness to

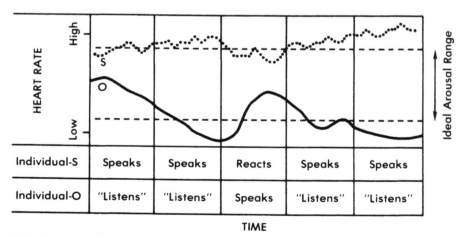

FIGURE 5. Heart rates/arousal of engaged Person S and disengaged Person O across speaking and listening turns during an interpersonal transaction.

his wife leads the wife to escalate her negative affect to the point that the husband eventually responds with negative affect.

Overt/Covert Engagement Style

This style has also been referred to as the dominant–submissive dyad (Strean, 1985). During such interactions, the overtly engaging (assertive) individual openly expresses views and feelings, whereas the covertly engaged spouse is emotionally engaged but is inhibited by internal or external processes from responding. A variety of factors, including differences in dominance, power, extraversion, and neuroticism, may promote the repeated occurrence of this pattern (Gilbert, 1981).

It is reasonable to hypothesize that introverts tend more often than extraverts to engage in patterns of covert engagement because they tend to prefer to avoid intense stimulation (Eysenck, 1967), are more concerned with avoiding potential punishments (Gray, 1981), and are more likely to experience anxiety than anger (Sipprelle *et al.*, 1977). Neurotic introverts are vulnerable in situations where assertiveness is important if one's needs are to be met. Such an individual in a close relationship with an assertive or aggressive partner is likely to experience difficulty in asserting his/her desires. Given this lack of assertion, the neurotic introvert or Type B individual is likely to experience repeated frustrations and feelings of being out of control, which, in turn, cause heightened autonomic arousal (Cornelius & Averill, 1980).

Figure 6 depicts the progressively increasing autonomic arousal of the covertly engaged individual O. Probably unaware of his/her partner's feel-

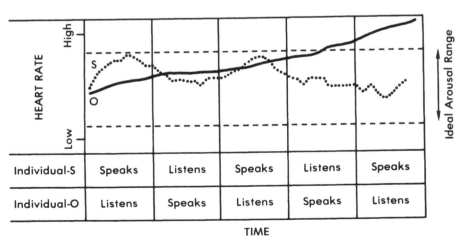

FIGURE 6. Heart rates/arousal of overtly engaged Person S and covertly engaged Person O across speaking and listening turns during an interpersonal transaction.

ings (or indifferent to them), the overtly assertive individual S becomes only mildly to moderately aroused and then, with the assurance of getting his/her way, quickly returns to baseline arousal. On the other hand, the autonomic arousal of the covertly engaged individual progressively escalates as a result of frustration, covert emotional preoccupation, and conflict between desires to assert and fears of the consequences of assertion. The lack of goal completion that the passive individual experiences creates a Zeigarnik effect (Marx & Hillix, 1973), an active and continuing processing of information related to the desired but uncompleted act of asserting one's desire and acquiring one's goals. This Zeigarnik effect is hypothesized to cause ongoing covert verbalizations and associated emotional self-statements and physiological arousal in a manner similar to that proposed by Ellis (1962). In Type A and neurotic individuals, this Zeigarnik-induced arousal is expected to be especially pronounced and to summate with externally generated sources of arousal, which, if high, send the neurotic introvert into such a high state of activation that an impulsive, seemingly irrational, burst of overt hostility is expressed.

FINAL COMMENTS

The PPS biosocial model outlined here suggests a number of interesting and testable experimental and clinical manipulations. The model is faithful to the complexity of human social behavior, yet predictions derived from the model are open to experimental falsification. The model builds on extensive noninteractive literatures and encourages the evaluation of personality × personality × setting interactions, as well as the integrated evaluation of the physiological, behavioral, and cognitive/subjective domains across time.

REFERENCES

Abbott, J., Sutherland, C., & Watt, D. (1987). Cooperative dyadic interactions, perceived control, and task difficulty in Type A and Type B individuals: A comparative study. *Psychophysiology, 24*, 1–13.

Abramson, L. Y., Seligman, M. E. P., & Teasdale, J. D. (1978). Learned helplessness in humans: Critique and reformulation. *Journal of Abnormal Psychology, 87*, 49–74.

Bell, R. A., & Daly, J. A. (1985). Some communicator correlates of loneliness. *Southern Speech Communication Journal, 50*, 121–142.

Bernstein, A. S., Schneider, S. J., Juni, S., & Pope, A. T. (1980). The effect of stimulus significance on the electrodermal response in chronic schizophrenia. *Journal of Abnormal Psychology, 89*, 93–97.

Berscheid, E. (1982). Attraction and emotion in interpersonal relations. In M. S. Clark & S. T. Fiske (Eds.), *Affect and cognition* (pp. 37–54). Hillsdale, NJ: Erlbaum.

Berscheid, E., Gangestad, S. W., & Kulakowski, D. (1984). Emotion in close relationships:

Implications for relationship counseling. In S. D. Brown & R. W. Lent (Eds.), *Handbook of counseling psychology* (pp. 435–476). New York: Wiley.

Birchler, G. R., Weiss, R. L., & Vincent, J. P. (1975). Multimethod analysis of social reinforcement exchange between maritally distressed and nondistressed spouse and stranger dyads. *Journal of Personality and Social Psychology, 31*, 349–360.

Blaney, N. T., Brown, P., & Blaney, P. H. (1986). Type A, marital adjustment, and life stress. *Journal of Behavioral Medicine, 9*, 491–502.

Bowers, K. (1973). Situationism in psychology: An analysis and critique. *Psychological Review, 80*, 307–336.

Bradbury, T. N., & Fincham, F. D. (1987a). Affect and cognition in close relationships: Towards an integrative model. *Cognition and Emotion, 1*, 59–87.

Bradbury, T. N., & Fincham, F. D. (1987b). The assessment of affect in marriage. In K. D. O'Leary (Ed.), *Assessment of marital discord* (pp. 59–108). Hillsdale, NJ: Erlbaum.

Buss, D. M. (1981). Predicting parent-child interactions from children's activity level. *Developmental Psychology, 17*, 59–65.

Byrne, D. G., Rosenman, E., Schiller, & Chesney, M. A. (1985). Consistency and variation among instruments purporting to measure the Type A behavior pattern. *Psychosomatic Medicine, 47*, 242–261.

Carlson, R. & Williams, J. (1984). Studies of Jungian typology. III: Personality and marriage. *Journal of Personality Assessment, 48*, 87–94.

Carment, D. W., & Miles, C. G. (1971). Persuasiveness and persuasibility as related to intelligence and extraversion. In H. J. Eysenck (Ed.), *Readings in extraversion-introversion: Vol. 2, Fields of application* (pp. 140–149). New York: Wiley.

Cegala, D. J., Savage, G. T., Brunner, C. C., & Conrad, A. B. (1982). An elaboration of the meaning of interaction involvement: Toward the development of a theoretical concept. *Communication Monographs, 49*, 229–248.

Chesney, M. A., Black, G. W., Chadwick, J. H., & Rosenman, R. H. (1981). Psychological correlates of the Type A behavior pattern. *Journal of Behavioral Medicine, 4*, 217–229.

Chesney, M. A., Eagelston, J. R., & Rosenman, R. H. (1980). The Type A structured interview: A behavioral assessment in the rough. *Journal of Behavioral Assessment, 2*, 255–272.

Claridge, G. (1986). Eysenck's contribution to the psychology of personality. In S. Modgil & C. Modgil (Eds.), *Han Eysenck: Consensus and controversy* (pp. 73–85). Philadelphia: Falmer Press.

Cooper, J., & Scalise, C. J. (1974). Dissonance produced by deviations from lifestyles: The interaction of Jungian typology and conformity. *Journal of Personality and Social Psychology, 29*, 566–571.

Cornelius, R. R., & Averill, J. R. (1980). The influence of various types of control on psychophysiological stress reactions. *Journal of Research in Personality, 14*, 503–517.

Davidson, J. R. (1984). Hemispheric asymmetry and emotion. In K. R. Scherer & P. Ekman (Eds.), *Approaches to emotion* (pp. 39–57). Hillsdale, NJ: Erlbaum.

Davis, H. C., Haymaker, D. J., Hermecz, D. A., & Gilbert, D. G. (1988). Marital interaction: Affective synchrony of self-reported emotional components. *Journal of Personality Assessment, 52*, 48–57.

Dollard, J., Doob, L. W., Miller, N. E., Mowrer, O. H., & Sears, R. R. (1939). *Frustration and aggression.* New Haven: Yale University Press.

Duckworth, D. H. (1975). Personality, emotional state, and perception of nonverbal communications. *Perceptual and Motor Skills, 40*, 325–326.

Easterbrook, J. A. (1959). The effect of emotion on cue utilization and the organization of behavior. *Psychological Review, 66*, 183–201.

Ellis, A. (1962). *Reason and emotion in psychotherapy.* New York: Stuart.

Eysenck, H. J. (1967). *The biological basis of personality.* Springfield, IL: Charles C Thomas.

Eysenck, H. J., & Eysenck, M. W. (1985). *Personality and individual differences: A natural sciences approach.* New York: Plenum Press.

Eysenck, H. J., & Wakefield, J. A. (1981). Psychological factors as predictors of marital satisfaction. *Advances in Behavior Research and Therapy, 3,* 151–192.

Eysenck, H. J., & Wilson, G. (1979). *The psychology of sex.* London: Dent.

Eysenck, M. W. (1982). *Attention and arousal: Cognition and performance.* New York: Springer.

Forsman, L. (1980). Habitual catecholamine excretion and its relation to habitual distress. *Biological Psychology, 11,* 83–97.

Froehlich, W. D. (1978). Stress, anxiety, and the control of attention: A psychophysiological approach. In C. D. Spielberger & I. G. Sarason (Eds.), *Stress and anxiety* (Vol. 5, pp. 99–130). Washington, DC: Hemisphere.

Gale, A. (1983). Electroencephalographic studies of Extraversion-Introversion: A case study in the psychophysiology of individual differences. *Personality and Individual Differences, 4,* 371–380.

Gale, A., Lucas, B., Nissim, R., and Harpham, B. (1972). Some EEG correlates of face-to-face contact. *British Journal of Social and Clinical Psychology, 11,* 326–332.

Gentry, W. D. (1970). Effects of frustration, attack, and prior aggressive training on overt aggression and vascular processes. *Journal of Personality and Social Psychology, 16,* 718–725.

Gilbert, B. O. (1985). *Physiological responsivity to venipuncture and speech giving in insulin-dependent diabetic adolescents at two levels of diabetes control and their nondiabetic peers.* Unpublished Dissertation, University of Florida.

Gilbert, D. G. (1981). *A biopsychosocial systems theory of communication and conflict in marriage and family.* Unpublished manuscript. Available on request from author. Southern Illinois University at Carbondale.

Gilbert, D. G. (1986). Marriage and sex: Moving from correlations to dynamic personality by personality interactions—Limits of monocular vision. In S. Modgil and C. Modgil (Eds.), *Hans Eysenck: Consensus and controversy* (pp. 287–299). Philadelphia: Falmer Press.

Gilbert, D. G. (1987). Effects of smoking and nicotine on EEG lateralization as a function of personality. *Personality and Individual Differences. 8,* 933–941.

Gilbert, D. G., & Spielberger, C. D. (1987). Effects of smoking on heart rate, anxiety, and feelings of success during social interaction. *Journal of Behavioral Medicine, 10,* 629–638.

Gilbert, D. G., Hermecz, D. A., & Davis, H. C. (1982). Heart rate and skin conductance responses during marital communication as a function of message and personality. *Psychophysiology, 19,* 562.

Gottman, J. M. (1979). *Marital interaction: Experimental investigations.* New York: Academic Press.

Gottman, J. M., & Levenson, R. W. (1984). Why marriages fail: Affective and physiological patterns in marital interaction. In J. C. Masters & K. Yarkin-Levin (Eds.), *Boundary areas in social and developmental psychology* (pp. 67–106). New York: Academic Press.

Gottman, J. M., & Levenson, R. W. (1986). Assessing the role of emotion in marriage. *Behavioral Assessment, 8,* 31–48.

Gottman, J. M., & Porterfield, A. L. (1981). Communicative dysfunction in the nonverbal behavior of married couples. *Journal of Marriage and the Family, 43,* 817–824.

Gottman, J. M., Notarius, C. N., Gonzo, J., & Markman, H. (1976). *A couple's guide to communication.* Champaign, IL: Research Press.

Gray, J. A. (1981). A critique of Eysenck's theory of personality. In H. J. Eysenck (Ed.), *A model for personality* (pp. 246–276). New York: Springer.

Graziano, W. G., Rahe, D. F., & Feldesman, A. B. (1985). Extraversion, social cognition, and the salience of aversiveness in social encounters. *Journal of Personality and Social Psychology, 49,* 971–980.

Gupta, U. (1984). Phenobarbitone and the relationship between extraversion and reinforcement in verbal operant conditioning. *British Journal of Psychology, 75*, 499–506.

Hawkins, J. L., Weisberg, C., & Ray, D. W. (1980). Spouse differences in communication style: Preference, perception, behavior. *Journal of Marriage and the Family, 42*, 585–593.

Henderick, C., & Brown, S. R. (1971). Introversion, extraversion, and interpersonal attraction. *Journal of Personality and Social Psychology, 20*, 31–36.

Henry, J. P. (1986). Neuroendocrine patterns of emotional response. In R. Plutchik & H. Kellerman (Eds.), *Emotion: Theory, research, and experience* (pp. 37–60). Orlando: Harcourt Brace Jovanovich.

Himadi, W. G., Arkowitz, H., Hinton, R., & Perl, J. (1980). Minimal dating and its relationship to other social problems and general adjustment. *Behavior Therapy, 11*, 345–352.

Hokanson, J. E., Willers, K. R., & Koropsak, E. (1968). The modification of autonomic responses during aggressive interchange. *Journal of Personality, 36*, 386–404.

Houston, B. K. (1983). Psychophysiological responsivity and Type A behavior pattern. *Journal of Research in Personality, 17*, 22–39.

Infante, D. A. (1987). Aggressiveness. In J. C. McCroskey & J. A. Daly (Eds.), *Personality and interpersonal communication* (pp. 157–192). Beverly Hills, CA: Sage.

Jacobson, N. S., & Holzworth-Munroe, A. (1986). Marital therapy: A social learning-cognitive perspective. In N. S. Jacobson & A. S. Gurman (Eds.), *Clinical handbook of marital therapy* (pp. 29–70). New York: Guilford Press.

Jacobson, N. S., & Margolin, G. (1979). *Marital therapy: Strategies based on social learning and behavior exchange principles.* New York: Brunner/Mazel.

Jacobson, N. S., Follette, W. C., & Elwood, R. W. (1984). Outcome research on behavioral marital therapy: A methodological and conceptual reappraisal. In K. Hahlweg & N. S. Jacobson (Eds.), *Marital interaction: Analysis & modification* (pp. 113–129). New York: Guilford Press.

Kaplan, H. S. (1987). *Sexual aversion, sexual phobias, and panic disorder.* New York: Brunner/Mazel.

Kaplan, H. B., Burch, N. R., & Bloom, S. W. (1964). Physiological covariation in small peer groups. In P. H. Leiderman & D. Shapiro (Eds.), *Physiological approaches to social behavior* (pp. 92–109). Stanford, CA: Stanford University Press.

Kelly, E. L., & Conley, J. J. (1987). Personality and compatibility: A prospective analysis of marital stability and marital satisfaction. *Journal of Personality and Social Psychology, 32*, 27–40.

Kline, P., & Barrett, P. (1983). The factors in personality questionnaires among normal subjects. *Advances in Behaviour Research and Therapy, 5*, 141–202.

Lacey, J. (1967). Somatic response patterning and stress: Some revisions of activation theory. In M. H. Appley & R. Trumbull (Eds.), *Psychological stress: Issues in research* (pp. 14–42). New York: Appleton-Century-Crofts.

Lansky, M. R. (1986). Marital therapy for narcissistic disorders. In N. S. Jacobson & A. S. Gurnam (Eds.), *Clinical handbook of marital therapy* (pp. 557–574). New York: Guilford Press.

Lewicki, P. (1986). *Nonconscious social information processing.* Orlando: Academic Press.

Lewinsohn, P. M., Steinmetz, J. L., Larson, D. W., & Franklin, J. (1981). Depression-related cognitions: Antecedent or consequence? *Journal of Abnormal Psychology, 90*, 213–219.

Lishman, W. A. (1972). Selective factors in memory: Part 1. Age, sex, and personality attrubutes. *Psychological Medicine, 2*, 121–138.

Lolas, F. (1987). Hemispheric asymmetry of slow brain potentials in relation to neuroticism. *Personality and Individual Differences, 8*, 969–971.

Long, J. M., Lynch, J. J., Machiran, N. M., Thomas, S. A., & Malinow, K. L. (1982). The effects of status on blood pressure during verbal communication. *Journal of Behavioral Medicine, 5*, 165–172.

Lynch, J. J., Long, J. M., Thomas, S. A., Malinow, K., & Katcher, H. (1981). The effects of talking on the blood pressure of hypertensive and normotensive individuals. *Psychosomatic Medicine, 43*, 25–33.

Lytton, H. (1980). *Parent-child interaction: The socialization process observed in twin and single families.* New York: Plenum Press.

Mandler, G. (1984). *Mind and body: Psychology of emotion and stress.* New York: Norton.

Markel, N. N., Phillis, J. A., Vargas, R., & Harvard, K. (1972). Personality traits associated with voice types. *Journal of Psycholinguistic Research, 1*, 249–255.

Martin, M. (1985). Neuroticism as predisposition toward depression: A cognitive mechanism. *Personality and Individual Differences, 6*, 353–365.

Martin, N. & Jardine, R. (1986). Eysenck's contributions to behavior genetics. In S. Modgil and C. Modgil (Eds.), *Hans Eysenck: Consensus and controversy* (pp. 13–47). Philadelphia: Falmer Press.

Marx, M. H., & Hillix, W. A. (1973). *Systems and theories in psychology* (2nd ed.). New York: McGraw-Hill.

May, J. R., & Johnson, H. J. (1973). Physiological activity to internally elicited arousal and inhibitory thoughts. *Journal of Abnormal Psychology, 82*, 239–245.

Matthews, K. A. (1982). Psychological perspectives on the Type A behavior pattern. *Psychological Bulletin, 91*, 293–323.

Naveteur, J, & Baque, E. F. (1987). Individual differences in electrodermal activity as a function of subjects' anxiety. *Personality and Individual Differences, 8*, 615–626.

Netter, P. (1985). Biochemical differences as related to differences in trait anxiety and neuroticism. *Personality and Individual Differences, 6*, XII, Poster session abstract.

Noller, P. (1984), *Nonverbal communication and marital interaction.* New York: Pergamon.

Norman, R. M. G., & Watson, L. D. (1976). Extraversion and reactions to cognitive inconsistency. *Journal of Research in Personality, 10*, 446–456.

Obrist, P. (1981). *Cardiovascular psychophysiology: A perspective.* New York: Plenum Press.

Parks, M. R. (1985). Interpersonal communication and the quest for personal competence. In M. L. Knapp and G. R. Miller (Eds.), *Handbook of interpersonal communication* (pp. 171–201). Beverly Hills, CA: Sage.

Patterson, G. R. (1982). *Coercive family process.* Eugene, OR: Castalia Press.

Patterson, M. L. (1976). An arousal model of interpersonal intimacy. *Psychological Review, 83*, 235–245.

Rands, M., Levinger, G., & Mellinger, G. D. (1981). Patterns of conflict resolution and marital satisfaction. *Journal of Family Issues, 2*, 297–321.

Raush, H. L., Barry, W. A., Hertel, R. K., & Swain, M. A. (1974). *Communication, conflict, and marriage.* San Francisco: Josey-Bass.

Rhodewalt, F., & Davison, J. (1983). Reactance and the coronary-prone behavior pattern: The role of self-attribution in responses to reduced behavioral freedom. *Journal of Personality and Social Psychology, 44*, 220–228.

Rimm, D. C., & Litvak, S. B. (1969). Self-verbalization and emotional arousal. *Journal of Abnormal Psychology, 74*, 181–187.

Roessler, R. (1973). Personality, psychophysiology, and performance. *Psychophysiology, 10*, 315–327.

Rule, B. G. & Hewitt, G. L. (1971). Effects of thwarting on cardiac response and physical aggression. *Canadian Journal of Behavioral Science, 3*, 174–182.

Sarason, I. G. (1972). Experimental approaches to test anxiety: Attention and the uses of information. In C. D. Spielberger (Ed.), *Anxiety: Current trends in theory and research* (Vol. 2, pp. 383–403). New York: Academic Press.

Satir, V. (1975). You as a change agent. In V. Satir, J. Stachowiak, & H. A. Taschman (Eds.), *Helping families to change* (pp. 37–62). New York: Jason Aronson.

Scarr, S., & McCartney, K. (1983). How people make their own environments: A theory of genotype → environment effects. *Child Development, 54*, 424–435.

Schill, T. R. (1972). Aggression and blood pressure responses of high- and low-guilt subjects following frustration. *Journal of Consulting and Clinical Psychology, 38,* 461.

Singer, M. T. (1974). Presidential address—Engagement-involvement: A central phenomenon in psychophysiological research. *Psychosomatic Medicine, 36,* 1–17.

Sipprelle, R. C., Ascough, J. C., Detrio, D. M., & Horst, P. A. (1977). Neuroticism, extroversion, and response to stress. *Behavior Research and Therapy, 15,* 411–418.

Smith, B. D., Wilson, R. J., & Jones, B. E. (1983). Extraversion and multiple levels of caffeine-induced arousal: Effects on overhabituation and dishabituation. *Psychophysiology, 20,* 29–344.

Strean, H. S. (1985). *Resolving marital conflicts: A psychodynamic perspective.* New York: Wiley.

Tecce, J. J. (1972). Contingent negative variation (CNV) and psychological processes in man. *Psychological Bulletin, 77,* 73–108.

Thorne, A. (1987). The press of personality: A study of conversations between introverts and extraverts. *Journal of Personality and Social Psychology, 53,* 718–726.

Tucker, D. M., & Williamson, P. A. (1984). Asymmetric neural control systems in human self-regulation. *Psychological Review, 91,* 185–215.

Tursky, B., Lodge, M., & Reeder, R. (1979). Psychophysical and psychophysiological evaluation of the direction, intensity, and meaning of race-related stimuli. *Psychophysiology, 16,* 452–462.

Vandenberg, S. G., Singer, S. M., & Pauls, D. L. (1986). *The heredity of behavior disorders in adults and children.* New York: Plenum Press.

Van Egeren, L. F. (1979). Social interactions, communications, and the coronary-prone behavior pattern: A psychophysiological study. *Psychosomatic Medicine, 41,* 2–18.

Ward, N. G., & Doerr, H. O. (1986). Skin conductance: A potentially sensitive and specific marker for depression. *The Journal of Nervous and Mental Disease, 174,* 553–559.

Watkins, P. L., & Eisler, R. M. (1988). The Type A behavior pattern, hostility, and interpersonal skill. *Behavior Modification, 12,* 315–334.

Watzlawick, P., Beavin, J. H., & Jackson, D. D. (1967). *Pragmatics of human communication: A study of interactional patterns, pathologies, and paradoxes.* New York: Norton.

Winter, W. D., Ferreira, A. J., & Bowers, N. (1973). Decision-making in married and unrelated couples. *Family Process, 12,* 83–94.

Zajonc, R. B. (1965). Social facilitation. *Science, 14,* 269–274.

Zajonc, R. B. (1984). On the primacy of affect. *American Psychologist, 39,* 117–123.

Zillmann, D. (1979). *Hostility and aggression.* Hillsdale, NJ: Erlbaum.

Zillmann, D. (1983). Transfer of excitation in emotional behavior. In J. T. Cacioppo & R. E. Petty (Eds.), *Social psychophysiology* (pp. 215–240). New York: Guilford Press.

CHAPTER SIX

Personality and Status

ROBERT HOGAN AND JOYCE HOGAN

INTRODUCTION

Stratification and status attainment have been major research topics in sociology for years (cf. Weber, 1946). Because status differences typify every human (and primate) group (Eibl-Eibesfeldt, 1989) and because these differences profoundly affect our lives, it is important to inquire about their origins.

Although status considerations are ubiquitous and consequential, psychologists have tended to avoid this topic. Actually they have not entirely ignored it, but when they analyze it, they often argue that people who seek status are emotionally unbalanced and in need of professional help. For example, the massive literature on Type A behavior (e.g., Strube, 1987) suggests that people who work hard and try to get ahead are prone to heart disease. Helmreich, Spence, Beane, Lucker, and Matthews (1980), in a study of achievement motivation, present data suggesting that competitive people are also neurotic. Berglas (1985) argues that ambitious people who finally succeed risk mental illness as a consequence. Finally, biographies of successful people are often searches for hidden and nasty psychiatric secrets (cf. Lynn, 1987), which are used as partial explanations for their success.

This essay examines the relationship between personality and status and argues that, although successful people in artistic professions may tend to be neurotic, they are exceptions. Success in most occupations is a function of energy, social skill, and desire to succeed.

ROBERT HOGAN AND JOYCE HOGAN • Department of Psychology, University of Tulsa, Tulsa, Oklahoma 74104.

Personality, Social Skills, and Psychopathology: An Individual Differences Approach, edited by David G. Gilbert and James J. Connolly. Plenum Press, New York, 1991.

137

SOME DEFINITIONS

The word *personality*, as MacKinnon (1944) pointed out some time ago, has two very different meanings. It is important to keep these meanings distinct because serious confusion results when they are confounded. On the one hand, personality refers to a person's reputation, to the manner in which other people describe and evaluate that person; this is personality from the perspective of the observer. On the other hand, personality refers to the processes and tendencies within a person that explain why he or she creates his or her unique reputation; this is personality from the perspective of the actor.

Concerning personality from the viewpoint of the observer, if observers rate actors on a series of personality dimensions, if these ratings are intercorrelated, and if the resulting matrix is factor-analyzed, then somewhere between three and seven (usually five) factors will emerge (cf. Norman, 1963). A similar set of factors reappear in study after study, and this has been recognized for over 25 years. Wiggins (1973) dubbed this finding the "Big 5" theory of personality structure. These factors provide a common and agreed-upon vocabulary for talking about personality. We have adopted the convention of describing actors' reputations in terms of six dimensions—these can be reduced to three more primary dimensions or expanded into over 40 microdimensions. These six dimensions, which are a slightly expanded version of Norman's five, are both evaluative and predictive. They can be used to evaluate or to predict an actor's social behavior, and they can be used to assess an actor's potential for achieving status and social acceptance. For the benefit of readers who may be unfamiliar with Big 5 theory, we describe the dimensions below:

1. *Intellectance.* At one pole of this dimension, actors are seen as having narrow interests, as being literal minded, unimaginative, and not curious. At the opposite pole, actors are seen as imaginative, curious, open-minded, and interested in education and ideas for their own sake. This is Norman's (1963) dimension of culture.

2. *Adjustment.* Actors at one end of this dimension are seen as anxious, unhappy, and emotionally unstable. At the other end, actors are seen as calm, poised, and self-assured. This is Norman's dimension of adjustment.

3. *Prudence.* At one pole of this dimension, people are described as impulsive, limit-testing, and unconventional; at the other pole, people are described as cautious, planful, and conscientious. This is Norman's dimension of conscientiousness.

4. *Ambition.* People at one end of this dimension (which Norman combines with sociability) are described as quiet, passive, and indifferent to material success. At the other end of this dimension, people

are described as hard working, competitive, achievement oriented, and materialistic.

5. *Sociability*. At one pole actors are described as shy, modest, and reserved; persons at the other pole are described as outgoing, exhibitionistic, and impulsive. Norman (1963) puts ambition and sociability together in a single dimension called Ascendance.

6. *Likeability*. Persons at one end of this dimension are seen as independent, tough, and critical; persons at the other end are described as congenial, cooperative, and tolerant. This is Norman's dimension of agreeableness.

Once again, reputations can be described and profiled in terms of these six dimensions of observers' evaluations and, as we will suggest, there are established empirical relationships between reputations coded in this way and individual status.

In contrast with what we know about the structure of personality from the observer's perspective, information regarding personality from the actor's perspective is less reliable and necessarily more speculative. The following comments are inferences based on a variety of sources; our goal is to try to specify structures within actors that might account for individual differences in the six dimensions of reputation just described. Earlier research suggests that personality from the actor's perspective can be conceptualized in terms of four broad categories of psychological variables: motives, temperament, intelligence, and strategy.

MOTIVES

All the evidence suggests that homo sapiens evolved as a group-living animal; we also know that every primate and human group has a status hierarchy (Eibl-Eibesfeldt, 1989). Human motivation is rooted in biology; in addition to needing food, water, oxygen, sleep, and shelter, it is reasonable to suppose the existence of biologically based needs for status and social acceptance. It is reasonable to assume the existence of these needs because persons with greater status and social acceptance have an advantage over those with less status and acceptance in terms of fitness—defined in terms of the number of a person's offspring who survive to maturity (Eibl-Eibesfeldt, 1989). Status is associated with control over material resources; social acceptance is associated with social support. Whether or not people are aware of having such tendencies, most people tend to be both self-seeking and affiliative, and these tendencies can (and often do) work at cross-purposes—that is, pursuing one may mean losing the other. Loss of status means loss of control; loss of acceptance leads to social isolation. Both kinds of losses are immensely stressful to normal humans, and this point is well documented in the literature of clinical psychology (cf. Bowlby, 1980).

In our view, status and approval seeking are primary motives in human affairs; how they are dealt with is a major theme in each person's life.

TEMPERAMENT

People differ from birth in terms of temperament. Some babies are more emotional than others; some babies are more active than others; and some babies are more cuddly than others. (cf. Buss & Plomin, 1984; Thomas & Chess, 1977). These innate differences in temperament set limits to adult aspirations and possibilities (Caspi, Elder, & Bem, 1987; Caspi, Elder, & Bem, 1988); they also determine the life course in a quiet but insistent manner. It is impossible to specify the number of temperaments at work in the human personality, but Buss and Plomin make a persuasive case for three: emotionality, activity, and sociability. Individual differences in these temperaments give a distinctive tone to a person's social conduct and contribute to the manner in which he or she is perceived by others.

INTELLIGENCE

Standardized cognitive tests (measures of vocabulary, reading comprehension, quantitative skills, spatial reasoning, etc.) are related to occupational success in every job that has been carefully studied; from clerk to architect, from police work to psychiatry, higher cognitive test scores are associated with greater occupational success (Ghiselli, 1973).

Intelligence is not typically regarded as part of personality. But the presence or absence of quick wits and sound judgment are important components of a person's reputation and, therefore, aspects of an actor's personality from the observer's perspective. This may in fact be one of the first evaluations that we make about other people. If, as we have argued, an actor's personality is composed of those psychological structures that explain his or her reputation, intelligence necessarily must be taken into account.

STRATEGY

As noted, we assume that people are biologically programmed to seek attention, acceptance, and approval as well as status, power, or control over resources (there are, of course, individual differences in these tendencies). As children, our parents provide us with these commodities. But as we move through adolescence and into adulthood, we increasingly must earn or negotiate acceptance and status. The methods and procedures that we develop for doing this are as interesting and varied as the stories of our lives. But certain themes are common to most lives. Specifically, for a normal life, we must establish a role for ourselves in our communities and social groups, we must carve out a niche in our social ecology in order to live and have families. And this is what the concept of identity is about: Everyone needs to be someone—a streetperson, a scientist, a gourmet cook, a rock musician—and a good bit of social interaction consists of telling others who we are and how we would like to be regarded (Goffman, 1958).

In early adolescence people begin to formulate identities for themselves; these are the desired public selves that they hope significant others will admire and respect, or at least not criticize. These images (identities, public selves) are taken from parents, peers, and the popular culture. Sometimes these identity choices can be used in adulthood. However, some young people return to the drawing board as when a skinny, uncoordinated boy discovers that he can't be a star athlete. Identities differ in many ways: Some are short term and superficial (e.g., a graduating senior in cap and gown); others are long lasting and consequential (e.g., a monk in a secluded religious order); some are easily attained and relatively undesirable (e.g., a terrorist); others are difficult to attain and quite desirable (e.g., a Nobel laureate). Despite their differences, identities are the mechanism by means of which we normally interact with others—outside of our public roles we often have surprisingly little to say to one another—and our identities are the principal mechanism by which we negotiate status and social acceptance.

Normal social interaction is usually based on an agenda or a pretext ("we need to talk this over") and roles for the interactants to play (the injured party and the accused). The actor's personal identity provides the context and guidelines for the manner in which he or she plays his or her roles during interaction. Although social interaction largely consists of role performances, this generalization should be qualified in certain important ways.

1. People are often unaware of the fact that social life requires attending to other's expectations during a series of conventional rituals (bank customer, student, car driver, tennis player); their lack of awareness is useful because self-consciousness leads to stilted, affected, and awkward role performances.
2. Some of what we do in social interaction is the unintentional product of habit (nervous throat clearing, finger drumming, gesticulating).
3. People are more conscious of these processes during consequential interactions (contract negotiations, courtroom testimony, romantic overtures) than during routine rituals.
4. Some people are generally more aware of these processes than others (e.g., extraverts vs. introverts).
5. Some occupations (e.g., sales) require more attention to these processes than others (e.g., mathematician).
6. Although it is usually a mistake to ignore the impressions that others form of us: (a) we aren't very good at evaluating how others react to us (DePaulo, Kenny, Hoover, Webb, & Oliver, 1987); and (b)

whatever we do, others will assume that we did it deliberately and evaluate us accordingly.

The larger point here is that one major source of variation in peoples' reputations is the identity that they have chosen and that guides and shapes their interpersonal behavior. This identity is part of a large and only partially conscious set of cognitive schemas that organizes behavior and forms part of what we call the "strategic" aspect of personality. A second set of strategic cognitive structures also affects status and social acceptance, and we refer to this as *interpersonal expertise*.

There are four interconnected components of interpersonal expertise. First, before intentionally doing or saying something, expertise requires trying to anticipate who will be affected by the action. Second, expert players will be able to anticipate who will be affected and how. Third, expertise entails using this information to guide or modify one's intended actions. And finally, expertise requires having the self-control to use the plan one has formulated.

Briefly, two of the four components of interpersonal expertise are dispositions or traits, and two are cognitive skills. Expertise requires being willing to take account of the wishes, expectations, and interests of one's counterplayers before undertaking an action and being disposed to use this information in subsequent actions. At the same time, when scanning the social environment, one should be able to read that environment correctly and, when incorporating that information into one's subsequent plans, one should incorporate it correctly. The process is analogous to strategic planning in business, sports, or war. Prior to a game, a coach should (a) review the strengths and weaknesses of the opponent; (b) correctly diagnose those strengths and weaknesses; (c) formulate an *appropriate* game plan based on that analysis; and (d) stay with the game plan until the game is over (or the situation changes). We suspect that success in one's career is based on similar processes.

People choose their identities for many reasons. At the individual level, there are as many identities as there are people. We find it useful to group identities in terms of related clusters of attitudes and values. The model for classifying identities that we find most helpful is Holland's (1985) type theory. Holland proposes that interests, values, and motives tend to come together in regular patterns. Specifically, he proposes that there are six generic occupational types, and he provides evidence (Gottfredson, Holland, & Ogawa, 1982) to suggest that this is an exhaustive classification of occupational choice.

PERSONALITY AND STATUS

We come finally to the heart of the chapter. To ask how personality is related to status and social acceptance is to ask too broad a question. In addition to defining personality (which we tried to do before), it is necessary to define status more closely.

We suggest that the determinants of status are relative to a person's occupation, that the determinants are different in different occupations. This means that the personality characteristics of a successful athlete will be different from those of a successful scientist, pianist, or financial analyst. Logically it would seem that there are as many determinants of status as there are occupational specialties (there are over 3,000 of these in the United States), and success within each of them is a function of a unique set of characteristics. Here is where Holland's theory can be helpful. Holland's model can be used to group occupations on the basis of similar psychological requirements and characteristics. This gives us six occupational categories to deal with—a system that is sufficiently complex to capture many of the valid distinctions between occupational categories but simple enough to be manageable. In the sections that follow, we will describe each occupational type, describe the personality characteristics associated with both normal performance and with success or status in that occupation; we will then review such evidence as is available to support our proposals.

REALISTIC

Realistic occupations include athletics, law enforcement, military service, and engineering. These occupations require attention to technical or practical detail, physical courage, the ability to work with others within a framework of rules, and conventionally masculine interests. They do not require a high degree of social skill or creativity. The choice of a "realistic" identity (and occupation) may be initially encouraged by recognition for physical talent or athletic achievement.

Table 1 translates Holland's (1985) data regarding the psychological requirements of the six occupational types into the language of "Big 5" theory (Norman, 1963). Table 1 suggests that persons with strong realistic interests or values are, relative to the other five types, the least interested in education, the most self-confident, the most adventuresome, and the least socially skilled. Successful realistic types (think of a fighter pilot) appear to be, therefore, exceptionally self-assured, risk taking, and independent. They seem to be highly autonomous and individualistic and relatively unconcerned with conventional worldly success. At the same time, Ghiselli's (1973, p. 471) review suggests that the more successful realistic persons are brighter than their peers. Hogan (1971), Hogan and Kurtines (1975), and Mills and Bohannan (1980) show that successful police officers are stable, self-controlled, and bright. Although realistic types are generally self-assured, risk taking, and independent, the higher status members are even more self-confident, self-disciplined, and bright than the lower status members. In Hogan's research on police effectiveness, for example, the best single predictor of performance was the Intellectual Efficiency scale of the

TABLE 1. The Relationship between Personality and Status Classified by Holland's Occupational Types

	Personality dimensions					
	Intellectance	Adjustment	Prudence	Ambition	Sociability	Likeability
Occupational type						
Realistic	Above average	High	Low	Average	Low	Average
Investigative	High	Average	Low	Average	Low	Low
Artistic	High	Low	Low	Average	Average	Average
Social	Above average	High	Average	Above average	High	High
Enterprising	High	High	Above average	High	High	High
Conventional	High	Average	High	High	Average	Average

California Psychological Inventory (CPI; Gough, 1987). This scale measures a syndrome that Gough (1968) describes as "(a) self-confidence and self-assurance . . . (b) effective social techniques and adjustment . . . (c) good physiological functioning . . . and (d) liking and respect for intellectual pursuits" (Gough, 1968, p. 71). Hogan (1971) notes that "good performance as a police officer seems to be related to a characteristic which can be loosely described as operational or effective intelligence" (p. 683). A study of the performance of Navy bomb-disposal technicians using the Hogan Personality Inventory (HPI) adds to this list an element of competitiveness (cf. Hogan, 1986, p. 19).

Summarizing the foregoing, among persons choosing a "realistic" identity, status is associated with being seen as bright, self-assured, leaderlike, a disciplined risk taker, and independent—perhaps even aloof. Among these kinds of people status is largely independent of persuasive skills, creativity, or interpersonal charm. Their independence and relative indifference to social approval suggests that realistic types don't avoid and perhaps even enjoy hostile confrontations, a capacity that is adaptive in the world of action but that is less adaptive in a corporate hierarchy.

INVESTIGATIVE

Investigative occupations include research, scholarship, and the development and critical analysis of theoretical and abstract systems. These occupations involve analytical thinking, curiosity, imagination, attention to detail, and a willingness to work alone (Holland, 1985). They require minimal social skills and an indifference toward financial gains. The choice of an "investigative" identity (and occupation) may be initially encouraged by praise for academic achievement.

Table 1 suggests that persons with strong investigative interests are, relative to the other five types, bright, curious, and educated. However, they do not seem necessarily well adjusted, self-disciplined, or socially engaging. Successful investigative types (think of Einstein) appear intelligent, curious, and fascinated by their own thought processes.

Cattell and Drevdahl (1955) studied 140 eminent contemporary researchers in physics, biology, and psychology using Cattell's Sixteen Personality Factor Questionnaire to analyze the sample. Cattell and Drevdahl describe the highly regarded scientist as rather cold, introspective, solemn, strong-willed, unconventional, serious about his or her work, and highly intelligent. Using the CPI, Gough (1961) characterizes a group of 45 research scientists studied at the Institute of Personality Assessment and Research (IPAR) in Berkeley as self-confident, nonconforming, bright, and introspective.

Persons who choose an "investigative" identity seem to be intelligent, creative, and committed to the search for knowledge. Successful scientists (as contrasted with the average scientist) are self-confident, introverted, hard working, unconventional, and independent; they tend to be well-suited for solitary laboratory or fieldwork but poorly suited for life in regulated organizations. Their hard work seems to come from a sense of commitment rather than from a desire for financial reward, and their status seems relatively independent of ambition or social skill.

We might note that psychologists as a group are investigative types (Holland, 1985), which means that they also tend to be introverted, self-confident, independent, and unconventional. This also means that they tend not to be model organizational citizens.

ARTISTIC

Artistic occupations include musician, painter, novelist, interior decorator, photographer, and fashion designer. People may initially adopt an "artistic" identity (and occupation) because, as children, they received praise and attention for their imaginative performances. Artistic work requires aesthetic sensibilities, sensitivity to issues of form and composition, a drive toward originality, and a high tolerance for ambiguity (Holland, 1985). It does not require self-discipline, great powers of analysis, or social skills. Pure artistic types tend to ignore organizational politics and to be somewhat careless about their finances, or financial gain.

Table 1 suggests that persons with strong artistic interests are, relative to the other types, bright, imaginative, and interested in pleasing others. On the other hand, they also may be somewhat moody and unconventional. Successful artistic types (think of Mozart or Vincent van Gogh) are often described as bright, egotistical, emotional, and nonconforming (Barron, 1965). Consequently, successful artists, as compared with typical artists, seem more concerned with pleasing themselves than others.

Cox (1926) describes eminent artists and writers as less intellectually talented than eminent scientists but higher in "aesthetic feelings" and "originality." They are lower in "common sense" and "the degree to which action and thought are dependent on reason"; they are, however, notably higher on the "amount of work spent on pleasures" (read for this, "self-indulgence"). Barron (1965) provides a brilliant summary of the IPAR creativity research—the definitive modern work on this topic. The basic methodology of that research was to compare groups of persons nominated for their demonstrated creativity with equally well-trained persons who were not so recognized. Among the Q-sort descriptions most highly correlated with creativity in writers, architects, scientists, and mathematicians were: "Thinks and associates to ideas in unusual ways," "tends to be rebellious and nonconforming," "genuinely values intellectual and cognitive matters," and "is self-dramatizing, histrionic." As Barron (1965) notes, "The emphasis is upon genuine unconventionality, high intellectual ability, vividness or even flamboyance of character, moodiness and preoccupation, courage, and self-centeredness" (p. 58). Barron also points out that a common thread running through test results and interviews for all creative groups is self-doubt: "The evidence is conveyed from a number of sources: creative individuals are very much concerned about their personal adequacy, and one of their strongest motivations is to prove themselves" (p. 61).

Artistic types are the one occupational group in which high-status persons are typified by a degree of maladjustment. Barron apologizes for this tendency in successful artists and suggests that they are both more neurotic and better adjusted than less creative artists. We would draw a different lesson from the fact that eminent artists are somewhat neurotic, namely, that this is the only occupational type for which a degree of maladjustment doesn't impede success. Consequently, biographical studies that depend on classic psychoanalysis (or other clinical theories) to interpret their subject matter are best reserved for persons with strong artistic proclivities. For the other five occupational types, self-confidence rather than self-doubt characterizes the successful person.

SOCIAL

Social occupations include teaching, nursing, social service, and other work motivated by altruism, empathy, and social concern (Holland, 1985). Such activities require idealism, selflessness, and (many times) an informal vow of poverty. They require tolerance rather than intellectual rigor, appreciation rather than critical thinking, social skill and personal warmth rather than competitiveness and ambition.

Table 1 suggests that persons with strong social interests are, relative to the other types, warm, sociable, and friendly. Persons adopting this identity pattern may have received attention and approval as children for their sheer conviviality and good humor. Table 1 also indicates that, despite the altruism, there is a moderate amount of ambition associated with social interests—social persons are in fact more ambitious than any type we have discussed so far. Successful social people (think of Gandhi or Martin Luther King) seem bright (but not brilliant), good-natured and self-accepting, socially at ease, tolerant and friendly, and willing to accept (however grudgingly) leadership roles.

Social types have been infrequently studied; they are less glamorous than athletes and military heroes (realistic), scientists and philosophers (investigative), or novelists and painters (artistic). Erikson's (1968) biographical study of Gandhi is an informative exception to this trend. Attracted to Gandhi's philosophy of nonviolent social change, Erikson was appalled to find that behind Gandhi's self-effacing public posture lurked a monster of narcissism and self-deception. The comment of another successful social type, Malcom X, sheds some light on this apparent paradox: In a moment of self-reflective candor, he remarked that "doing good is a hustle too."

Hogan, Hogan, and Busch (1984) asked 101 nursing aides working at a large Baltimore hospital to complete the Hogan Personality Inventory (HPI). These women, who worked at a prototypical social occupation, were also rated for their performance. Subcomponents (adjustment, sociability and likeability) of the HPI were correlated with these ratings, leading to the development of a measure of "service orientation." This measure allows us to study the relationship between personality and status in social occupations. Specifically, we find that persons with high scores for service orientation perform very well in social occupations, and they are described by others as conforming and self-controlled, tolerant and good natured, self-accepting, idealistic, and a bit competitive.

ENTERPRISING

Enterprising occupations include management, politics, law, and other work that depends on persuasion, coalition building, negotiation, and leadership. Such activities require energy, self-confidence, enthusiasm, and social skill; conversely, deference, shyness, and sensitivity to criticism are handicaps in enterprising occupations (cf. Holland, 1985).

Table 1 suggests that persons with enterprising interests are, relative to the other types, ambitious, assertive, and self-dramatizing—they are the most ambitious of the types (as defined by scores on measures of ambition—Hogan, 1986). In addition, they appear convivial, friendly, outgoing, and intellectually quick. One suspects that, as children, their sunny and gregarious dispositions brought these naturally popular people approval and peer status. Successful enterprising people (think of Lee Iacocca or John Kennedy) appear to be bright, self-assured, and decisive. They also typically seem impatient with details, abstractions, or prolonged rumination, but also affable, outgoing, and competitive (Holland, 1985; Hogan, 1986).

Enterprising types have been studied in substantial detail; there is vast biographical literature describing famous politicians, generals, and statesmen. These biographies are interesting in their own right, but they are designed to highlight the unique features of their subjects' lives, and we find it difficult to draw many general conclusions from them.

On the other hand, there is an extensive literature in industrial/organizational psychology regarding effective management. Campbell, Dunnette, Lawler, and Weick (1970) provide perhaps the best single review of this topic. From their detailed and comprehensive study we would abstract four points. First, research at Standard Oil of New Jersey (Sparks, 1966) shows that there is a distinct syndrome that can be called "general potential for management." Second, measured intelligence is related to managerial effectiveness in virtually every study that has examined the issue (Ghiselli, 1973). Third, there is a distinctive, lifelong pattern of interests that characterize successful enterprising types. As Campbell *et al.* (1970) note: "The more effective manager prefers activities which do not demand much regimentation. He dislikes technical and agricultural activities and prefers not to spend lengthy periods concentrating on close or detailed tasks. He enjoys being with other people, especially in relationships wherein he is dominant to them; thus, he is not solely service-oriented. He prefers physical and social recreations, as opposed to aesthetic or cultural forms of entertainment" (p. 132). Finally, with regard to what motivates successful enterprising people, Campbell *et al.* (1970) conclude: "Better managers tend to show a life time pattern of high achievement, power, and economic motivation. In addition, they are more dominant . . . and tend to score higher on the political and economic scale of the Allport–Vernon–Lindzey test [a measure of Spranger's types]. They are interested in directing others and they have strong desires for status and prestige" (p. 361).

Lombardo, Ruderman, and McCauley (1987) compared two groups of senior managers ($N = 160$), half of whom had "derailed" and half of whom were successful. The successful managers were seen as significantly higher on all six of the primary dimensions of personality description; the following are the items used to describe them, and the corresponding personality dimensions: (a) "Is a source of good ideas"—intellectance; (b) "is emotionally stable"—adjustment; (c) "is loyal to the company"—prudence; (d) "is ambitious"—ambition; and (e) and (f) "is able to build a team." "Can get along with all kinds of people."—sociability and likeability (or social skill).

Enterprising types are overrepresented among the high-status persons in every organization. Moreover, the personological attributes of success in enterprising occupations are reasonably well defined—namely successful enterprising types seem to have more of everything. Nonetheless, they do have some disconcerting characteristics: Like all people with high self-esteem, they tend to ignore valid criticism, to take more credit for success than is warranted, to blame their failures on circumstances rather than on themselves, and to exploit other people. None of the six Holland types is a vision of moral perfection; each has a set of distinctive strengths and shortcomings, but we tend to be more forgiving of the shortcomings that we ourselves embody.

CONVENTIONAL

Conventional occupations include data management, record keeping, and rule enforcement. Such activities require orderliness, attention to detail, and a scrupulous regard for ceremonial adequacy. On the other hand, creativity, informality, and aesthetic sensitivity are unimportant if not actually detrimental to performance in conventional occupations (cf. Holland, 1985).

Table 1 shows that conventional people are the most conforming and prudential of the types. As a group, they also tend to be bright and ambitious—second only to enterprising types in this regard. It is hard to think of a well-known conventional person, but former President Jimmy Carter comes to mind. Carter is bright, well organized, meticulous, and attentive to details. He is also conventionally religious, self-disciplined, and proper. Social skills are not especially crucial for conventional careers; hard work, intelligence, and mastery of detail are more important.

The literature regarding the characteristics of successful conventional types is modest to nearly nonexistent. One of our earlier studies may give the flavor of success in this identity pattern. We tested 107 clerks (all women) in a very large insurance firm using the HPI. The clerks were then rated for their performance by their supervisors. The most successful clerks, as defined by supervisors' ratings, were seen as well adjusted, conforming, bright, and ambitious, in that order (cf. Hogan, 1986, pp. 38–39). They were not, however, especially charming or self-dramatizing.

CONCLUDING COMMENTS

The foregoing discussion leads to four general conclusions that, in this final section, we would like to reemphasize. First, personality is related to status, but the relationship is not monolithic, and it is substantially clarified when one takes a differentiated perspective with regard to that relationship. Being perceived as bright seems universally important. After that, however, the relevant personality characteristics depend on the identity (or occupational) category in question. Successful realistic types tend to be self-assured, disciplined risk takers, with an abrupt interpersonal style. Successful investigative types appear bright, self-confident, dedicated, unconventional, introverted, and independent. Successful artistic types are imaginative, histrionic, nonconforming, insecure, and lacking common sense. Successful social types tend to be idealistic, selfless, warm, and friendly. Successful enterprising types seem to be energetic, self-confident, decisive, and leaderlike. Finally, successful conventional types appear to be conforming, bright, and ambitious.

Second, many prominent theories of personality see achievement as motivated by negative adjustment. High achievers are often described as driven by various private demons (existential terror, revenge, deep feelings of inadequacy), and they are believed to pay for their public success in terms of inner torment. Inner tranquility is thought to be achieved by renouncing fame and fortune. As it turns out, there is some merit to this analysis. Successful artists are in fact characterized by feelings of inadequacy and concerns about their personal worth. This is a statistical generalization, and there will be exceptions—that is, there will be artists who are not especially neurotic—but relative to the other five identity (and occupational) types, artistic people show signs of mild to moderate psychopathology. But this is the only identity type to which this generalization applies. In every other case, adjustment is positively related to status.

In a moderator variable study, Hobarth and Dunnette (1967) show that, in organizations, adjustment moderates the effect of intelligence on success. Persons who are poorly adjusted perform less well than their talent would predict, whereas persons who are well adjusted perform better than their talent would predict. The explanation of this, we suspect, is interpersonal rather than intrapsychic; that is, persons who are poorly adjusted are unpleasant to deal with because they are depressed, anxious, self-absorbed, moody, and complaining. Over time, the small animosities that they engender in coworkers, subordinates, and supervisors accumulate and turn into lost opportunities for career development. The opposite conclusion is not true, however; although poor adjustment will constrain almost any career, success requires more than self-confidence. Adjustment is a necessary but insufficient condition for status achievement.

Our third conclusion concerns the role of interpersonal expertise or self-presentational skills in the attainment or loss of status. We defined this earlier as the ability to anticipate correctly the needs and expectations of one's interactional partners and to guide one's behaviors accordingly. Persons who pursue social or enterprising careers need self-presentational skills on a daily basis. For the other identity choices, self-presentational skills are not central to what those people do each day. Nonetheless, we suspect (although we have no data to substantiate the point) that self-presentational skills are related to success in every occupational endeavor. Military personnel and athletes (realistic types) often need to be able to behave in a dominant way, and that behavior is a self-conscious performance. Well regarded academics (investigative types) must be able to present their ideas well in a public forum. Successful artists (artistic types) must be able to sell their products to potential patrons. Successful ministers (social types) are more colorful and charismatic than less successful ministers. Ronald Reagan (a prototypical enterprising type) owes his vast personal popularity to his masterful self-presentational skills. Again, some careers require more of this than others, but successful people, regardless of their occupational specialities, normally have well-developed self-presentational skills.

Our final point concerns the fact that successful people, regardless of their identity category, work much harder than less successful people (Barron, 1965; Bloom, 1984). The question is, why do they work so hard? One reason may be that they enjoy what they do, and that they like to test their skills.

A second reason why successful people work so hard may be that they have a great deal of natural energy. Many of the successful academics and businessmen that we know typically sleep 5 hours a night and start work very early in the morning. When Jimmy Carter campaigned for the democratic presidential nomination, political journalists remarked that he had an advantage, relative to the other contenders, because he simply had more energy than they did. And so it goes in art, finance, science, and politics; naturally energetic people have an advantage from the outset.

A final reason why successful people work so hard may be that, as children, adults (parents, teachers, coaches) encouraged them to work hard. Bloom (1984), in his interesting study of young prodigies from a variety of fields, shows that behind every prodigy are some adults who push, prompt, and encourage the youngster to succeed. In the introduction to their edition of Jones's biography of Freud, Trilling and Marcus (1961, pp. viii–xi) note that Freud's family frankly and explicitly expected him to be successful; as a consequence, he was intensely ambitious, and "overtly and without apology, Freud hoped to be a genius."

There is a tendency to think that status is attractive only if it is achieved with minimal effort (Goffman, 1958). By and large, however, successful people work very hard at their careers. That much we know. But our standard assessment methodologies are not designed to illuminate the reasons why people work hard. The ambition scale of the HPI reflects competitiveness and the desire for status, but responses to items such as "I am a hard worker" are not very helpful because virtually everyone endorses them. We are left then to speculate about the origins of the willingness to work hard. Until such time as firm data are available, we propose that it is a function of a desire to test one's skills, animal energy, and parental guidance. We also suggest that clinical psychology and traditional depth psychology, as conceived by Freud, Jung, Adler, have historically done a disservice to high-status persons by attributing their strivings to personal insecurity.

REFERENCES

Barron, F. (1965). The psychology of creativity. *New Directions in Psychology*, II, 1–134. New York: Holt, Rinehart & Winston.
Berglas, S. (1985). *The success syndrome*. New York: Plenum Press.
Bloom, B. S. (Ed.). (1984). Developing talent in young people. New York: Ballantine.
Bowlby, J. (1980). *Attachment and Loss, III*. London: Hogarth.
Buss, A. H., & Plomin, R. (1984). *Temperament: Early developing personality traits*. Hillsdale, NJ: Erlbaum.
Campbell, J. P., Dunnette, M. D., Lawler, E. E., & Weick, C. E. (1970). *Managerial behavior, performance, and effectiveness*. New York: McGraw-Hill.
Caspi, A., Elder, G. H., & Bem, D. J. (1987). Moving against the world: Life course patterns of explosive children. *Developmental Psychology, 22*, 303–308.

Caspi, A., Elder, G. H., & Bem, D. J. (1988). Moving away from the world: Life course patterns of shy children. *Developmental Psychology, 24*, 824–831.

Cattell, R. B., & Drevdahl, J. F. (1955). A comparison of the personality profile of eminent researchers with that of eminent teachers and administrators and that of the general population. *British Journal of Psychology, 46*, 248–261.

Cox, C. (1926). The early mental traits of 300 geniuses. *Genetic studies of genius* (Vol II). Stanford: Stanford University Press.

DePaulo, B. M., Kenny, D. A., Hoover, C. W., Webb, W., & Oliver, P. V. (1987). Accuracy of person perception: Do people know what kinds of impression they convey? *Journal of Personality and Social Psychology, 52*, 303–315.

Eibl-Eibesfeldt, I. (1989). *Human ethology.* New York: Aldine de Gruyter.

Erickson, E. H., (1968). *Gandhi's truth.* New York: Norton.

Gardner, H., (1983). *Frames of mind.* New York: Basic Books.

Ghiselli, E. E. (1973). The validity of aptitude tests in personnel selection. *Personnel Psychology, 26*, 461–477.

Goffman, E. (1958). *The presentation of self in everyday life.* New York: Anchor.

Gottfredson, G. D., Holland, J. L., & Ogawa, D. K. (1982). *Dictionary of Holland occupational codes.* Palo Alto, CA: Consulting Psychologists Press.

Gough, H. G. (1961). *Techniques for identifying the creative research scientist.* In Conference on the Creative Person, Berkeley: Institute of Personality Assessment and Research.

Gough, H. G. (1968). An interpreter's syllabus for the California Psychological Inventory. In P. McReynolds (Ed.), *Advances in psychological assessment* (Vol. I, pp. 55–79). Palo Alto, CA: Science and Behavior Books.

Gough, H. G. (1987). *Manual for the California Psychological Inventory.* Palo Alto, CA. Consulting Psychologists Press.

Helmreich, R. L., Spence, J. T., Beane, W. E., Lucker, G. W., & Matthews, K. A. (1980). Making it in academic psychology: Demographical and personality correlates of attainment. *Journal of Personality and Social Psychology, 39*, 896–908.

Hobart, R., & Dunnette, M. D. (1967). Development of moderator variables to enhance the prediction of managerial effectiveness. *Journal of Applied Psychology, 51*, 50–64.

Hogan, R. (1971). Personality characteristics of highly rated policemen. *Personnel Psychology, 24*, 679–686.

Hogan, R. (1986). *Manual for the Hogan Personality Inventory.* Minneapolis: National Computer Systems.

Hogan, R., & Kurtines, W. (1975). Personological correlates of police effectiveness. *Journal of Psychology, 91*, 289–295.

Hogan, R., Hogan, J., & Busch, C. (1984). How to measure service orientation. *Journal of Applied Psychology, 69*, 167–173.

Holland, J. L. (1985). *Making vocational choices.* Englewood Cliffs, NJ: Prentice-Hall.

Jung, C. G. (1971). Psychological types. In *Collected works* (Vol. 6). Princeton, NJ: Princeton University Press. (First German Edition, 1921)

Lombardo, M. W., Ruderman, M. N., & McCauley, C. D. (1987). *Success and derailment in upper-level management positions.* Greensboro, North Carolina: Center for Creative Leadership.

Lynn, K. S. (1987). *Hemingway.* New York: Simon & Schuster.

MacKinnon, D. W. (1944). The structure of personality. In J. McV. Hunt (Ed.), *Personality and the behavior disorders* (Vol. I, pp. 3–48). New York: Ronald Press.

Mills, C. J., & Bohannan, W. E. (1980). Personality characteristics of effective state police officers. *Journal of Applied Psychology, 65*, 680–684.

Norman, W. T. (1963). Toward an adequate taxonomy of personality attributes: Replicated factor structure in peer nomination personality ratings. *Journal of Abnormal and Social Psychology, 66*, 574–583.

Sparks, C. P. (1966). *Personnel development series: Humble Oil & Refining Co.* Unpublished mimeographed report, Bayonne, NJ: Humble Co.

Spranger, E. (1928). *Types of men.* Halle: Niemeyer.

Sternberg, R. J. (1985). *Beyond IQ: A triarchive theory of human intelligence.* New York: Cambridge University Press.

Strube, M. J., (1987). A self-appraisal model of the Type A behavior pattern. In R. Hogan & W. H. Imes (Eds.), *Perspectives in personality* (Vol. II; pp. 201–250). Greenwich, CT: SNI.

Trilling, L., & Marcus, S. (Eds.). (1961). *The life and work of Sigmund Freud,* by Ernest Jones. New York: Doubleday.

Thomas, A., & Chess, S. (1977). *Temperament and development.* New York: Brunner/Mazel.

Weber, M. (1946). *Max Weber: Essays in sociology* (H. Gerth & C. W. Mills, trans. & eds.). New York: Norton.

Wiggins, J. S. (1973). *Personality and prediction.* Reading, MA: Addison-Wellesley.

PART TWO

SOCIAL SKILLS AND SPECIFIC PSYCHOPATHOLOGIES

CHAPTER SEVEN

Interpersonal Factors in Depression

JACK E. HOKANSON AND MARK P. RUBERT

INTRODUCTION

The aim of this chapter is to review theories and lines of research that implicate interpersonal processes in depression. To begin, principal theories of depression that emphasize interpersonal factors will be presented. This section includes a review of the specific conceptual questions that are pertinent to each theory. The second portion of the chapter presents a critical review of the empirical literature, along with commentary on methodological problems in this area of research. The chapter concludes with an evaluation of the current status of the literature and suggestions for future work.

THEORETICAL PERSPECTIVES

Research on the roots of depression is far from complete, and therefore the development of a comprehensive theory has not yet been possible. As an introduction to the partial theories to be presented, let us first review some of the data coming from large-scale studies on the incidence of depression. These data will highlight the importance of interpersonal factors in depression and also serve to indicate some of the major conceptual issues to be resolved.

In their community survey of Camberwell, England, Brown, and Har-

JACK E. HOKANSON AND MARK P. RUBERT • Department of Psychology, Florida State University, Tallahassee, Florida 32306.

Personality, Social Skills, and Psychopathology: An Individual Differences Approach, edited by David G. Gilbert and James J. Connolly. Plenum Press, New York, 1991.

ris (1978) found that about 8% of their sample had developed new cases of depression during the preceding year and that 9% of their sample could be identified as chronically depressed. Replication studies by Bebbington, Sturt, Tennant, and Hurry (1984), Costello (1982), and Campbell, Cope, and Teasdale (1983) found essentially the same incidence rates in other community studies. Brown and Harris (1978) also found that in approximately 90% of the new cases of depression the episode was preceded by stressful life events, and a strong majority (88%) of these "provoking agents" involved some sort of interpersonal disruption or loss. Similar results involving social stress have been found in other epidemiological studies (e.g., Paykel, 1979; Paykel, Myers, Dienelt, Klerman, Lindenthal, & Pepper, 1969).

Findings such as these implicate interpersonal problems in a significant proportion of cases of depression, and they raise a number of general theoretical questions. When faced with distressing life events, why do some people become depressed whereas others continue to function adequately? What are the psychological/interpersonal mechanisms that result in a depressive disorder rather than some other form of psychopathology? What impact does an individual's depression have on other people? Do others' reactions to the depressed individual have an effect on either lessening or intensifying the depression? The theories to be presented attempt to answer these questions from the perspective of interpersonal processes. As such, they pay little attention to genetic predispositions, biochemical factors, or the possible role of infectious disease in the etiology of depressive symptoms. Hence they must necessarily be viewed as only parts of a far more complex set of processes that contribute to the development of the disorder.

Theory development concerning the role of interpersonal factors in depression was initiated by several key individuals in recent times, the principal ones being P. M. Lewinsohn and J. C. Coyne in the United States, and G. W. Brown, in England. Although many others have contributed to the ideas of these workers, the theories presented will focus on these major figures. Each theorist addresses different aspects of the depressive process. Lewinsohn's conceptualization emphasizes the social processes that play a role in the development of depression. The contributions of Coyne (1976a) focus on interpersonal processes that occur after the onset of depression that maintain or intensify the disorder. A third perspective, by Brown and Harris (1978) addresses, in part, social factors that make individuals vulnerable to developing a depressive reaction.

LEWINSOHN

Central to Lewinsohn's (1974) behavioral approach is the proposition that a low rate of response-contingent positive reinforcement from the social environment elicits a variety of reactions that are ordinarily considered to be depressive: statements of dysphoria and pessimism, reduced rates of verbal behavior, and generally lowered activity level. In situations where the low rate of positive reinforcement is long term, the individual's general activity level is, in effect, on a prolonged extinction schedule. The relatively few positive reinforcements that may occur, for example in the form of sympathy and concern from others, are viewed as strengthening the depressive behaviors. An underlying assumption of this conceptualization is the idea that happy, active, optimistic responding is maintained by high rates of positive reinforcement from the environment and that in the absence of such environmental influences, "depression" is a natural consequence.

What are the determinants of a low rate of positive reinforcement? Lewinsohn acknowledges that a variety of environmental circumstances could be involved, such as the loss of important (reinforcing) people through death or separation or negative living conditions as in chronic poverty or isolation. He also proposes that an especially important set of factors that are causally related to a low rate of positive reinforcement are deficiencies in social skills in the individual. Lewinsohn suggests that the inability to emit social behaviors (because of lack of training, ignorance, inhibitions) that normally result in positive reinforcement from others plays a central role in the development of depression. Lewinsohn, Hoberman, Hautzinger, and Teri (1982) have expanded this formulation to include the notion that the persistent inability to elicit environmental reinforcement results in a state of heightened "self-awareness" that is characterized by negative affect, self-criticism, and behavioral withdrawal. This is hypothesized to set in motion a "vicious cycle" that serves to maintain the depressive state.

Lewinsohn's approach has a simple elegance in that the notion of a low rate of positive reinforcement can be applied to a wide variety of tragic life circumstances. The loss of a loved one can obviously create a sudden and major void in one's life. At the same time, this formulation of depression can handle the slow and progressive erosion of reinforcing life events that might occur with an individual who simply is unskilled in forming friendships or in developing intimate relations with others. This approach is also attractive in the sense that its constructs are clearly specified and measurable, thereby making it amenable to research evaluation.

Propositions within Lewinsohn's formulation lend themselves to empirical tests along the lines of the following research questions: (1) Do states of depression vary in a systematic and inverse fashion with rates of positive reinforcement from the environment?; (2) Are individuals who develop depression likely to be deficient in social skills?; (3) Do other people react to these deficient social skills with relatively low rates of positive behaviors?; (4) Are the processes outlined specific to the development of depression?; or alternatively, (5) Do they represent a set of factors that play a role in the development of a wide variety of psychopathology? A review of research pertaining to these questions will be presented later in this chapter.

COYNE

Communication patterns that evolve between a depressed person and others in the environment are a central feature in Coyne's (1976a) formulation. His analysis focuses on social events that occur after an individual has become depressed, and it attempts to identify interpersonal processes that may prolong or intensify the depression. Coyne argues that variations in the intensity of depressed behavior over time cannot be understood by simply studying the depressed person in isolation. Rather, it requires an analysis of changes that take place in significant relationships in the depressive's life. A similar point of view has been proposed by Coates and Wortman (1980).

In summary form, Coyne proposes that depression-maintaining social interactions are likely to proceed along the following lines. Initial communications of depressive symptoms (verbal and nonverbal messages of sadness, hopelessness, inactivity, distress, etc.) exert a strong influence on people around the depressed person and are likely to elicit expressions of support and reassurance from them. The depressed person is now faced with the problem of how to interpret these messages. Do others, in fact, have the view that the depressive is worthy and acceptable, or are expressions of support given merely because the situation calls for them? Faced with this ambiguity, Coyne suggests that the depressed person emits more depressive symptoms to seek additional reassurance, whereas at the same time continuing to question the genuineness of others' feedback.

A second phase of this process occurs as others begin to experience the persistence of depressive symptoms as aversive. However, the obvious distress and suffering of the depressed person generally serves as an inhibitor of direct expressions of annoyance or frustration by others. This state of affairs is viewed by Coyne as producing an increasing discrepancy between the reassuring verbal content of others' speech and their nonverbal communications (such as tone of voice) that now take on a progressively negative quality. Such "mixed messages" prompt greater insecurity in the depressive and presumably result in displays of more symptoms.

At this point in the process, Coyne suggests that several subsequent interactional patterns are possible. Other people may begin to withdraw, finding suitable excuses to spend less time with the depressed individual. Becoming aware of this withdrawal, the depressive presumably becomes even more insecure, and the expression of symptoms takes on a more urgent quality. Those who do not withdraw enter into a pattern of mutual "manipulation" with the despondent person, using token verbalizations of support to provide temporary reassurance, whereas the depressive maintains symptom displays to elicit such responding. The prolonged nature of this interactional pattern is thought to generate more frequent occasions of open hostility, accusation, and conflict by both participants.

We see here a set of interpersonal processes that prompt increasing insecurity and depression in the depressed individual, along with increasing frustration and distress among those close to the depressed person. The eventual possible outcomes appear bleak: (1) the complete withdrawal of those persons who are important in the depressive's life; (2) stabilization of relationships in a mutually unhappy, insecure, manipulative mode; (3) escalation of the depression to the point where family or other intimates cannot manage the situation alone, and responsibility for care is shifted to a therapeutic facility.

Research questions that emanate from Coyne's theory may be framed as follows. Do displays of depressive symptoms have a negative impact on others? Early in the interactive process, do others respond to depressive communications with reassurance and support (and an inhibition of negative reactions)? Does the depressed person show evidence of "confusion" as to the genuineness and validity of these positive communications from others, and is a persistence of depressive symptoms the likely response to this confusion? As depression persists, do others display increasingly discrepant reactions (reassuring verbal content, but with negative tone)? In later stages of the process, is there an escalation in depressive symptomatology and progressively more overt negative communications and/or withdrawal by others? As was the case with Lewinsohn's theory, the question of whether the processes outlined by Coyne are specific to depression represents an important research issue.

BROWN AND HARRIS

The formulation proposed by Brown and Harris (1978) is an outgrowth of their large-scale study of the incidence of depression in the Camberwell community of London. They theorize that the development of depression can be related to three broadly defined groups of factors. The first one, termed *provoking agents*, refers to severely stressful life events such as death of a loved one, serious marital problems, substandard living conditions, and so forth. Although such provoking agents can bring about considerable distress, Brown and Harris suggest that the actual occurrence of depression is dependent on two other sets of mediating variables: symptom formation factors and vulnerability factors. The former refer to a conglomerate of personal or historical variables, such as prior episodes of depression, early loss of a parent, or family history of affective disorder, which play a role in determining the form in which psychological disturbance is expressed. On the other hand, they use the term *vulnerability factors* to designate the absence of ongoing social supports in one's life, which, they suggest, increase susceptibility to maladaptive reactions. In effect, then, Brown and Harris propose that severely negative life events produce a general condition of distress. When this disturbance is coupled with the appropriate symptom formation factors (e.g., family history, early loss), there is an increased likelihood that the distress will be manifested as depressive symptoms. Further, they posit that a lack of adequate social supports heightens the individual's vulnerability to a depressive reaction, and conversely, that the presence of social supports protects against the development of depression.

The notion of social support is obviously relevant to the subject matter of this chapter, and research questions regarding the interaction between stress, social support, and depression are particularly germane. Because the constructs employed by Brown and Harris (1978) are fairly global, research efforts are required to elucidate the specific processes that are involved. Are there certain types of social support that play a protective role with regard to depression?; for example, having a wide network of acquaintances versus being in a close, intimate relationship? By what mechanisms does social support exert beneficial effects? For example, is the protective process mediated by supportive persons who provide help and consultation in managing stressful life events, or does their presence have some direct effect in enhancing self-esteem and a sense of well-being? Is the relationship between social support and beneficial outcomes a linear function, or can too much support have detrimental effects, as, for example, in being overprotected? These and related questions have prompted an extensive body of research, and a summary of findings will be presented toward the end of this chapter.

RESEARCH FINDINGS

Interestingly, the theories described when considered together, seem to cover the entire range of the depressive process; that is, social factors that may contribute to the onset of an episode, those that are involved in the maintenance of depression, and, factors that may protect an individual from developing the disorder. Research studies relating interpersonal issues to depression frequently cut across these conceptual areas, and hence the reviewer is faced with the problem of how to most effectively organize the empirical findings. This chapter will divide the literature into three general sections: (1) studies that assess the social behaviors of depressed persons; (2) research that investigates the effects of depression on interpersonal relations; and (3) investigations that evaluate the interplay between stress and social support in the development of depression.

BEHAVIOR OF DEPRESSED PERSONS IN SOCIAL SITUATIONS

Research methodologies vary considerably in the study of depressives' interpersonal behaviors. Important differences occur with regard to (1) the severity of depression (subclinical college students, clinically depressed patients), (2) the social context in which the behavior is being investigated (meeting a stranger in a quasi-laboratory situation, a discussion group with acquaintances, intimate relationships), (3) the method of data collection (behavioral observation by independent judges, self-reports by depressed persons), and (4) the temporal relationship between the collection of data assessing social behaviors and the depressive state (concurrent, prior to, postdepression). Such subject, contextual, and temporal variables are relevant to theory with regard to identifying the conditions under which "depressive social behaviors" occur and in assessing whether they play an antecedent role in the development of depression or are merely concomitants of the disorder.

General Social Skills

This category of responding refers to a broad class of social behaviors that would commonly be labeled as interpersonally effective. It includes such skills as being pleasant and personable with others, responding in an appropriately assertive fashion when necessary, and being a good conversationalist as well as a good listener. This level of analysis has relevance to Lewinsohn's notion of "social skills deficits" in depression-prone individuals, and, indeed, Lewinsohn and his colleagues have conducted much of the research on this question.

A number of studies involve the use of trained observers to rate social behaviors produced in dyadic and group interaction settings. Results using this observer methodology indicate that depressed persons, relative to control subjects, are rated lower on desirable social attributes such as friendliness, warmth, clarity of communication, reasonableness, interest in others, and the like (Lewinsohn, Mischel, Chaplin, & Barton, 1980; Youngren & Lewinsohn, 1980). Depressives also appear to emit fewer behaviors than controls, express more general negative content, and direct less positive communications to others (Blumberg & Hokanson, 1983; Gotlib & Robinson, 1982; Libet & Lewinsohn, 1973; Youngren & Lewinsohn, 1980). Nonverbal aspects of social communication appear to be problematic as well, with depressed individuals generally displaying less eye contact, facial pleasantness, adaptive gestures, along with slower and more monotonous speech than control subjects (Ekman & Friesen, 1974; Gotlib & Robinson, 1982; Hinchliffe, Lancashire, & Roberts, 1971; Youngren & Lewinsohn, 1980).

It is of interest to note that relative deficiencies in general social skills have been observed in subclinical, college student samples (e.g., Blumberg & Hokanson, 1983; Gotlib & Robinson, 1982) as well as in outpatients seeking help for depression (e.g., Lewinsohn *et al.*, 1980; Youngren & Lewinsohn, 1980). These findings are supplemented by self-report data from depressed individuals that indicate that they judge themselves to be, relative to nondepressed control subjects, less competent, comfortable, assertive, and outgoing in social situations (Altman & Wittenborn, 1980; Cofer & Wittenborn, 1980; Hokanson & Meyer, 1984; Lewinsohn *et al.*, 1980; Lewinsohn, Steinmetz, Larson, & Franklin, 1981; Youngren & Lewinsohn, 1980). These negative self-appraisals appear to improve with remission of depressive symptoms (Lewinsohn *et al.*, 1980; Zeiss, Lewinsohn, & Munoz, 1979).

The self-report format has been an important vehicle for studying the relationships between social skills, the occurrence of positive reinforcement in daily life events, and depression. Lewinsohn and colleagues have developed three psychometric instruments in this regard: the Pleasant Events Schedule (MacPhillamy & Lewinsohn, 1976); the Unpleasant Events Schedule (Lewinsohn, 1975); and the Interpersonal Events Schedule (Youngren, Zeiss, & Lewinsohn, 1975). On each instrument, subjects rate the frequency of occurrence of a wide variety of life events during a defined interval (e.g., 1 month) and also assign an impact rating to each event (how enjoyable or aversive it was). Multiplication of frequency and impact ratings for each event is assumed to be an estimate of positive reinforcement (or aversiveness) for the period of time being studied. Of special interest to the present discussion is the Interpersonal Events Schedule, which is divided into eight rationally derived scales: Social Activity, Assertion, Cognition, Conflict, Give Positive, Receive Positive, Give Negative, and Receive Negative.

Lewinsohn's group has conducted several relatively large studies using these instruments with depressed outpatients. The designs of these investigations include a group of subjects who display nondepressive psychopathology, thus permitting an assessment of those problems that are specific to depression. Youngren and Lewinsohn (1980) found that depressives differed from normal and other-pathology control groups in their reports of lowered frequency and comfort in social interactions, in giving and receiving positive interpersonal responses, assertiveness, and in the overall social reinforcement derived from social exchanges. Also related to depression were a high frequency of negative cognitions about social events and excessive discomfort while engaging in such cognitions. This study also noted that depressed subjects differed from normals (but not from the other-pathology controls) in reports of a higher frequency of interpersonal conflict and in giving and receiving negative social responses. Using the same measures in a treatment study, Lewinsohn, Youngren, and Grosscup (1979) found essentially the same results. In addition, this investigation found that the problematic social patterns for depressives improved to levels not significantly different from those of normals following successful treatment.

Interpersonal Problem Solving

An important component of general social skills is the ability to manage interpersonal difficulties when they arise. Gotlib and Asarnow (1979) addressed this issue by comparing subclinically depressed and normal college students on two measures: anagram performance (a measure of nonsocial problem solving) and the Means–Ends Problem-Solving Procedure (MEPS), a measure of skills in dealing with interpersonal problems (Platt & Spivack, 1975). These investigators found that both mildly and moderately depressed subjects displayed deficient performance on the MEPS relative to normal controls, but no group differences were found on anagram performance or on a general measure of intelligence. Similar findings using the MEPS have been obtained by Zemore and Dell (1983) and Wierzbicki (1984). The Wierzbicki 1984 study is of special interest in that relatively unskilled performance on the MEPS was related to elevated depression 2 months later. This correlation was obtained after controlling for initial level of depression.

Coyne, Aldwin, and Lazarus (1981) periodically assessed depressed and nondepressed middle-age subjects over a period of a year with respect to the thoughts and actions they used in coping with stressful episodes in their lives. Occurrences of stress were categorized into four general areas: health, work, family matters, and other. Thus the findings in this study are not entirely specific to interpersonal problem solving. Results, based on self-reports, indicate that depressed persons appraised stressful situations as requiring more information in order for them to act, and their coping efforts were characterized by elevated seeking of emotional and informational support from others and by heightened wishful thinking. The groups did not differ however in problem-focused coping behaviors. Within the category of stressful family matters (more specifically interpersonal problem situations), depressives reported a relatively high occurrence of wishful thinking and self-blame as coping responses.

Billings, Cronkite, and Moos (1983) compared some 400 subjects entering treatment for unipolar depression with a demographically matched sample of nondepressed individuals with regard to life stressors and methods of coping. As in Coyne et al. (1981) results are not reported specifically in terms of interpersonal stressors; however, the findings have relevance to the present discussion in that "family arguments" is included as one source of stress. The findings indicate that depressed individuals not only reported higher levels of stress (including those involving family relationships) but also that depressives were found to be less likely to use problem solving and more likely to use emotion-focused coping responses ("emotional discharge") in reaction to life problems.

Folkman and Lazarus (1986) found that depressed subjects did not differ from controls in "planful problem solving" with regard to stressful life events. Those high in depressive symptoms, however, indicated a higher personal stake in stressful encounters, used more confrontive coping, self-control, and escape-avoidance and responded with more anger and worry than did controls.

Overall, the line of research dealing with interpersonal problem solving by depressed individuals suffers from the use of different methodologies across studies, and hence the data do not as yet present a coherent picture. The MEPS (Platt & Spivack, 1975), which has been employed in several investigations, measures subjects' abilities to generate solutions to hypothetical social problems. The findings of Gotlib and Asarnow (1979), Zemore and Dell (1983), and Wierzbicki (1984) using subclinically depressed college students, suggest that even with such relatively benign subjects, deficits in knowing how to solve interpersonal problems (cognitive deficits) can be discerned. On the other hand the findings of Coyne *et al.* (1981) and Folkman and Lazarus (1986), based on self-reports by community samples of depressed individuals, indicate that depressives and normal controls do not differ on measures of planful, problem-focused responding when faced with stressful social or nonsocial situations. These studies also found, however, that depressed persons reacted to stress with relatively strong negative affect and with a variety of emotionally focused behaviors (avoidance, wishful thinking, support seeking, emotional discharge). As a whole, these data leave us unclear as to the determinants of depressives' apparent deficits in social problem solving. One hypothesis suggests that they are due to cognitive deficits (having insufficient knowledge, being unable to adequately analyze problem situations, or to formulate appropriate plans of action). An alternate viewpoint, which may be termed *the behavioral interference hypothesis*, suggests that depressed individuals are not cognitively deficient, but rather, that the execution of effective problem-solving behaviors is hampered by maladaptive emotional responding during times of stress. The ambiguity posed by these alternative hypotheses has led Welker (1986) to propose a two-stage procedure for future studies: first evaluating whether subjects can conceptualize a solution to an interpersonal problem and thereafter assessing subjects' abilities to carry out the solution in an actual problem situation.

Communication of Symptoms in Social Relations

Thus far, this review of depressive interpersonal behaviors has focused on general social skills. In this next section, the research literature regarding behaviors that are usually associated with depression at a clinical level will be inspected; that is, communications of dysphoria, self-blame, pessimism, helplessness, and so forth. There is some risk of engaging in circular reasoning with regard to this subset of behaviors because such symptomatic responding is also used to define a depressive condition. However, the question here is to what degree such behaviors occur in routine engagements with the social environment, and as we shall see in a later section, what effects these behaviors may have on others. Consideration of these questions is important with respect to both Lewinsohn's (1974) and Coyne's (1976a) theories. In the former, Lewinsohn proposes that such behaviors may result in positive reinforcement from others, thereby inadvertently fostering depressive responding. Coyne posits that persistent symptomatic responding is aversive and frustrating to others and is likely to elicit nongenuine expressions of support and/or withdrawal—reactions to which the depressive presumably responds with an escalation of symptom displays.

A number of studies have performed content analyses of subclinically depressed college students' conversations and written communications with new acquaintances in brief laboratory encounters. It might be expected that under such artificial conditions, the elicitation of symptomatic behaviors is unlikely. Nevertheless reliable effects have been obtained, with depressed subjects expressing relatively high frequencies of general negative content and self-devaluation in conversational behavior (Blumberg & Hokanson, 1983; Gotlib & Robinson, 1982). As described in an earlier section, this dysphoric content appears to be accompanied by negative nonverbal behaviors as well, such as unpleasant facial expression, monotonous speech, and less eye contact (Gotlib & Robinson, 1982; Youngren & Lewinsohn, 1980). Several laboratory studies have also assessed messages sent between subjects via The Communications Checklist, a series of rating scales that subjects exchange and through which feelings can be communicated on such dimensions as anger, friendliness, self-devaluation, helplessness, and the like (Hokanson, Sacco, Blumberg, & Landrum, 1980). Results using this more indirect form of communication indicate that depressed students send stronger messages of self-devaluation, sadness, and helplessness to their newly acquainted laboratory partners than do normal controls (Blumberg & Hokanson, 1983; Hokanson et al., 1980). Several studies using self-reports by clinically depressed subjects provide similar results regarding self-blame and self-devaluation behaviors in relationships with others (Cofer & Wittenborn, 1980; Coyne et al., 1981; Hokanson & Meyer, 1984).

In an attempt to obtain naturalistic data, Hokanson, Loewenstein, Hedeen, and Howes (1986) studied the relationship that depressed students developed with their college roommates over a 3-month interval. The Interpersonal Checklist (ICL; LaForge & Suczek, 1955) was used to gather descriptive data regarding each roommates' behavior toward the other. Depressed subjects were found to be more passive, dependent, self-effacing, and distrustful at the beginning of the relationship. Among those depressives who did not improve, these interpersonal behaviors became more extreme over the 3-month duration of the study. Among initially depressed subjects whose symptoms did remit, scores on passivity and self-devaluation continued to remain elevated relative to normal controls.

Studies of marriages in which one spouse is depressed also bear on the question of depressives' maladaptive responding. Although the data in these investigations tend to be more global than those described earlier, a reasonably consistent picture of distressed interactions emerges, which can be characterized by inhibited communication, resentment, perceived inequity, and unresolved conflicts between partners (Hinchliffe, Hooper, Roberts, & Vaughan, 1975; Paykel, Emms, Fletcher, & Rassaby, 1980; Rounsaville, Prusoff, & Weissman, 1980; Weissman & Paykel, 1974). Evidence of disturbed marital relations has been found prior to the onset of depression (Brown & Harris, 1978; Lewinsohn et al., 1981; Paykel et al., 1969) as well as after depressive symptoms have remitted (Billings & Moos, 1986; Rounsaville et al., 1980; Rounsaville, Weissman, Prusoff, & Herceg-Baron, 1979; Weissman & Paykel, 1974).

Descriptions of disturbed marital relationships do not provide a clear picture of depressed persons' behavioral contribution to the distress. To gather such information Coyne, Kessler, Tal, Turnbull, Wortman, and Greden (1987) evaluated the psychological problems experienced by the spouses of currently depressed or remitted depressed persons. A more complete description of this study will be presented in a later section; however, for present purposes, a listing of depressives' behaviors that spouses found most disturbing is informative. Among currently depressed persons these were: lack of energy, expressions of worthlessness and helplessness, constant worrying, and communications of sadness.

Expectations about Interpersonal Events

Cognitive theory as applied to depression posits that negative appraisals and expectancies about the self and the future are central attributes of the disorder (Beck, Rush, Shaw, & Emery, 1979). This general postulate has prompted several investigations of depressed persons' cognitions about life events. Results of these studies are fairly uniform in finding that currently clinically depressed individuals do display, relative to nondepressed controls, negative evaluations of their own competencies and pessimistic outlook for the future (Altman & Wittenborn, 1980; Cofer & Wittenborn, 1980; Hollon et al., 1986; Hollon, Kendall, & Lumry, 1986; Zeiss et al., 1979). Lewinsohn et al. (1981) also found that negative cognitions were not antecedents of a depressive episode, nor were they in evidence with persons in remission. One problem with respect to the present discussion is that the instruments used to assess cognitions in these studies intermix items involving social and nonsocial events. Hence we can only assume, for the moment, that negative expectancies are in evidence for both classes of events.

Some clarification of this issue is provided by investigations that specifically assess depressives' cognitions in interpersonal situations. Lewinsohn et al. (1980) found that depressed subjects' relatively low ratings of their own social behaviors matched the low ratings given by external observers. In a similar vein, Strack and Coyne (1983) observed that depressives correctly anticipated rejection by new acquaintances after a brief social encounter. Hokanson and Meyer (1984) used a specially constructed self-report instrument to evaluate depressed outpatients' expectancies regarding future social events. The instrument included subscales to assess expectations about how intimates (family and close friends) would behave toward them in the future, as well as expectations about the behavior of other people in general. Results indicated that depressed patients expressed a more pessimistic outlook on both scales relative to nondepressed outpatients and to normal controls.

Summary and Critique

Taken together, the research results provide a fairly consistent picture of the social behaviors of persons in a depressed state. The evidence points to a constellation of problematic social attributes ranging from relatively gloomy, unresponsive, and generally unskilled responding in encounters with acquaintances, to frequent communications of the full range of depressive symptoms to others in family situations. Depressed persons appear to be well aware of these interpersonal attributes, and indeed, the evidence suggests that considerable rumination, worry, and discomfort accompany self-appraisal in this area. Related to this are apparent pessimistic expectations about the outcomes of current and future social relationships. Paralleling these problematic behaviors and cognitions is evidence of relative deficiencies in being able to engage in effective interpersonal problem solving.

This summary of depressive social characteristics needs to be viewed in the context of several methodological difficulties in this line of research. Some of these research problems seem to be overcome by the sheer weight of the data and the variety of methodologies that have been used. For example, many studies use self-reports by depressives regarding their own behavior and the occurrence of various life events. Such data are prone to the operation of response biases and situational demand characteristics (see, for example, Coyne & Gotlib, 1983). However, results from self-report studies appear to be paralleled by similar findings in investigations using independent, trained observers, thus lending credence to the overall set of findings. Similarly, the results of laboratory studies, which can be criticized for lack of ecological validity, generally are replicated by research utilizing observations in naturalistic settings. Finally a considerable number of studies in this area used subclinical college students as subjects. Questions have been raised as to whether such subjects represent the low end of a depression continuum or if they indeed represent a population that is qualitatively different from clinically depressed individuals (see for example, Gotlib, 1984). Here again, an overview of the empirical results suggests that similar forms of problematic social behaviors (though perhaps differing in intensity) are observed in both groups of subjects.

There are, however, at least two major methodological problems in this literature that have resulted in important gaps in knowledge and have forestalled the resolution of several key theoretical issues. First, the research designs of most studies compare the responses of depressed subjects with those of normal control subjects. In the absence of nondepressed–other psychopathology control groups, it is impossible to evaluate whether the problem behaviors evidenced by depressed subjects are attributable to depression *per se* or are the result of general deviancy (i.e., would be displayed in other pathological conditions as well). Recall that in the introduction to this chapter, one of the broad conceptual questions posed concerned the factors that lead some people to become depressed, whereas others develop a different set of symptoms. Without the use of research designs that include other psychopathologies, this important issue will remain unresolved. Cognizant of this deficiency, Youngren and Lewinsohn (1980) urged the use of such control groups with some consequent improvements having occurred in more recent studies.

The second important and persistent problem in this line of study is the use of concurrent, cross-sectional research designs. The majority of investigations assess subjects' social behaviors at one point in time; that is, when individuals are in a depressed state. This approach, of course, provides information about the interpersonal concomitants of depression but offers little data regarding the antecedent social patterns that might play a contributory role in the development of the disorder. Thus theories such as Lewinsohn's (1974) that propose that social skills deficits are one of the avenues leading to reduced rates of positive reinforcement (and therefore a depressed state) remain essentially untested. As urged by a number of reviewers (e.g., Monroe & Steiner, 1986), what is needed are prospective, longitudinal research designs that evaluate subjects' interpersonal characteristics before the onset of depression.

REACTIONS OF OTHERS TO DEPRESSED PERSONS

Each of the theories cited at the beginning of this chapter in one fashion or another involve the role of other people in either the development or the maintenance of depression. In this next section, research pertaining to the responses of other people to depression will be reviewed. As with the previously cited work, research approaches range from brief laboratory encounters with mildly depressed students to assessments of the effects of clinical depression on family interactions. The material will be divided into several subsections covering (1) others' willingness to have future interaction with a depressed person, (2) their social–behavioral responses to the depressive, and (3) psychological effects of having contact with a depressed person.

Willingness for Future Contact

Virtually all the studies that assess preferences for future interaction with a depressed person involve brief encounters between strangers in laboratory situations. Within this genre of study, methodologies vary considerably, particularly with respect to the way in which the depressed person is presented to subjects (role enactments by trained accomplices, observing videotapes, written descriptions of case histories, direct conversation with a depressed person). It would be expected, therefore, that the stimulus conditions that occur in these studies can be quite different in terms of such qualities as the severity of symptoms that are portrayed and the emotional impact of the "encounter." Given this lack of standardization, it is surprising that reasonably consistent results have been obtained, with most studies demonstrating reduced preference for future contact with the depressed person (a rejection effect) (Coyne, 1976b; Hammen & Peters, 1977, 1978; Howes & Hokanson, 1979; Marks & Hammen, 1982; Pond, 1986; Sacco, Milana, & Dunn, 1985; Stephens, 1986; Strack & Coyne, 1983), but with several notable exceptions (Gotlib & Robinson, 1982; King & Heller, 1984).

Within this literature, efforts have also been directed toward studying the factors that may mediate the rejection effect in encounters with a depressed person. One prominent hypothesis (Coyne, 1976a) proposes that interaction with a depressed person induces negative emotions, which subjects then try to avoid by reducing further contact. A number of studies have observed elevated feelings of depression, anxiety, and anger in subjects after brief interaction with a depressed person (Coyne, 1976b; Hammen & Peters, 1978; Marks & Hammen, 1982; Sacco et al., 1985). In a related vein, Youngren and Lewinsohn (1980) and Strack and Coyne (1983) found that depressed individuals were given relatively low ratings on such personal characteristics as friendliness, pleasantness, and warmth by subjects with whom they had recently had a conversation. The evidence regarding the elicitation of negative emotions in others, however, is not entirely consistent, with several studies being unable to demonstrate such effects (Gotlib & Robinson, 1982; Howes & Hokanson, 1979; King & Heller, 1984).

A variable of apparent importance in the rejection effect is the type of relationship that takes place between interactants. Marks and Hammen (1982) found that induced negative mood was significantly attenuated when the subject adopted a "helper" role—an effect that was also modestly associated with lower rejection. Stephens (1986) also had subjects adopt a helper role and found relatively high rejection and induced negative emotions but high levels of support and advice giving as well. A similar finding was obtained by Sacco et al. (1985) who asked subjects to assume that they were acquainted with a hypothetical depressed person. Subjects displayed a conflicted pattern similar to that observed by Stephens (1986); that is, heightened tendencies to reject and expressions of concern and willingness to help.

Studies reviewed thus far do not go into the specific social patterns that occur in long-term relationships with depressives, nor do they describe the reactions of other people in such relationships. A series of studies by Hokanson and colleagues provide preliminary data on such relationship questions. The college roommates of depressed persons perceived their depressed partners as becoming progressively more passive, dependent, and self-effacing over a 3-month period of living together (Hokanson *et al.*, 1986). During this interval, the initially normal roommates displayed increasing scores on the Beck Depression Inventory themselves (Howes, Hokanson, & Loewenstein, 1985) and also indicated strong feelings of dissatisfaction with the relationship and desires to find a new roommate (Howes, 1983).

Behavioral Responses to Depressed Persons

Relatively few studies have investigated the actual social behaviors that others direct toward depressed individuals. The data that have been collected appear to parallel the results described in the previous section that dealt with others' emotional reactions to depression.

Several studies indicate that in interactions between new acquaintances, other people direct fewer social responses with less positive content to depressives than are communicated to normal controls (Gotlib & Robinson, 1982; Libet & Lewinsohn, 1973; Pond, 1986; Stephens, 1985). Gotlib and Robinson (1982) also observed that negatively toned behaviors by others occurred in both verbal content and in nonverbal responding (facial expressions, gestures, etc.). The picture may well be more complicated, however, in that several other studies indicate conflicted patterns of responding. Howes and Hokanson (1979) found elevations in both negative and supportive expressions directed to experimental accomplices playing a depressed role. Hokanson *et al.* (1980) observed greater amounts of both extrapunitive and ingratiating communications toward depressed subjects. In the "Roommate Studies" cited in the previous section (Hokanson *et al.*, 1986; Howes, 1983; Howes *et al.*, 1985), it was found that the dormitory roommates of unremitted depressives evidenced increasing signs of distress (elevated Beck Depression Inventory scores, perception of the relationship as unsatisfactory). Despite these signs of negative reaction, the normal roommates also displayed progressive increases in caretaking behaviors toward their depressed partners over the 3-month course of the study.

Such observations of conflicted reaction patterns appear to be consistent with clinical impressions of depressives' effects on others and with the reports by the spouses of depressed persons (e.g., Coyne *et al.*, 1987; Hinchliffe *et al.*, 1975) where a sense of obligation and caring share the spotlight with feelings of worry, resentment, guilt, and inequity. These mixed response patterns have an obvious bearing on Coyne's (1976a) interactional theory of depression maintenance; however, the data as yet are too scanty to permit an evaluation of this formulation. As with the literature concerning depressives' behaviors, research on others' responses suffers from an absence of longitudinal designs, careful microanalyses of depressive-other interactional patterns, and assessment of some of the subtle forms of behaviors that are presumably involved (e.g., others' communications of nongenuine support or depressives' difficulties in interpreting expressions of caring by others).

Psychological Effects of Contact with a Depressed Person

Laboratory studies investigating the psychological/emotional effects of brief contact with a depressed person have already been reviewed in this chapter, and the mixed results of these investigations are difficult to interpret because of methodological variations across studies. Naturalistic investigations, involving ongoing relationships between depressed persons and family members represent another sphere of analysis, and here, the emerging data appear to be generally consistent (although not without methodological problems). Depressed individuals and their spouses report a full range of family problems including elevations in marital conflict, resentment, perceived inequity in managing responsibilities, as well as declines in family cohesiveness (Billings & Moos, 1983, 1986; Hinchliffe et al., 1975; Paykel et al., 1980; Rounsaville et al., 1980; Weissman & Paykel, 1974). Continuing marital conflict also appears to be a negative prognostic indicator with respect to treatment (Keller, Klerman, Lavori, Coryell, Endicott, & Taylor, 1984; Rounsville et al., 1979; Vaughn & Leff, 1981).

Coyne et al. (1987), following up on earlier work by Targun, Dibble, Davenport, and Gershon (1981), have presented descriptive data regarding the specific "burdens" experienced by the spouses of depressed individuals. Sources of distress were divided into those that prompted disruptions in family activities (objective burdens) and those that involved psychological strains on the spouse (subjective burdens). In the former category, disruptions in household routines and social life, inability to plan, and financial strains discriminated families with a currently depressed person from those in which the depressed individual was in remission. In the subjective burdens category, spouses reported relatively intense personal distress about such specific symptoms in the patient as expressions of hopelessness, worthlessness, noncommunicativeness, constant worrying and nervousness, and lack of interest in social activities. Reports of their own symptoms indicated that about 40% of the spouses of currently depressed individuals would be suitable for therapeutic intervention themselves.

Disruptions in family patterns and the psychological strains on the spouse might be expected to affect the children of a depressed parent as well. Billings and Moos (1983) compared the psychological adjustment of children with a currently depressed parent with that of children with nondepressed parents. Adjustment measures involved a broad range of functions including psychological symptoms, physical problems, behavior difficulties, academic and school discipline problems, and disruptions in peer relations. Children with a depressed parent scored significantly higher than controls on all these measures. Within-group analyses also revealed that the quality of the family environment in "depressed" households had appreciable effects on children's adjustment. Those families who managed to maintain relatively high cohesiveness despite a parent's depression showed less disturbance in the children. A 1-year follow-up of these families (Billings & Moos, 1986) indicated that among nonremitted parents, the children (and the family environment) continued to manifest disturbance. The children of remitted parents also showed residual adjustment problems relative to normal controls. As in the earlier data, correlational analyses revealed that the children's adjustment at the follow-up assessment was significantly related to family support and cohesiveness. Similar relationships between family social climate and the adjustment of adolescents with a depressed parent were observed by Hirsch, Moos, and Reischl (1985).

A common methodological problem shared by virtually all the studies in this section involves the use of self-report data. Thus group differences could reflect a systematic bias in the information and judgments provided by respondents. In studies where several different aspects of data are gathered by self-report methods (e.g., reporting on children's symptoms and reporting on family cohesiveness) correlations may be inflated because of shared measurement method variance (Monroe & Steiner, 1986). Some attempts to check on these potential confounds have been made. For example, Billings and Moos (1983) compared the reports of both parents in depressed families on indexes of family stress and resources and found correlations that were generally in the .50s. They also found that ratings of children's functioning by the depressed parent were not significantly different from those made by the nondepressed parent. Further discussion of these methodological issues will be presented at the end of the next section.

SOCIAL SUPPORT, STRESSFUL LIFE EVENTS, AND PERSONAL RESOURCES IN DEPRESSION

Recent years have seen a proliferation of large-scale studies that have attempted to elucidate the relationships between stressful life events, social supports, personal resources (e.g., self-esteem, methods of coping), and depressive symptoms. These investigations are largely outgrowths of the Brown and Harris work in 1978. Two general types of studies are involved: (1) communitywide surveys that attempt to identify individuals who display significant depressive symptoms on standardized assessment instruments; (2) evaluations of currently depressed patients, with retrospective analysis of life circumstances prior to the onset of depression, and in some investigations, follow-up study of remitted and nonremitted cases. Most of these investigations rely on interview and self-report data to assess stressful life circumstances, amount and quality of social support, and depressive symptoms.

Correlational Findings

The current status of this literature appears to be unsettled. Some general trends are reasonably consistent; however, analyses of the interrelationships between stress, support, and depression have thus far produced inconclusive results. Among the relatively stable findings are several of significance: Depression is positively correlated with amount of life stress and negatively correlated with level of social support (Aneshensel & Stone, 1982; Billings et al., 1983; Brown & Harris, 1978; Costello, 1982; Lin, Dean, & Ensel, 1986; Monroe, Bromet, Connell, & Steiner, 1986; O'Neal, Lancee, & Freeman, 1986; Paykel et al., 1980; Pearlin, Lieberman, Menaghan, & Mullan, 1981). As cited earlier, currently depressed individuals also display deficits in personal resources related to coping skills when faced with stressful or problematic life events (Billings et al., 1983; Coyne et al., 1981; Gotlib & Asarnow, 1979; Folkman & Lazarus, 1986; Zemore & Dell, 1983; Wierzbicki, 1984). Several treatment outcome studies provide supplements to these general results. Monroe, Bellack, Hersen, and Himmelhoch (1983) found a negative relationship between pretreatment stress and clinical outcomes among depressed patients. Billings and Moos (1985) found at a 12-month posttreatment follow-up that remitted patients approached normal levels in the occurrence of stressful events and social supports, whereas nonremitted patients remained subject to heightened stressors and relatively low levels of support. Remitted patients also displayed improvements in such personal resources as self-esteem and adequacy of coping responses, whereas nonremitters did not improve on these measures.

Ambiguities in this literature arise when we try to specifically identify how and under what circumstances stress, social support, personal resources, and depression interact with each other. Interpretive difficulties are compounded by the global nature of these concepts and by some of the associated measurement problems (Cohen & Wills, 1985; Monroe & Steiner, 1986). Untangling these interrelationships have been attempted from several points of view, and in the next several paragraphs, the research questions, but no firm conclusions, will be highlighted.

How Is Social Support Helpful?

One question that has drawn attention is whether social support serves to protect against depression only during periods of high stress (the "buffer" hypothesis); or alternatively, whether social support and depression are negatively correlated regardless of stress level ("main effect" hypothesis). The buffer model suggests that social support operates to ameliorate the potentially adverse effects of stressful events, whereas the latter model points toward direct beneficial effects of social support in promoting well-being. Reviews of research that bear on this question specifically with regard to depression (Lin, Dean, & Ensel, 1986; Oatley & Bolton, 1985) or with regard to general health issues (Cohen & Wills, 1985) suggest that social support can operate both to mediate the effects of stressful life events and to directly ameliorate depressive symptoms. Support for each hypothesis appears to be dependent on the type of social support being considered. The buffer hypothesis is supported when others are perceived as providing some form of help that is related to coping with negative life events, whereas the main-effect hypothesis derives support when measures focus on how well the individual is embedded in a wide social network (Cohen & Wills, 1985).

The relationship between social support and stress deserves some elaboration in order to convey the interpretive complexities in this area. Some studies suggest that social support buffers stress because individuals appraise negative life events in a more benign fashion (Gore, 1978; Karasek, Triantis, & Chaudhry, 1982), or they experience enhanced feelings of self-esteem and mastery (Billings & Moos, 1985; Mitchell, Billings, & Moos, 1982; Pearlin et al., 1981). Several studies in which various types of support were assessed (e.g., emotional, instrumental, informational) found a buffering effect because others provide actual help or consultation on how to effectively cope with stressors (Cohen & Hoberman, 1983; Lin et al., 1986; Paykel et al., 1980; Wilcox, 1981). The reciprocal nature of the support–stress relationship is highlighted by several studies that suggest that the occurrence of stressful events seems to elicit increases in helping behaviors by others (Aneshensel & Frerichs, 1982; Barrera, 1981; McFarlane, Norman, Streiner, & Roy, 1983). Underlying these trends is the occasional finding in longitudinal studies that individuals who are assessed as having high levels of support experience fewer subsequent negative events than do persons with low levels of support (McFarlane et al., 1983; Turner & Noh, 1982).

An important and recurrent finding in a number of studies is the importance of having an intimate relationship with a confidante (marital relationship, close friendship, etc.) as opposed to a network of superficial relations. Several investigators suggest that such a form of support is critical in protecting an individual from depression (Brown & Harris, 1978; Costello, 1982; Lin et al., 1986; O'Neal et al., 1986; Pearlin et al., 1981). An intimate, confiding relationship, it would seem, can potentially provide a variety of the support functions that were outlined before: helping the troubled person appraise negative live events in a less threatening manner; offering direct assistance or information in coping with stress; and the enhancement of self-esteem.

Methodological Considerations

Several reviewers of the literature relating stress, social support, and psychopathology (e.g., Cohen & Wills, 1985; Depue & Monroe, 1986;

Monroe & Steiner, 1986) point out important methodological problems. First, it should be noted that most studies in this area are correlational and that the constructs being assessed are global and relatively ill-defined. These characteristics pose a number of basic difficulties that Monroe and Steiner (1986) categorize as measurement redundancy, conceptual problems, and limitations of research design. *Measurement redundancy* refers to overlap among the dependent variables being assessed on two or more measuring instruments. In the present context, an example of such a redundancy might be the death of a loved one (on a measure of stressful life events) and the absence of an intimate confidante (on a measure of supportive relationships). The item on the measure of stress refers to the same life circumstance that is being tapped by the measure of support—a procedure that contributes to a spurious correlation between the assessment instruments. At the level of *conceptual problems*, a similar lack of precision in differentiating among constructs can be noted in this literature. The theoretical distinction between such notions as marital stress, having a nonsupportive spouse, and the depressive symptom of inability to derive pleasure from intimate relations are difficult to discern. *Limitations of research design* refers to the fact that most studies in this area are cross-sectional; that is, the factors that presumably contribute to the depression and the depressive symptoms themselves are assessed at the same time. With such procedures, it is virtually impossible to infer cause-and-effect relationships or to describe the temporal sequencing among variables.

In summary, then, research efforts to understand the relationships between depression, support, stress, and coping are provocative and important. Refinement of concepts and measures are called for, as well as the ever-present need for prospective studies.

EVALUATION OF THE LITERATURE AND FUTURE DIRECTIONS

An overview of the research reviewed in this chapter prompts a number of speculations regarding the role of interpersonal processes in depression. In this concluding section, these speculations will be put in the form of questions, to be followed by judgments as to whether or not sufficient data are available to answer them.

Do Social Skills Deficits Contribute to the Development of Depression?

This question, an outgrowth of Lewinsohn's (1974) theory, raises the possibility that some individuals have stable, traitlike deficient or inappropriate social behaviors that play a causal role in the development of depressive symptoms. Implied in this question is the notion that such stable patterns of social responding interfere with the development of sound interpersonal relationships, and more generally, diminish the possibility of successful adjustment to the environment. Three possible mechanisms may be identified. (1) The skills deficits produce a progressive isolation from others resulting in declining rates of positive reinforcement and an associated lowered sense of well-being. (2) The skills deficits reduce the availability of social support, hence increasing vulnerability to stressful life events. (3) The social skills deficits not only alienate potential sources of support, but by their very nature create stressful circumstances for the individual.

Evidence that social skills deficits play a causal role in depression would have to come from studies that demonstrate existing social skill deficiencies prior to the onset of depression, and thus far no such studies have apparently been conducted. Intuitively, these ideas seem to have some relevance for a subclass of individuals who are labeled as chronic or intermittent depressives; but in the absence of long-term prospective studies, these notions remain in the realm of interesting hypotheses.

Do Problematic Interpersonal Relationships Accompany Depression?

The relatively large number of studies on this issue indicate that currently depressed individuals communicate dysphoria, passivity, pessimism, and self-devaluation during interpersonal encounters. Such responding has been observed in subjects that range from mildly depressed college students to clinically depressed patients. These behavior patterns seemingly contribute to problematic social relationships in that they have a strong impact on other people, eliciting negative evaluations of the depressed person, desires to reduce further contact, and/or a conflict between tendencies to withdraw versus wanting to help. The evidence also indicates considerable strife in marital relationships in which one spouse is depressed, as well as adjustment problems in the children of such families.

There are several important gaps in this literature. The principal theory of depressive–other relationships (Coyne, 1976a) focuses on problems that develop between a depressed individual and intimates such as family members or close friends. The majority of studies, however, investigate social interactions between strangers (typically college students) in brief laboratory encounters. Coyne's theory also posits that interpersonal difficulties evolve over time, going through several defined stages. Evaluation of theory, therefore, requires longitudinal research designs. Virtually all studies in this area utilize a cross-sectional approach, assessing depressive–other relationships at a single point in time. Last, Coyne's formulation suggests that a significant portion of the variance related to remission–nonremission of depression can be attributed to individual differences in how others respond to the depressive's behaviors. Interestingly, few studies have systematically investigated variations in others' responding, and hence a clear picture of what would be "therapeutic" versus "pathogenic" reactions by others has not yet emerged in the empirical literature.

ARE SOCIAL SKILLS DEFICITS SPECIFIC TO DEPRESSION?

This question does not appear to have been addressed sufficiently in the research literature and therefore must remain unanswered. Relatively few studies employ control subjects who display nondepressive psychopathology, and the few studies that have utilized such controls have produced mixed results. Therefore, any social skills deficits that are displayed by depressed subjects may be attributable to psychological deviancy rather than specifically to a depressed state.

Part of the problem also appears to be conceptual. The construct of "social skills deficits" may be too broad to relate specifically to depression. It can be argued that many psychopathological conditions involve interpersonal difficulties (e.g., McLemore & Benjamin, 1979), and hence the task faced by depression researchers is to identify specific social behavioral patterns that are unique to the disorder, along with careful analyses of the interpersonal consequences of such behaviors.

An additional research task is to identify the precursors of these behaviors. Sporadic attempts have been made in this direction (e.g., relating depression proneness to early interpersonal loss) without significant success. Efforts to relate symptomatic social behaviors to such processes as early modeling of a depressed parent or socialization practices that reinforce helpless and self-devaluating responding would add a significant dimension to this area of research.

IS DEPRESSION PART OF A LARGER SYNDROME OF DIFFICULTIES IN COPING WITH STRESSFUL LIFE EVENTS?

There is insufficient data to answer this concluding question; however, the question itself appears to raise some interesting possibilities for future research. Studies that have investigated depressives' coping style suggest that ineffective adjustive behaviors occur in response to both social and nonsocial stressors. Such findings open the door to the entire realm of psychophysiological reactions to prolonged stress. Anisman and Zacharko (1982), in a provocative review of the interrelationships between stress, brain biochemistry, and depression, suggest that when behavioral means of coping with stress are ineffective or when stress is perceived as uncontrollable, an increased burden is placed on endogenous neurochemical mechanisms. Amine utilization increases substantially, which may lead to possible depletion of several neurotransmitters such as norepinephrine, dopamine, and serotonin. Such depletion in turn may promote or intensify dysphoric mood.

The foregoing may be related to interpersonal processes in the following manner. Research reviewed toward the end of this chapter indicates that supportive interpersonal relationships can temper the effects of stress. The specific mechanisms that are involved are as yet unclear; however, preliminary findings suggest that stressful events may be appraised as less threatening, and/or the individual may experience an enhanced sense of efficacy, in the presence of social supports. If indeed the perception of stressful events is mediated by interpersonal factors, then a linkage between social relationships and neurochemical processes is a viable hypothesis. Because depression is fundamentally an *affective* disorder, research aimed at understanding the relationships between stressful life events, interpersonal relations, and their psychophysiological substrates seems to be fundamental to the area.

REFERENCES

Altman, J. H., & Wittenborn, Jr. (1980). Depression-prone personality in women. *Journal of Abnormal Psychology, 89*, 303–308.

Aneshensel, C. S., & Frerichs, R. R. (1982). Stress, support, and depression: A longitudinal causal model. *Journal of Community Psychology, 10*, 363–376.

Aneshensel, C. S., & Stone, J. D. (1982). Stress and depression: A test of the buffering model of social support. *Archives of General Psychiatry, 39*, 1392–1396.

Anisman, H., & Zacharko, R. M. (1982). Depression: The predisposing influence of stress. *Behavioral and Brain Sciences, 5*, 89–137.

Barrera, M., Jr. (1981). Social support in the adjustment of pregnant adolescents: Assessment issues. In B. H. Gottlieb (Ed.), *Social networks and social support* (pp. 69–96). Beverly Hills, CA: Sage.

Bebbington, P. E., Sturt, E., Tennant, C., & Hurry, J. (1984). Misfortune and resilience: A community study of women. *Psychology Medicine, 14*, 347–363.

Beck, A. T., Rush, A. J., Shaw, B. F., & Emery, G. (1979). *Cognitive therapy of depression.* New York: Guilford Press.

Billings, A. G., & Moos, R. H. (1983). Comparisons of children of depressed and nondepressed parents: A socio-environmental perspective. *Journal of Abnormal Child Psychology, 11*, 463–485.

Billings, A. G., & Moos, R. H. (1985). Psychosocial processes of remission in unipolar depression: Comparing depressed patients with matched community controls. *Journal of Consulting and Clinical Psychology, 53*, 314–325.

Billings, A. G., & Moos, R. H. (1986). Children of parents with unipolar depression: A controlled 1-year follow-up. *Journal of Abnormal Child Psychology, 14*, 149–166.

Billings, A. G., Cronkite, R. C., & Moos, R. H. (1983). Social-environmental factors in unipolar depression: Comparisons of depressed patients and nondepressed controls. *Journal of Abnormal Psychology, 92*, 119–133.

Blumberg, S. R., & Hokanson, J. E. (1983). Effects of response style on behavior in depression. *Journal of Abnormal Psychology, 91*, 196–204.

Brown, G. W., & Harris, T. (1978). *Social origins of depression: A study of psychiatric disorders in women.* London: Tavistock.

Campbell, E. A., Cope, S. J., & Teasdale, J. D. (1983). Social factors and affective disorder: An investigation of Brown and Harris's model. *British Journal of Psychiatry, 143*, 548–553.

Coates, D., & Wortman, C. B. (1980). Depression maintenance and interpersonal control. In A. Baum & J. Singer (Eds.), *Advances in environmental psychology* (Vol. 2, pp. 149–182). Hillsdale, NJ: Erlbaum.

Cofer, D. H., & Wittenborn, J. R. (1980). Personality characteristics of formerly depressed women. *Journal of Abnormal Psychology, 89*, 309–314.

Cohen, S., & Hoberman, H. M. (1983). Positive events and social supports as buffers of life change stress. *Journal of Applied Social Psychology, 13*, 99–125.

Cohen, S., & Wills, T. A. (1985). Stress, social support, and the buffering hypothesis. *Psychological Bulletin, 98*, 310–357.

Costello, C. G. (1982). Social factors associated with depression: A retrospective community study. *Psychological Medicine, 12*, 329–339.

Coyne, J. C. (1976a). Toward an interactional description of depression. *Psychiatry, 39*, 28–40.

Coyne, J. C. (1976b). Depression and the response of others. *Journal of Abnormal Psychology, 85*, 186–193.

Coyne, J. C., & Gotlib, I. H. (1983). The role of cognition in depression: A critical appraisal. *Psychological Bulletin, 94*, 472–505.

Coyne, J. C., Aldwin, C., & Lazarus, R. S. (1981). Depression and coping in stressful episodes. *Journal of Abnormal Psychology, 90*, 439–447.

Coyne, J. C., Kessler, R. C., Tal, M., Turnbull, J., Wortman, C. B., & Greden, J. (1987). Living with a depressed person: Burden and psychological distress. *Journal of Consulting and Clinical Psychology, 55*, 347–352.

Depue, R. A., & Monroe, S. M. (1986). Conceptualization and measurement of human disorder in life stress research: The problem of chronic disturbance. *Psychological Bulletin, 99*, 36–51.

Ekman, P., & Friesen, W. V. (1974). Nonverbal behavior and psychopathology. In R. J. Friedman and M. M. Katz (Eds.), *The psychology of depression: Contemporary theory and research* (pp. 84–101). New York: Wiley.

Folkman, S., & Lazarus, R. S. (1986). Stress processes and depressive symptomology. *Journal of Abnormal Psychology, 95*, 107–113.

Gore, S. (1978). The effect of social support in moderating the health consequences of unemployment. *Journal of Health and Social Behavior, 19*, 157–165.

Gotlib, I. H. (1984). Depression and general psychopathology in university students. *Journal of Abnormal Psychology, 93*, 19–30.

Gotlib, I. H., & Asarnow, R. B. (1979). Interpersonal and impersonal problem-solving skills in mildly and clinically depressed university students. *Journal of Consulting and Clinical Psychology, 47*, 86–95.

Gotlib, I. H., & Robinson, L. A. (1982). Responses to depressed individuals: Discrepancies between self-report and observer-rated behavior. *Journal of Abnormal Psychology, 91*, 231–240.

Hammen, C. L., & Peters, S. D. (1977). Differential responses to male and female depressive reactions. *Journal of Consulting and Clinical Psychology, 45*, 994–1001.

Hammen, C. L., & Peters, S. D. (1978). Interpersonal consequences of depression: Response to men and women enacting a depressed role. *Journal of Abnormal Psychology, 87*, 322–332.

Hinchliffe, M., Hooper, D., Roberts, F. J., & Vaughn, P. W. (1975). A study of the interaction between depressed patients and their spouses. *British Journal of Psychiatry, 126*, 164–172.

Hinchliffe, M. K., Lancashire, M., & Roberts, F. J. (1971). A study of eye-contact in depressed and recovered psychiatric patients. *British Journal of Psychiatry, 119*, 213–215.

Hirsch, B. J., Moos, R. H., & Reischl, T. M. (1985). Psychosocial adjustment of adolescent children of a depressed, arthritic, or normal parent. *Journal of Abnormal Psychology, 94*, 154–164.

Hokanson, J. E., & Meyer, B. E. B. (1984). Interpersonal expectancies and preferences for various types of social behaviors of depressed outpatients. *Journal of Personal and Social Relationships, 1,* 279–292.

Hokanson, J. E., Lowenstein, D. A., Hedeen, C., & Howes, M. J. (1986). Dysphoric college students and roommates: A study of social behaviors over a three-month period. *Personality and Social Psychology Bulletin, 12,* 311–324.

Hokanson, J. E., Sacco, W. R., Blumberg, S. R., & Landrum, G. C. (1980). Interpersonal behavior of depressive individuals in a mixed-motive game. *Journal of Abnormal Psychology, 89,* 320–332.

Hollon, S. D., Kendall, P. C., & Lumry, A. (1986). Specificity of depressotypic cognitions in clinical depression. *Journal of Abnormal Psychology, 95,* 52–59.

Howes, M. J. (1983). *Depression and the development of interpersonal relationships.* (Doctoral dissertation, Florida State University, Tallahassee, 1982) *Dissertation Abstracts International, 43* (9), 3031.

Howes, M. J., & Hokanson, J. E. (1979). Conversational and social responses to depressive interpersonal behavior. *Journal of Abnormal Psychology, 88,* 625–634.

Howes, M. J., Hokanson, J. E., & Loewenstein, D. A. (1985). Induction of depressive affect after prolonged exposure to a mildly depressed individual. *Journal of Personality and Social Psychology, 49,* 1110–1113.

Karasek, R. A., Triantis, K. P., & Chaudhry, S. C. (1982). Coworkers and supervisor support as moderators of associations between task characteristics and mental strain. *Journal of Occupational Behavior, 3,* 181–200.

Keller, M. B., Klerman, G. L., Lavori, P. W., Coryell, W., Endicott, J., & Taylor, J. (1984). Long-term outcome of episodes of major depression: Clinical and public health significance. *Journal of the American Medical Association, 252,* 788–792.

King, D. A., & Heller, K. (1984). Depression and the response of others: A re-evaluation. *Journal of Abnormal Psychology, 93,* 477–480.

Laforge, R., & Suczek, R. (1955). The interpersonal dimension of personality: III. Interpersonal checklist. *Journal of Personality, 24,* 94–112.

Lewinsohn, P. M. (1974). A behavioral approach to depression. In R. J. Friedman & M. M. Katz (Eds.), *The psychology of depression: Contemporary theory and research* (pp. 157–178). New York: Wiley.

Lewinsohn, P. M. (1975). *The Unpleasant Events Schedule: A scale for the measurement of aversive events.* Unpublished memo, University of Oregon.

Lewinsohn, P. M., Steinmetz, J. L., Larson, D. W., & Franklin, J. (1981). Depression-related cognitions: Antecedent or consequence? *Journal of Abnormal Psychology, 90,* 213–219.

Lewinsohn, P. M., Mischel, W., Chaplin, W., & Barton, R. (1980). Social competence and depression: The role of illusory self-perceptions. *Journal of Abnormal Psychology, 89,* 203–212.

Lewinsohn, P. M., Hoberman, H. M., Hautzinger, M., & Teri, L. (1982). *Cognitive distortion: Consequence rather than cause of depression.* Paper presented at the 16th American Association of Behavior Therapy Convention, Los Angeles, California.

Lewinsohn, P. M., Youngren, M. A., & Grosscup, S. J. (1979). Reinforcement and depression. In R. A. Depue (Ed.), *The psychobiology of depressive disorders: Implications for the effects of stress* (pp. 291–316). New York: Academic Press.

Libet, J. M., & Lewinsohn, P. M. (1973). Concept of social skill with special reference to the behavior of depressed persons. *Journal of Consulting and Clinical Psychology, 40,* 304–312.

Lin, N., Dean, A., & Ensel, W. M. (1986). *Social support, life events, and depression.* London: Academic Press.

Marks, T., & Hammen, C. L. (1982). Interpersonal mood induction: Situational and individual determinants. *Motivation and Emotion, 6,* 387–399.

MacPhillamy, D. J., & Lewinsohn, P. M. (1976). *Manual for the Pleasant Events Schedule.* Unpublished manuscript, University of Oregon.

McFarlane, A. H., Norman, G. R., Streiner, D. L., & Roy, R. J. (1983). The process of social stress: Stable, reciprocal, and mediating relationships. *Journal of Health and Social Behavior, 24,* 160–173.

McLemore, C. W., & Benjamin, L. S. (1979). Whatever happened to interpersonal diagnosis? *American Psychologist, 34,* 17–34.

Mitchell, R. E., Billings, A. G., & Moos, R. H. (1982). Social support and well-being: Implications for prevention programs. *Journal of Primary Prevention, 3,* 77–98.

Monroe, S. M., & Steiner, S. C. (1986). Social support and psychopathology: Interrelations with preexisting disorder, stress, and personality. *Journal of Abnormal Psychology, 95,* 29–39.

Monroe, S. M., Bellack, A. S., Hersen, M., & Himmelhoch, J. M. (1983). Life events, symptom course, and treatment outcome in unipolar depressed women. *Journal of Consulting and Clinical Psychology, 51,* 604–615.

Monroe, S. M., Bromet, E. J., Connell, M. M., & Steiner, S. C. (1986). Social support, life events, and depressive symptoms: A 1-year prospective study. *Journal of Consulting and Clinical Psychology, 54,* 424–431.

Oatley, K., & Bolton, W. (1985). A social-cognitive theory of depression in reaction to life events. *Psychological Review, 92,* 372–388.

O'Neil, M. K., Lancee, W. J., & Freeman, S. J. J. (1986). Psychosocial factors and depressive symptoms. *Journal of Nervous and Mental Disease, 174,* 15–23.

Paykel, E. S. (1979). Causal relations between clinical depression and life events. In J. E. Barrett, R. M. Rose, & G. L. Klerman (Eds.), *Stress and mental disorder* (pp. 71–86). New York: Raven Press.

Paykel, E. S., Myers, J. K., Dienelt, M. N., Klerman, G. L., Lindenthal, J. J., & Pepper, M. P. (1969). Life events and depression: A controlled study. *Archives of General Psychiatry, 21,* 753–760.

Paykel, E. S., Emms, E. M., Fletcher, J., & Rassaby, E. S. (1980). Life events and social support in puerperal depression. *British Journal of Psychiatry, 136,* 339–346.

Pearlin, L. I., Lieberman, M. A., Menaghan, E. G., & Mullan, J. T. (1981). The stress process. *Journal of Health and Social Behavior, 22,* 337–356.

Platt, J. J., & Spivack, G. (1975). *Manual for the Means-Ends Problem-Solving Procedure (MEPS): A measure of interpersonal cognitive problem-solving skill.* Philadelphia: Hahnermann Medical College and Hospital.

Pond, C. A. (1986). *The effect of expectations about depression on perception and behavior in dyadic interactions.* (Unpublished doctoral dissertation, University of Saskatchewan, Canada, 1985) *Dissertation Abstracts International, 48* (01B), 273.

Rousanville, B. J., Prusoff, B. A., & Weissman, M. M. (1980). The course of marital disputes in depressed women: A 48-month follow-up study. *Comparative Psychiatry, 21,* 111–118.

Rousanville, B. J., Weissman, M. W., Prusoff, B. A., & Herceg-Baron, R. L. (1979). Marital disputes and treatment outcome in depressed women. *Comprehensive Psychiatry, 20,* 483–490.

Sacco, W. P., Milana, S., & Dunn, V. (1985). Effects of depression level and length of acquaintance on reactions of others to a request for help. *Journal of Personality and Social Psychology, 49,* 1728–1737.

Stephens, R. S. (1985). *Factors mediating responses to depressed interpersonal behavior.* (Unpublished doctoral dissertation, Florida State University, Tallahassee, 1985) *Dissertation Abstracts International, 46* (11), 461.

Strack, S., & Coyne, J. C. (1983). Social confirmation of dysphoria: Shared and private reactions to depression. *Journal of Personality and Social Psychology, 44,* 798–806.

Targun, S. D., Dibble, E. D., Davenport, Y. B., & Gershon, E. S. (1981). The family attitude questionnaire: Patient and spouses views of bipolar illness. *Archives of General Psychiatry, 38,* 562–568.

Turner, R. J., & Noh, S. (1982). *Social support, life events, and psychological distress: A three wave panel analysis*. Paper presented at the meeting of the American Sociological Association, San Francisco.

Vaughn, C. E., & Leff, J. (1981). Patterns of emotional response in the relatives of schizophrenic patients. *Schizophrenia Bulletin, 7,* 43–44.

Welker, R. A. (1986). *The coping behavior of depressives in social situations.* Unpublished master's thesis, Florida State University, Tallahassee.

Weissman, M. S., & Paykel, E. S. (1974). *The depressed woman: A study of social relationships.* Chicago: University of Chicago Press.

Wierzbicki, M. (1984). Social skills deficits and subsequent depressed mood in students. *Personality and Social Psychology Bulletin, 10,* 605–610.

Wilcox, B. L. (1981). Social support, life stress, and psychological adjustment: A test of the buffering hypothesis. *American Journal of Community Psychology, 9,* 371–386.

Youngren, M. A., & Lewinsohn, P. M. (1980). The functional relation between depression and problematic interpersonal behavior. *Journal of Abnormal Psychology, 89,* 333–341.

Youngren, M. A., Zeiss, A., & Lewinsohn, P. M. (1975). *Interpersonal Events Schedule.* Unpublished manuscript, University of Oregon.

Zeiss, A. M., Lewinsohn, P. M., & Munoz, R. F. (1979). Nonspecific improvement effects in depression using interpersonal skills training, pleasant activities, schedules, or cognitive training. *Journal of Consulting and Clinical Psychology, 47,* 427–439.

Zemore, R., & Dell, L. W. (1983). Interpersonal problem-solving skills and depression proneness. *Personality and Social Psychology Bulletin, 9,* 231–235.

CHAPTER EIGHT

Development and Maintenance of Aggressive Behavioral Patterns

MICHAEL A. MCCOLLOCH AND BRENDA O. GILBERT

INTRODUCTION

In its examination of persistent aggressive behavior patterns and the factors maintaining aggressivity, this chapter places special emphasis on individual, social-skill, and social-system variables. For our purposes, aggression is viewed as the utilization of aversive and negative behaviors that threaten or inflict psychological or physical damage on people or property.

AGGRESSIVITY AS A TRAIT

Individuals differ in the amount and intensity of their aggressive behavior (Olweus, 1977, 1979; Patterson, 1976). In addition, aggressive persons tend to use various aversive behaviors interchangeably, presumably based on their similarity in effect. It has been shown, for example, that children who fight also frequently engage in verbal attacks, complaining, crying, and other obnoxious behaviors (Patterson, 1976). Consistent with this interchangeability principle, factor analytically devised rating scales show aversive behaviors such as temper tantrums, crying, fighting, meanness and cruelty to others, and destruction of property to correlate highly

MICHAEL A. MCCOLLOCH • Private Practice, 3779 Vest Mill Road, Winston-Salem, North Carolina 27103.   BRENDA O. GILBERT • Department of Psychology, Southern Illinois University at Carbondale, Carbondale, Illinois 62901-6502.

Personality, Social Skills, and Psychopathology: An Individual Differences Approach, edited by David G. Gilbert and James J. Connolly. Plenum Press, New York, 1991.

with each other (Achenbach & Edelbrock, 1983). Furthermore, the distribution of individuals' rates of aggressivity is bimodal instead of bell-shaped (Achenbach & Edelbrock, 1983). Utilizing parent and teacher ratings on behavioral checklists, most students have few if any of the aggressive items endorsed, whereas the youngsters identified as aggressive have the majority of such items endorsed. Similar bimodal distributions are found in observational studies in the home and other settings (Patterson, 1982). With increasing age, the discrepancy in amount of aggressive behavior between the aggressive and normal child increases. Thus it becomes an increasingly easy task to identify the aggressive child.

Aggressivity in males tends to be moderately consistent across time. Olweus (1977, 1979) reviewed 16 longitudinal studies of aggression in males and found consistent support for stability of aggression over time. Initial ages varied from 2 to 18 years old and the follow-up periods ranged from 6 months to 21 years with an average interval of 5.7 years. Measures of aggression included peer nominations, peer ratings, teacher ratings, clinical ratings, and direct behavioral observations. Stability coefficients ranged from .26 to .98 with an overall mean correlation of .49. Longer delays were associated with lower correlation coefficients.

In addition to the significant consistencies across time, the higher correlations between concurrent teacher, parent, and peer ratings support the conclusion that the rank order of people on aggression is stable cross-situationally. Other data have shown high correlations between self and other ratings (Olweus, 1973, 1975). More evidence of cross-situational stability is provided by the finding of high correlations between peer nomination measures and overt aggressive behavior in a contrived naturalistic setting (Winder & Wiggings, 1964) and behavior in an experimental cooperative game (Williams, Meyesson, Eron, & Sender, 1967). In conclusion, for males there is strong evidence attesting to the stability of aggression in individuals across time and situation.

The level of consistency of aggression in woman is less well established. Kagan and Moss (1962) found limited stability in females' level of aggressivity from childhood to adulthood, presumably due to the lack of environmental support for female aggression. A review by Olweus (1984) questions these conclusions. In the studies reviewed, mean female age was 7 years and the follow-up period varied from 6 months to 10 years. The mean stability correlation was .44, which is very similar to the mean correlation for males. However, unlike the Kagan and Moss study, the Olweus review did not include studies of adult women. Because the magnitude of the stability correlations of female aggressivity declines significantly in adulthood (Parke & Slaby, 1983), the long-term outcomes of aggressivity between childhood and maturity in women are unclear. The adult behavior patterns of females high in child and adolescent aggression need study.

DEVELOPMENTAL TRENDS IN AGGRESSION

The frequency of aggression tends to gradually decrease during the preschool years. As early as 1931, Goodenough had the mothers of preschoolers keep daily diaries on the frequency of their children's outbursts. After an initial peak at a year and a half, the frequency slowed gradually until age 5. Likewise Patterson (1982) observed the frequency of aversive behaviors of normal children in their homes and reported a gradual reduction in aversive behaviors between the ages of 2 and 4 and 9 and 10. Aggressive youngsters had considerably higher levels of aggressive behavior from about age 5–6 and failed to show a gradual decrease with age. In fact, aggressive children at 11 and 12 years of age showed as high a frequency of aversiveness as 2- to 4-year-old normal children.

The form and goals of aggression change over time. Between the ages of 2 and 4, physical aggression begins to decrease, whereas verbal aggression shows an increase (Goodenough, 1931). Similarly, with increasing age, aggression becomes more hostile. Several authors (Buss, 1966; Feshbach, 1964; Hartup, 1974) have made a distinction between hostile aggression (where the aggression is aimed at another person) and instrumental aggression (where the goal is obtaining some object or other noninterpersonal outcome). Hartup's research (1974) demonstrated that the increased level of aggression in preschoolers compared to 6- and 7-year-olds is due totally to the reduction of instrumental aggression. Hartup speculated that these age trends continue and that instrumental aggression becomes a relatively unimportant form of aggression by adolescence and adulthood.

One presumed reason children exhibit less hostile aggression at earlier ages is that younger children are less able to perceive negative intent in other persons. With increased age, children develop the ability to evaluate intention as important in their responses to aggression. Shantz and Voydanoff (1973) found that 9- and 12-year-olds made less severe aggressive reactions to accidental provocation as compared to intentional provocation, whereas 7-year-olds responded equally severely to either. Older children may make an even more subtle distinction with regard to aggressive intent. Ferguson and Rule (1980) found that eighth graders not only saw intended aggression as more reprehensible than unintentional aggression but viewed foreseeable but unintentional aggression as more reprehensible than either justified or accidental and unforeseeable aggression.

A parallel developmental change is the ability to use information about aggressive intent to predict future behavior. Second and fourth graders have been found to predict that the intentionally aggressive child was more likely to be aggressive in future situations, whereas the kindergarten child made no discrimination based on the intentionality of aggression (Rotenberg, 1980). Overall, evidence supports the occurrence of developmental changes in the perception of aggressive intent and the relevancy of these perceptions to aggressive responses.

The form of hostile aggression to different elicitors also changes over time. Hartup (1974) found that in response to derogation, half of the younger group (4- and 5-year-olds) hit the derogater compared to only 22% of the older group (6- and 7-year-olds). The same pattern of hostile aggression did not emerge when examining hostile aggression elicited by blocking attainment of a goal. There were no changes in frequency or type of response with age. For both age groups, about 25% responded with verbal attacks and tattling on this type of elicitor. These findings point to the complex interactions among forms of aggression, elicitors of aggression, and developmental changes.

The next sections of the chapter deal with factors contributing to the development and maintenance of aggression.

CONSTITUTIONAL FACTORS IN AGGRESSION

GENETIC INFLUENCES

There is little direct support for genetic effects upon human aggression, although information is available on other variables associated with aggressivity. For example, the evidence for genetic influence upon criminality is stronger. By studying the thorough records available in Denmark, Mednick, Gabrielli, and Hutchings (1984) determined that the criminality of the biological fathers of adoptive boys had significant influence upon the criminality of their sons. However, the criminality of the adoptive father also had an influence.

Another presumed genetic effect that has been highly publicized is the XYY syndrome. A greater than expected frequency of males with an extra male chromosome has been found in a mental–penal setting (2% vs. 0.11% in the general population) (McClearn, 1970). However, upon further investigation, most of the increased probability of criminality can be accounted for by the lower intelligence of this group (Witkin, Mednick, Schulsinger, & Owen, 1976).

TEMPERAMENT

Temperament refers to a child's normative style of behaving—their characteristic ways of responding to different types of situations. There appears to be a high degree of stability in temperament from an early age regardless of the assessment procedure. Thomas and Chess (1977, 1980) and Thomas, Chess, and Birch (1968) rated babies on nine aspects of temperament (e.g., activity level, intensity of reactions, approach to new stimuli). Based on the intercorrelations between scales and the stability of ratings over time, three types of children were identified: the easy, difficult, and slow-to-warm-up babies. The difficult child who is irregular in biological function, slow to adapt to environmental change, very expressive of negative moods and highly intense in reactions has the temperament pattern most associated with aggression. For example, Bates, Olson, Pettit, and Bayles (1982) identified difficult children at an early age (6 months to 2 years) through observational techniques. These youngsters were much higher in their level of resistance to parental efforts at control, in their failure to respond to requests to stop, and in their expression of negative affect.

Temperament can be predictive of subsequent behavioral problems. Thomas and Chess (1980) found that 10 of 14 "difficult" children developed subsequent behavioral disorders, a much higher percentage than in the other two groups. One of the frequent behavioral problems displayed by the difficult children was aggressiveness. However, this aggression was one of a cluster of problem behaviors listed, and it is uncertain what number of difficult children actually displayed persistent aggression. More direct evidence of the possible role of temperament is Olweus's (1980) retrospective study of the temperament ratings of aggressive children by their mothers. A positive correlation between early troublesome temperament and peer-rated aggression was found. A serious limitation of this study is the danger of negatively distorted memories of mothers with problematic children.

Temperament may also indirectly influence aggression by affecting parental behavior. Thomas and Chess (1980) found that initially the behavior of parents toward their difficult children did not differ from other parents' behavior. However, by the time the difficult children reached late childhood and early adolescence, their parents were much more negative and aversive in their interactions with their children than other parents.

BIOLOGICAL MECHANISMS

Specific areas of the brain are especially associated with aggressive behavior. Lesion and stimulation experiments in several types of animals and humans have shown that the amygdala, septum, hippocampus, hypothalamus, and brain-stem regions are involved in the regulation of emotion and aggression (Moyer, 1986). In addition to the actual anatomical structure of the brain, electrocortical activity of the brain has been hypothesized to be related to aggression. More specifically, it is suggested that aggressive behavior, as well as sociopathic behavior, is partly a function of impulsivity associated with the inadequate development of inhibitory controls related to low cortical arousal associated with slow formation of classically conditioned responses (Eysenck & Eysenck, 1985; Newman, Widom, & Nathan, 1985). Another hypothesis related to inadequate cortical arousal is that deficits in verbal information processing are produced from inadequate cortical arousal that are related to aggression proneness (Hare & Jutai, 1988). However, few studies have assessed EEG activity in aggressive adolescents or children. One study that did (Gilbert, Johnson, McColloch, & Gilbert, in press) failed to find lower levels of EEG arousal in aggressive adolescents; in fact, their aggressive group had a higher level of EEG arousal. One other relevant study is that of Lewis, Pincus, Shanok, and Glaser (1982). These researchers found abnormal EEGs and other signs suggestive of psychomotor epilepsy in 18 of 97 incarcerated adolescent delinquents, 89 of whom were violent.

Differences between aggressive and nonaggressive humans have been found in hormonal levels. Plasma testosterone concentrations have been found to be related to aggressiveness and criminal behavior (Kreuz & Rose, 1972; Persky, Smith, & Basn, 1971). However, other studies have failed to confirm this relationship (Mattsson & Kim, 1982; Olweus, Mattsson, Schalling, & Low, 1980). The Olweus study found a significant relationship between plasma testosterone concentrations and self-reports of aggression but not between this hormone and actual adolescent antisocial behavior. These differences in findings point to the need to relate hormonal levels to specific types of aggression. It should be pointed out that aggressive acts may result in increased levels of testosterone; thus any cause–effect relationship cannot be assumed. Aggression could cause testosterone increases or a third, unidentified variable could cause increases in both.

Effects of early exposure to high levels of male or female hormones upon subsequent aggression have received considerable attention. For humans, hormonal effects on aggression are unclear (Tieger, 1980). Although male hormones may masculinize females in certain ways, the level of aggressiveness does not appear to be changed (Ehrhardt & Baker, 1974). Tieger has concluded that hormones can have effects on organizing behavior but do not act in a way to predispose humans to behave aggressively. However, other researchers express a different view. Reinisch (1981) reported that early exposure to progestin did increase the probability of physical aggression. As it stands, the effects of early exposure to male or female hormones on aggressivity is unclear.

Other biological factors such as attractiveness may influence aggression. Unattractive 5-year-olds were found to be more aggressive than attractive 5-year-olds, though attractiveness was unrelated to aggression in 3-year-olds (Langlois & Downs, 1979). Unattractiveness may be an example of a biological factor that is not a necessary condition for aggression but, by influencing peers' and others' acceptance and expectations, could contribute to the development of aggressivity in some youngsters.

ENVIRONMENTAL FACTORS

DEMOGRAPHIC VARIABLES

There is little relationship between socioeconomic class and aggression. Although the delinquency conviction ratio for lower-class to upper- or middle-class children is 5:1, respectively, it drops to 1½ to 1 when self-report of delinquency acts are utilized. When aggression instead of delinquency is examined, the link with social class is even weaker. Feshbach (1970) found no consistent relationship between teacher or parent-rated aggression and social class. Likewise, Olweus (1979) found no significant correlation between peer-rated aggression and socioeconomic status.

The relationship of a variety of family variables to aggression has been examined. In the Isle of Wight study (Rutter, Tizard, & Whitmore, 1970), family size was directly related to antisocial behavior. However, IQ is inversely related to family size (Rutter et al., 1970; Zajonc, 1976). After IQ was partialed out, Rutter found only a small relationship between family size and antisocial behavior. Another study that found a positive relationship between family size and physical aggression discovered that the larger the family, the less parent–child interaction and the more peer interaction occurred (Burgess & Conger, 1978). Greater peer interactions, combined with less parent monitoring, may help account for the greater physical aggression. These studies suggest that family size may influence aggressivity through the mechanisms of lowered intelligence, increased peer interaction, and reduced parental monitoring.

There has been much speculation that broken homes lead to more aggressive children. Rutter et al. (1970) found that living in a broken home increased the probability of child psychiatric disorders, but the incidence of antisocial disorders was not increased. In contrast, two studies (Hetherington, Cox, & Cox, 1977; Wallerstein & Kelly, 1976) showed that following divorce and the father leaving the home, child aggression increases. Patterson (1982) found evidence suggesting that father-absent homes produce the most severe antisocial children. The presumed cause of greater aggression is the disruption in parental management of the child caused by divorce and its accompanying stress.

Ordinal sibling position is related to aggression. The middle child is most likely to be persistently aggressive (Anderson, 1969; Rutter et al., 1970). Patterson (1982) suggests that the ideal way to learn aggression is to have an older sibling model for aggression and a younger potential victim on which to practice. Patterson's model provides an explanation for why larger family size is associated with increased aggression.

The presence of antisocial parents in the home increases the likelihood of antisocial behavior in children. For example, Robins (1979) found that for whites with an antisocial parent, the probability of being delinquent was 28%; for those without an antisocial parent, 13%. For black families with an antisocial parent, the chance of being delinquent was 43%; for other black families, 0%!

GENDER

Males are more aggressive than females and the differences between them emerge at a very early age (Feshbach, 1970; Maccoby & Jacklin, 1974; Mischel, 1966; Parke & Slaby, 1983; Patterson, 1982). Observational studies in preschool settings have consistently shown males to engage in more child-to-child aggression than females (Maccoby & Jacklin, 1974). Sex difference occur for both physical and verbal aggression, though even for preschoolers, girls rely more on verbal than physical aggression, whereas boys are equally likely to use physical or verbal aggression. Observational data (Reid, 1978), as well as teacher and parent reports (Rutter *et al.*, 1970), confirm the greater aggressiveness of males in elementary school. Patterson's systematic observations in the home (1982) confirm these sex differences. In middle childhood and adolescence these differences in the frequency of aggression result in more boys than girls being referred to clinics for the treatment of conduct disorders (Achenbach, 1982). Furthermore, adolescent boys are much more likely to commit violent crimes than adolescent girls (Gibbons, 1976; Johnson, 1979).

This sex difference in aggression is not restricted to a particular social class or culture. Maccoby and Jacklin (1974) reported sex differences across social classes. Omark and Edelman (1975) studied American, Swiss, and Ethiopian preschoolers through the third grade and found males were more physically aggressive than females in all three cultures. Whiting and Whiting (1975) studied six different cultures and also found greater male aggression in all cultures. For younger children, this result was true for both physical and verbal aggression, whereas the sex difference was limited to verbal aggression for older children in underdeveloped countries.

PARENTING INFLUENCES

A major hypothesis in the field is that ineffective parenting techniques are a necessary ingredient to the development of persistent aggression. Although some authors describe parents as permissive and others talk about parental ineffectiveness, both seem to be referring to the same parental behavior (failure to control the child's behavior) that has the same ultimate outcome (increasing the probability that the child will not follow parental directives).

These two descriptions imply different interpretations of parental motivation and skill. Permissiveness presumes that the parent allows the child to misbehave, possibly because of lack of motivation or values, whereas parental ineffectiveness typically implies a skill deficit. These interpretations have different implications for treatment. Lack of motivation suggests that parents have an appropriate level of parental skill but, due to affect/motivation, fail to adequately apply their skills. On the other hand, a skill deficit suggests training parents in the parenting skills and their application. Parental consistency appears to be closely allied to parent effectiveness. Parke and Slaby (1983) point out that parental inconsistency may refer to intra-agent inconsistency (lack of consistency of a single agent or parent) or interagent inconsistency (lack of consistency between agents or parents).

Family system theorists have focused on interagent inconsistency. Haley (1978) hypothesized that the cause of most child problems is a disrupted family hierarchy, which results when one parent aligns with a child against the other parent. The presumed cause of this cross-generational alliance is a troubled marital relationship. The evidence for marital discord leading to interparent inconsistency is minimal, even though the hypothesis may seem logical (Rutter, 1976).

Studies are needed that relate independent measures of marital discord to interparent consistency in disciplining their children. The most likely relationship is that marital discord can increase the probability of parental inconsistency. However, it seems likely that inconsistency between parents in discipline can occur without severe marital discord. Regardless of the cause, this inconsistency is associated with and probably contributes to the likelihood of a variety of child misbehavior, including aggression.

The evidence for intraparent inconsistency in aggressive families is stronger. Patterson (1982), in particular, has explored in great detail the use of consequences by aggressive and antisocial families. In general, the aggressive parent is likely to use punishment more frequently and in more severe forms. However, compared to normal families, in terms of percentages, this punishment is less likely to be used contingently with aversive behavior. Likewise, the punishment is more likely to be used contingently with prosocial behavior as compared to normal families. In short, in aggressive families there is a failure to adequately differentiate positive from aversive behavior and administer consequences to the child's behavior accordingly. In addition, the aggressive parent has a higher probability of what Patterson calls nattering—which is the use of threats, complaints, and other aversive behaviors that are ineffective in controlling the child. The parents and children in an aggressive family are more likely to engage in what Patterson refers to as a coercion process described as follows: The aggressive youngster periodically will stop his/her obnoxious behavior when the parent reaches a high level of aversive consequences, thus reinforcing the parent for aversiveness. Likewise, the parent's threats or demands to the child may be met with high levels of child aversive behavior that cause parental withdrawal of the demand, thus reinforcing the young-ster for his/her aversiveness. This process escalates over time resulting in high levels of aversive interactions between parent and child. Over time, the child develops pain control—which means that the aggressive child utilizes pain or aversive behavior to control others.

Overall, there is consistent evidence supporting the hypothesis that the parents of aggressive children are inconsistent and ineffectual in their use of discipline. Though longitudinal data pinpointing the onset of the inconsis-tent and ineffectual discipline is lacking, from observation studies, we know the parental inconsistency begins at least by preschool (Patterson, 1982).

A major question concerns what causal relationship these related char-acteristics have in the formation of aggressive traits. Parke and Slaby (1983) reviewed the literature on power-assertive disciplinary practices—which is the use of both verbal and physical punishment to control behavior. They question whether such practices are necessary for the development of ag-gression. Eron's longitudinal work on aggression (Eron, Walder, & Lefkowitz, 1971; Lefkowitz, Eron, Walder, & Huesmann, 1977) did not show parental punitiveness to be closely related to child aggression. More specifically, Lefkowitz et al. (1977) found that the current level of aggression was related to parental punitiveness only for high-aggression children with moderate parental identification. In a 10-year follow-up study of the same children, Lefkowitz et al. (1977) found that earlier parental punitiveness was not predictive of subsequent child aggression. Other studies (Johan-neson, 1974; Sears, 1961) confirm these findings.

Although these results fail to support the belief that parental power disciplinary tactics are important for the development of aggressivity in children, these findings do not eliminate the possible importance of parental negativity toward the child. The term *negativity* as used here has a broader connotation than simply punitiveness. Negativity also includes criticalness, personalized rejection, lack of acceptance, and a general expression of nega-tive affect toward the child. Most studies of aggressiveness have found some form of parental negativity in aggressive families. Maccoby and Martin (1983) identified two patterns of parental characteristics associated with child aggression. Although differing in specifics, both patterns involved low acceptance and high parental punitiveness by at least one parent. More direct evidence of the importance of parental negativity is provided by a path model constructed by Olweus (1980). Based on prior theory and re-search, Olweus assigned primary causal roles in the development of ag-gressive traits to mother's negativism and the child's temperament and secondary roles to mother's permissiveness and use of parental power as-sertive methods. In accord with Olweus's model, McColloch, Gilbert, and Johnson (1991) found observational ratings of negative affect toward the child during adolescent problem discussions to be one of the largest dif-ferences between aggressive and control families. Overall, these findings indicate that parental negativity is important and possibly essential to the development of most aggressive traits.

SOCIAL SYSTEMS INFLUENCES

It is important to remember that all single variables, such as a specific parental characteristic, have their effects within the context of the social system, and other system variables have an impact upon that variable and its influence. The simplest example of this is how feedback from the child or the child's temperament may have a substantial influence on the way the parent interacts with the child. The overall family systems model proposes that individuals and their behaviors have mutual effects upon each other, and specific behaviors have mutual effects upon each other. Furthermore, a specific behavior has multiple causal agents and is the result of the interactions of many factors. Instead of thinking in linear causality, social systems theory proposes that behavior can best be explained by circular or mutual influences among components (Haley, 1978). In addition to family systems relationships, other external social systems, such as school and work environment, can influence family functioning and the development of aggressive behavior.

TEMPERAMENT AND ELICITED SOCIAL RESPONSE

Earlier the possible influence of a "difficult" temperament upon the development of aggression was discussed. A problem with *temperament* is that the term is used so generally—to cover regularity, attentiveness, severity of response to stimuli, activity level, and the like. It would be very useful to have more information about the degree to which high negative levels of these different components of temperament are predictive of parental negativity toward the child. For example, the effect of activity level alone has been studied. Stevens-Long (1973) had adults observe videotapes of children with different activity levels, and when the child misbehaved, the observer had to choose a disciplinary tactic. Overactive children were found to elicit more severe punishments than underactive or moderately active children.

THE FAMILY SYSTEM

Patterson's work shows the advantage of a social systems perspective. As mentioned earlier, his studies demonstrate how frequent aversive exchanges among aggressive family members escalate into physical aggression and how ineffective parenting and pain control are important in the development of aggressive traits. Gottman (1979) has shown that distressed marital couples are more likely to reciprocate negative affect, and the same appears true for aggressive families.

Other family systems theorists have focused on the idea of cross-generational alliances between a parent and child as a cause of child problems. The alliance between parent and child is seen as weakening the parents' ability to act jointly in disciplining the child. This lack of parental cooperation is hypothesized to disrupt the ability of the parents to set limits and leads to the retardation of the social development of the child (Haley, 1978). However intuitively appealing, presently this theory lacks empirical support.

OTHER SOCIAL SYSTEMS

Other social systems can impact on the development of persistent aggression. One way this might occur is by external systems modifying family functioning. The most obvious influence upon family functioning is external stress. One general effect of stress is to increase emotionality and the likelihood of negative or hostile behavior toward others. Given this effect, chronic stress in parents would be expected to increase the probability of aggression due to the association between parental negativity and aggression. Little evidence has been directly gathered on the relationship between stress and aggression. However, there is evidence suggesting a positive relationship between highly stressed parents and the physical abuse of their children (Wolfe, 1985).

Although not always replicated, studies have found that preschool children in full-time day care are rated as more aggressive than children in part-time day care or raised at home. For example, children with extensive time in cognitively orientated preschools were rated by their teachers during the first 2 or 3 years of grade school. Those from the preschools were more aggressive than their peers raised at home, but the effects tended to diminish over time (Haskins, 1985). Overall, the results suggest that day care may influence the development of aggressiveness, but other factors are necessary to maintain this characteristic over time.

PEER INFLUENCES ON OTHERS

Peers have a substantial influence on the development of aggression. Exposure to aggressive peer models has been found to have a greater immediate impact upon child aggression than exposure to aggressive adult models (Hicks, 1965). Furthermore, peers can reinforce aggressive behavior and thus increase the likelihood of subsequent aggression. The ability of peers to positively reinforce aggression has been demonstrated in naturalistic (Charlesworth & Hartup, 1967) and laboratory settings (Hartup, 1964) and with trained confederates (Wahler, 1967). In a process very similar to that described previously, peers can negatively reinforce aggressive behavior. Patterson *et al.* (1976) found that the initiation of a counterattack by a child halted the aggressive attack by a peer in almost three out of four cases. This result means that aggression is generally successful in eliminating a negative stimuli, and thus the likelihood of subsequent counterattack increases. Interestingly, losing may also increase the probability of subsequent aggression. Hay and Ross (1982) found that losing a fight to a peer was more predictive of subsequent aggression toward peers than winning a fight.

INDIVIDUAL PROCESSES

This section will explore the perceptual, affective, and cognitive processes underlying the aggressive response and, in addition, will examine the relationship of an individual's social skills and personality characteristics in relation to the development of aggression.

PERCEPTUAL AND COGNITIVE PROCESSES

A major hypothesis regarding hostile aggression is that the aggressor must perceive negative intent to harm or threaten his or her self-esteem or welfare by the victim (Hartup, 1974). Because this is presumed to be true for all hostile aggressive acts, it follows that individuals who become chronically aggressive should generally perceive negative intent in others and feel that their self-esteem and welfare are threatened. There is empirical support for both of these notions. Dodge (1980) exposed aggressive and nonaggressive boys in the second through fourth grades to a frustrating negative outcome caused by a peer with either a hostile, benign, or ambiguous intent. Both types at all ages reacted with more aggression to the hostile than benign intent. However, in the ambiguous intent situation, the aggressive boys were more likely to attribute hostile intentions and to respond with aggressive behavior than the nonaggressive boys. These results suggest that aggressive boys engage in greater cue distortion in the direction of negative intent. Although this study does not address whether a change in attribution followed or preceded the development of an aggressive trait, it suggests that a tendency to perceive negative intent in others may be predictive of subsequent aggression.

Several factors contribute to the child's negative outlook. A child's view about perceived mistreatment often is similar to his/her parental views, at least for settings outside the home. Both may see the world as more hostile toward themselves than others do. These parental views then contribute to the maintenance of the child's negative attributional processes. Additionally, the high frequency of negative experiences would likely affect the perception of negative intent. For example, Patterson's work in the home has illustrated the prevalence of aversive interactions among family members. Similarly, aggressive boys not only initiate more unprovoked aggressive acts but are subject to more aggressive attacks by peers than nonaggressive boys (Dodge & Frame, 1982). Thus a confluence of experiences at home and school may operate to create a perceptual mode bent toward the anticipation of mistreatment from others.

Olweus (1975) confirmed that aggressive children develop a negative view of others. The more a child perceives negative intent, the more he/she will be aggressive. As a consequence of aggression, he/she will receive negative responses from others that in turn reinforce the perceptions that others intend the aggressive person harm. Besides developing a perception of negative intent, aggressive children also seem to develop an antisocial attitude that justifies aggression against others as the only possible response to perceived mistreatment (Patterson, 1982). Overall, it appears that the environmental conditions associated with the development of aggressive behavior also contribute to the development of a prevalent perception of negative intent by others.

AFFECT

The differentiation among negative affect, anger, and anxiety is often unclear in aggression research; however, anger appears to be the crucial affective state associated with hostile aggression. McColloch et al. (1991) found that aggressive families showed no deterioration in problem solving or increases in negative or aggressive behavior with higher levels of anxiety (when anger was not higher) than control families. Furthermore, Zillman and his associates found that heightened arousal did not contribute to subsequent aggression toward a confederate unless the experimental situation allowed them to mislabel the arousal as anger (Zillman, Johnson, & Day, 1974).

One way anger may influence aggression is by changing an individual's goals. Hostile aggression has the goal of injuring someone. What is new is not whether the reinforcement processes apply, but a change in goals. The goals may include physical damage or broader psychological damage such as defeat, humiliation, or anxiousness for perceived mistreatment by others. Some evidence supports this hypothesized change in goals. For example, studies show that pain feedback often inhibits an aggressor's attack (Baron, 1971; Milgram, 1974). One interpretation of this inhibition is that the pain feedback tells the aggressor that the retaliatory goal has been obtained, and therefore the attack is terminated. Also, Hay and Ross (1982) examined the effect of winning and losing conflicts with peers upon the subsequent initiation of conflict with peers. The prior outcome influenced subsequent conflict, with the loser of the prior conflict much more likely to initiate a conflict.

Another affective variable requiring consideration is the effect of an individual's aversive and aggressive behavior upon the affect of others. Patterson's (1982) research shows that over two-thirds of coercive chains initiated by the antisocial or aggressive child are unprovoked. This means that the parents of aggressive children and likely others in their environment are frequently dealing with largely unpredictable aversive events. One emotion the child's aversive behavior elicits from others is anger that in turn may influence the aggressive child's emotional state. This behavioral and emotional interactive pattern is likely to operate to maintain the anger and hostile world view of the aggressive youngster.

SOCIAL SKILLS

Aggressive behavior and social skills clearly covary (see Patterson, 1982, for review). Aggressive children have poor academic, interpersonal, and self-control skills. Three primary models of the relationship between social skills and aggression have been proposed. One is that aggressive characteristics occur and lead to the development of social skills deficits (Patterson, 1982). The child is seen as showing an early (preschool) aggressive characteristic that becomes the preferred mode of coping with conflict. This tactical choice is effective in the home and other environments—primarily in providing escape from parental demands. Once established, its consistent use prevents the development of other skills. This model assumes that social skill deficits are not important in the development of aggression but are significant in the maintenance of an aggressive pattern.

The second model assumes a more parallel development of social skill deficits and aggressive behavioral characteristics. Lack of social skills in certain situations might cause anger that, in turn, leads to aggressive actions. The development of social skill deficits and the tendency to respond to frustration with aggression would occur independently and would largely be controlled by different variables. The link between them would be the affective response of frustration or anger. Within this model, it is important to know how social skills develop in order to prevent the development of aggression.

Similar to the first model, the third model hypothesizes a direct causal link between social skills deficits and aggression. However, this model proposes that skills deficiencies precede aggression. Social skills deficits that could increase aggressivity include the abilities to take another's perspective, to empathize with others, to delay gratification, or to use verbal mediation to inhibit impulses and to anticipate possible consequences.

PERSONALITY

Several personality traits are related to aggressivity. Low need achievement, high trait anxiety, and extraversion are more characteristic of aggressive boys than nonaggressive ones (Camp, 1977). Additionally, persons with Type A personality behavior patterns generally behave more aggressively than Type B persons. However, Holmes and Will (1985) found that when not angered, Type A's and B's did not differ in their level of aggression. After inducing anger, however, the Type A's used higher levels of punishment than Type B's. Overall, most of these personality characteristics that have been identified as being associated with aggression appear to increase the probability of anger reactions. Anger and, specifically, anger without instrumental contingencies appears to mediate the aggressiveness.

MAINTENANCE OF THE AGGRESSIVE TRAIT

The following discussion explores factors that help predict which children will remain aggressive and/or develop other major problems.

PARENT AND FAMILY VARIABLES

Parental deficits in disciplining the child appear basic to the development and maintenance of an aggressive trait. Social learning theory predicts that if the parent(s) are highly inconsistent and harsh in their discipline, it would be predictive of continued aggression. Even with substantial improvement in parenting skills, the child may not change easily because the pattern is well established. Working with parents, one often sees substantial resistance by the aggressive child to treatment efforts. Even after successful treatment, relapses are frequently observed (Patterson, 1982).

Furthermore, the characteristics of the parent are related to poor parent–child interactions and problematic child behavior. Kagan and Moss (1962) found that parents of aggressive children to be angry individuals. These parents showed deficiencies in cognitive, social, and parenting skills and a general inability to cope with problems. In these cases, not only is the parent a poor model for social competence and positive affect but a contributor to the general negative interactional style within the family. As mentioned earlier, a high rate of negativity among aggressive family members appears to be important in the development and maintenance of aggressive traits.

It appears likely that the low level of positive interactions between the child and his or her parent(s) or others needs to be overcome if changes in aggressivity are to occur. Clinical observations suggest that when the aggressive child feels no support or warmth from the parent, he/she is unmotivated to reduce negative behavior. Supportive of this conclusion, Alexander (1973) examined communications within families and found that a son's aggressiveness was negatively correlated with both his mother's and father's supportiveness. The level and effect of positive interactions, as well as the relationship of these interactions to feelings of support and rejection, should be a focus of future investigations.

A barrier to more positive parental attitudes and interactions with the child is the child's aversive behavior itself. The parent of the conduct-disordered child combines rejection of the child, frequent use of physical punishment, and withdrawal of privileges with a lack of confidence in the child's morality and self-control (Hetherington, Stouwie, & Ridberg, 1971). These parental views, which are based on the child's behavior, serve to maintain the family structure and perception of the problem.

A lack of clarity in the standards for behavior is another problem that maintains the child's misbehavior and aggressiveness. The aggressive home tends to be chaotic, with an absence of clear expectations regarding child responsibilities and roles (Garmezy, 1974; Hetherington, Cox, & Cox, 1977). The difficulties with consistency in disciplinary consequences (Patterson, 1982) and consistency between parents (McCord & McCord, 1959) have the effect of clouding expectations. The process of the child continually resisting parental demands until the parents give up seems to make parental expectations appear changeable. Continual stress placed on the family may lead the parents to change their reactions and thresholds for response, which again will increase inconsistency.

In this type of home atmosphere, poor problem solving is not surprising. The child participates minimally in family interactions and decision making and often fails to reach agreement with his/her parents when discussing personally relevant material (McColloch *et al.*, 1991). These problem-solving difficulties are a mechanism for preventing the resolution of differences in a nonaggressive fashion and, again, serve to maintain the family system and the aggressiveness of the child.

PEER VARIABLES

A consistent finding is that children with persistent aggression are rejected by peers, presumably because of the severity and inappropriateness of their aggression (Parke & Slaby, 1983). Even when placed in a new group, the aggressive child continues to behave aggressively and again suffers peer rejection (Coie & Kupersmidt, 1983). Once a pattern of rejection by peers is established, it is highly resistant to change even when the aggressive child's behavior greatly improves (Ollendick & Cerny, 1981). This ingrained response and continued rejection by peers is undermining to the previously aggressive youngster's new behavior patterns and, in general, contributes to the likelihood of a relapse to previous behavior patterns.

In addition to peer rejection, other peer variables may be important. Peer reinforcement, modeling, and eliciting of aggression almost certainly help maintain the aggressive trait. Related to this is peer group norms that may value aggressivity. Gang aggression is a good example. In highly aggressive gangs, group members obtain higher levels of status for aggressive behavior and are encouraged to be threatening and tough. Frequent belligerent encounters provide the opportunity of aggression modeling and pull for aggressive responses. As long as one participates in a group that highly values aggressivity, aggressive behavior patterns may be expected to continue.

OTHER SYSTEM VARIABLES

Systems outside the home and eternal to peer groups respond in ways that may either detract or contribute to the continuance of aggression. For example, beginning at an early age, parents receive feedback about the aversive behavior of their child from baby-sitters, relatives, and preschool programs. At some point in time, the message will be that "something must be done." Concurrently, a continuum of responses ranging from excluding the child from that system to providing help in changing the child will be offered to the parent(s). The exclusionary response may increase the probability of the child's remaining aggressive by raising parental negative emotionality toward the him or her and, thus, perpetuating their inconsistent, severe, and ineffective approach to discipline. Likewise, the response furthers the parents' feelings of isolation and their perceptions of mistreatment by a hostile world. Offering appropriate help to the family may increase the probability that parents will improve in their parenting abilities and reduce the problematic behavior of their child.

PERCEPTUAL AND COGNITIVE PROCESSES

The youngster's perceptual and attributional propensities and styles have clear implications for maintenance of aggressive behavior patterns. Dodge (1980) showed that aggressive boys were more likely to perceive ambiguous cues as indicating negative intent and suggested several ways in which these biased perceptions might be enhanced and exacerbated over time. One way involves hostile perceptions as a self-fulfilling prophecy. Perceptions lead to behavior that elicits hostile reactions in others. Another avenue proposes that the child is prepared to respond affectively to any conditioned provocative cue with an aggressive response. In a final way, the child's biased information processing proclivities operate to isolate him from information contrary to his hostile view of others. Thus corrective feedback does not occur. Additionally, Dodge found that aggressive boys were twice as likely as nonaggressive boys to attribute hostile intent in hypothetical situations and to suggest that the appropriate response to these situations would be to retaliate aggressively. This original work of Dodge (1980) showed that a hostile attributional bias for aggressive children occurs only with ambiguous cues. More recent work (Dodge & Frame, 1982) indicates that aggressive children show more hostile interpretations of motives than nonaggressive children when there is a clear negative outcome. However, this is likely to occur only when the potential recipient of a negative outcome is the aggressive child. That is, the aggressive child interprets or expects negative behavior to be accompanied by hostile intent when it happens to him/her but does not interpret the same hostile intent when the negative outcome happens to others.

Dodge and Frame (1982) explored some possible causes of this negative attributional bias. One general explanation is that the bias is based on a personalized paranoid view of the world. This explanation depends upon underdeveloped skill in information processing (for example, poor social role-taking skill) or having been subject to some bias-inducing circumstances. This explanation does not assume other differences in information processing between aggressive and nonaggressive individuals. Another explanation proposes that the normal processing of information is disrupted by negative emotional reactions that cause the processing to be biased. This explanation views irrational informational processing as occurring in response to specific cues in order to account for the attributional bias. One hypothesis from this perspective is that aggressive children are perceptually ready to attribute hostility. In other words, hostile explanations are "more available" to explain events than nonhostile explanations. This position is supported by a study by Dodge and Newman (1981) where children listened to child-taped testimonies before deciding intent. The aggressive children listened to less than half as many testimonies before deciding than did the nonaggressive group and attributed a higher proportion of negative intent to the events.

Another hypothesis pertains to the possible biasing effects of emotional states. From this perspective, an emotional state is expected to short-circuit usual information processing and lead directly to hostile attributions. For example, in a study by Dodge and Frame (1982), aggressive boys were no different from nonaggressive boys in attributing hostile intent when provocation was directed at a peer. However, when the provocation was directed at the aggressive youngster, he was much more likely to attribute hostile intentions than his nonaggressive peers. One difference in this scenario is that the person receiving the provocation would be emotionally aroused. Less direct support for this hypothesis comes from other data regarding emotional arousal. When in a negative emotional state, children are more likely to choose a small, immediate reward over a larger delayed reward (Seeman & Schwarz, 1974; Schwarz & Pollach, 1977) and less likely to resist temptation and to consider alternative courses of action (Mischel & Baker, 1975).

AFFECT

McColloch *et al.* (1991) showed that families with an aggressive adolescent displayed negative and competitive behavior when angry, but when not angry (even when high in anxiety), their negativeness and problem solving were not different from those of control families. As part of their study of adult influence on the emotions and aggression of young children, Cummings, Rannotti, and Zahn-Waxler (1985) examined the behavior of the more aggressive youngsters. Compared to other conditions, the highly aggressive group showed over four times as much aggression after exposure to conflict and anger between adults. Presumably, this exposure elicited hostility in these children. Also, Cummings *et al.* found that, for all children, a second exposure to this adult conflict and anger substantially increased child distress and aggression over the first exposure. Thus hostility-eliciting cues do not lose their potency in provoking anger. It seems clear that anger plays a major mediating role for the chronically aggressive.

Other emotional reactions may indirectly influence aggressive behavior. Aggressive children report feelings of loneliness and social isolation. These feelings, and the accompanying perception of mistreatment, may increase the likelihood of perceiving those situations in which they are excluded or not included as incidents of hostile rejection and, in turn, responding to these situations with aggression. Again, the aggressive reactions perpetuates the pattern by resulting in more exclusion by peers, more feelings of loneliness and more subsequent aggression.

SOCIAL SKILLS

Children with aggressive characteristics are widely reported to have many deficiencies in the area of social skills. One explanatory model is that early development of an aggressive style operates to minimize the development of other social-skill and problem-solving techniques (Patterson, 1982). In problem situations, the child draws on those skills he/she has developed. In short, this model suggests that due to lack of other social skills to handle problem situations, the aggressive youngster falls back on aggressivity. This, in turn, operates to prevent the development of new, nonaggressive skills.

Another model focuses on the social cognitive skills necessary to inhibit aggression. These skills might generally be referred to as self-control skills and may include such specific abilities as empathy, perspective taking, delay of gratification, anticipation of long-term consequences, cognitive control of affective responses, prosocial values, and feelings of responsibility for actions. This model has an intuitive appeal for those working with aggressive adolescents (Pulkkinen, 1984). These youngsters appear to lose their ability to control themselves when angered and seem deficient in understanding or empathizing with others' feelings or to regret their actions. Some research support for this position has already been presented.

A problem for models describing the relationship between social skill and aggressive behavior is that the apparent lack of skill in a situation may primarily reflect a lack of motivation. Pulkkinen (1984) has said that "the difficulty for the aggressive boys seems to be one of implementing the skills they possess." Studies are needed where adequate incentives are provided for the subjects to demonstrate their repertoire of social skills, including behavioral and social cognitive skills.

SITUATIONAL INFLUENCES

Situational differences between conditions where anger is or is not elicited points to the importance of personal relevancy of the situation. McColloch et al. (1991) examined the impact of situational influences upon task performance for families with aggressive adolescents and control families. The aggressive families showed more negativeness and poorer problem solving during the adolescent problem discussions but did not differ in problem solving from control families in discussing the marital problems. A major finding was that anger appeared to be the crucial mediator of negative and competitive behavior and poorer problem solving for aggressive families. These results are congruent with Hartup's (1974) hypotheses that threat to self-esteem would be crucial for the elicitation of anger and the occurrence of hostile aggression.

SUMMARY

This chapter has reviewed the primary theories and relevant research pertaining to aggressive behavior patterns. The focus has been divided into two parts—the first part on the development of aggressive behavior patterns and the second on its maintenance. From these overall perspectives, the influence of constitutional factors, environmental and family factors, and individual factors has been explored.

In approaching the topic of aggressivity in this manner, it becomes apparent that the phenomena of aggressivity is a product of the interaction of psychological, biological, social, and ecological factors. To discuss one of these factors in isolation of the others limits the validity and generalizability of the findings. Both model building and research will be more productive and relevant when viewed from this larger perspective.

REFERENCES

Achenbach, T. M. (1982). *Developmental psychopathology* (2nd ed.). New York: Wiley.
Achenbach, T. M., & Edelbrook, C. (1983). *Manual for the Child Behavior Checklist and*

Revised Child Behavior Profile. Burlington: University of Vermont, Department of Psychiatry.

Alexander, J. F. (1973). Defensive and supportive communications in normal and deviant families. *Journal of Consulting and Clinical Psychology, 40,* 223–231.

Anderson, L. M. (1969). Personality characteristics of neurotic, aggressive, and normal preadolescent boys. *Journal of Consulting and Clinical Psychology, 33*(5), 575–581.

Baron, R. A. (1971). Magnitude of victim's pain cues and level of prior anger arousal as determinants of adult aggressive behavior. *Journal of Experimental Social Psychology, 2,* 343–355.

Baron, R. A. (1977). *Human aggression.* New York: Plenum Press.

Bates, J. E., Olson, S. L., Pettit, G. S., & Bayles, K. (1982). Dimensions of individuality in the mother-infant relationship at six months of age. *Child Development, 53,* 446–461.

Burgess, R., & Conger, R. (1978). Family interaction in abusive, neglectful, and normal families. *Child Development, 49,* 1163–1173.

Buss, A. H. (1966). Instrumentality of aggression feedback and frustration as determinants of physical aggression. *Journal of Personality and Social Psychology, 1,* 249–255.

Camp, B. W. (1977). Verbal mediation in young aggressive boys. *Journal of Abnormal Psychology, 86,* 145–153.

Charlesworth, R., & Hartup, W. W. (1967). Positive social reinforcement in the nursery school peer group. *Child Development, 38,* 993–1002.

Coie, J. D., & Kupersmidt, J. B. (1983). A behavioral analysis of emerging social status in boys groups. *Child Development, 54*(6), 1400–1416.

Constanzo, P. R., & Dix, T. H. (1983). Beyond the information processed: Socialization in the development of attributional processes. In E. T. Higgings, D. N. Ruble, and W. W. Hartup (Eds.), *Social cognition and social development: A sociocultural perspective* (pp. 63–81). New York: Cambridge University Press.

Cummings, E. M., Rannotti, R. J., & Zahn-Waxler, C. (1985). Influence of conflict between adults on the emotions and aggression of young children. *Developmental Psychology, 21*(3), 495–507.

Deur, J. L., & Parke, R. D. (1970). Effects of inconsistent punishment on aggression in children. *Developmental Psychology, 2,* 403–411.

Dodge, K. (1980). Social cognition and children's aggressive behavior. *Child Development, 51,* 162–170.

Dodge, K. A., & Newman, J. P. (1981). Biased decision making processes in aggressive boys. *Journal of Abnormal Psychology, 90,* 375–379.

Dodge, K. A., & Frame, C. L. (1982). Social cognitive biases and deficits in aggressive boys. *Child Development, 53,* 620–635.

Dumas, J. E., & Wahler, K. G. (1985, March). Indiscriminate mothering as a contextual factor in aggressive-oppositional child behavior: "Damned if you do and damned if you don't." *Journal of Abnormal Child Psychology, 13*(1), 1–17.

Ehrhardt, A. A., & Baker, S. W. (1974). Fetal androgens, human central nervous system differentiation and behavior sex differences. In R. Rubart, R. Friedman, R. Richart, & R. Wanda Wiele (Eds.), *Sex differences in behavior* (pp. 33–51). New York: Wiley.

Eron, L. D., & Huesmann, L. R. (1984). The relation of prosocial behavior to the development of aggression and psychopathology. *Aggressive Behavior, 10*(3), 201–211.

Eron, L. O., Walder, L. O., & Lefkowitz, M. M. (1971). *Learning of aggression in children.* Boston: Little, Brown & Co.

Eysenck, H. J., & Eysenck, M. W. (1985). *Personality and individual differences: A natural sciences approach.* New York: Plenum Press.

Ferguson, T. J., & Rule, B. G. (1980). Effects of inferential set, outcome severity, and basis of responsibility on children's evaluations of aggressive acts. *Developmental Psychology, 16,* 141–146.

Feshbach, S. (1964). The function of aggression and the regulation of aggressive drive. *Psychological Review, 71,* 257–272.

Feshbach, S. (1970). Aggression. In P. H. Mussen (Ed.), *Carmichaels manual of child psychology* (Vol. 2, pp. 159–259). New York: Wiley & Sons.

Garmezy, N. (1974). The study of competence in children at risk for severe psychopathology. In E. J. Anthony & C. Koupernik (Eds.), *The child in his family: Children at psychiatric risk. III* (pp. 77–98). New York: Wiley.

Gibbons, D. C. (1976). *Delinquent behavior* (2nd ed.), Englewood Cliffs, NJ: Prentice-Hall.

Gilbert, D. G., Johnson, S., McColloch, M. A., & Gilbert, B. (in press). Electro-cortical and electro-dermal activities differences between aggressive adolescents and controls. *Journal of Personality & Social Behavior.*

Goodenough, F. L. (1931). *Anger in young children.* Minneapolis: University of Minnesota Press.

Gottman, J. M. (1979). *Marital interaction: Experimental investigations.* New York: Academic Press.

Haley, J. (1978). *Problem solving therapy.* San Francisco: Jossey-Bass.

Hare, R. D., & Jutai, J. W. (1988). Psychopathy and cerebral asymmetry in semantic processing. *Personality and Individual Differences, 9,* 329–337.

Hartup, W. W. (1964). Friendship status and the effectiveness of peers as reinforcing agents. *Journal of Experimental Child Psychology, 1,* 154–162.

Hartup, W. W. (1974). Aggression in childhood: Developmental perspectives. *American Psychologist, 29,* 336–339.

Haskins, R. (1985, June). Public school aggression among children with varying day-care experience. *Child Development, 56*(3), 689–703.

Hay, D. F., & Ross, H. S. (1982). The social nature of early conflict. *Child Development, 53,* 105–113.

Hetherington, E. M., Stouwie, R. J., & Ridberg, E. H. (1971). Patterns of family interaction and child-rearing attitudes related to three dimensions of juvenile delinquency. *Journal of Abnormal Psychology, 78*(2), 160–176.

Hetherington, E. M., Cox, M., & Cox, R. (1976). Divorced fathers. *Family Coordination, 25,* 417–428.

Hetherington, E. M., Cox, M., & Cox, R. (1977). The aftermath of divorce. In J. Stevens & M. Mathews (Eds.), *Mother-child, father-child relations* (pp. 149–176). Washington, DC: National Association for the Education of Young Children.

Hicks, D. J. (1965). Imitation and retention of film-mediated aggressive peer and adult models. *Journal of Personality and Social Psychology, 2,* 97–100.

Holmes, D. S., & Will, M. J. (1985). Expression of interpersonal aggression by angered and nonangered persons with the Type A and Type B behavior patterns. *Journal of Personality and Social Psychology, 48*(3), 723–727.

Isen, A. M., & Shalker, T. E. (1982). The effect of feeling state on evaluation of positive, neutral, and negative stimuli: When you "accentuate the positive," do you "eliminate the negative"? *Social Psychology Quarterly, 45*(1), 58–63.

Johanneson, A. (1974). Aggressive behavior among school children related to maternal practices in early childhood. In J. deWit & W. W. Hartup (Eds.), *Determinants and origins of aggressive behavior.* The Hague: Mouton.

Johnson, R. E. (1979). *Juvenile delinquency and its origins.* New York: Cambridge University Press.

Kagan, J., & Moss, H. (1962). *Birth to maturity.* New York: Wiley.

Kreuz, L. E., & Rose, R. M. (1972). Assessment of aggressive behavior and plasma testosterone in a young criminal population. *Psychosomatic Medicine, 34,* 321–332.

Langlois, J., & Downs, C. (1979). Peer relations as a function of physical attractiveness: The eye of the beholder or behavioral reality? *Child Development, 50,* 409–418.

Lefkowitz, M. M., Eron, L. D., Walder, L. O., & Huesmann, L. R. (1977). *Growing up to be violent: A longitudinal study of the development of aggression.* New York: Pergamon Press.

Lewis, D. O., Pincus, J. H., Shanok, S. S., & Glaser, G. H. (1982). Psychomotor epilepsy and violence in a group of incarcerated adolescent boys. *American Journal of Psychiatry, 139,* 882–887.

Maccoby, E., & Jacklin, C. (1974). *The psychology of sex differences.* Stanford: Stanford University Press.

Maccoby, E., & Martin, J. (1983). Socialization in the context on the family: Parent-child interaction. In E. M. Hetherington (Ed.), *Socialization, personality, and social development* (Vol. 4), *Handbook of child psychology* (pp. 1233–1486). New York: Wiley.

Mattsson, A., & Kim, S. P. (1982). Blood disorders. *Psychiatric Clinics of North America, 5*(2), 345–356.

McClearn, G. E. (1970). Genetic influences on behavior and development. In P. H. Mussen (Ed.), *Carmichael's Manual of Child Psychology* (Vol. 1; pp. 421–484). New York: Wiley.

McColloch, M. A., Gilbert, D. G., & Johnson, S. (1991). Effects of situational variables on the interpersonal behavior of families with an aggressive adolescent. *Personality and Individual Differences, 11,* 1–11.

McCord, W., & McCord, J. (1959). *Origins of crime.* New York: Columbia University Press.

Mednick, S., Gabrielli, W., & Hutchings, B. (1984). Genetic influences in criminal convictions: Evidence from an adoption cohort. *Science, 224,* 891–894.

Milgram, S. (1974). *Obedience to authority.* New York: Harper & Row.

Mischel, W. (1966). A social-learning view of sex differences in behavior. In E. Maccoby (Ed.), *The development of sex differences* (pp. 56–81). Stanford, CA: Stanford University Press.

Mischel, W., & Baker, L. (1975). Cognitive transformations of reward objects through instructions. *Journal of Personality and Social Psychology, 31,* 254–261.

Moyer, K. E. (1986). Biological bases of aggressive behavior. In P. Peutchik & H. Kellerman (Eds.), *Emotion: Theory, research and experience* (pp. 103–142). Orlando: Academic Press.

Newman, J. P., Widom, C. S., & Nathan, S. (1985). Passive avoidance in syndromes of disinhibition, psychopathy and extraversion. *Journal of Personality and Social Psychology, 48,* 1316–1327.

Ollendick, T., & Cerny, J. (1987). *Clinical behavior therapy with children.* New York: Plenum Press.

Olweus, D. (1973). Personality and aggression. In J. K. Cole and D. D. Jensen (Eds.), *Nebraska Symposium on Motivation, 1972* (pp. 261–321). Lincoln: University of Nebraska Press.

Olweus, D. (1975, June). *'Modern' interactionism in personality psychology and the analysis of variance components approach. A critical examination.* Paper presented at the Symposium on Interactional Psychology, Saltsjöbaden, Sweden.

Olweus, D. (1977). Aggression and peer acceptance in adolescent boys: Two short-term longitudinal studies of ratings. *Child Development, 48,* 1301–1313.

Olweus, D. (1979). Stability of aggressive reaction patterns in males: A review. *Psychological Bulletin, 86*(4), 852–875.

Olweus, D., Mattsson, A., Schalling, D., & Low, H. (1980). Testosterone, aggression, physical and personality dimensions on normal adolescent males. *Psychosomatic Medicine, 42,* 253–269.

Olweus, D. (1980). Familial and temperamental determinants of aggressive behavior in adolescent boys: A causal analysis. *Developmental Psychology, 16,* 644–666.

Olweus, D. (1982). Development of stable aggressive reaction pattern. In R. J. Blanchard & C. Blanchard (Eds.), *Advances in the study of aggression* (Vol. 1, pp. 103–134). New York: Academic Press.

Omark, D. R., & Edelman, M. S. (1975). Formation of dominance hierarchies in young children:

Attention and perception. In T. Williams (Ed.), *Psychological anthropology*. The Hague: Mouton Press.

Parke, R. D., & Slaby, R. G. (1983). In P. H. Mussen (Ed.), *Handbook of child psychology*. New York: Wiley.

Patterson, G. R. (1976). The aggressive child: Victim and architect of a coercive system. In E. J. Mash, L. A. Hamerlynck, & L. C. Handy (Eds.), *Behavior modification and families* (Vol. 1). New York: Brunner/Mazel.

Patterson, G. R. (1982). *A social learning approach to family intervention. Vol. 3. Coercive family process*. Eugene, OR: Castalia.

Patterson, G. R., Littman, R. A., & Bricker, W. (1984). Assertive behavior in children: A Step toward a theory of aggression. *Monographs of the Society for Research in Child Development, 32*(5), 1–43.

Persky, H., Smith, K. D., & Basn, G. K. (1971). Relation of psychological measures of aggression and hostility to testosterone production in man. *Psychosomatic Medicine, 33*, 265–277.

Persky, H. (1974). Reproductive hormones, moods, and the menstrual cycle. In R. C. Friedman, R. M. Richart, & R. L. Vande Wiele (Eds.), *Sex differences in behavior* (pp. 455–466). New York: Wiley.

Pulkkinen, L. (1984). The inhibition and control of aggression. *Aggressive Behavior, 10*(3), 221–225.

Reid, J. B. (Ed). (1978). *A social learning approach to intervention. Vol. 2. Observation in home settings*. Eugene, OR: Castalia.

Reinisch, J. M. (1981). Prenatal exposure to synthetic progestins increases potential for aggression in humans. *Science, 211*, 1171–1173.

Robins, L. N. (1979). Follow-up studies. In H. C. Quay & J. S. Werry (Eds.), *Psychopathological disorders of childhood* (2nd ed.). New York: Wiley.

Rotenberg, K. J. (1980). Children's use of intentionality in judgments of character and disposition. *Child Development, 51*, 282–284.

Rule, B. G., & Nesdale, A. R. (1976). Emotional arousal and aggressive behavior. *Psychological Bulletin, 83*(5), 851–863.

Rutter, M. (1976, May). Isle of Wight studies 1964–1974. *Psychological Medicine, 6*(2), 313–332.

Rutter, M., Tizard, J., & Whitmore, R. (1970). *Education, health, and behavior*. New York: Wiley.

Schwarz, J. C., & Pollack, P. R. (1977, June). Affect and delay of gratification. *Journal of Research in Personality, 11*(2), 147–164.

Sears, R. R. (1961). Relation of early socialization experiences to aggression in middle childhood. *Journal of Abnormal & Social Psychology, 63*, 466–492.

Seeman, G., & Schwarz, J. C. (1974). Affective state and preference for immediate versus delayed reward. *Journal of Research in Personality, 7*(4), 384–394.

Shantz, D. W., & Voydanoff, D. A. (1973). Situational effects on retaliatory aggression at three age levels. *Child Development, 44*, 149–153.

Stevens-Long, J. (1973). The effect of behavioral context on some aspects of adult disciplinary practice and effect. *Child Development, 44*, 476–484.

Thomas, A., & Chess, S. (1977). Evolution of behavior disorders into adolescence. *Annual Progress in Child Psychiatry and Child Development*, 489–497.

Thomas, A., & Chess, S. (1980). *The dynamics of psychological development*. New York: Brunner/Mazel.

Thomas, A., Chess, S., & Birch, H. (1968). *Temperament and behavior disorders in children*. New York: New York University Press.

Tieger, T. (1980). On the biological basis of sex differences in aggression. *Child Development, 51*, 943–963.

Wahler, R. G. (1967). Child-child interactions in five field settings: Some experimental analyses. *Journal of Experimental Child Psychology, 5*, 278–293.

Wallerstein, J. S., & Kelly, J. B. (1976). The effects of parental divorce: Experiences of the child in later latency. *American Journal of Orthopsychiatry, 46*(2), 256–269.

Whiting, B. B., & Whiting, J. M. (1975). *Children of six cultures.* Cambridge: Harvard University Press.

Williams, J. F., Meyesson, L. J., Eron, L. D., & Sender, I. J. (1967). Peer-related aggression and aggressive responses elicited in an experimental situation. *Child Development, 38*, 181–190.

Winder, C. L., & Wiggins, J. S. (1964). Social reputation and social behavior: A further validation of the Peer Nomination Inventory. *Journal of Abnormal and Social Psychology, 68*, 681–684.

Witkin, H., Mednick, S., Schulsinger, F., & Owen, D. (1976). Criminality in XYY and XXY men. *Science, 193*, 547–555.

Wolfe, D. (1985). Child abusive parents: An empirical review and analysis. *Psychological Bulletin, 97*, 462–482.

Zajonc, R. B. (1976). Family configuration and intelligence. *Science, 192*, 227–236.

Zillman, D., Johnson, R. C., Day, K. D. (1974). Attribution of apparent arousal and proficiency of recovery from sympathetic activation affecting excitation transfer to aggressive behavior. *Journal of Experimental Social Psychology, 10*(6), 503–515.

CHAPTER NINE

Social Skills Training for Alcoholics

Conceptual, Methodological, and Treatment Issues

EMIL CHIAUZZI

INTRODUCTION

Nancy Reagan's "Just Say No" campaign focused much attention on the needs for refusal skills and self-assertion in resisting drug and alcohol abuse (Diamint, 1988). Many substance abuse treatment programs routinely include assertiveness training as part of treatment. Authors writing about adult children of alcoholics also stress the need for open expression of feelings in interpersonal contexts (Beattie, 1987). The interpersonal emphasis of these trends suggests a need to reexamine the contribution of social skills theories to alcoholism treatment.

The social skills theory has been particularly prominent in behavioral conceptualizations of alcoholism. Behavioral psychologists have theorized that interpersonal skills deficits increase the likelihood of abusive drinking in sober alcoholics (Nathan, 1985) and that interpersonal situations requiring appropriate social skills may provoke anxiety or tension that precipitate abusive drinking in the absence of other behavioral alternatives (Hamburg, 1975). There also appears to be a modeling effect, as Collins and Marlatt (1981) have found that an individual's consumption of alcohol will vary to match that of a drinking partner. Overall, it seems clear that because alcohol use is a socially mediated activity, there should be assessment and intervention developed in this area.

EMIL CHIAUZZI • Northeast Psychiatric Associates, Brookside Hospital, Nashua, New Hampshire 03063.

Personality, Social Skills, and Psychopathology: An Individual Differences Approach, edited by David G. Gilbert and James J. Connolly. Plenum Press, New York, 1991.

This chapter will evaluate the conceptual, methodological, and treatment issues involved in social skills training for alcoholics. For the purposes of this chapter, the terms *social skills* and *assertiveness* will be used interchangeably. Reviewers in the field (e.g., Van Hasselt, Hersen, & Milliones, 1978) generally equate the two because most studies focus on open expressions of feeling when using the term *social skills*. Broader uses of this term (to include moral behavior or social "strategy") are not found in the alcoholism literature. In addition, this review will be confined to studies of alcoholics and problem drinkers and the nature of the relationship between drinking and social interaction. This chapter will address the following three questions:

1. In comparison to other populations, do alcoholics have social skills deficits and what is the nature of these deficits?
2. Is there a causal link between alcoholism and social skills deficits?
3. Are social skills treatments effective in improving social skills of alcoholics and if so, does it affect their abusive drinking?

THE SOCIAL SKILLS CONCEPTS

BEHAVIORAL THERAPY

The behavioral approach to treatment in general involves three major concepts: (1) the concept of skill; (2) situational specificity; and (3) reinforcement maximation (Bellack & Morrison, 1982).

In terms of the skill concept, the behavioral approach considers maladaptive behavior to result from inadequate skill development. It does not consider maladaptive behavior to be a function of particular personality traits, which may possibly be resistant to remediation. Instead, each individual's deficits are conceptualized within a learning model and therefore taught the components of skills required to eliminate the problem behavior. For instance, in terms of social skills, an alcoholic may have difficulty making eye contact in peer pressure situations. The behavior therapist would seek to train this behavior in order to help the alcoholic articulate his or her concerns in a more direct manner.

Situational specificity is a very important part of behavioral treatment of alcoholism. Rather than assuming that an individual behaves similarly in all situations (connoting a personality trait), the behavioral approach suggests that each individual varies his or her behavior as a function of his environment. In the case of the alcoholic, this may mean that he or she is socially skilled in certain situations and unskilled in others. The alcoholic may have no difficulty asserting himself with his wife, but when it comes to asking for a raise, may experience a great deal of activity. The behavioral approach would seek to target those situations in which the alcoholic has difficulty rather than taking a global approach.

The behavioral approach seeks to maximize reinforcement. This means that the therapist will attempt to train behaviors that are most likely to be reinforced by others, are frequent, and have a high probability of resulting in reinforcement. For instance, the behavior therapist would not spend much time working on a situation that occurs once a year (such as visits from relatives on holidays) but would seek to establish a linkage between frequent drinking and related social skills situations (such as drinking when feeling socially anxious).

COMPONENTS

Bellack, Hersen, and Himmelhoch (1978) have described the major components of social skills. For the purposes of this chapter, Hersen and Bellack's (1977) definition of social skills will be used:

> We therefore emphasize an individual's ability to express both positive and negative feelings in the interpersonal context without suffering consequent loss of social reinforcement. Such skill is demonstrated in a large variety of interpersonal contexts . . . and involves the coordinated delivery of appropriate verbal and nonverbal responses. In addition, a socially skilled individual is attuned to the realities of the situation and is aware when he/she is likely to be reinforced for his/her efforts. Thus, at times, the socially skilled individual may have to forego the expression of "hostile" assertiveness if such expression is likely to result in punishment or social censure. (p. 512)

On the basis of this definition, Bellack *et al.* have divided social skills into four basic categories: (1) expressive elements; (2) receptive elements; (3) interactive balance; and (4) cognitive factors.

Expressive Elements

Expressive elements can be further subdivided into speech content, paralinguistic cues, and nonverbal cues. Speech content simply consists of what a person says. Paralinguistic cues refer to voice quality, the manner in which a person speaks. Paralinguistic cues mainly consist of intonation but can also represent any other feature that communicates emotion or inflection. Nonverbal cues refer to the ways in which people use their bodies when speaking. Examples are eye contact, facial expressions, kinesics (such as hand gestures), and proxemics (the physical distancing and learning between people).

Receptive Elements

These elements can be divided into attention and decoding, which represent the sensing, processing, and interpretation of information. Within this category, it will also be important to remember the importance of contextual factors and cultural mores as social "filters."

Interactive Balance

This category refers to the timing of responses within a social interchange. Because communication is a dynamic process, it is important for individuals to time their responses at particular points in a conversation and also be able to take turns within a conversation. If an individual is constantly interrupting or if there is a long lag between communications of the individual and his or her partner, there will be an alteration in the meaning of the communications.

Cognitive Factors

This is an extremely broad category and needs to be carefully considered when training social skills. There are five major subcategories within cognitive factors of social skill training: (1) socialization messages; (2) self-efficacy; (3) self-statements; (4) social perception; and (5) faulty discrimination. Socialization messages are extremely critical in how a person evaluates a message (Lange & Jakubowski, 1976). These messages may involve slang, idioms, or attitudes internalized during an individual's developmental years. Self-efficacy refers to an individual's self-evaluation that he or she can perform a particular behavior (Bandura, 1977). An individual may have all the requisite social skills but if there is a lack of confidence or self-esteem in one's ability to perform the appropriate response, the individual may not perform the response. The third factor, self-statements, refers to the internal "talk" that an individual may utilize during a difficult situation (Meichenbaum, 1977). The final factor, faulty discrimination, involves the production of a socially skilled response in inappropriate context (Rich & Schroeder, 1976). The features of the response may be performed adequately and internally consistent, but if an individual does not produce the behavior in a socially normative manner, it would not be considered socially skilled.

The previously mentioned description of social skills components suggests the complexity faced by therapists in training social skills. It is this writer's experience that social skills trainers seldom recognize this level of complexity in the application of social skills training programs. In addition, many alcoholics have social skills deficits, although the patterns of these deficits are widely divergent. The heterogeneity of the alcoholic population is probably the major contributor to the lack of many definitive findings in the extant research.

SOCIAL SKILLS DEFICITS OF ALCOHOLICS

TYPE OF SOCIAL SKILLS DEFICITS

Most comparative studies have evaluated the differences between alcoholic and nonalcoholic clinical populations. Miller and Eisler (1977) compared alcoholics to psychiatric patients on self-report and behavioral measures of assertiveness. Alcoholic patients were significantly more assertive than nonalcoholic patients in self-reports of assertiveness, but both groups were equally unassertive on a behavioral role-playing test when negative assertion was required. However, alcoholics tended to rate higher in assertiveness on scenes requiring positive assertion. Monti, Corriveau, and Zwick (1981) compared alcoholics to psychiatric outpatients. They found that alcoholics tended to evidence greater overall skill than did the psychiatric outpatients. It should be noted that all patients had been referred into treatment because their primary therapist had considered them to have interpersonal difficulties, rather than through rigorous screening.

Other studies have compared relapsers to nonrelapsers. Rist and Watzl (1983) compared these populations 3 months after treatment. The relapsers tended to evaluate social pressure situations as more difficult and experienced greater discomfort than did abstainers. Rosenberg's (1983) study produced similar results. He noted that relapsers were more compliant in problem situations than nonrelapsers. He also found that nonrelapsers experienced fewer negative life events and more positive life events than did relapsers.

Parker, Gilbert, and Speltz (1981) compared alcoholics and social drinkers under instructional sets for assumed sobriety and assumed intoxication. The completed assertiveness questionaires and behavioral findings indicated that alcoholics reported more assertiveness under the assumed intoxication situations and that social drinkers were not influenced by the instructional set. This is an interesting finding, considering that both score equally under the assumed sobriety condition. O'Leary, O'Leary, and Donovan (1976) compared "prealcoholic" (high risk), light, and nondrinking male adolescents and found that the prealcoholic males were less socially skilled than the other groups. They also reported that these individuals seemed to lack appropriate models for masculine behavior early in life.

Other studies have examined alcoholics' social skills within a family relationship context. Jacob, Ritchey, Cvitkovic, and Blane (1981) observed alcoholic and nonalcoholic families in a communication task during both drinking and nondrinking conditions. They found that alcoholics expressed more negative and less positive affect and had less task-relevant communication in family discussions than did nonalcoholic individuals. In addition, their disagreements with other family members increased as consumption increased, but this did not occur in nonalcoholics.

Supporting this finding, Frankenstein, Hay, and Nathan (1985) determined that alcoholics spoke more than their spouses but had fewer positive nonverbal behaviors when they were intoxicated. Interestingly, they had *more* problem-solving statements when they were intoxicated. Mendelson and Mello (1985) found non-self-disclosing alcoholics who engaged in short social interactions became more socially active, independent, and assertive when drinking. However, they did not become noticeably more self-disclosing when drinking.

Several conclusions can be made. First, there is no consistent evidence that alcoholics as a group are less assertive than nonalcoholic psychiatric inpatients or outpatients. At present, there are no conclusive data suggesting that baseline rates of alcoholics' assertiveness are lower than nonclinical populations. Second, assertiveness appears to provide a buffer against relapse. Third, alcoholics may perceive the potential for greater assertiveness when drinking, but family communication studies suggest that *meaningful* assertive communication (task relevance and self-disclosure) may not be affected. Paralinguistic factors such as speech duration *may* be increased. Alcohol appears, therefore, to disinhibit, but not necessarily to organize, communication.

SOCIAL SKILLS DEFICITS AS A CAUSAL FACTOR

There are three major behavioral theories of alcoholism, all of which have implications for social skills deficits as a causal factor: (1) social learning; (2) tension reduction; and (3) expectancy (cognitive factors). The social learning approach focuses on the observation that drinking is often a socially mediated activity (Bandura, 1969). Vicarious learning, modeling, and positively reinforcing properties of alcohol may serve to increase the probability of drinking (rather than socially skilled communication) as a way of handling interpersonal relationships. Because parental drinking habits are often predictive of drinking patterns of adolescents (Goodwin, 1988), inappropriate styles of coping with emotional and environmental pressures may be inadvertently passed on (Collins & Marlatt, 1983). These inappropriate styles may preclude adaptive coping styles and therefore set the stage for adolescents' drinking. There is also the possibility that the media plays a role because Lowery (1980) found that the majority of portrayals of alcohol use in daytime soap operas involved social *facilitation*, with escape from reality and crisis management second and third in frequency.

Despite these findings, Goodwin (1988) reports that there is no consistent information that children of alcoholics (who have presumably been exposed to socially unskilled behavior) have more mental or emotional problems than children of nonalcoholics (who have presumably been exposed to more socially skilled behavior). This would argue against a social skills interpretation of alcoholism. In addition, exposure to heavy drinking models does tend to influence consumption more in heavy drinkers than in light drinkers (Lied & Marlatt, 1979). This suggests that both model and "subject" factors are important in social learning. However, it is unclear whether drinking increases as a result of social facilitative or competitive factors.

The second theory, the tension-reduction hypothesis, states that alcohol serves to reduce tension and therefore reinforces further alcohol use. Any experience of tension or stress may set the stage for excessive alcohol use. Because these stressors are often interpersonal (Marlatt & Gordon, 1985), poor social skills may theoretically increase the probability of alcohol use. This hypothesis has received little support for these reasons: (1) alcoholics are a heterogenous group—some are tense and some are not; (2) alcohol has a biphasic effect—light to moderate doses may actually act as a *stimulant*, whereas larger doses are more likely to be depressant (Russell & Mehrabian, 1975); and (3) alcohol can *increase* stress. The latter reason is supported by a recent report (*Norwich Bulletin*, 1987) in which S. A. Lisman found that two drinks produced marked social impairment and four drinks seriously restricted conversational ability in shy male drinkers. Under the influence, they misjudged their own effectiveness and believed that alcohol had indeed made them better socializers. The gap between their actual and perceived abilities suggests that the effects of alcohol may decrease perceptual rather than behavioral components of stress. As a result, it seems that stress can *result* from drinking and that, even when it precedes drinking, may not be reduced by drinking.

The third theory, expectancy, refers to beliefs about alcohol held by a person or group. Many social drinkers and alcoholics expect alcohol to have positive effects on mood and social behavior (Brown & Crowell, 1974). To separate the physiological and expectancy effects of alcohol, researchers utilize a "balanced placebo" design (Rohsenow & Marlatt, 1981). Subjects are given vodka and tonic or tonic alone (indistinguishable from each other) and placed in one of four groups—expect alcohol/receive alcohol, expect alcohol/receive tonic, expect tonic/receive alcohol, expect tonic/receive tonic. Using the design in a communication task with a female confederate, Wilson and Abrams (1977) found that moderate drinking male subjects who believed they had consumed alcohol showed *decreases* in heart rate relative to subjects who believed they had consumed tonic alone. Subjects expecting alcohol also rated themselves as less anxious. This study was repeated with a male confederate and female subjects. Abrams and Wilson (1979) found that females expecting alcohol experienced *increased* anxiety. The differences between males and females may be due to differing social messages regarding behavior (i.e., more "taboo" in females).

Taken together, there is no strong evidence that social skills deficits in the form of poor role modeling or tension reduction represent primary causal factors in alcoholism. There is stronger evidence that *beliefs* about alcohol and its relationship to social behavior are more powerful factors. These results suggest a bidirectional rather than a unidirectional relationship between social skills and alcoholism in some individuals. Some individuals actually become more withdrawn, anxious, and self-effacing under the influence of alcohol.

THE SOCIAL SKILLS TREATMENT OF ALCOHOLISM

COMPONENTS

There are a number of primary components in social skills treatment. The therapist must first determine the patient's baseline skill level and determine which components need the most work. As a first step, the therapist provides *instructions* in order to focus the patient on target skills. This helps the patient to begin conceptualizing his or her difficulties in smaller, more manageable units of behavior rather than as a global trait. The next step is modeling, which is one of the most widely used treatment components in social skills training. Twentyman and Zimering (1979) found that over 70% of the studies that they reviewed made use of a role model to perform a particular behavior that was then imitated by the patient. Modeling helps convey the instructions in a concrete observable manner. Although most treatment uses a live version of modeling, some treatments use audiotaped and/or videotaped modeling. This component of treatment is especially important in light of the findings of Collins and Marlatt (1981) because the modeling of drinking behavior seems to be a possible mode of transmission.

After the patient has received information via instructions and modeling, it is important to practice these new responses in order to add a new response to the behavioral repertoire or, if the response is present, increase the probability of its occurrence. The patient typically follows the lead of the model and focuses on the areas of deficiency. After the patient completes the role play, he or she is typically asked to evaluate his or her performance and then receives feedback from the therapist or group. When the performance matches that of the model, the patient receives social reinforcement.

On the basis of his or her performance, the patient is then usually asked to try to practice this response several times to achieve a criterion level of performance. This process underscores the importance of viewing deficits within a skill-building model. This helps the patient to become more confident about remediating these deficits and applying them to his or her natural environment. After the criterion level is reached, the patient is asked to complete "homework" that involved production of the response in a real-life situation. The patient reports back to the therapist and/or group about his or her performance and further suggestions are given. As responses are mastered, the patient begins to work on new responses.

OUTCOME STUDIES

Individual Treatment

Eisler, Hersen, and Miller (1974) evaluated the effects of social skills training on a 34-year-old, twice-divorced male with a history of alcoholism. They conducted a pretreatment role-playing assessment, and in a multiple baseline design across behaviors found that social skills training resulted in marked improvements in social skills. Specifically, instructions and feedback improved eye contact, verbal affect, and assertive demeanor, with a reduction in frequency of problem drinking.

Foy, Miller, Eisler, and O'Toole (1976) used social skills training to teach refusal behavior in alcoholics. Utilizing multiple baseline design with two chronic alcoholics, these researchers targeted behaviors such as requests for change, offering alternatives to drinking, changing the subject of conversation, duration of looking, and affect. In a nine-session treatment conducted over a 2-week period, both men improved ratings on all target behaviors at posttreatment and maintained these improvements at a 3-month follow-up.

Eisler, Miller, Hersen, and Alford (1974) utilized assertiveness training with a 52-year-old automotive mechanic with a history of episodic drinking. Because his difficulty was related to marital conflict, the couple was videotaped before and after the husband received training. The target behaviors selected for modification were duration of looking, duration of speech, requests for the interpersonal partner to change her behavior, and response latency. Therapists included instructions, behavioral rehearsal, role playing, and feedback and found that training was effective in producing positive changes for all target behaviors. Both spouses reported a sharp decrease in the husband's drinking after training.

Martorano (1974), in a study that disputed the effectiveness of social skills training, found that despite the fact that alcoholics were less anxious and aggressive following assertiveness training, they also tended to drink more alcohol. However, this study was performed on "skid-row" alcoholics, and there was probably a need for more extensive treatment.

Overall, it appears that individual social skills training for alcoholics can be effective in improving various expressive elements in communication, but there are relatively few studies that have systematically evaluated the components of treatment within tight single-subject designs. In addition, the effects of improved social skills on the target behavior (drinking) were unclear. Assessment of the *link* between alcoholics' social skills and drinking is necessary in order to determine whether increased skill levels will increase, decrease, or produce no change in drinking behavior.

Group Treatment

Adinolfi, McCourt, and Geoghegan (1975) trained six socially isolated, unassertive male alcoholics with a combination of role playing, modeling, and behavior rehearsal. Patients were also given *in vivo* assignments that required a transfer of newly learned assertive behavior. Postassessment indicated an improvement in assertiveness scores, assertive skill, and good social and vocational adjustment. At an 11-month follow-up, three of the subjects were totally abstinent, whereas the others engaged in episodic drinking ranging from 3 days to several weeks.

Scherer and Freedberg (1976) provided six 2-hour workshops to alcoholics in a 3-week inpatient program. One group received role playing with videotaped feedback, a second group received role playing with no videotaped feedback, and one group received no treatment at all. Both treatment groups improved in their levels of assertiveness, with a maintenance of skills differences at 3-, 6-, and 12-month follow-ups.

Chaney, O'Leary, and Marlatt (1978) assigned 40 inpatient alcoholics to a skill training group, discussion group, or no-additional-treatment control group. In their social skills training, they included instructions, modeling, behavioral rehearsal, and coaching for both overt behavior and problem solving. They evaluated the subjects with role-play assessments and found a significant improvement at posttreatment for the training group as compared with the control groups. They also found that at a 1-year follow-up, patients in the skill training group experienced a decreased duration and severity of relapse episodes.

Hirsch, von Rosenberg, Phelan, and Dudley (1978) compared a 10-hour assertion training group comprising role playing, feedback, and other assertive training components with minimal (2 hours of lectures) and control groups on three measures of assertiveness (involving paper-and-pencil and role-playing assessments). They found that the assertiveness group was significantly better in response duration, total assertiveness, latency, and measures of verbal and nonverbal assertiveness. However, there was no follow-up to determine whether these changes were maintained over time or if they related to drinking behavior.

Oei and Jackson (1980) compared group social skills training, individual social skills training, group traditional supportive treatment, and individual traditional supportive treatment. They found that patients receiving social skills treatments improved more than patients receiving traditional supportive treatment. The group social skills approach also seemed to fare better than the individual social skills approach. Oei and Jackson (1982) refined their treatment in a later study by comparing four groups: (1) social skills training; (2) cognitive restructuring; (3) social skills training plus cognitive restructuring; and (4) traditional supportive therapy. Cognitive restructuring, whether combined with social skills training or not, was more successful in producing lasting social skills changes and decreasing alcohol consumption over a 12-month follow-up. Although these results suggest the importance of cognitive restructuring, they provide no firm support for the inclusion of social skills training within a treatment regimen.

Jones, Kanfer, and Lanyon (1982) compared three groups: (1) a skill training group, which consisted of behavioral rehearsal of coping responses generated for potential relapse-precipitating events; (2) a control group, which received no additional treatment; and (3) a discussion control group, which discussed the potential relapse-precipitating events without rehearsing specific responses. The authors found that both the skilled training and discussion groups were superior to the no-treatment control group and did not differ from each other. This result tended to disagree with the Chaney *et al.* (1978) study that found the skill training package to be superior to both control groups.

Greenwald, Kloss, Kovaleski, Greenwald, Twentyman, and Zibung-Huffman (1980) compared an assertiveness training group that sought to improve drink refusal and positive assertion behaviors with a no-training control group. Although there were no pre–post role-play differences, they found significant effects in untrained categories. However, all patients were hospitalized, and presumably all improved their ability to refuse drinks because of this treatment.

Ferrell and Galassi (1981) evaluated the effects of milieu therapy plus assertion training with milieu therapy plus human relations training. The goal was to increase interpersonal skills and reduce drinking behavior of chronic alcoholics in an alcoholic rehabilitation center. Both treatments led to comparable sobriety rates at a 6-week follow-up, but the treatment group that contained assertion training demonstrated significant improvements in interpersonal skills.

Nelson and Howell (1982) randomly assigned alcoholic inpatients at a VA hospital to one of three groups: (1) rehearsal group; (2) modeling group; and (3) discussion control group. There were six 1-hour group assertiveness training sessions held over a 2-week period. Upon completion of assertiveness training, trained subjects performed significantly better in assertiveness than did controls, and they received more regular discharges from the hospital. The patients in this study responded best to rehearsal-based treatment. At 2-month follow-up, patients in the assertiveness training group reported less drinking and more abstinent days than did controls, although the differences were not statistically significant. Reports from collaterals suggested slightly less favorable results.

Eriksen, Bjornsted, and Gotestam (1986) assigned inpatient alcoholics to a social skills training group or control group. At a 1-year follow-up, patients in the social skills group were reported to be drinking one-third less than the control patients were drinking. The social skills group also had twice as many sober and working days. The average length of abstinence for the social skills training group was significantly higher than the control group.

It is apparent that group methods have been more widely researched than individual methods of social skills training. At present, it appears that social skills training produced better results than supportive treatment, discussion groups or no treatment, particularly if cognitive restructuring is included. However, these studies suffer from deficiencies such as a lack of follow-up assessments of social skills related to drinking situation (e.g., drink refusal), a lack of a convincing initial connection between subject's drinking and social skills, and lack of specificity in evaluating components of the treatment regimens.

Marital Treatment

The relative paucity of studies does not allow any firm conclusions to be drawn about the effectiveness of social skills training in remediating communications deficiencies between alcoholics and their spouses. Hedberg and Campbell (1974) assigned 49 outpatient alcoholics to behavioral family counseling, systematic desensitization, covert sensitization, or electrical shock aversion. Assertiveness training was incorporated within the rehearsal behavioral family counseling. Behavior *rehearsal* was used in an attempt to enhance the quality of verbal interchanges between patients and family members. The authors found that the behavioral family counseling group had the highest percentage of subjects achieving their goal of either abstinence or controlled drinking.

Eisler, Miller, Hersen, and Alford (1974), in a study mentioned earlier, found that assertiveness training helped an alcoholic improve his speech duration, eye contact, verbal requests for behavioral change between his wife and him, and verbal references to drinking.

Based upon this limited research, it appears that the development of socially skilled behavior between alcoholics and their spouses is potentially useful. Because many alcoholic patients appear at treatment centers as a result of marital or family problems related to poor communication a greater focus on the social skills of the *spouse* may enhance the alcoholic's recovery.

DISCUSSION

Reviewers in the social skills field have commented often on the lack of valid measures for measuring social skill (Heimberg, Montgomery, Madsen, & Heimberg, 1977; Rich & Schroeder, 1976; Twentyman & Zimering, 1979). Most social skills questionnaires have been developed with college, nonclinical, or psychiatric populations. At present, there is no specific social skills assessment measure with reliability and validity data for alcoholics. Callner and Ross (1976) have developed one for drug addicts, but it has not achieved widespread acceptance even within that population.

Other major problems with these studies regarding alcoholism are typical of the difficulties inherent in social skills research in general. Van Hasselt, Hersen, and Milliones (1978) have described some of these difficulties. First, the generalization of training effects from a hospital environment to a patient's natural environment has seldom been accomplished or even systematically evaluated. Researchers tend to assume a relationship between drinking and social skills deficits in general and then develop groups based upon spontaneously generated problem behaviors that may or may not be related to drinking. They further compound these problems by utilizing global, rather than social skills, assessments at follow-up.

The next difficulty relates to the validity of role playing as an assessment device. Bellack (1983) and McNamara and Blumer (1982) have questioned the validity of role plays as an assessment device and treatment outcome. There is only a modest correspondence between behavior in role-play and naturalistic settings. There have been few attempts made to study differences in role-play format and how they affect the ecological validity of role-play procedures. For example, role plays can be presented by a live person, audiotape, or videotape, and there is minimal data on the validity of responses given on the subject as a result of these presentations. There is also a great deal of differences between individuals in role-playing ability. Are we measuring indicators of actual social skills, or are we measuring acting ability? There appear to be no established norms about what constitutes socially skilled behavior or how broadly it should be defined. Van Hasselt, Hersen, and Milliones (1978) suggest an expansion of our present definition to include social skills in job interviews and social interactions with non-drug users. For instance, Sisson and Azrin (1989) report successful use of a "community reinforcement approach," which is a broad-based multicomponent package including a "job club," social skills training, marriage counseling, and advice on social and recreational activities.

Another difficulty with social skills training research is the fact that there are so many different components and there is relatively little research on the longitudinal development of social skills and their relationship to substance abuse. There are inherent dangers in attributing causality to any psychological or behavioral dimension within the field of alcoholism, because of the wide diversity of the alcoholic population.

Finally, these studies are hampered by the fact that behavioral psychologists differ on the ultimate goals of treatment. Some believe that controlled drinking is a suitable goal, whereas others view abstinence as essential. As a result, some studies mentioned earlier were judged successful because they resulted in a significant decrease in drinking rather than in abstinence.

When one considers all these difficulties within the social skills field in general, it is readily apparent that these difficulties are magnified within social skills interventions for alcoholism. This is because the alcoholism research appears to be about 10 years behind research in the field as a whole. This development may be further hampered by the lack of involvement of behavior therapy in mainstream treatment settings, which typically espouse an abstinence philosophy and xenophobic attitudes toward research.

Perhaps the best approach has been suggested by Marlatt (1983), who said that a relapse-prevention model is best when treating the alcoholic. Social skills training can then be construed as a method with which an individual can reduce the likelihood that he or she will drink in response to a high-risk situation. Marlatt and Gordon (1985) have developed a comprehensive relapse-prevention approach based on recognition and coping with such high-risk situations. In fact, they have estimated that 16% of all relapses occurred as a result of interpersonal conflict and that 20% resulted from social pressure. It would seem that social skills training combined with a cognitive treatment approach would be extremely promising in the treatment of alcoholism. Future studies should try to compare these interventions in individual and group formats.

Social skills training offers much promise as an intervention that allows an integration of behavioral techniques in traditional settings. A barrier has arisen due to the fact that many behavioral treatments such as social skills training are thought to necessarily espouse a controlled drinking philosophy. In fact, many behavioral psychologists utilize an abstinence philosophy, and there is a great deal of similarity between an Alcoholics Anonymous philosophy and behavioral approaches using social skills training (McCrady & Sher, 1983). For example, AA and social skills training both agree that environmental management (avoiding bars, limiting contact with drinking friends) is an important feature of recovery. AA encourages communication between recovering individuals and stresses the importance of changing cognitive content that is related to drinking ("stinking thinking"). Social skills training focuses on these same cognitive factors and also works to help people with communicating their ideas. AA stresses a "here-and-now" approach, suggested by the slogan "1 day at a time." Social skills training focuses on proximal rather than distal goals until the patient seems ready to link learned behavior into more complex chains. Most importantly, both approaches are relatively atheoretical. AA does not support any rationalization for drinking but simply states that "people drink because they're alcoholics." Social skills training also focuses on the drinking behavior, rather than an underlying motivation or personality trait, as the primary focus of change.

Taken together, these similarities suggest much potential for rapprochement between the self-help and behavioral models. Because alcoholism presents such a great challenge to the treatment field, it is certainly time to eliminate theoretical struggles and find mechanisms to improve outcome.

REFERENCES

Abrams, D. B. & Wilson, G. T. (1979). Effects of alcohol on social anxiety in women: Cognitive versus physiological process. *Journal of Abnormal Psychology, 88*, 161–173.

Adinolfi, A. A., McCourt, W. F., & Geoghegan, S. (1975). Group assertiveness training for alcoholics. *Journal of Studies on Alcohol, 37*, 311–320.

Alcohol: A poor solution for the shy. *Norwich Bulletin*, April 9.

Bandura, A. (1969). *Principles of behavior modification*. New York: Holt.

Bandura, A. (1977). Self-efficacy: Toward a unifying theory of behavior change. *Psychological Review, 84*, 191–215.

Beattie, M. (1987). *Codependent no more.* New York: Harper/Hazelden.

Bellack, A. S. (1983). Recurrent problems in the behavioral assessment of social skill. *Behavior Research and Therapy, 21,* 29–41.

Bellack, A. S. & Morrison, R. L. (1982). Interpersonal dysfunction. In A. S. Bellack, M. Hersen, & A. E. Kazdin (Eds.), *International handbook of behavior modification and therapy* (pp. 717–747). New York: Plenum.

Bellack, A. S., Hersen, M., & Himmelhoch, J. M. (1978). Social skills training for depression: A treatment manual. Washington, DC: JSAS Catalog of Selected Documents in Psychology.

Brown, J. S., & Crowell, C. R. (1974). Alcohol and conflict resolution: A theoretical analysis. *Quarterly Journal of Studies on Alcohol, 35,* 66–85.

Callner, D. A. & Ross, S. M. (1976). The reliability and validity of three measures of assertion in a drug addict population. *Behavior Therapy, 7,* 659–667.

Chaney, E. F., O'Leary, M. R., & Marlatt, G. A. (1978). Skill training with alcoholics. *Journal of Consulting and Clinical Psychology, 46,* 1092–104.

Collins, R. L., & Marlatt, G. A. (1981). Social modeling as a determinant of drinking behavior: Implications for prevention and treatment. *Addictive Behaviors, 6,* 233–239.

Collins, R. L., & Marlatt, G. A. (1983). Psychological correlations and explanations of alcohol use and abuse. In B. Tabakoff, P. B. Sutker, & C. L. Randall (Eds.), *Medical and social aspects of alcohol abuse* (pp. 273–308). New York: Plenum Press.

Diamint, A. (1988). The big lie. *Boston Magazine,* August.

Eisler, R. M., Hersen, M., & Miller, P. M. (1974). Shaping components of assertive behavior with instructions and feedback. *American Journal of Psychiatry, 131,* 1344–1347.

Eisler, R. M., Miller, P. M., Hersen, M., & Alford, H. (1974). Effects of assertive training on marital interaction. *Archives of General Psychiatry, 30,* 643–649.

Eriksen, L., Bjornstad, S., & Gotestam, K. G. (1986). Social skills training in groups for alcoholics: One year treatment outcome for groups and inidviduals. *Addictive Behaviors, 11,* 309–329.

Ferrell, W. L., & Galassi, J. P. (1981). Assertion training and human relations training in the treatment of chronic alcoholics. *International Journal of the addictions, 16,* 959–968.

Foy, D. W., Miller, P. M., Eisler, R. M., & O'Toole, D. H. (1976). Social skills training to teach alcoholics to refuse drinks effectively. *Journal of Studies on Alcohol, 37,* 1340–1345.

Frankenstien, W., Hay, W. M., & Nathan, P. E. (1985). Effects of intoxication on alcoholics' marital communication and problem-solving. *Journal of Studies on Alcohol, 46,* 1–6.

Goodwin, D. W. (1988). *Is alcoholism hereditary?* New York: Ballantine.

Greenwald, M. A., Kloss, J. D., Kovaleski, M. E., Greenwald, D. P., Twentyman, C. T., & Zibung-Huffman, P. (1980). Drink refusal and social skills training with hospitalized alcoholics. *Addictive Behaviors, 5,* 227–228.

Hamburg, S. (1975). Behavior therapy in alcoholism: A critical review of broad-spectrum approaches. *Journal of Studies on Alcohol, 36,* 69–87.

Hedberg, A. G. & Campbell, L. A. (1974). Comparison of four behavioral treatments of alcoholism. *Journal of Behavior Therapy and Experimental Psychiatry, 5,* 251–256.

Heimberg, R. G., Montgomery, D., Madsen, C. H., & Heimberg, J. S. (1977). Assertion training: A review of the literature. *Behavior Therapy, 8,* 953–971.

Hersen, M., & Bellack, A. S. (1977). Assessment of social skills (1977). In A. R. Ciminero, K. S. Calhoun, & H. E. Adams (Eds.), *Handbook of behavioral assessment.* New York: Wiley.

Hirsch, S. M., von Rosenberg, R., Phelan, C., & Dudley, H. R. (1978). Effectiveness of assertiveness training with alcoholics. *Journal of Studies on Alcohol, 39,* 89–97.

Jacob, T., Ritchey, D., Cvitkovic, J. F., & Blane, H. T. (1981). Communication styles of alcoholic and nonalcoholic families when drinking and not drinking. *Journal of Studies on Alcohol, 42,* 466–482.

Jones, S. L., Kanfer, R., & Lanyon, R. I. (1982). Skill training with alcoholics: A clinical extension. *Addictive Behaviors, 7,* 285–290.

Lange, A. J., & Jakobowski, P. (1976). *Responsible assertive behavior: Cognitive-behavioral procedures for trainers*. Champaign, IL: Research Press.

Lied, E. R., & Marlatt, G. A. (1979). Modeling as a determinant of alcohol consumption: Effect of subject sex and prior drinking history. *Addictive Behaviors, 4*, 47–54.

Lowery, S. A. (1980). Soap and booze in the afternoon. *Journal of Studies on Alcohol, 41*, 829–838.

Marlatt, G. A. (1983). The controlled-drinking controversy: A commentary. *American Psychologist, 38*, 1097–1110.

Marlatt, G. A., & Gordon, J. R. (1985). *Relapse prevention*. New York: Guilford.

Martorano, R. D. (1974). Mood and social perception in four alcoholics: Effects of drinking and assertion training. *Quarterly Journal of Studies on Alcohol, 35*, 445–457.

McCrady, B. S., & Sher, K. J. (1983). Alcoholism treatment approaches: Patient variables, treatment variables. In B. Tabakoff, P. B. Sutker, & C. L. Randall (Eds.), *Medical and social aspects of alcohol abuse* (pp. 309–373). New York: Plenum Press.

McNamara, J. R., & Blumer, C. A. (1982). Role-playing to assess social competence: Ecological validity considerations. *Behavior Modification, 6*, 519–549.

Meichenbaum, D. (1977). *Cognitive-behavior modification*. New York: Plenum Press.

Mendelson, J. H., & Mello, N. K. (1985). *Alcohol: Use and abuse in America*. Boston: Little, Brown and Company.

Miller, P. M., & Eisler, R. M. (1977). Assertive behavior of alcoholics: A descriptive analysis. *Behavior Therapy, 8*, 146–149.

Miller, P. M., Hersen, M., Eisler, R. M., & Hilsman, G. (1974) Effects of social stress on operant drinking of alcoholics and social drinkers. *Behavior Research and Therapy, 12*, 65–72.

Monti, P. M., Corriveau, D. P., & Zwick, W. (1981). Assessment of social skill in alcoholics and other psychiatric patients. *Journal of Studies on Alcohol, 92*, 526–528.

Nathan, P. E. (1985). Alcoholism: A cognitive social learning approach. *Journal of Substance Abuse Treatment, 2*, 169–173.

Nelson, J. E., & Howell, R. I. (1982). Assertiveness training using rehearsal and modeling with male alcoholics. *American Journal of Drug and Alcohol Abuse, 9*, 309–323.

Oei, T. P. S., & Jackson, P. (1980). Long-term effects of group and individual social skills training with alcoholics. *Addictive Behaviors, 5*, 129–136.

Oei, T. P. S., & Jackson, P. (1982). Social skills and cognitive-behavioral approaches to the treatment of problem drinking. *Journal of Studies on Alcohol, 43*, 532–547.

O'Leary, D. E., O'Leary, M. R., & Donovan, D. M. (1976). Social skill acquisition and psychosocial development of alcoholics: A review. *Addictive Behaviors, 1*, 11–120.

Parker, J. C., Gilbert, G., & Speltz, M. L. (1981). Expectations regarding the effects of alcohol on assertiveness: A comparison of alcoholics and social drinkers. *Addictive Behaviors, 6*, 29–33.

Rich, A. R., & Schroeder, H. E. (1976). Research issues in assertiveness training. *Psychological Bulletin, 83*, 1031–1096.

Rist, F., & Watzl, H. (1983). Self assessment of relapse risk and assertiveness in relation to treatment outcome of female alcoholics. *Addictive Behaviors, 8*, 121–127.

Rohsenow, D. M., & Marlatt, G. A. (1981). The balanced placebo design: Methodological considerations. *Addictive Behaviors, 6*, 107–122.

Rosenberg, H. (1983). Relapsed versus non-relapsed alcohol abusers: Coping skills, life events, and social support. *Addictive Behaviors, 8*, 1983–1986.

Russell, J. A., & Mehribian, A. (1975). The mediating role of emotions in alcohol use. *Journal of Studies on Alcohol, 36*, 1508–1531.

Scherer, S. E., & Freedberg, E. J. (1976). Effects of group videotape feedback on development of assertiveness skills in alcoholics: A follow-up study. *Psychological Reports, 39*, 983–992.

Sisson, R. W., & Azrin, N. H. (1989). The community reinforcement approach. In R. R. Hester & W. R. Miller (Eds.), *Handbook of alcoholism treatment approaches* (pp. 242–258). Elmsford, NY: Pergamon Press.

Sturgis, E. T., Calhoun, K. S., & Best, C. L. (1979). Correlates of assertive behavior in alcoholics. *Addictive Behaviors, 4,* 193–197.

Twentyman, C. T., & Zimering, R. T. (1979). Behavioral training of social skills: A critical review. In M. Hersen, R. M. Eisler, & P. M. Miller (Eds.), *Progress in behavior modification* (Vol. 7, pp. 319–400). New York: Academic Press.

Vaillant, G. E. (1983). *The natural history of alcoholism.* Cambridge: Harvard University Press.

Van Hasselt, V. B., Hersen, M., & Milliones, J. (1978). Social skills training for alcoholics and drug addicts: A review. *Addictive Behaviors, 3,* 221–233.

Wilson, G. T., & Abrams, D. B. (1977). Effects of alcohol use on social anxiety and physiological arousal: Cognitive versus pharmacological processes. *Cognitive Therapy and Research, 1,* 195–210.

CHAPTER TEN

Stimulant Medication and the Social Interactions of Hyperactive Children

Effects and Implications

STEPHEN P. HINSHAW AND JAMES P. MCHALE

INTRODUCTION

In the past decade investigators have begun to emphasize the clinical, prognostic, and theoretical importance of hyperactive children's social interactions (Barkley, 1982; Campbell & Paulauskas, 1979; Milich & Landau, 1982; Pelham & Bender, 1982; Whalen & Henker, 1985). Indeed, such social and interpersonal phenomena as disruptive interactions in classrooms, aggression against children and adults, noncompliance with parental directions, and disturbed peer relationships are currently considered to be as central to hyperactivity as are the "core" features of inattention, impulsivity, and motor overactivity (Barkley, 1985b; Hinshaw, 1987a; Pelham & Milich, 1984). Indeed, because of their tendencies to elicit undesirable reactions from others, hyperactive children have been characterized as "negative social catalysts" (see Whalen, Henker, Castro, & Granger, 1987a). Furthermore, the deficient social skills and disturbed interpersonal relationships of these children are likely to be implicated in their relatively poor prognoses with respect to adolescent and young adult functioning (Barkley, Fischer, Edelbrock, & Smallish, 1990; Gittelman, Mannuzza, Shenker, & Bonagura, 1985; Satterfield, Hoppe, & Schell, 1982; Weiss, Hechtman, Milroy, & Perl-

STEPHEN P. HINSHAW AND JAMES P. MCHALE • Department of Psychology, University of California, Berkeley, California 94720.

Personality, Social Skills, and Psychopathology: An Individual Differences Approach, edited by David G. Gilbert and James J. Connolly. Plenum Press, New York, 1991.

man, 1985). Clearly, no consideration of hyperactivity can ignore the social domain.[1]

The most frequently employed treatment for hyperactive children is stimulant medication. Surveys indicate that a majority of youngsters diagnosed as hyperactive will receive stimulant treatment during their school years (see Gadow, 1986). Although a multitude of well-controlled reports document the short-term benefits of stimulants on attention span, impulse control, and disruptive behavior (e.g., Donnelly & Rapoport, 1985), the long-term efficacy of these medications is questionable (Hechtman, Weiss, & Perlman, 1984). It has been speculated that this lack of long-range benefit may relate to a dearth of direct effects of stimulants on critical social behaviors (Pelham & Bender, 1982). Until recently, however, data have been sparse; only in the past several years have investigators begun to evaluate, in systematic fashion, the effects of these medications on social interactions.

In our review of the effects of stimulants on social behavior, we will be asking whether, and to what extent, these drugs alter the social functioning of the hyperactive child. We will focus on hyperactive children's social interactions in three major domains: classrooms, families, and peer environments. (For comprehensive coverage of more general aspects of hyperactivity and stimulant treatment, please see the reviews of Barkley, 1989; Gadow, 1986; Klein, Gittelman, Quitkin, and Rifkin, 1980; Ross & Ross, 1982; and Whalen, 1989). A particular focus of this chapter will be the reciprocal effects of stimulants on the behaviors and perceptions of the significant others with whom hyperactive children interact—namely teachers, parents, and peers. Only through understanding the reactions of such social partners to the acute shifts in behavior induced by stimulants can an integrative perspective on both hyperactivity and the medication process be attained (see Whalen & Henker, 1980).

In order to gain a deeper understanding of the effects of stimulants on social interactions, we will then discuss some pertinent issues in social development. As we explore developmental changes in social behaviors, peer relationships, and social networks, we will highlight the increasing importance of the peer domain across the school-age years and emphasize the complex interpersonal matrices in which medication effects take place. Our concluding comments emphasize (a) the need for consideration of broad developmental and social competence issues when evaluating medication effects on social behaviors, (b) methodologic and interpretive issues regarding medication studies, and (c) the role of multiple-modality interventions in the treatment of the interpersonal difficulties of hyperactive children.

---

[1]In this chapter, the term *hyperactivity* will refer to the entire constellation of behaviors subsumed under the current nosologic category of *attention-deficit-hyperactivity disorder*, or *ADHD* (American Psychiatric Association, 1987).

HYPERACTIVE CHILDREN'S SOCIAL INTERACTIONS

A brief overview of the social functioning of hyperactive children will help to place discussion of medication effects in context. Traditionally, classroom environments have been the loci of many of the core problems of hyperactivity. Examination of the teacher rating scales and classroom behavioral observation systems used to define hyperactive behavior reveals a substantial proportion of items that reflect social and interpersonal conflict: disruptive, interfering, and negativistic behaviors; noncompliance with teachers; and verbal and nonverbal aggression (e.g., Abikoff, Gittelman-Klein, & Klein, 1977; Conners, 1973; Quay & Peterson, 1983; Whalen, Henker, Collins, Finck, & Dotemoto, 1979a). With respect to systematically recorded observations, hyperactive children have been distinguished from their nonlabeled classmates not only by inattentive/off-task behavior but also on the basis of such socially related categories as disruption, verbalization, and interference (Abikoff, Gittelman, & Klein, 1980; Whalen, Collins, Henker, Alkus, Adams, & Stapp, 1978). Furthermore, even when compared to other clinic-referred children, hyperactive youngsters show increased rates of negative peer interactions in classrooms (Milich & Fitzgerald, 1985). In short, socially disruptive classroom behaviors are a pertinent feature of hyperactivity.

In addition, even when blind to diagnostic status, teachers tend to be more intense and controlling toward unmedicated hyperactive children than toward nonhyperactive peers (Whalen, Henker, & Dotemoto, 1980, 1981a). Such a finding speaks to the truly transactional nature of hyperactive children's classroom behavior and to the need for embedding hyperactive/acting-out behavior and its treatment in relevant interpersonal contexts.

At home, the most salient underlying feature of the behavioral style of hyperactive children is noncompliance. Such noncompliance is exemplified across many different aspects of the home setting, particularly those involving interactions with parents and demands for restraint (Barkley, 1985b). Along with well-documented difficulties in complying with classroom demands, such a noncompliant and non-self-controlled posture at home has led Barkley (1985a) to characterize hyperactive children as suffering from a fundamental deficit in rule-governed behavior.

More specific aspects of parent–child interactions have emerged from detailed analyses of laboratory-based playroom encounters. Overall, hyperactive children are less likely to sustain compliance, are less frequently on task, and are more negative than their nonhyperactive peers; parents of hyperactive children are, in turn, more controlling and negative than are parents of comparison youngsters (Barkley, Karlsson, & Pollard, 1985; Campbell, 1975; Cunningham & Barkley, 1979; Mash & Johnston, 1982;

Tallmadge & Barkley, 1983). Such effects are particularly salient when structured tasks are to be performed; free play observations reveal far fewer differences between hyperactive and control children. Once again, attention-disordered and hyperactive behavior is seen to be embedded in a reciprocally interactive interpersonal context. The "directionality" of these parent–child interactions—that is, which behaviors elicit which responses—will be addressed specifically in the subsequent section on medication effects.

When the peer culture is considered, the true extent and severity of hyperactive children's social difficulties emerge. Not only do hyperactive youngsters tend to display aggressive behavior toward peers, but they are also overzealous, intrusive, and inappropriate in playgroup situations (Pelham & Bender, 1982). A recent "catalogue" of the interpersonal deficits and excesses that hyperactive children display with peers is provided by Whalen and Henker (1985), who note the wide variety of both behavioral content and environmental settings that characterize such children's peer difficulties.

Classmates and playmates of hyperactive children are sensitive monitors of such behaviors. In fact, peer ratings of hyperactive children conform closely to adult characterizations of inattentive and hyperactive behavioral features (Glow & Glow, 1980). Most critically, hyperactive children are extremely unpopular with and rejected by peers (Milich & Landau, 1982; Pelham & Bender, 1982). Given the predictive power of such sociometric ratings and nominations (Parker & Asher, 1987), it is not surprising that hyperactive children are at risk for continued behavioral and social problems during adolescence and adulthood (Gittelman et al., 1985; Satterfield et al., 1982). An ongoing research task for the field is the determination of the specific behavioral problems—and peer responses—that contribute to the noteworthy unpopularity and rejection experienced by hyperactive children.

Before leaving this brief discussion of the social difficulties of hyperactive children, several related issues bear discussion. First, the preceding paragraphs have hinted at the tendencies toward aggression in these children. Indeed, the linkage is of sufficient magnitude that some investigators have claimed hyperactivity to be merely a subset of general conduct disturbance (Quay, 1979; Sandberg, Rutter, & Taylor, 1978). Although clear overlap in the two behavioral domains does exist, separate dimensions emerge from factor analytic studies, and each dimension predicts uniquely to important criterion measures (Hinshaw, 1987b; Milich, Loney, & Landau, 1982). Furthermore, consensus has emerged that the attempt to separate subgroups of hyperactive (or inattentive), aggressive, and hyperactive–aggressive children is worthwhile (Loney & Milich, 1982; Milich & Landau, 1989; Quay, 1986). Thus, whereas aggressive social interactions are common in most samples of hyperactive children and are important prognostically

(Milich & Loney, 1979), hyperactivity is not inevitably linked with aggressive behavior, and hyperactive children have social problems that transcend aggression (Pelham & Bender, 1982). We will discuss stimulant effects on both aggressive and nonaggressive interpersonal encounters in this chapter.

Second, lest the reader be left with an overwhelmingly negative picture, we must note that there are areas of normality and even strength in the social repertoires of hyperactive children. In the first place, these youngsters are far from asocial; they may actually be more prone to seek social contact than are their peers (Whalen & Henker, 1985). Problems often emerge from the rather unsophisticated and overzealous strategies employed by these children when they interact. In addition, tantalizing evidence exists that the social awareness displayed by hyperactive children is quite acute. For instance, data provided by Dotemoto (1984) point to the equivalent, and on occasion superior, predictive power of the peer ratings made by hyperactive children compared with those made by nonlabeled peers. Finally, clinical vignettes and parental reports attest to the often poignant efforts made by hyperactive children to be helpful or accepted (see Whalen & Henker, 1985). Certainly, no hyperactive child is always socially clumsy, intrusive, or aggressive. Yet, the social responses of this group are among the most salient and severe forms of their psychopathology.

MEDICATION EFFECTS ON SOCIAL BEHAVIORS AND SOCIAL INTERACTIONS

Several properties of psychostimulant medications render them ideal agents for research on social interactions.[2] First, the time-response properties of methylphenidate and dextroamphetamine are such that their behavioral effects are usually noted within an hour (e.g., Swanson, Kinsbourne, Roberts, & Zucker, 1978). Thus, initial data in the medicated state can typically be collected quite acutely, as opposed to the days or weeks required for many other psychotropic medications. Also, because of the short half-lives of stimulants, crossover designs can be performed on an extremely tight schedule. In fact, although some investigators have crossed over methylphenidate and placebo within a single day (Swanson & Kinsbourne, 1976), the usual "washout" period ranges from overnight to several days. Such properties allow for the independent variable of medication status to be manipulated acutely, yielding analysis of the effects of

[2]The most commonly prescribed medications for hyperactive children are the stimulants methylphenidate (Ritalin) and dextroamphetamine (Dexedrine). Pemoline (Cylert) is less frequently employed. The particular drug used in a given study, along with the dosages employed (if indicated), will be indicated in the review. Furthermore, unless noted, all cited studies employed double-blind procedures for medication trials.

pharmacologic status on social interactions without the confounding variable of maturation over extended periods of time. Several investigators have taken advantage of these properties to make causal inferences as to the direction of effect—that is, parent to child versus child to parent—in social interactions (see Barkley, 1981).

Also relevant to methodology is the potential for bias in detection of medication effects by observers or raters. This crucial question was addressed by Henker, Whalen, and Collins (1979). In this report, whereas raters in double-blind conditions guessed the medication versus placebo status of hyperactive children at above-chance rates, their behavioral ratings were indistinguishable from those of triple-blind raters, who were completely unaware that medication trials were being held. It thus appears that observer-detected medication effects cannot be attributed to "halo" effects or other biases.

Space does not permit initial discussion of such other important methodologic issues as does response curves, ecological validity of medication trials, and individual subject differences that might mediate medication response. These issues will be raised subsequently, however, as we turn now to key studies of medication effects on social interactions.

CLASSROOMS

As noted earlier, the many classroom studies of medication employing rating scales as outcome measures have consistently revealed positive drug effects. Such rating scales typically contain items reflecting noncompliance or social disruption (which tend to load on factorial scales entitled "hyperactive" or "conduct problem"), fueling the contention that medication does reduce global measures of disruptive social behavior (see Pelham, 1986). In the interests of obtaining a finer-grained look at the specific behaviors affected by medication, we will focus solely on research employing behavior observation strategies (as opposed to rating strategies) for the coding of both child and teacher behaviors. This "policy" of focusing on observed rather than rated behavior will be followed throughout the chapter.

In a multidimensional intervention study, Gittelman, Abikoff, Pollack, Klein, Katz, and Mattes (1980) demonstrated that moderately high dosages of methylphenidate ($M = .6$ mg/kg) improved the classroom behavior of a carefully diagnosed sample of hyperactive children over an 8 week period. Employing the behavioral observation code from Abikoff et al. (1977), these investigators showed significant reductions in the socially relevant category of disruption, which includes the "interfering" behaviors of calling out and interrupting other children during work periods. Next, Pelham, Bender, Caddell, Booth, and Moorer (1985) showed linear dose response effects of methylphenidate (at .15, .30, and .60 mg/kg) on a large category of negative classroom behaviors, which included destruction of property, disturbing others, name calling, and teasing. Although specific condition comparisons were not reported, all dosages showed sizable reductions from placebo on this composite measure.

Using preexisting dosages that averaged about .30 mg/kg, Whalen *et al.* (1978) and Whalen *et al.* (1979a) also found reductions in hyperactive children's socially disruptive classroom behavior. In these studies, the categories of disruption, negative verbalization, and social initiation were normalized—that is, reduced to levels essentially equivalent to those of normal comparison youngsters—with active medication. In light of the claims of some (see Rie, Rie, Stewart, & Ambuel, 1976) that medication may diminish the social interest of hyperactive children, one might ask whether reductions in verbalization and social initiation are actually negative effects of medication. First, the classrooms in the studies of Whalen *et al.* (1978, 1979a) emphasized task completion during the observation periods, so that inappropriate verbalization to teachers or peers and initiation of social contacts were not functional. Second, the stimulants did not totally squelch such behavior but rather brought it into the normal range. Third, additional studies in both classroom and outdoor settings have *not* revealed that stimulants increase categories of nonsocial behavior or social isolation (Hinshaw, Henker, & Whalen, 1984a; Whalen, Henker, Swanson, Granger, Kliewer, & Spencer, 1987b; Hinshaw, Henker, Whalen, Erhardt, & Dunnington, 1989b). We will continue to be sensitive to the potential for possible negative effects of stimulants on social functioning in later portions of this chapter.

What are the implications of these medication-induced effects for teacher–child interactions? In two related reports, Whalen *et al.* (1980, 1981a) presented analyses of the teacher's responses to the children in the Whalen *et al.* (1978, 1979a) studies. The particular teacher involved was blind not only to the medication versus placebo status of the hyperactive participants but also to the issues that a medication trial was being conducted and that some children were formally diagnosed as hyperactive. Videotaped recordings of the entire classroom area allowed for coding of the function (regular and controlling contacts), modality (verbal, physical), and intensity of the teacher's interactions with the children, as well as the number of times that she verbalized the children's names.

In the more comprehensive report, Whalen *et al.* (1981a) found that the teacher's responses to students on placebo were more controlling and intense across all four replications of this study; she was more verbal to placebo youngsters in three of the four. Furthermore, the teacher more frequently employed placebo children's names for purposes of control in three of the replications, with the fourth just missing significance. Although generalization to other classrooms and teachers is certainly required, these groundbreaking results clearly suggest that the positive effects of stimulants on hyperactive children's task-appropriate and socially regulated behavior are salient to teachers, who respond, in turn, with a less controlling and punitive style. The results are particularly encouraging in their indica-tion that teachers do not stereotype or negatively halo the misbehaviors of hyperactive children to such an extent that they fail to notice and respond differentially to improvement. Finer-grained sequential analyses of the spe-cific transactions between teacher and child are required in order to under-stand more fully the nature of these powerful medication effects.

PARENT–CHILD INTERACTIONS

The first controlled study assessing the effects of stimulants on parent–child social interactions was performed by Humphries, Kinsbourne, and Swanson (1978), who administered methylphenidate or placebo to 26 hyper-active children in a blind trial. All children had been previously identified as positive responders to medication. Each mother–child pair performed one easy and one difficult task, both of which forced cooperation between the members of the dyad (i.e., each partner controlled one dial of an Etch-A-Sketch). With active medication (average dose of 12.5 mg), (a) children gave more directions to mothers, (b) both partners responded with less criticism and more praise, and (c) parent–child dyads made fewer errors in complet-ing the Etch-A-Sketch mazes. Most medication effects were stronger for the more difficult maze. The interpretation of Humphries *et al.* (1978) was that mothers were sensitive to the facilitation of their children's task-oriented behavior by medication, as evidenced by less frequent maternal direction giving and criticism and increased use of praise. It may be that maternal overcontrol is a result (and not a proximal cause) of hyperactive children's misbehavior.

In a programmatic series of studies, Barkley, Cunningham, and col-leagues have replicated and extended such findings. Particularly noteworthy in this work are the use of Mash, Terdal, and Anderson's (1973) Re-sponse Class Matrix, which permits coding of reciprocal behavioral transactions, and the progression to designs that include the independent variables of medication dosage and child age. In the basic design, a parent–child dyad interacts in a small playroom, with the first 15 minutes devoted to unstructured play and the remaining 15 minutes to structured workbook tasks and clean-up. For the observation system, one coder records child behaviors—both those initiated by the child and those emitted in response to a particular parental behavior—whereas the other records parent behav-iors in a parallel format. These procedures allow for such categories as "child's negative response to mother's command" and "mother praises child's task-related behavior," yielding data on the reciprocal nature of the interac-tion process.

In the first study of the series (Barkley & Cunningham, 1979), a meth-ylphenidate-placebo crossover was employed with 20 mother–child dyads. In the free-play interaction, a somewhat disturbing medication effect was noted: The hyperactive boys decreased their self-initiated interactions with their mothers and increased their independent play. Yet, mothers responded more appropriately to the social interactions that *were* initiated by the boys. Furthermore, an unlabeled control group was not employed, rendering inconclusive the severity of this apparent medication-related decrease in social interest. More positively, in the structured interactions, medication produced an increase in the boys' sustained compliance to maternal demands, a decrease in the controlling behavior (commands, negative responses) of the mothers, and an increase in contingent maternal praise. Echoing the conclusions of Humphries *et al.* (1978), Barkley and Cunningham (1979) stated that the mothers "appear to shift readily to a less coercive and more positive style of management when the children are given methylphenidate" (p. 207).

In subsequent studies, the important factors of dosage and child age have been systematically examined. Barkley, Karlsson, Strzlecki, and Murphy (1984) studied 54 hyperactive children between 4.0 and 9.9 year, with methylphenidate dosages of placebo, .15, and .50 mg/kg. Although findings were minimal in the free-play interactions, the structured interactions yielded both age effects—with increased child compliance and decreased maternal control related to increasing age—and medication effects. Regarding the latter, at both dosages the children's compliance and on-task behavior were increased over baseline levels, but only at the higher dose did maternal direction giving and negative interactions decrease. In a partial replication (Barkley, Karlsson, Pollard, & Murphy, 1985), 60 new 5- to 9-year-olds were studied at placebo as well as .30 and .70 mg/kg of methylphenidate. Again, free-play interactions did not yield medication effects, but in the structured period, child compliance increased at the higher dosage, and maternal commands/disapproval decreased at both dosages. Despite age effects, no age by medication interactions emerged. Significantly, evidence was *not* found in this report for a medication-related decrease in the sociability of the hyperactive children.

In sum, systematic, laboratory-based studies of mother–child interactions have revealed that stimulants simultaneously increase child compliance (particularly the ability to sustain compliance) and decrease parental control and negativity. Also, in some reports, *positive* parental behaviors have increased following their child's medication. The acuteness of the medication-related alterations in parental responsiveness to child behavior allows for the conclusion that parental overcontrol *results from* (rather than causes) child noncompliance and inattention, at least in the short run, calling to mind the theoretical formulations of Bell (1968) and Bell and Harper (1977) regarding bidirectional causation in parent–child interactions (see also Houts, Shutty, & Emery, 1985). The ecological validity of these playroom studies is clearly an issue, however; more naturalistic medication studies on social interaction are mandated.

PEER INTERACTIONS

We have seen that stimulant-induced improvements in the behavior of hyperactive children are often accompanied by reciprocal shifts in the responses of adults. Because the situation with regard to peers is less clear cut, however, the current section will involve a more detailed level of discussion. We will begin by discussing the types of peer-related behaviors that have been shown to benefit from stimulant medication, moving to investigations of peer interactions and then to peer evaluations.

In the first place, stimulants positively affect several peer-related classes of behavior. For example, methylphenidate has been shown to suppress broad categories of negative social behavior in structured and less structured play settings (Hinshaw et al., 1984a; Whalen et al., 1987b). Methylphenidate also facilitates some stylistic aspects of hyperactive children's dyadic communication and small-group interaction with age-mates (Whalen, Henker, Collins, McAuliffe, & Vaux, 1979b; Whalen, Henker, Dotemoto, Vaux, & McAuliffe, 1981b). Given the central role of aggressive behavior in hyperactivity (see earlier discussion), a critical question is whether stimulants decrease aggressive interactions. Until quite recently, rating scales comprised the sole outcome measures regarding this question. Amery, Minichiello, and Brown (1984) did find that dextroamphetamine reduced laboratory and projective indexes of aggression in hyperactive children; the more naturalistic study of Murphy, Pelham, and Lang (1986) showed that relatively low doses of methylphenidate decreased observed aggression and conduct problems. More recently, Hinshaw et al. (1989b) performed systematic observations of 25 hyperactive boys' aggressive interactions in naturalistic classroom and playground settings. In a crossover design, both .30 mg/kg and .60 mg/kg dosages of methylphenidate effected statistically significant reductions of verbal and physical aggression over placebo. Furthermore, the active medication decreased aggression to levels that were indistinguishable from those of normal comparison boys. Thus stimulants do not merely decrease socially noncompliant and disruptive behavior but also dramatically reduce aggressive interactions (see also Hinshaw, Buhrmester, & Heller, 1989a).

Several reports have addressed the issue of reciprocal changes in behavior and/or peer status as a function of stimulants. In the first investigation to document such effects, Cunningham, Siegel, and Offord (1985) examined the dyadic interactions of hyperactive children and normal peers. Forty-two aged-matched pairs were observed in free play, cooperative task, and simulated school settings; the crossover design involved placebo, .15, and .50 mg/kg dosages. Among 4- to 6- and 7- to 9-, but not 10- to 12-year-olds, medication reduced the frequency of dominating and controlling behaviors displayed by the hyperactive children in the simulated classroom. These reductions were accompanied by a reciprocal decrease in the controlling behaviors of the normal partners. The optimal effect was witnessed at the lower dosage, with no additional benefit at .50 mg/kg. Methylphenidate also reduced simulated-classroom activity level and enhanced on-task behavior in both hyperactive boys *and* their peers, with maximal improvement at the higher dosage. Unlike parents, however, the peers did not increase their positive responses to hyperactive children as a function of medication status.

In contrast, Pelham and Bender (1982) employed an unsupervised small-group format (one hyperactive child with four normal control children), in which free and cooperative play were the sole "tasks." Following two initial sessions without medication, they found that methylphenidate dosages of .30 and .60 mg/kg in subsequent playgroups did not alter the high rate of negative behavior in the hyperactive youngsters, nor did medication reciprocally change the behavior of the nonhyperactive playmates. A post hoc analysis did reveal that the medication *was* effective in reducing the aggressive behavior of a subgroup with high initial levels of negative verbalizations, yet whether this subgroup effect was accompanied by reciprocal changes in peer behavior was not examined.

With regard to the issue of peer evaluations, data are not plentiful. The Cunningham *et al.* (1985) study was conducted with dyads; sociometric data were not obtained. In the Pelham and Bender (1982) report, medication did not influence negative ratings assigned by normal playmates. Because, however, the hyperactive children's social behavior was not (as a group) influenced by methylphenidate, it is possible that peers were accurately responding to the aversive behavior of the target children. Alternatively, the negative reputations developed by the hyperactive children during the two premedication sessions may have been sufficiently powerful that any short-term behavioral improvement could not have altered them. Indeed, following these initial sessions, all nine hyperactive children were rated as the "least liked" children in their groups. Thus the negative reputations earned by hyperactive children are both quick to emerge and pervasive; it is possible that strong medication effects (which were not found in this report) may be insufficient to overcome them.

In a crossover study, Pelham, Bender, Caddell, and Booth (reported in Pelham, 1980) revealed nonsignificant effects of .15, .30, and .60 mg/kg methylphenidate on the evaluations of medicated hyperactive children *by* medicated peers. A significant medication effect did emerge, however, when peer ratings obtained during the hyperactive child's "best dose" were contrasted with ratings from the placebo period, suggesting that peers were sensitive to alterations in the behavior of optimally medicated hyperactive children. This possibility is particularly interesting in light of reports that hyperactive children may, in some instances, be more acutely aware of inappropriate peer behavior than are normal peers (Whalen & Henker, 1985). Nonetheless, the shifts in peer perception reported in Pelham (1980) were quite small, even for children who showed dramatic improvement with medication as indexed by adult ratings and observations.[3]

What factors can be called upon to explain such negative findings? Perhaps age-mates simply do not notice medication-related improvements in the behavior of medicated hyperactive children. This state of affairs was largely discounted, however, by Whalen et al. (1987a), who found that normal sixth graders (blind to diagnostic and to medication status) readily discerned medication–placebo differences in the behavior of videotaped hyperactive youngsters, as indexed by ratings relevant to hyperactivity, conduct problems, and school difficulties. Importantly, however, a rating category of popularity did not reveal medication effects. Also, as mentioned, it is possible that stimulant effects, even if strong, are not sufficient to overcome the quickly developing negative reputations of hyperactive children. Furthermore, evidence suggests that only rather high dosages of medication enhance the *acquisition* of critical social and interpersonal skills in hyperactive children (see Hinshaw, Henker, & Whalen, 1984b; Hinshaw et al., 1989a). Not only must negative and intrusive behaviors be decreased in the peer arena, but positive approach behaviors must be learned and developed. Research exploring the efficacy of stimulants for such acquisition is a priority.

The first set of clearly positive findings with regard to medication effects on peer status has appeared quite recently. With the same sample as that from the Hinshaw et al. (1989b) report, Whalen, Henker, Buhrmester, Hinshaw, Huber, and Laski (1989) discovered that .30 mg/kg and .60 mg/kg of methylphenidate, investigated as part of a 3-week crossover with placebo, effected significant increases in the number of friendship nominations received by hyperactive boys. In addition, medication increased the number of nominations of the descriptor categories of "cooperates" and "fun to be with." Noteworthy, however, is the finding that most of these increases were not sufficient to raise the sociometric status of the hyperactive sample to a level comparable to that of normal comparison children. Thus the clinically significant decreases in observed aggression (Hinshaw et al., 1989b) were not sufficient to improve peer nominations to normative levels, placing analyses of the *reasons for* and *predictors of* peer nominations and ratings for hyperactive children as a major topic for subsequent research.

---

[3]A caveat is in order with regard to peer evaluations of medication-induced changes. Pelham and Bender (1982) reported that dramatic decreases in aggressive behavior were found for one hyperactive child at the .6 mg/kg dosage. This same child also showed large decreases in all other interactions, however, and was rated by the staff as clearly overmedicated. Yet the peers of this child rated him quite positively on this day, suggesting that peer ratings may not discriminate beneficial from adverse medication effects. We must be careful to ensure that drug-induced improvement in peer status does not come at the expense of all interaction.

SUMMARY

Stimulant medications have pervasive effects on the social behavior of hyperactive children. In addition to (or perhaps, in consonance with) the effects of such drugs on the core symptoms of inattention, impulsivity, and hyperactivity, stimulants both reduce social disruptiveness and enhance socially appropriate behavior in classrooms, parent–child interactions, and some peer environments. Furthermore, the parents and teachers of hyperactive children respond to stimulant treatment with decreases in negative and controlling behavior. Peer response—a particularly important variable, given its strong relationship with subsequent outcome—is less definitive. Although age-mates of hyperactive children can detect medication effects, actual medication-related behavioral changes in familiar peers are less striking than those for adults (Cunningham et al., 1985); and only recently have stimulant effects on the sociometric status of hyperactive children been shown (Whalen et al., 1989). Unresolved issues in this area include (a) the potential for negative effects on sociability in some children and (b) the efficacy of stimulants with respect to the *acquisition* of needed social skills. In addition, the sufficiency of stimulant treatment should not be inferred from this discussion, particularly in light of the sparse evidence for any long-term efficacy of these drugs (e.g., Hechtman et al., 1984). Nonetheless, stimulants exert powerful, if incomplete, short-term effects on critical social interactions and transactions.

DEVELOPMENTAL CONSIDERATIONS

SOCIAL DEVELOPMENT AND PEER INTERACTIONS

In an attempt to provide a fresh perspective on the many findings presented so far, we will shift to discussion of some pertinent developmental theory, particularly in the realm of social development in the peer domain. This discussion will illuminate the "journey" taken by the hyperactive child from preschool through adolescent years, as his or her social world greatly widens and as peers play an increasingly important role in development. Our brief elaboration of this topic will lead to a reframing of the prior discussion of medication effects on hyperactive children's social behavior.

During the preschool years, youngsters enter into fairly constant groups of same-aged children for the first time.[4] At this point, children who

---

[4]Although shifts in cognitive development facilitate this major transition, there are striking individual differences in the facility with which children negotiate their early peer relationships. The longitudinal data from infancy through elementary school of Sroufe and colleagues at the University of Minnesota reveal that the quality of early parent–child attachment is an important factor in determining children's success in peer and teacher relationships during the preschool years (see Sroufe, 1979, 1983; and Bretherton, 1985, for details).

are able to exchange information successfully, to establish common activities, and to manage minor conflicts are more likely to develop acquaintances with agemates (Gottman, 1983). Whereas more is known about the initial development of friendships among preschoolers than about factors that maintain such ties, children of this age describe friendships in concrete terms, primarily by what other children *do*. They cite common activities, general play, and possession of interesting items as reasons for liking another child; aggression and rule violations head the list of reasons for disliking a peer (Hayes, 1978). Along this line, significant associations between observed behavior and sociometric status are more common in preschool samples than in older groups (Asher & Hymel, 1981).

With respect to the behaviors that facilitate entry into ongoing social play situations among young children, Putallaz and Gottman (1983) report that disagreements, question asking, and other behaviors that call attention to the self are displayed by unpopular children (who are often rejected regarding group entry), whereas acceptance is mediated in popular children by the ability to approach slowly, adapt the group's frame of reference, and thus maintain continuity with the ongoing activity. Such subtle yet crucial social-approach skills deserve more attention in the literature on child psychopathology and social skills training.

The early elementary-school years represent a significant transition period for children's peer relations and their conceptions of friendships. First, 6- to 8-year-olds continue to define friendships in concrete, behavioral terms—friends are those who play with or share materials with you (see Youniss, 1980)—and aggression and intrusiveness continue to lead to rejection. Toward the end of this age period, however, and coincident with the general decline in egocentrism, children begin to describe friends as those who assist one another or show acts of kindness. Another interesting cognitive development takes place at this time: Children begin to call upon their knowledge of peers' past behavior to predict how those peers will behave in the present (Livesly & Bromley, 1973; Rholes & Ruble, 1984). Although few studies have focused on the transitional years of first or second grade, it is quite possible that this cognitive advance sets the stage for the greater stability of sociometric ratings that are found during the elementary-school years. In a relevant report by Hymel (1986), second- (as well as fifth- and tenth-) grade children attributed the *positive behaviors* of *liked* (but not disliked) and the *negative behaviors* of *disliked* (but not liked) peers to stable, dispositional causes. It may be the case that such attributional processes or "biases" in peer interpretations of social behavior may contribute to the stability of social acceptance and rejection in children by the second grade.

As children move into middle childhood, they begin to develop more accurate and abstract conceptualizations of their peers and begin to leave behind the physical, contact-dominated descriptions that predominated earlier. During these years, the behaviors that contribute to friendship become complex and idiosyncratic, perhaps accounting for the decline in the association between sociometric status and observed behavior with age (Asher & Hymel, 1981). In addition, aggression *per se* is no longer the most salient factor in differentiating low- from high-status peers: A variety of deviant but nonaggressive behaviors, including dishonesty, irritation, and immaturity, take precedence (Dor & Asher, cited in Asher & Hymel, 1981).

Throughout childhood, children spend increasing amounts of time with peers. By adolescence, peers predominate as the prime agents of socialization (Medrich, Rosen, Rubin, & Buckley, 1982). In keeping with this trend, children increasingly extract information about themselves from their relationships with peers, creating more articulated self-definitions from this knowledge. Parental judgments fade as the primary source of information about the self during development through childhood (Rosenberg, 1979); by adolescence, deliberately chosen friends provide the chief source of evaluation.

At the same time, the social hierarchy within peer groups becomes more rule governed and less flexible. Whereas membership in preschool playgroups may fluctuate from day to day, with few implicit or explicit norms for behavior, group membership becomes more stable and rule-governed as children progress toward adolescence. Furthermore, children above the ages of 7 or 8 find it particularly difficult to leave behind the negative images of peers that have been forged. Indeed, Hymel (1986) has reported that adolescents may actually be less likely to alter their negative attitudes toward disliked peers than are younger children.

IMPLICATIONS FOR HYPERACTIVITY

This brief foray into social development raises several key points regarding the main topic of stimulant medication and hyperactivity. First, as discussed earlier, teachers and parents respond reciprocally to medication-induced improvements. They are therefore likely to be satisfied with stimulant intervention, particularly if behavioral disruption is diminished and compliance and self-regulation are enhanced. The many reports employing teacher and/or parent ratings of global improvement attest to such satisfaction with medication treatment.

With regard to peers, however, the situation is less clear: Children in dyadic interactions do not seem to behave more positively toward medicated hyperactive peers, although their interactions are less controlling (Cunningham *et al.*, 1985). Also, in the sole report that has documented medication-related increases in sociometric status, the gains were often not of sufficient magnitude to induce a normal level of peer reputation (Whalen *et al.*, 1989). Thus, a child who is perceived by adults to be responding quite favorably to stimulant treatment may not be receiving the same level of critically important peer feedback.

This scenario may be particularly salient for older hyperactive children, whose negative reputations have, in all probability, become more consolidated over the years. Furthermore, extrapolating from Hymel's (1986) findings, it is likely that even on those occasions that peers do recognize favorable changes in the behavior of hyperactive age-mates, whether or not induced by stimulant treatment, they may tend to attribute the positive behavior to situational factors and not to positive features or efforts of the children themselves. Such events are occurring, it should be reiterated, at the precise times that peers are becoming the prime agents of socialization; the critical importance of peer exposure, acceptance, and interchange for subsequent social and personal development cannot be overstated (Hartup, 1983; Parker & Asher, 1987). Persons wishing to intervene with the social and interpersonal deficits and excesses of hyperactive children must be aware of the wider peer context in which improved behavior mut be attempted and reciprocated.

A second consideration is that, even with younger hyperactive children whose peer relations are much more tied to observable, ongoing behavior, stimulant-related changes in behavioral style or reductions in negative behavior and aggression should not be expected to translate directly or automatically into improved functioning with peers. Children who attain preferred status within peer groups are effective at initiating social interaction and acknowledging the overtures of others (see previous discussion). They are often appropriately tentative when entering a group activity, first observing and attempting to comprehend the play that is transpiring, and then only gradually moving into the group. Whereas medication may temper the vigor of hyperactive children's approach behavior and even reduce aggression, there is little evidence to suggest that the skills required for successful peer functioning will emerge as a function of these reductions. In short, medication may not be sufficient to enhance key social approach behaviors in the hyperactive child. Determination of the precise cognitive, affective, and behavioral skills that are necessary for proactive social initiation is a key agenda item for investigators and practitioners in the field.

Overall, the preceding discussion has emphasized that any consideration of medication effects on social behavior with peers must take into account such variables as social competence, initiation of behavior, development of reputation, and attributions for behavior change. Indeed, investigations must be multidisciplinary and transactional if we are to obtain full understanding of the role that medications play in facilitating social skill and social adjustment. Furthermore, investigators must be increasingly concerned with the ecological validity of the research that is performed, so that we may be sure that the responses of social partners to stimulant-related improvement do indeed occur in the real world. Research on the effects of stimulants on key social interactions is in a budding stage of development; the field must not lose sight of the roles that environments, social partners, and reciprocal interchanges play in the study of medication effects.

CONCLUDING COMMENTS

The question of whether stimulant medication exerts important effects on the social behavior of hyperactive children was raised at the outset of this chapter. As should be apparent, the answer to this question is a decided "yes." Stimulants enhance social compliance and task orientation in social interchanges with teachers and parents, who respond, in turn, with a less controlling style. In peer settings, stimulants decrease negative social behavior and aggression; and recent evidence suggests some effects on reciprocal peer behavior as well as on peer status. Yet these latter effects may well fall short of clinical significance. Overall, then, stimulants exert clear effects on key elements of the social functioning of children labeled hyperactive or ADHD, although the ultimate clinical significance of such effects does not appear to be strong, as evidenced by the less-than-optimal long-term outcomes for many medicated hyperactive children (Hechtman et al., 1984).

ADDITIONAL ISSUES REGARDING STIMULANTS

Several features of such medication effects that were not emphasized in the preceding review should be highlighted. First, in any given hyperactive child, medication response is *not* a unitary variable. That is, enormous within-subject variability in clinical response to stimulant drugs exists, even in children who are globally labeled as *positive responders* to stimulants. For instance, a hyperactive child may show greatly improved "on-task" behavior with stimulants but little reduction in impertinent comments to parents; another child who becomes more cooperative with peers may not display increased impulse control in the classroom. In short, medication response does not constitute a meaningful variable in a global sense; one must examine specific responsiveness in discrete behavioral domains to determine whether the medication is effective (Gualtieri & Hicks, 1985).

Perhaps, in part, because of the lack of unitary medication response in hyperactive children, the search for predictors of stimulant medication responsiveness has provided little yield (Barkley, 1976; Gualtieri & Hicks, 1985). Thus, whether a child will respond to medication is best determined through a medication trial rather than a prediction equation. An empirical approach is the only justifiable one for scientific or clinical purposes.

We should also emphasize that, despite the many significant *group* effects of stimulant medication that have been cited, (a) some hyperactive children are unresponsive to stimulants and (b) some significant effects are actually rather small in magnitude (e.g., Whalen et al., 1979b; Whalen et al., 1987b). (On the other hand, as shown by Hinshaw et al., 1989b, the magnitude of stimulant-related reductions in such key variables as aggression is often large for individual children, even at relatively low dosages.) In sum, despite the real and robust group effects of medications on key social behaviors, the sufficiency of medication treatment for social outcomes cannot be assumed.

Studies of the role of medication *dosage* on social behaviors have appeared only within the last decade. Such reports as Sprague and Sleator (1977), Halliday, Gnauck, Rosenthal, McKibben, & Callaway (1980), Pelham *et al.* (1985), Barkley *et al.* (1985b), Whalen *et al.* (1987b), and Hinshaw *et al.* (1989b) have typically found indications of linear dose response curves with respect to social behavioral outcomes, with moderate to high dosages of methylphenidate (.60 to .80 mg/kg) often producing greater behavioral change than lower dosages (.15 to .30 mg/kg). Such linear effects are not consistently replicated, however, across outcome measures, subsamples, or investigations (see Barkley *et al.*, 1984); indeed, surprisingly strong effects are often found at relatively low dosages (e.g., Pelham *et al.*, 1985). In addition, dose-response effects that are apparent in group data may be reflected only rarely when individual subjects are examined (Hinshaw *et al.*, 1989b). Dosage is one of many variables that must be better controlled in subsequent research on hyperactive children's social interactions.

ADJUNCTIVE INTERVENTIONS

Because of the lack of sufficiency of stimulant medications, stimulants should regularly be associated with supplementary interventions, particularly in the peer domain. Yet what should such adjunctive treatments constitute? This is a thorny issue for the clinician/investigator. Although existing research certainly points to the viability of behavioral interventions for hyperactive children, the often-cited problems of generalization and maintenance are clearly an issue (Mash & Dalby, 1979). Furthermore, typical "social skills training" interventions are not likely to facilitate clinically significant improvements in the interpersonal realm for these children (e.g., Berler, Gross, & Drabman, 1982); and cognitive–behavioral interventions for hyperactivity have not lived up to their initial promise of clinical benefits (Abikoff, 1987; Hinshaw & Erhardt, 1991). In short, despite the call for alternative or adjunctive treatments, extant interventions have limitations, and studies tend to favor stimulants when medications and alternatives are contrasted "head to head" (e.g., Gittelman *et al.*, 1980).

On the other hand, there is growing hope (and some evidence) that *adding* behavioral or cognitive–behavioral interventions to medication regimens will facilitate greater gains than will medication alone (Pelham & Murphy, 1986). We do not have time to debate the evidence on this topic; the extant data are far from resolved in this regard. We will state, however, that one promising area for investigation involves the active inclusion of peers in treatment programs for hyperactive children's social difficulties. Because peers may be the last to "accept" the social benefits of stimulant medications and because the acquisition and rehearsal of social approach behaviors are probably best performed with age-mates rather than exclusively with adults, we advocate the exploration of creative uses of peers in intervention programs for hyperactive children's serious social and interpersonal problems.

As one example of such use, peers may be enlisted to motivate hyperactive children to enter treatment (see Henker, Whalen, & Hinshaw, 1980). They can also serve as agents for the rehearsal of newly learned social strategies (Hinshaw *et al.*, 1984b; see also Bierman, Miller, & Stabb, 1987, for an example of the use of peers in interventions for socially rejected children). In addition, age-mates may, under skilled clinical direction from trainer/therapists, be in the best position to help hyperactive children realistically appraise the impact of their (often negative) social behavior (e.g., Hinshaw *et al.*, 1984a). The potential roles for peers in treatment programs for hyperactive children are both variegated and of potential clinical importance.

The call for peers to be regular additions to treatment programs for hyperactive children is not dissimilar to the plea, several decades ago, for parents and teachers to be the mainstays of behavioral interventions for behavior disordered children. There are severe limitations to what the individual therapist can do for any externalizing child who is treated alone in the playroom or therapy setting; the field has come to accept that parents and/or teachers will act, in many respects, as the primary change agents for such children. (The use of parent-directed interventions is particularly salient for hyperactive children, given that medications are typically given for the schoolday only and that parents may see no effects whatsoever of medications during late afternoons or evenings.) There are certainly ethical issues to be considered if peers are to be included in hyperactive children's treatment programs, particularly if nonlabeled age-mates (and not just other referred youngsters) are enlisted to serve as facilitators of intervention programs. Yet the field must come to grips with the realization that hyperactivity does not exist in a vacuum and that peers cannot be ignored as potential treatment targets and agents.

In emphasizing both the peer difficulties of hyperactive children and the need for inclusion of age-mates in intervention programs, we should remember that even as the peer culture increases in importance over time, it is impossible to extricate peer influences on development from those of families and schools (Hartup, 1983). Thus robust interventions must continue to incorporate input from and involvement with teachers and parents, as these are the adults who are in key positions to promote generalization to home and school environments. Although difficult to evaluate (see Satterfield, Satterfield, & Cantwell, 1981), truly multimodal interventions are mandated for the comprehensive treatment of the hyperactive child.

In sum, the social and interpersonal problems of hyperactive children are quite severe. Indeed, it is impossible to separate the diagnostic category of "hyperactivity" from the social contexts in which it occurs. Although medication effects on social behaviors with adults and children are pervasive, their limitations and lack of sufficiency must motivate us to work actively to seek adjunctive interventions that incorporate the efforts of parents, teachers, and peers. It is only through such systematic, painstaking, and long-term intervention that the course of hyperactivity is likely to be altered.

REFERENCES

Abikoff, H. (1987). An evaluation of cognitive behavior therapy for hyperactive children. In B. B. Lahey & A. E. Kazdin (Eds.), *Advances in clinical child psychology* (Vol. 10, pp. 171–206). New York: Plenum Press.

Abikoff, H., Gittelman-Klein, R., & Klein, D. F. (1977). Validation of a classroom observation code for hyperactive children. *Journal of Consulting and Clinical Psychology, 45,* 772–783.

Abikoff, H., Gittelman, R., & Klein, D. F. (1980). Classroom observation code for hyperactive children: A replication of validity. *Journal of Consulting and Clinical Psychology, 48,* 555–565.

American Psychiatric Association. (1987). *Diagnostic and statistical manual of mental disorders* (3rd ed., revised). Washington, DC: Author.

Amery, B., Minichiello, M. D., & Brown, G. L. (1984). Aggression in hyperactive boys: Response to d-amphetamine. *Journal of the American Academy of Child Psychiatry, 23,* 291–294.

Asher, S. R., & Hymel, S. (1981). Children's social competence in peer relations: Sociometric and behavioral assessment. In J. D. Wine & M. D. Smye (Eds.), *Social competence* (pp. 125–157). New York: Guilford Press.

Barkley, R. A. (1976). Predicting the response of hyperkinetic children to stimulant drugs: A review. *Journal of Abnormal Child Psychology, 4,* 327–348.

Barkley, R. A. (1981). The use of psychopharmacology to study reciprocal influences in parent-child interaction. *Journal of Abnormal Child Psychology, 9,* 303–310.

Barkley, R. A. (1982). Guidelines for defining hyperactivity in children: Attention deficit disorder with hyperactivity. In B. B. Lahey & A. E. Kazdin (Eds.), *Advances in clinical child psychology* (Vol. 5, pp. 137–180). New York: Plenum Press.

Barkley, R. A. (1985a). The parent-child interaction patterns of hyperactive children: Precursors to aggressive behavior? In M. Wolraich & D. K. Routh (Eds.), *Advances in developmental and behavioral pediatrics* (Vol. 6, pp. 117–150). Greenwich, CT: JAI Press.

Barkley, R. A. (1985b). The social behavior of hyperactive children: Developmental changes, drug effects, and situational variation. In R. McMahon & R. Peters (Eds.), *Childhood disorders* (pp. 218–243). New York: Brunner/Mazel.

Barkley, R. A. (1989). Attention deficit hyperactivity disorder. In E. J. Mash & R. A. Barkley (Eds.). *Treatment of childhood disorders* (pp. 39–72). New York: Guilford Press.

Barkley, R. A., & Cunningham, C. E. (1979). The effects of methylphenidate on the mother-child interactions of hyperactive children. *Archives of General Psychiatry, 36,* 201–208.

Barkley, R. A., Karlsson, J., Strzelecki, E., & Murphy, J. V. (1984). Effects of age and Ritalin dosage on the mother-child interactions of hyperactive children. *Journal of Consulting and Clinical Psychology, 52,* 750–758.

Barkley, R. A., Karlsson, J., & Pollard, S. (1985a). Effects of age on the mother-child interactions of ADD-H and normal boys. *Journal of Abnormal Child Psychology, 13,* 631–637.

Barkley, R. A., Karlsson, J., Pollard, S., & Murphy, J. V. (1985b). Developmental changes in the mother-child interactions of hyperactive boys: Effects of two dose levels of Ritalin. *Journal of Child Psychology and Psychiatry, 26,* 705–715.

Barkley, R. A., Fischer, M., Edelbrock, C. S., & Smallish, L. (1990). The adolescent outcome of hyperactive children diagnosed by research criteria: I. An 8-year prospective follow-up study. *Journal of the American Academy of Child and Adolescent Psychology, 29,* 546–557.

Bell, R. Q. (1968). A reinterpretation of the direction of effects in studies of socialization. *Psychological Review, 75,* 81–95.

Bell, R. Q., & Harper, L. V. (1977). *Child effects on adults.* Hillsdale, NJ: Erlbaum.

Berler, E. S., Gross, A. M., & Drabman, R. S. (1982). Social skills training with children: Proceed with caution. *Journal of Applied Behavior Analysis, 15,* 41–53.

Bierman, K. L., Miller, C. L., & Stabb, S. D. (1987). Improving the social behavior and peer acceptance of rejected boys: Effects of social skill training with instructions and prohibitions. *Journal of Consulting and Clinical Psychology, 55,* 194–200.

Bretherton, I. (1985). Attachment theory: Retrospect and prospect. In I. Bretherton & E. Waters (Eds.), Growing points of attachment theory and research (pp. 3–25). *Monographs of the Society for Research in Child Development, 50,* Serial No. 209(1–2).

Campbell, S. B. (1975). Mother-child interaction: A comparison of hyperactive, learning disabled, and normal boys. *American Journal of Orthopsychiatry, 45,* 51–57.

Campbell, S. B., & Paulauskas, S. (1979). Peer relations in hyperactive children. *Journal of Child Psychology and Psychiatry, 26,* 233–246.

Conners, C. K. (1973). Rating scales for use in drug studies with children. *Psychopharmacology Bulletin* (Special issue: *Pharmacotherapy of children*), 24–84.

Cowen, E. L., Pederson, A., Babigian, H., Izzo, L. D., & Trost, M. A. (1973). Long-term follow-up of early detected vulnerable children. *Journal of Consulting and Clinical Psychology, 41,* 438–446.

Cunningham, C. E., & Barkley, R. A. (1979). The interactions of normal and hyperactive children with their mothers in free play and structured tasks. *Child Development, 50,* 217–224.

Cunningham, C. E., Siegel, L. S., & Offord, D. R., (1985). A developmental dose-response analysis of the effects of methylphenidate on the peer interactions of attention deficit disordered boys. *Journal of Child Psychology and Psychiatry, 26,* 955–971.

Donnelly, M., & Rapoport, J. L. (1985). Attention deficit disorders. In J. M. Weiner (Ed.), *Diagnosis and psychopharmacology of childhood and adolescent disorders* (pp. 179–197). New York: Wiley.

Dotemoto, S. (1984). *Peer status and peer relations of hyperactive and normal boys: Peer and adult perceptions.* Unpublished doctoral dissertation, University of California, Los Angeles.

Gadow, K. D. (1986). *Children on medication* (Vol. 1). San Diego, College-Hill Press.

Gittelman, R., Abikoff, H., Pollack, E., Klein, D. F., Katz, S., & Mattes, J. (1980). A controlled trial of behavior modification and methylphenidate in hyperactive children. In C. K. Whalen & B. Henker (Eds.), *Hyperactive children: The social ecology of identification and treatment* (pp. 221–243). New York: Academic Press.

Gittelman, R., Mannuzza, S., Shenker, R., & Bonagura, N. (1985). Hyperactive boys almost grown up: I. Psychiatric status. *Archives of General Psychiatry, 42,* 937–947.

Glow, R. A., & Glow, P. H. (1980). Peer and self-rating: Children's perception of behavior relevant to hyperkinetic impulse disorder. *Journal of Abnormal Child Psychology, 8,* 471–490.

Gottman, J. M. (1983). How children become friends. *Monographs of the Society for Research in Child Development, 48,* Serial No. 201(3).

Gualtieri, C. T., & Hicks, R. E. (1985). Neuropharmacology of methylphenidate and a neural substrate for childhood hyperactivity. *Psychiatric Clinics of North America, 8,* 875–892.

Halliday, R., Gnauck, K., Rosenthal, J. R., McKibben, J. L., & Calloway, E. (1980). The effects of methylphenidate dosage on school and home behavior of the hyperactive child. In R. M. Knights & D. J. Bakker (Eds.), *Treatment of hyperactive and learning disordered children: Current research* (pp. 237–247). Baltimore: University Park Press.

Hartup, W. W. (1983). Peer relations. In P. H. Mussen (Ed.), *Handbook of child psychology: Socialization, personality, and social development* (Vol. 4, 4th ed., pp. 103–196). New York: Wiley.

Hayes, D. S. (1978). Cognitive bases for liking and disliking among preschool children. *Child Development, 49*, 906–909.

Hechtman, L., Weiss, G., & Perlman, T. (1984). Young adult outcome of hyperactive children who received long-term stimulant treatment. *Journal of the American Academy of Child Psychiatry, 23*, 261–269.

Henker, B., Whalen, C. K., & Collins, B. E. (1979). Double-blind and triple-blind assessments of medication and placebo responses in hyperactive children. *Journal of Abnormal Child Psychology, 7*, 1–13.

Henker, B., Whalen, C. K., & Hinshaw, S. P. (1980). The attributional contexts of cognitive intervention strategies. *Exceptional Education Quarterly, 1*, 17–30.

Hinshaw, S. P. (1987a). Hyperactivity, attention deficit disorders, and learning disabilities. In V. B. van Hasselt & M. Hersen (Eds.), *Psychological evaluation of the developmentally and physically disabled* (pp. 213–260). New York: Plenum Press.

Hinshaw, S. P. (1987b). On the distinction between attentional deficits/hyperactivity and conduct problems/aggression in child psychopathology. *Psychological Bulletin, 101*, 443–463.

Hinshaw, S. P., & Erhardt, D. (1991). Attention-deficit hyperactivity disorder. In P. C. Kendall (Ed.), *Child and adolescent therapy: Cognitive-behavioral procedures* (pp. 98–128). New York: Guilford Press.

Hinshaw, S. P., Henker, B., & Whalen, C. K. (1984a). Cognitive-behavioral and pharmacologic interventions for hyperactive boys: Comparative and combined effects. *Journal of Consulting and Clinical Psychology, 52*, 739–749.

Hinshaw, S. P., Henker, B., & Whalen, C. K. (1984b). Self-control in hyperactive boys in anger-inducing situations: Effects of cognitive-behavioral training and of methylphenidate. *Journal of Abnormal Child Psychology, 12*, 55–77.

Hinshaw, S. P., Buhrmester, D., & Heller, T. (1989a). Anger control in response to verbal provocation: Effects of stimulant medication for boys with ADHD. *Journal of Abnormal Child Psychology, 17*, 393–407.

Hinshaw, S. P., Henker, B., Whalen, C. K., Erhardt, D., & Dunnington, R. E. (1989b). Aggressive, prosocial, and nonsocial behavior in hyperactive boys. Dose effects of methylphenidate in naturalistic settings. *Journal of Consulting and Clinical Psychology, 57*, 636–643.

Houts, A. C., Shutty, M. S., & Emery, R. E. (1985). The impact of children on adults. In B. B. Lahey & A. E. Kazdin (Eds.), *Advances in clinical child psychology* (Vol. 8, pp. 267–307). New York: Plenum Press.

Humphries, T., Kinsbourne, M., & Swanson, J. (1978). Stimulant effects on cooperation and social interaction between hyperactive children and their mothers. *Journal of Child Psychology and Psychiatry, 19*, 13–22.

Hymel, S. (1986). Interpretations of peer behavior: Affective bias in childhood and adolescence. *Child Development, 57*, 431–445.

Klein, D. F., Gittelman, R., Quitkin, F., & Rifkin, A. (1980). *Diagnosis and drug treatment of psychiatric disorders: Adults and children* (2nd ed.). Baltimore, MD: Williams & Wilkins.

Livesly, W. J., & Bromley, D. B. (1973). *Person perception in childhood and adolescence*. London: Wiley.

Loney, J., & Milich, R. (1982). Hyperactivity, inattention, and aggression in clinical practice. In M. Wolraich & D. K. Routh (Eds.), *Advances in developmental and behavioral pediatrics* (Vol. 3, pp. 113–147). Greenwich, CT: JAI Press.

Mash, E. J., & Dalby, J. T. (1979). Behavioral interventions for hyperactivity. In R. L. Trites (Ed.), *Hyperactivity in children: Etiology, measurement, and treatment implications* (pp. 161–216). Baltimore: University Park Press.

Mash, E. J., & Johnston, C. (1982). A comparison of the mother-child interactions of younger and older hyperactive and normal children. *Child Development, 53*, 1371–1381.

Mash, E. J., Terdal, L., & Anderson, K. (1973). The Response Class Matrix: A procedure for recording parent-child interactions. *Journal of Consulting and Clinical Psychology, 41*, 163–164.

Medrich, E. A., Rosen, J., Rubin, V., & Buckley, S. (1982). *The serious business of growing up.* Berkeley: University of California Press.

Milich, R., & Fitzgerald, G. (1985). Validation of inattention/overactivity and aggression ratings with classroom observations. *Journal of Consulting and Clinical Psychology, 53*, 139–140.

Milich, R., & Landau, S. (1982). Socialization and peer relations in hyperactive children. In K. D. Gadow & I. Bialer (Eds.), *Advances in learning and behavioral disabilities* (Vol. 1, pp. 283–339). Greenwich, CT: JAI Press.

Milich, R., & Landau, S. (1989). The role of social status variables in differentiating subgroups of hyperactive children. In L. M. Bloomingdale & J. M. Swanson (Eds.), *Attention deficit disorder* (Vol. 4, pp. 1–16). Oxford: Pergamon Press.

Milich, R., & Loney, J. (1979). The role of hyperactive and aggressive symptomatology in predicting adolescent outcome among hyperactive children. *Journal of Pediatric Psychology, 4*, 93–112.

Milich, R., Loney, J., & Landau, S. (1982). Independent dimensions of hyperactivity and aggression: A validation with playroom observation data. *Journal of Abnormal Psychology, 91*, 183–198.

Murphy, D. A., Pelham, W. E., & Lang, A. R. (1986, August). *CNS stimulant effects on aggression in ADD and ADD/Aggressive children.* Paper presented at the meeting of the American Psychological Association, Washington, D.C.

Parker, J. G., & Asher, S. R. (1987). Peer relations and later personal adjustment: Are low-accepted children at risk? *Psychological Bulletin, 102*, 357–389.

Pelham, W. E. (1980, September). Peer relationships in hyperactive children: Description and treatment effects. In R. Milich (Chair), *Peer relationships among hyperactive children.* Symposium held at the meeting of the American Psychological Association, Montreal.

Pelham, W. E. (1986, August). Peer relationships in children with hyperactivity/attention deficit disorder: Their nature and the effects of psychostimulant drugs. In S. Johnson (Chair), *Childhood chronic conditions in the social context.* Symposium held at the meeting of the American Psychological Association, Washington, DC.

Pelham, W. E., & Bender, M. E. (1982). Peer relationships in hyperactive children: Description and treatment. In K. D. Gadow & I. Bialer (Eds.), *Advances in learning and behavioral disabilities* (Vol. 1, pp. 365–436). Greenwich, CT: JAI Press.

Pelham, W. E., & Milich, R. (1984). Peer relations in children with hyperactivity/attention deficit disorder. *Journal of Learning Disabilities, 17*, 560–567.

Pelham, W. E., & Murphy, H. A. (1986). Attention deficit and conduct disorders. In M. Hersen (Ed.), *Pharmacological and behavioral treatments: An integrative approach* (pp. 108–148). New York: Wiley.

Pelham, W. E., Bender, M. E., Caddell, J., Booth, S., & Moorer, S. H. (1985). Methylphenidate and children with attention deficit disorder: Dose effects on classroom academic and social behavior. *Archives of General Psychiatry, 42*, 948–952.

Putallaz, M., & Gottman, J. M. (1983). Social skills and group acceptance. In S. R. Asher & J. M. Gottman (Eds.), *The development of children's friendships* (pp. 116–149). New York: Cambridge University Press.

Quay, H. C. (1979). Classification. In H. C. Quay & J. S. Werry (Eds.), *Psychopathological disorders of childhood* (2nd ed., pp. 1–42). New York: Wiley.

Quay, H. C. (1986). Classification. In H. C. Quay & J. S. Werry (Eds.), *Psychopathological disorders of childhood* (3rd ed., pp. 1–34). New York: Wiley.

Quay, H. C., & Peterson, D. R. (1983). *Interim manual for the Revised Behavior Problem Checklist* (1st ed.). Unpublished manuscript, University of Miami.

Rholes, W. S., & Ruble, D. N. (1984). Children's understanding of dispositional characteristics of others. *Child Development, 55*, 550–560.

Rie, H. E., Rie, E. D., Stewart, S., & Ambuel, J. P. (1976). Effects of methylphenidate on underachieving children. *Journal of Consulting and Clinical Psychology, 44*, 250–260.

Rosenberg, M. (1979). *Conceiving the self.* New York: Basic Books.

Ross, D. M., & Ross, S. A. (1982). *Hyperactivity: Current issues, research, and theory.* New York: Wiley.

Sandberg, S. T., Rutter, M., & Taylor, E. (1978). Hyperkinetic disorder in psychiatric clinic attenders. *Developmental Medicine and Child Neurology, 20*, 279–299.

Satterfield, J. H., Hoppe, C. M., & Schell, A. M. (1982). A prospective study of delinquency in 110 adolescent boys with attention deficit disorder and 88 normal adolescent boys. *American Journal of Psychiatry, 139*, 795–798.

Satterfield, J. H., Satterfield, B. T., & Cantwell, D. P. (1981). Three-year multimodality treatment study of 100 hyperactive boys. *Journal of Pediatrics, 98*, 650–655.

Sprague, R. L., & Sleator, E. K. (1977). Methylphenidate in hyperkinetic children: Differences in dose effects on learning and social behavior. *Science, 198*, 1274–1276.

Sroufe, L. A. (1979). The coherence of individual development. *American Psychologist, 34*, 834–841.

Sroufe, L. A. (1983). Infant-caregiver attachment and patterns of adaptation in preschool: The roots of maladaptation and competence. In M. Perlmutter (Ed.), *Minnesota Symposium in Child Psychology* (Vol. 16, pp. 41–81). Hillsdale, NJ: Erlbaum.

Swanson, J. M., & Kinsbourne, M. (1976). Stimulant-related state-dependent learning in hyperactive children. *Science, 192*, 1354–1356.

Swanson, J., Kinsbourne, M., Roberts, W., & Zucker, K. (1978). Time-response analysis of the effect of stimulant medication on the learning ability of children referred for hyperactivity. *Pediatrics, 61*, 21–29.

Tallmadge, J., & Barkley, R. A. (1983). The interactions of hyperactive and normal boys with their fathers and mothers. *Journal of Abnormal Child Psychology, 11*, 565–579.

Weiss, G., Hechtman, L., Milroy, T., & Perlman, T. (1985). Psychiatric status of hyperactives as adults: A controlled perspective 15-year follow up of 63 hyperactive children. *Journal of the American Academy of Child Psychiatry, 24*, 211–220.

Whalen, C. K. (1989). Attention deficit and hyperactivity disorders. In T. H. Ollendick & M. Hersen (Eds.), *Handbook of child psychopathology* (2nd ed., pp. 131–169). New York: Plenum Press.

Whalen, C. K., & Henker, B. (1980). The social ecology of psycho-stimulant treatment: A model for conceptual and empirical analysis. In C. K. Whalen & B. Henker (Eds.), *Hyperactive children: The social ecology of identification and treatment* (pp. 3–51). New York: Academic Press.

Whalen, C. K., & Henker, B. (1985). The social worlds of hyperactive (ADDH) children. *Clinical Psychology Review, 5*, 447–478.

Whalen, C. K., Collins, B. E., Henker, B., Alkus, S. R., Adams, D., & Stapp, J. (1978). Behavior observations of hyperactive children and methylphenidate (Ritalin) effects in systematically structured classroom environments: Now you see them, now you don't. *Journal of Pediatric Psychology, 3*, 177–187.

Whalen, C. K., Henker, B., Buhrmester, D., Hinshaw, S. P., Huber, A., & Laski, K. (1989). Does stimulant medication improve the peer status of hyperactive children? *Journal of Consulting and Clinical Psychology, 57*, 545–549.

Whalen, C. K., Henker, B., Castro, J., & Granger, D. (1987a). Peer perceptions of hyperactivity and medication effects. *Child Development, 58*, 816–828.

Whalen, C. K., Henker, B., Collins, B. E., Finck, D., & Dotemoto, S. (1979a). A social ecology of hyperactive boys: Medication effects in structured classroom environments. *Journal of Applied Behavior Analysis, 12*, 65–81.

Whalen, C. K., Henker, B., Collins, B. E., McAuliffe, S., & Vaux, A. (1979b). Peer interaction in a structured communication task: Comparisons of normal and hyperactive boys and of methylphenidate (Ritalin) and placebo effects. *Child Development, 50*, 388–401.

Whalen, C. K., Henker, B., & Dotemoto, S. (1980). Methylphenidate and hyperactivity: Effects on teacher behaviors. *Science, 208*, 1280–1282.

Whalen, C. K., Henker, B., & Dotemoto, S. (1981a). Teacher response to the methylphenidate (Ritalin) versus placebo status of hyperactive boys in the classroom. *Child Development, 52*, 1005–1014.

Whalen, C. K., Henker, B., Dotemoto, S., Vaux, A., & McAuliffe, S. (1981b). Hyperactivity and methylphenidate: Peer interaction styles. In K. D. Gadow & J. Loney (Eds.), *Psychosocial aspects of drug treatment for hyperactivity* (pp. 295–324). Boulder, CO: Westview Press.

Whalen, C. K., Henker, B., Swanson, J. M., Granger, D., Kliewer, W., & Spencer, J. (1987b). Natural social behaviors in hyperactive children: Dose effects of methylphenidate. *Journal of Consulting and Clinical Psychology, 55*, 187–193.

Youniss, J. (1980). *Parents and peers in social development: A Sullivan-Piaget perspective.* Chicago: University of Chicago Press.

PART THREE

STATISTICAL APPROACHES TO SOCIAL INTERACTION ANALYSIS

CHAPTER ELEVEN

The Analysis of Sequence in Social Interaction

THOMAS N. BRADBURY AND FRANK D. FINCHAM

INTRODUCTION

Although all behaviors occur over time, it is relatively uncommon for the temporal order or sequence of behaviors to be a matter of great interest in psychological research. Thus sequence, an intrinsic feature of all behavioral phenomena, has been largely ignored in attempts to explore and understand these phenomena. It is particularly noteworthy that this oversight occurs in research on social interaction, where investigators often claim to study reciprocity, patterns, processes, systems, and cycles. Rather than examine the sequential dependencies among behaviors that are strongly implied by these terms, simple rates of behavior are often studied instead. This practice is deficient because it fails to capture the dynamic qualities of social interaction and also promotes inferential error: A behavior that emerges from the combined actions of two individuals is often viewed as being solely determined by the one individual exhibiting the behavior. More generally, "efforts to analyze given actions while ignoring their interactive context seem misdirected, error prone, and noise generating" (Duncan, Kanki, Mokros, & Fiske, 1984, p. 1346).

The purpose of this chapter is to present two approaches to the analysis of social interaction data that permit the sequence, and thus the interactive

THOMAS N. BRADBURY • Department of Psychology, University of California, Los Angeles, California 90024. FRANK D. FINCHAM • Department of Psychology, University of Illinois at Urbana–Champaign, Champaign, Illinois 61820.

Personality, Social Skills, and Psychopathology: An Individual Differences Approach, edited by David G. Gilbert and James J. Connolly. Plenum Press, New York, 1991.

context, of behavior to be examined. The two approaches, log-linear analysis and lag sequential analysis, were chosen because they have been developed most fully and are the most commonly used methods to study sequence in the social sciences. A third technique, time-series analysis, is not reviewed here for two reasons. First, the topic is too complex to be treated adequately in a short chapter, particularly when other methods are also reviewed. (For comprehensive discussions see Catalano, Dooley, & Jackson, 1983; Chatfield, 1980; Gottman, 1981; McCain & McCleary, 1979; McCleary & Hay, 1980). Second, time-series analysis is most appropriate when continuous measurements are taken, yielding a form of data rarely available in social interaction research (for noteworthy exceptions see Levenson & Gottman, 1983, 1985; Gottman & Levenson, 1985). Instead, our focus is on the analysis of *categorical* data (also referred to as nominal, qualitative, or discrete data), a form of data that is typically generated in observational investigations of social interaction.

This chapter introduces the fundamental features of log-linear and lag sequential analysis in simple, nontechnical language. Our intent is to provide a basic yet sound introduction to these topics and to direct the reader to other more detailed papers and texts so that a practicable knowledge of sequential analysis may eventually be achieved.[1] Log-linear and lag sequential analysis are presented using examples from the study of marital interaction. This bias reflects the context in which we are most familiar with sequential methods rather than any limit on the domain to which the techniques can be applied. In fact, the methods are described in general terms so that they can be applied to a diverse array of topics in clinical, social, educational, and developmental psychology, as well as in ethology and communication sciences.

The remainder of this chapter is organized into three main sections. The first two sections cover log-linear and lag sequential analysis, respectively. For each, the method is introduced and discussed in terms of a concrete example concerning the analysis of marital interaction. In the final section an overview of the two analytic strategies is offered.

LOG-LINEAR ANALYSIS

INTRODUCTION

Marital interaction is a common context for investigating interpersonal processes, where a primary aim has been to distinguish the interactions of distressed couples from those of nondistressed couples. The paradigm employed in the study of marital interaction usually involves inviting married

---

[1]References to further reading on log-linear and lag sequential analysis are available in appendices to this chapter.

couples to a laboratory where data are collected in the form of individuals' self-reports of marital satisfaction as well as videotapes of each couple discussing an issue they have identified as a major problem in their marriage. Verbatim transcripts of each interaction are then generated and coders, well versed in a particular coding system, work with the videotape and transcript to assign a code from the system to each meaningful unit of speech (e.g., a complete thought or sentence). A typical coding system might have three categories (for behaviors positive, neutral, and negative in affective tone), each of which can be given to either of the two interactants (husband, wife), for a total of six possible codes.

The assigned codes represent a behavioral record of the interaction and can be subjected to sequential analysis. When analyses of this sort are conducted in this paradigm, a widely replicated finding is that, compared to nondistressed spouses, distressed spouses are more likely to reciprocate their spouses' negative behaviors (e.g., Gottman, 1979; Margolin & Wampold, 1981; Revenstorf, Vogel, Wegener, Hahlweg, & Schindler, 1980; Schaap, 1982; Ting-Toomey, 1983). The capacity to identify patterns of this sort is an obvious advantage of sequential methodology, one that is not available when only the simple rates of behaviors are analyzed.

By considering another body of research on marriage, the study of attributions or explanations for spouse behaviors, we will expand upon the negative reciprocity findings in a hypothetical example and introduce the principles of log-linear analysis. The investigation of explanations by spouses in marriage builds upon the social psychological framework of attribution theory (Heider, 1944, 1958; Jones & Davis, 1965; Kelley, 1967) and identifies two classes of attributions—the first might be called *benevolent* in that one's spouse is given credit for positive behaviors (e.g., behaviors are ascribed to internal factors and the causes of the behaviors are seen as stable and globally influential in the marriage), whereas negative behaviors are discounted (e.g., they are attributed to factors outside the person, and their causes are seen as unstable and specific to that behavior). In the second, *malevolent* style the opposite pattern occurs, as positive behaviors are discounted and spouses are "given credit" for their negative actions. An empirical association between attributions, as dependent variables assessed via self-report, and marital satisfaction has been demonstrated, with distressed couples tending to employ malevolent attributions and nondistressed couples using benevolent attributions (e.g., Holtzworth-Munroe & Jacobson, 1985; Fincham, Beach, & Nelson, 1987; Fincham & O'Leary, 1983; for reviews see Bradbury & Fincham, 1990; Fincham & Bradbury, 1991). In the present example, however, both attributions and marital satisfaction will be treated as independent grouping factors with which to study marital interaction.[2]

---

[2]The notion of *attributional style* in marriage has been assumed rather than demonstrated. The term is used here solely for illustrative purposes.

TABLE 1. A 2 × 2 × 6 × 6 Contingency Table Describing Relationships
among Four Variables

Marital satisfaction/ attributional style	Antecedent code	Consequent code					
		H+	H0	H−	W+	W0	W−
Distressed/malevolent	H+						
	H0						
	H−						
	W+						
	W0						
	W−						
		H+	H0	H−	W+	W0	W−
Distressed/benevolent	H+						
	H0						
	H−						
	W+						
	W0						
	W−						
		H+	H0	H−	W+	W0	W−
Nondistressed/malevolent	H+						
	H0						
	H−						
	W+						
	W0						
	W−						
		H+	H0	H−	W+	W0	W−
Nondistressed/benevolent	H+						
	H0						
	H−						
	W+						
	W0						
	W−						

Note. H = husband; W = wife; + = positive code; 0 = neutral code; − = negative code.

The question thus arises, what is the association between marital satisfaction (with two levels, distressed and nondistressed couples), attributions (with two levels, malevolent and benevolent couples), and the sequences of positive, neutral, and negative behaviors (and particularly negative affect reciprocity) in the problem-solving discussions of married couples? Because all four variables in this example are defined in categorical terms, the problem is amenable to log-linear analysis. Table 1 shows a 2 (marital satisfaction) × 2 (attributional style) × 6 (antecedent codes) × 6 (consequent codes) contingency table that depicts the relationship among these four variables. For each of the four groups that results from fully crossing marital satisfaction and attributional style, there is a unique 6 × 6 matrix that allows for all possible combinations of antecedent and consequent codes.

CONSTRUCTING DATA TABLES

Before discussing how the raw behavioral records can be scanned to fill the cells in the four antecedent–consequent subtables, we first introduce the concepts of marginals, marginal tables, and conditional tables. These three concepts all involve summing over ("collapsing over") or selectively disregarding some variable or variables in the 2 × 2 × 6 × 6 design. In each case, the table is simplified because some variable or combination of variables is excluded. First, the marginal values (or *marginals*) for a variable can be obtained by summing over all other variables. There is a marginal for each level of the variable. For example, in Table 1, the six marginals (one for each behavioral code) for the consequent code variable can be found by summing down (i.e., ignoring antecedent codes), within columns, across all four marital satisfaction by attribution subtables. Three variables, marital satisfaction, attributions, and antecedent codes, are ignored. Similar procedures could be used to find the three marginals for the three ignored variables.

Second, a *marginal table* is obtained by combining two sets of marginals. For example, a marginal table of antecedent codes by consequent codes could be derived from Table 1 by summing corresponding entries over the four marital satisfaction by attribution subtables. Note that the relationship between antecedent and consequent codes is retained in this table and that any information about how this relationship might be different at different levels of marital satisfaction or attributions is now lost. Five other marginal tables, each representing a separate pairwise relationship, can be found by summing over all possible combinations of two variables.

Finally, *partial* or *conditional tables* can be formed. Collapsing over marital satisfaction, for example, would yield two antecedent code by consequent code subtables, one for each type of attribution. In this case, the antecedent–consequent table is said to be *conditional upon* attributional style. That is, these two 6 × 6 subtables show the relationship between antecedent and consequent codes, controlling for class of attribution. Three other conditional tables can be derived from Table 1, each of which ignores one variable and shows the conditional relationship among the remaining three variables.

These basic ideas about the marginals and tables embedded in multidimensional contingency tables (also known as cross-classifications or cross-tabulations) are introduced here because they capture certain relationships among variables while ignoring others and because they are central to log-

TABLE 2. Hypothetical
Behavioral Record from a Coded
Problem-Solving Interaction

Unit	Speaker	Code
1	*H*	*+*
2	*W*	*0*
3	*H*	*0*
4	*W*	*0*
5	*W*	*—*
6	*H*	*—*
7	*W*	*—*
8	*H*	*0*
9	*W*	*—*
10	*H*	*0*
11	*W*	*0*
12	*H*	*0*
13	*H*	*+*
14	*W*	*+*
15	*H*	*0*
.	.	.
.	.	.
.	.	.

Note. H = husband; W = wife; $+$ = positive
code; 0 = neutral code; $-$ = negative code.

linear analysis. Although it can be a bit overwhelming to think about all of
these tables and what they might mean, log-linear analysis is a technique
that can simplify the task by describing the tables and providing a strategy
that allows important relationships to be identified.

A next step is to discuss how the behavioral codes assigned to the units
in the interaction can be examined so that they can be entered into one of
the four 6×6 marital satisfaction by attribution subtables shown in Table 1.
Consider the behavioral record shown in Table 2, which might be generated
in the first few minutes of a problem-solving discussion by a distressed
couple in which both spouses use benevolent attributions. Treating the husband's positive code in Unit 1 as the antecedent code and the wife's neutral
code in Unit 2 as the consequent code, a count of 1 is added to the cell
defined by Antecedent Code H+ and Consequent Code W0 in the distressed
by benevolent subtable. Proceeding in similar form, all antecedent–consequent code pairs in the behavioral record can be represented. The next pair
to consider is Unit 2 with Unit 3—note that Unit 2 is being used twice, first
as the consequent code and here as the antecedent code. For this pair, a
count would be added to the Antecedent Code *W0*, Consequent Code *H0*
cell. Working through all 15 units (or 14 pairs of units) in this manner results

TABLE 3. Antecedent Code × Consequent Code Table Derived from
Hypothetical Data in Table 2

Antecedent code	Consequent code					
	$H+$	$H0$	$H-$	$W+$	$W0$	$W-$
$H+$				1	1	
$H0$	1				2	1
$H-$						1
$W+$		1				
$W0$		2				1
$W-$		2	1			

Note: H = husband; W = wife; $+$ = positive code; 0 = neutral code; $-$ = negative code.

in the distressed by benevolent contingency table shown in Table 3. Continuing in this way, for all units and for all couples in each of the four groups, would fill in Table 1 and produce what are known as *observed* values. It will be seen that an important component of log-linear analysis is the comparison of observed values with values that are *expected* on the basis of the investigator's hypotheses.

FITTING MODELS TO THE DATA

The goal of log-linear analysis is to use the categorical variables to account for the differential distribution of the observed counts. The elements used to account for the data are referred to as *parameters*, which are merely the categorical variables themselves or some combinations of them. In the present example there are four variables, marital satisfaction (M), attributional style (S), antecedent codes (A), and consequent codes (C). They can be considered as parameters, either individually,

$$[M] \, [S] \, [A] \, [C],$$

in combination with one other variable,

$$[MS] \, [MA] \, [MC] \, [SA] \, [SC] \, [AC],$$

in combination with two other variables,

$$[MSA] \, [MSC] \, [MAC] \, [SAC],$$

or in combination with three other variables,

$$[MSAC].$$

Note that the first group of parameters corresponds to the marginals, the second group to the marginal tables, and the third group to the conditional tables, as discussed above—each represents a relationship among variables while disregarding others. In the final parameter, [MSAC], no variables are disregarded and the table it represents, sometimes know as the *saturated table*, is the table of observed counts that would appear in Table 1.

Models are created when parameters are combined in certain ways; they are distinguished by the relationships they specify among the parameters. It is helpful to think of models as hypotheses or guesses about which relationships among the variables might be most important in explaining the distribution of the observed counts. For example, the following model could be proposed if marital satisfaction [M] was thought to be unimportant for these data: [SAC]. The corresponding hypothesis is that an understanding of the relationship between antecedent [A] and consequent [C] codes is conditional upon attributional style [S]. Note that the models tested are constrained by the particular variables under investigation. In general, the model [ABC] indicates that the [AB] relationship is conditional upon [C], that the [AC] relationship is conditional upon [B], and that the [BC] relationship is conditional upon [A].

An important constraint on models is that they are *hierarchical*, meaning that certain lower-order parameters are necessarily implied by the higher-order parameters that are in the model.[3] That is, the model [SAC] implies that the lower-order parameters [SA] [SC] [AC] are present, which in turn imply that [S] [A], and [C] are also present. Thus, writing [SAC] is a unique and convenient representation of the model

$$[SAC] \, [SA] \, [SC] \, [AC] \, [S] \, [A] \, [C],$$

and the two forms are entirely equivalent.

From the 4 dimensions of Table 1, the 15 resulting parameters that have been identified can be combined to form 113 different hierarchical models. The complexity of these models ranges from the simple *equiprobability model*, which uses no parameters and predicts (using the grand mean of the cell counts) that all cells will be equal, to the *saturated model*, [MSAC], which includes all the parameters. As noted, the saturated model is not a "model" or simplification at all, as it contains all possible marginals and thus duplicates the original table of data. Thus neither of these two models is very practical for accounting for the observed values. The more likely candidates will fall between these two extremes and will include some relationships among parameters while excluding others.

The problem arises, however, of how to choose among the more than 100 remaining models. Recall that the goal is to identify a model that provides a reasonable account of the data; selecting a model that is also par-

---

[3]Nonhierarchical models can be tested, but the procedure for doing so is more complex, and their interpretation is not straightforward. More information on nonhierarchical models can be found in the references of Appendix I.

simonious and interesting are important secondary considerations. As with any hypothesis, each of the possible models can be used to generate predictions, known as *expected values*, for how the $2 \times 2 \times 6 \times 6$ table would appear if those relationships reflected in the parameters of the model were present in the data. That is, each model represents a unique set of parameters, which in turn reflect an hypothesis about which relationships may be best able to account for the observed values. Based upon this combination of parameters, a table of expected values can be generated. These expected values include only those relationships that are indicated by the model. In log-linear analysis, the method that is used to produce the expected values is known as *iterative proportional fitting*. For each possible model, iterative proportional fitting serves to construct a table of expected values in which some set of marginals is said to be *fixed* in such a way that they are identical to the corresponding marginals in the table of observed values. Remaining marginals are left free to vary. The marginals that are fixed are those that reflect the relationships specified by the parameters in the model.

An overview of log-linear analysis is shown in Figure 1, which both summarizes the discussion to this point and provides an outline of what is to follow.

Knowing that the end product of iterative proportional fitting is a table of expected values for each model, the question of how to choose among models can now be addressed. The essential comparison is between the values that are observed and those that are expected on the basis of some model. A model will be considered good to the extent that it "fits the data" or to the extent that the expected values it generates approximate the values found in the actual data. The tool that allows this comparison to be made is the *likelihood ratio statistic*, which is abbreviated as G^2 and is often referred to as a "goodness of fit" statistic. The likelihood ratio statistic is defined as

$$G^2 = 2 \sum (\text{observed}) \log (\text{observed/expected}) \qquad \text{(Eq. 1)}$$

where "log" means natural logarithm and the summation is over all cells in the table. G^2 is distributed approximately as chi-square with the general formula for degrees of freedom being

$$\text{d.f.} = \text{number of total cells} - \text{number of parameters fitted. (Eq. 2)}$$

A single G^2 value can be calculated for each model, with higher values indicating greater discrepancies between observed and expected data. Comparing the obtained G^2 value to the chi-square distribution with appropriate degrees of freedom will indicate the level of statistical significance, with larger values being less likely to occur. In log-linear analysis one seeks models with small, *nonsignificant* G^2 values, as these indicate that the observed values are well approximated by the expected values. As a rough

Research question involving
categorical variables is proposed

↓

Collection of data yields observed values

↓

Data are represented in a contingency table
(diagnostic tests of stationarity, homogeneity, and order
may be performed)

↓

Variables are considered individually or in combinations
to form parameters

↓

Parameters are combined to form models

↓

Each model, via iterative proportional fitting,
yields a table of expected values

↓

In model fitting, expected and observed values are
compared with the likelihood ratio statistic, G^2

↓

Forward selection and backward elimination may be
used to identify best-fitting model

↓

The contribution of an individual parameter is determined
by subtracting G^2 values of models that include
and exclude the parameter

↓

Goodness of fit in individual cells is assessed with
standardized residuals or Freeman–Tukey residuals

FIGURE 1. Overview of log-linear analysis.

criterion, models with a probability level *above* .05 provide a reasonably good fit of the data. This would imply that the parameters excluded from the model probably do not contribute to an understanding of the observed values—even without the excluded parameters (and the relationships among variables they reflect), the model manages to generate expected values that do not diverge greatly from the data that were actually collected.

At the conclusion of the model-fitting stage of log-linear analysis, the investigator will have a general appreciation of which models can be used to understand the differential distribution of counts. For instance, in the present example, some resolution to the question concerning the role of attributional style in furthering knowledge of behavioral sequences in marital interaction will have been attained. It is quite possible, however, that two or more models fit the data, at which point it is common to weigh G^2 (i.e., goodness of fit) values against the complexity of the models. If several models fit the data to roughly the same degree, it will be more desirable to retain the simpler model. On the other hand, the argument could be made for adopting a more complicated model if it affords a substantially better fit.

These general guidelines may be helpful when there are only a few competing models, yet they will not be of much use when more models are under consideration. For these latter situations, a model selection strategy known as *forward selection* is often employed. With this procedure, a model is selected by starting with the worst possible model (i.e., the equiprobability model, already described) and systematically adding relationships so that the fit is improved. The second step would probably involve adding in all four single variable marginals, [M] [S] [A] [C]. If this *main effects* model did not fit much better than the previous model (as indicated by a significant G^2 value), then the six marginal tables, [MS] [MA] [MC] [SA] [SC] and [AC] might be added; this model is known as the *pairwise association* model. If this model were inadequate, then the four *three-way associations*, [MSA] [MSC] [MAC] and [SAC], would be included.

Assume that the discrepancy between the model and the data was found to be nonsignificant when the three-way associations were added. Although this is important, it is not clear that all four of the three-way associations are contributing to the improved fit. The next step would then be to drop back to the pairwise association model and reexamine this model four times, once with each of the four three-way terms. Given the previous result, that the model with all three-way associations gave a good fit, it is quite likely that at least one of the three-way terms should be added to the all pairwise associations model. If this were done, the final step might then be to independently drop out pairwise associations (while keeping in the others and the most important three-way terms or terms), to determine if they are needed in fitting the model to the data. As the models being tested are hierarchical, not all of the pairwise associations can be dropped, as they are necessarily implied by the three-way association(s) kept in the model. If

a pairwise association is deleted in this manner without any adverse consequences to the fit of the model, then that association can be dropped from
the model.

Readers familiar with multiple regression analysis will recognize the
forward selection procedure, and the basic ideas are the same: A number of
models are examined and compared, with the goal being to find one that is
both parsimonious and well fitting. A less frequently used strategy, *backward elimination*, follows similar procedures but starts with the best possible model (i.e., the saturated model, [*MSAC*]) and deletes the least important term at each stage. Regardless of which procedure is used (and even if
both are used), neither is without shortcomings. Briefly, these include (a)
the fact that there is no assurance that a unique or particularly meaningful
model will emerge; (b) that some models are never examined; and (c) that
the investigator's criteria for a satisfactory model are ignored by these
mechanical procedures. Nonetheless, in practice, these steps provide a
useful means of identifying an appropriate model.

EVALUATING THE STRENGTH OF RELATIONSHIPS

The selection of a model for a particular data set does not imply that all
parameters in the model are of equal importance. This is because the statistical significance of a model is calculated using actual frequencies and thus
reflects not only the strength of the relationships in the model but also the
size of the sample. With a large enough sample, even trivial effects may be
included in a model that fits the data well. Thus, following identification of
an adequate model, a next step in log-linear analysis is to determine which
of the relationships specified by the parameters in the model are of greatest
importance in explaining the data. Such a step would be undertaken to
facilitate clearer interpretation of the model or to further refine the model
that has been proposed. Because they are insensitive to sample size, propor-
tions rather than actual frequencies are used to estimate the strength of
relationships.

The procedure used to assess the strength of a relationship in log-linear
analysis is known as *screening* (Brown, 1976) and can be described as a
simple operation in which the goodness of fit statistics for two models are
compared. That is, the G^2 value of a larger model, which includes the parameter of interest, is compared with the G^2 model of a smaller model that
excludes the parameter. The importance of the tested parameter will be
reflected in the magnitude of the *difference* between the two G^2 values: An
important parameter (i.e., a relationship among variables) will yield a large
difference in G^2 values, whereas an unimportant parameter will show a
relatively small difference in G^2 values. Stated differently, if a relationship
is of importance for understanding the observed data, then a model including that relationship will fit much better than a model that excludes the

relationship. The difference in goodness of fit is therefore large and will be reflected in the difference between G^2 values. In contrast, if a relationship is not very important, then a model including that relationship will produce a fit similar to that of a model excluding the relationship. In this case the difference between G^2 values will be small.

Having selected a parameter to test and given that there are many pairs of models that differ only by that parameter, an obvious question arises: Which pair of models should be compared? It can be reasoned that if a relationship were important independent of the other relationships in the model, then it would not matter which models were compared, as long as they differed in the parameter of interest. However, as one might expect, the capacity of a relationship to account for the observed values is conditional upon the other relationships in the model that are being used to explain the data. Thus, because the decision of which pair of models to compare is not an arbitrary one, log-linear data analysts will typically examine two pairs of models that differ in the tested parameter; one pair will be simple, with few parameters, and the other will be complex, with many parameters.

Returning to the example, suppose that one were interested in knowing how important the association between marital satisfaction and attributional style, [MS], was in understanding the data. A first step would be to identify two simple models that differ in this parameter,

$$(1) \quad [MS] \quad [M] \quad [S]$$
$$(2) \qquad\qquad [M] \quad [S]$$

and compare their goodness of fit values,

$$\Delta\, G^2 = G^2(2) - G^2(1) \qquad\qquad\qquad \text{(Eq. 3)}$$

with

$$\Delta\, \text{d.f.} = \text{d.f.}(2) - \text{d.f.}(1) \qquad\qquad\qquad \text{(Eq. 4)}$$

This is known as a *test of marginal association* and should always yield a nonnegative value. It yields a measure of association that one would find if nothing were known about the influence of other variables. The significance of $\Delta\, G^2$ can be assessed from the chi-square distribution for Δ d.f., with larger, statistically significant differences indicating that the parameter should be kept in the model.

To conduct a *test of partial association*, two complex models that differ in the [MS] parameter can be compared in the same way:

$$(1) \quad [MAC] \quad [MS] \quad [MA] \quad [MC] \quad [AC] \quad [M] \quad [S] \quad [A] \quad [C]$$
$$(2) \quad [MAC] \qquad\qquad [MA] \quad [MC] \quad [AC] \quad [M] \quad [S] \quad [A] \quad [C],$$

again computing $\Delta\, G^2$ and Δ d.f. and referring to the chi-square distribution. This measure of association is more refined than that described, as it reflects the association while controlling for the other variables in the model. Further analysis might take the form of comparing models between these two extremes. In this way, the importance of a parameter can be determined systematically. Similar tests could then be performed on other parameters in the model. Working through the parameters in this manner provides an assessment of the relative strength of the relationships in the model and may suggest directions for further model selection. In addition, screening can be used as a valuable starting point for model building, followed by the forward selection–backward elimination procedures discussed.

Assessing Goodness of Fit in Individual Cells

Just as there is variability in the strength of relationships among parameters in a model, so, too, is there variability in how well the expected values approximate the observed values across individual cells in the data table. Knowing the location of large discrepancies between observed and modeled values provides information about which antecedent code–consequent code sequences are contributing to G^2 and where the parameters in the model are having a pronounced effect. That the model does not provide a uniform fit of data for each cell is a valuable realization because in the present example it permits examination of a substantive question raised earlier. Specifically, how do the four groups (i.e., two levels of marital satisfaction crossed with two levels of attributional style) compare in their tendency to reciprocate negative affect? For any couple, there are two ways to reciprocate negative affect (W- followed by H- and H- followed by W-), and, because there are four groups to compare, this means that a total of eight negative affect reciprocity cells in Table 1 could be examined.

Two tools are commonly used to identify cells in which expected values differ significantly from the observed values. The first, *standardized residuals* (*SR*), are computed with the following equation:

$$SR = (\text{observed} - \text{expected})/\sqrt{\text{expected}}. \qquad \text{(Eq. 5)}$$

It is interesting to note that summing the squared standardized residuals over all cells results in the likelihood ratio statistic, G^2. That is,

$$G^2 = \sum (\text{standardized residual})^2.$$

The second tool, *Freeman-Tukey deviates* (*FT*), are computed as follows,

$$FT = \sqrt{\text{observed}} + \sqrt{\text{observed} + 1} - \sqrt{4(\text{expected}) + 1} \qquad \text{(Eq. 6)}$$

and is particularly appropriate for smaller samples.

A desirable feature of both standardized residuals and Freeman–Tukey deviates is that they approximate a standardized normal distribution (mean = 0, variance = 1). Because about 95% of all values fall between -2 and 2 in this distribution, computed values smaller than -2 or larger than 2 can be regarded as statistically rare events. The computed SR or FT values are not independent, however, and this convention can be offered only as a rough guide; interpretation of individual deviates and residuals should take into account the entire range of observed values. Significant positive values indicate that the observed frequency of counts in the cell is greater than that expected by the model (i.e., the cell was underestimated), and significant negative values indicate that fewer counts were observed than expected (i.e., the cell was overestimated).

Either of these two techniques could be applied to all cells in the present example, with particular attention upon the eight negative-affect cells. The fit of these eight cells would be expected to vary with marital satisfaction (e.g., distressed couples may show larger deviations), with attributional style (e.g., couples with malevolent styles may show larger deviations), or some combination of the two. Further, differences may arise according to which spouse is reciprocating or delivering the negative consequent code. The significance of these and other comparisons can be addressed with z and F tests.

Diagnostic Tests of Sequential Data

The purpose of this section is to examine critically three assumptions that were made of the data in the foregoing discussion. Ordinarily these assumptions would be considered *before* constructing the final table of counts to be analyzed (e.g., Table 1; see Anderson & Goodman, 1957); however, in order to understand them, the likelihood ratio statistic and the model fitting procedure had to first be introduced. Each of the assumptions will be considered in turn.

Stationarity

First, it was assumed that the expected counts derived from a particular model would be representative of all parts of the interaction between spouses. This is the assumption of stationarity and is equivalent to saying that the underlying structure of the interaction process is essentially the same through the duration of the interaction.

To test this assumption, the data are divided into a number of subtables that are then compared to the overall table. The tables differ according to which part of the interaction they represent. A first step is to divide the units in the interaction into a workable number of parts—two halves, three thirds, or four quarters might be reasonable starting points. Because there is evidence that marital interactions can be described in three parts (i.e., agenda building, arguing, and negotiation; see Gottman, 1979, p. 112), this division will be used here. Across couples, three tables of expected values can be constructed, one for each third of the interaction. To test for stationarity, each of these *individual* tables (E_i) is compared, with the likelihood ratio statistic, to the *composite* (E_c) or original table of expected values:

$$G^2 = 2 \sum (E_c) \log (E_c/E_i) \qquad\qquad \text{(Eq. 7)}$$

with

$$\text{d.f.} = \text{d.f. of composite} - \text{d.f. of individual.} \qquad \text{(Eq. 8)}$$

(Note the similarity of this statistic to Equation 1.) This procedure will yield one G^2 value for each individual part of the data (three in this instance), which are then referred to the chi-square distribution with appropriate degrees of freedom. Three nonsignificant values would indicate that the individual tables do not differ reliably from the composite table and that the assumption of stationarity is indeed sound. A significant value, in contrast, is usually less desirable and would indicate statistical independence of an individual table from the composite table. Further analysis of the lack of stationarity (e.g., by examining individual cells, by dividing the data into fewer or more parts) could be pursued to identify the source of independence.

Homogeneity

Rather than assume there is no difference across *time* in the interaction, as is done in stationarity, the assumption of homogeneity maintains that there are no outstanding differences in the sequential structure across *groups*. That is, the assumption is made that there are no radically different groups being modelled.

Testing the homogeneity assumption is very similar to testing the stationarity assumption: Subdivisions of the data, in this case the four individual marital satisfaction by attributional style groups, are compared to the composite table. Again the likelihood ratio statistic is used (Equation 7) and the interpretation of significant and nonsignificant values takes similar form. Most investigators will seek support for the assumption of homogeneity so that their data can be analyzed according to the original grouping variables. If this assumption is not met, lag sequential analyses, described later, can be performed to examine the interaction of each couple individually.

Order

Apart from the general assumption that guides the study of sequence in social interaction, that the current state of an interaction is a function of recent past states, a slightly more subtle assumption has been made in the present analysis. Specifically, it has been assumed that marital interaction can be captured by behavioral sequences that are limited to two codes in length (see Table 1). The possibility remains that additional information can be recovered by considering longer sequences of behavioral codes before each consequent code. Technically speaking, a *first-order* model has been assumed (i.e., one code was considered before the consequent), even though *zero-order* (i.e., zero codes before the consequent, reflecting a total absence of sequential structure), *second-order* (i.e., two codes considered before the consequent), or higher-order models may provide a more thorough representation of the dependencies in the data.

Testing for order involves fitting models of increasing order to the data and checking at each point the corresponding likelihood ratio value, G^2. If adding parameters (i.e., relationships among antecedent and consequent codes) significantly improves the fit of the model, then the G^2 value will drop and the ΔG^2 between a pair of models will be statistically significant (see related discussion of Equation 3). This indicates that the parameter is needed in the model and that the higher order of data should be analyzed.

In the present example, an investigator might begin by asking whether the data are zero-, first-, or second-order. A next step would be to construct a table to accommodate these three orders, with a dimension for the consequent code, [C], and one for each of the two antecedent codes, [A1] and [A2]. This arrangement is shown in Table 4. It can be seen that the data have been collapsed across the four groups in Table 1 and that the dimensions of the table are now 6 (Antecedent 2, [A2]) × 6 (Antecedent 1, [A1]) × 6 (Consequent, [C]). Note that expanding this table to test a third-order model, thus considering three codes before the consequent, would multiply it sixfold, from 216 to 1296 cells.

In this example the first model to be fitted would be the zero-order model, [A2] [A1] [C]. It is unlikely that this model would fit the data, as it would imply that the interactants are responding to one another in random fashion; no consideration has yet been given to the sequence of their behaviors. Thus the first-order model is fitted next, introducing two new parameters: [A2] [A1] [C] [A2 A1] [A1 C]. The significance of these two new parameters is determined by subtracting G^2 (first-order) from G^2 (zero-order) and referring the difference to the chi-square distribution. The first-order model will probably fit better than the zero-order model (i.e., the tested parameter will be statistically significant), but it is necessary to continue and determine whether more information can be gained by considering sequences three codes in length. This is accomplished by the second-order model, which adds one further parameter, [A2] [A1] [C] [A2 A1] [A1 C] [A2 C]. If the difference observed in subtracting G^2 (second-order) from G^2 (first-order) is significant, then the data are at least second order, and the second-order model should be compared in a similar way with the third-order model (i.e., considering three codes before the consequent). However,

TABLE 4. 6 × 6 × 6 Table to Test for Order in Marital Interaction Data

[A2]	[A1]	[C]					
		$H+$	$H0$	$H-$	$W+$	$W0$	$W-$
$H+$	$H+$						
	$H0$						
	$H-$						
	$W+$						
	$W0$						
	$W-$						
		$H+$	$H0$	$H-$	$W+$	$W0$	$W-$
$H0$	$H+$						
	$H0$						
	$H-$						
	$W+$						
	$W0$						
	$W-$						
		$H+$	$H0$	$H-$	$W+$	$W0$	$W-$
$H-$	$H+$						
	$H0$						
	$H-$						
	$W+$						
	$W0$						
	$W-$						
		$H+$	$H0$	$H-$	$W+$	$W0$	$W-$
$W+$	$H+$						
	$H0$						
	$H-$						
	$W+$						
	$W0$						
	$W-$						
		$H+$	$H0$	$H-$	$W+$	$W0$	$W-$
$W0$	$H+$						
	$H0$						
	$H-$						
	$W+$						
	$W0$						
	$W-$						
		$H+$	$H0$	$H-$	$W+$	$W0$	$W-$
$W+$	$H+$						
	$H0$						
	$H-$						
	$W+$						
	$W0$						
	$W-$						

Note: [A2] = Antecedent code two lags before consequent; [A1] = antecedent code one lag before consequent; [C] = consequent code. H = husband; W = wife; $+$ = positive code, 0 = neutral code, $-$ = negative code.

if the difference between the first-order and second-order models is not significant, then it can be inferred that no new information about the consequent code is to be gained from its association with the code two steps back [A2] and that the data are first order. Log-linear analysis could then proceed by fitting models to the 2 [M] × 2 [S] × 6 [A2] × 6 [A1] × 6 [C] table, in the manner described above. Nevertheless, it cannot be concluded that there is nothing to be derived from the examination of behaviors two steps back if a different approach is taken, particularly one in which codes intervening between an antecedent and a consequent are systematically ignored. Such an approach is lag sequential analysis, which is described in the next section.

SUMMARY

To this point we have introduced the basic principles of log-linear analysis, as applied to sequential categorical data. The discussion has addressed the fitting of models to the data, with the likelihood ratio statistic (G^2); evaluating the strength of relationships represented in the model, with differences between likelihood ratio values; and assessing the goodness of fit of the model in individual cells, with standardized residuals and Freeman–Tukey deviates. Finally, the assumptions of stationarity, homogeneity, and order were introduced, and procedures for testing them were reviewed. An overview of these principles is shown in Figure 1.

In sum, log-linear analysis is a valuable tool for exploring relationships among variables and testing specific hypotheses. Although the foregoing discussion has focused largely on a particular research question in the study of marital interaction, log-linear analysis is actually a set of rather general and flexible techniques that can be used to explain the distribution of frequency counts in multidimensional tables.

LAG SEQUENTIAL ANALYSIS

INTRODUCTION

Log-linear analysis is being used more frequently to examine the sequence of behaviors in social interaction. However, it is an unwieldy task to apply log-linear analysis to long behavioral sequences and to data derived from complicated coding schemes. For example, a relatively modest study of dyadic interaction with a coding system comprising 10 codes for sequences up to 5 codes in length would generate a staggering $(2 \times 10)^5$ or 3,200,000 unique sequences. Of course, many of these sequences would never occur, and most cells in the resulting contingency table would be empty, thus precluding most forms of data analysis.

Lag sequential analysis, initially proposed by Sackett (1979), overcomes these difficulties and can serve as a valuable complement to log-linear analysis in the study of social interaction. It allows the examination of longer sequences of behavior, which often provide a better impression of the underlying phenomenon than do shorter sequences. For example, Gottman, Markman, and Notarius (1977) used this method and found an association between marital satisfaction and patterns of interaction (up to seven codes in length) following certain coded behaviors. In one analysis, it was determined that, in response to the husband's description of his feelings or statement about a problem (delivered with neutral affect), nondistressed couples were likely to cycle twice through a *validation* sequence (wife agrees, husband continues to describe feelings or comment on problem), whereas distressed couples were likely to cycle three times through a *cross-complaining* sequence (wife then describes her feelings or views on the problem, husband reciprocates). Thus it can be seen that lag sequential analysis can be useful in describing interaction. Additional strengths are that the computations are simple, that hypotheses can be tested, and that the method can be applied to the interactions of individual dyads.

Despite their differences, log-linear analysis and lag sequential analysis are also similar in two important respects. The most obvious similarity, alluded to before, is that both methods can be used to study sequential dependencies among coded behaviors, thereby preserving the dynamic quality of interpersonal exchanges. A second common feature is that statements of statistical significance are based upon comparisons between observed and expected values. In log-linear analysis, this refers to the approximation of collected data by values predicted from some model, as reflected in the likelihood ratio statistic. In lag sequential analysis the expected values, referred to as *unconditional probabilities*, are subtracted from observed values, or *conditional probabilities*, and this difference is divided by an error term to produce a statistic resembling a z-score.

Before elaborating upon the z-score test statistic and the procedure for conducting lag sequential analysis, the notion of conditional and unconditional probabilities will be briefly discussed. Consider once again the behavioral record from Table 2, reproduced here:

Unit: 1   2   3   4   5   6   7   8   9   10   11   12   13   14   15
Code: $H+$ $W0$ $H0$ $W0$ $W-$ $H-$ $W-$ $H0$ $W-$ $H0$ $W0$ $H0$ $H+$ $W+$ $H0$

The unconditional probability or base rate of a code is the number of times it occurs out of the total number of units. For example, $H0$ has an unconditional probability of $5/15 = .33$. In contrast, the conditional probability of a code is the number of times it occurs, given that some other specified code occurred before it. For example, 3 of the 15 units are coded as $W-$, and of these three units, two are followed by $H0$. Thus the probability of $H0$ occurring given that $W-$ occurred in the preceding unit is $2/3 = .67$. Because the conditional probability of $H0$ given $W-$ is greater than its expected or unconditional probability, it might be proposed that there is something about $W-$ that makes $H0$ more likely to occur in the following unit. The uncertainty in knowing when $H0$ would occur is reduced by knowing that $W-$ was the immediately preceding event.

When conditional probabilities involve only consecutive units they are referred to as lag 1 probabilities. (Note that Table 1 is constructed for lag 1 or antecedent–consequent frequency counts, which could easily be translated into conditional probabilities.) Conditional probabilities of higher lags can be computed in a similar way, by displacing the two codes of interest by some number of units. The specified code that occurs earlier in time is called the *criterion* code and the later code is called the *target* code. A lag 3 conditional probability, for instance, is computed by allowing two codes to intervene between the criterion and the target. In the data shown, the lag 3 conditional probability of $H0$ occurring given that $W-$ occurred three units before is ⅓ = 1.0. With longer behavioral records, relatively stable conditional probabilities of all codes at several lags could be determined. It is these two simple computations, of unconditional (expected) probabilities and lagged conditional (observed) probabilities, that are the basic elements of lag sequential analysis.

Returning again to the example introduced at the outset of the log-linear section, it can be seen that the same hypothetical data set can now be approached from an entirely different analytic perspective. Rather than using the two independent grouping factors, marital satisfaction and attributional style, and the antecedent–consequent code pairs to explain the distribution of frequency counts in the contingency table, the goal of lag sequential analysis is to identify nonrandom sequences of codes that might distinguish the four groups. More specifically, given that a certain code has occurred, what are the most likely events to follow in the next several units? Do these events occur more often than might be expected from the unconditional probabilities? Are any resulting sequences different across groups? Reconsidering the negative affect reciprocity data, we can now ask: Given that one spouse has been coded for negative affect, what is the likely sequence of events that will follow? Do the four groups tend to handle negative affect in fundamentally different ways? Do husbands differ from wives in their propensity to reciprocate negative affect, at different lags from the initial negative code? Questions such as these are readily addressed by lag sequential analysis. The specific steps that are taken to perform these analyses are described in the following section.

CONDUCTING LAG SEQUENTIAL ANALYSIS

Step 1

Calculate the unconditional probability of occurrence of each coded event. Although lag sequential analysis can be performed on data from

individual dyads as well as on aggregate data (e.g., summed over all dyads
in a particular group), the procedure will be illustrated here on data from a
hypothetical distressed couple with a benevolent attributional style. The
unconditional probabilities of the six codes are shown in the last column on
the right side of Table 5a.

Step 2

Designate one code as the criterion. In practice, all codes will take their
turn as the criterion in a complete lag sequential analysis. The criterion code
represents the first code in the sequence to be studied and in Table 5a, $W-$
will first serve in this role.

Step 3

Calculate the conditional probability of each target code at all lags of
interest. This is done by dividing the number of times the target code occurs
at a specified lag by the number of times the code selected in step 2 occurs.
Repeat this procedure using each code in turn as the criterion code. In Table
5a, six conditional probabilities (one for each code) are computed at each of 4
lags, resulting in 24 lagged conditional probabilities. The small number of
lags used here is chosen for illustrative purposes; ordinarily, and particularly in the early stages of data analysis, conditional probabilities would be
determined for many more lags. Each conditional probability reflects the
probability of the target code occurring, given that the criterion code occurred before it at a specified number of lags.

Step 4

Identify the largest conditional probabilities at each lag. These values
are underlined in Table 5a, and they seem to suggest the following pattern:

$$W- \rightarrow H- \rightarrow W- \rightarrow H0 \rightarrow W0$$

The initial reciprocation of negative codes, characteristic of distressed couples, is followed by neutral units by the husband and the wife. Based upon
this and other sequences (i.e., from other groups), an investigator may start
to suspect that marital distress is associated with the likelihood of a negative exchange, whereas the duration of that exchange (or the likelihood of
exiting such a sequence) may be a function of the second independent factor,
attributional style. Hypotheses of this sort can thus be generated and tested
with lag sequential analysis. At the end of step 4 then, a preliminary appreciation of the sequential dependencies (as reflected in the lagged conditional
probabilities) that may exist in the data is established. However, the sequence identified reflects only the conditional probabilities associated with a

TABLE 5. Lag Sequential Analysis Tables for Hypothetical Data from an Individual Dyad

a. Conditional probabilities

Criterion	Target	Lag				P(T)
		1	2	3	4	
W−	H+	.19	.11	.05	.11	.02
	H0	.24	.11	.40	.08	.33
	H−	.34	.12	.11	.12	.14
	W+	.06	.09	.07	.12	.05
	W0	.17	.20	.19	.38	.34
	W−	.00	.37	.18	.19	.12

b. Conditional probabilities

H−	H+	.13	.17	.09	.18	
	H0	.17	.29	.10	.16	
	H−	.00	.25	.13	.17	
	W+	.05	.12	.16	.14	
	W0	.27	.06	.32	.18	
	W−	.38	.11	.20	.17	

c. Z-statistics

W−	H+	1.17	1.32	0.43	0.61	
	H0	−1.41	−1.62	2.23*	−1.74	
	H−	2.64*	−0.12	−0.28	−0.12	
	W+	0.72	0.39	0.47	1.50	
	W0	−1.27	−1.19	−1.78	2.16*	
	W−	−0.66	2.77*	0.84	1.10	

Note: H = husband; W = wife; + = positive code; 0 = neutral code; − = negative code; P(T) = unconditional probability of target code; highest conditional probabilities for each lag are underlined; * = statistically significant z-statistic, p < .05.

single criterion behavior. It is therefore important to examine the *transitional probabilities* of the dependencies that exist between adjacent codes in the sequence. This is done in the following step.

Step 5

To test the transitional probabilities associated with the sequence identified in step 4, one begins by designating the code with the highest conditional probability at lag 1 as the new criterion. Further support for the sequential relationship among the first three codes in the pattern identified is obtained if the most probable code at lag 2 with the original criterion now becomes the most probable code at lag 1 with the new criterion. This is shown in Table 5b. Because the code with the highest conditional probability at lag 1 in Table 5a was $H-$, this code then becomes the criterion in Table 5b. Evidence for the sequence

$$W- \rightarrow H- \rightarrow W-$$

will be obtained if the largest conditional probability following the $H-$ criterion is that of $W-$. It can be seen that this is in fact the case in Table 5b. The next step would be to designate $W-$ as the criterion (as this is the next code in the tentative sequence) and inspect the recomputed lag conditional probabilities to determine if $H0$ is the most likely consequent at lag 1. An informal assessment of the sequence found in Table 5a is made by following this basic procedure, for all lags.

The sequence of behaviors identified at this point is based entirely upon the use of conditional probabilities. However, it is reasonable to question whether an understanding of the interaction is increased beyond that obtained by knowledge of the base rates (unconditional probabilities) of the behaviors. Indeed, the sequence represented by conditional probabilities alone may be spurious unless the conditional probabilities differ significantly from their associated unconditional probabilities. Step 6 describes how the difference between conditional and unconditional probabilities can be tested for significance.

Step 6

At each lag, compare the conditional (observed) probability with the unconditional (expected) probability, using a z-statistic. The formal test of comparing conditional and unconditional probabilities was originally proposed by Sackett (1979; see also Gottman, 1979). However, this test was found by Allison and Liker (1982; see also Wampold & Margolin, 1982) to be too conservative in estimating the significance of the conditional probabilities. Instead, the appropriate statistic in lag sequential analysis is

$$z = \frac{P_{T/C} - P_T}{\sqrt{\dfrac{P_T(1 - P_T)(1 - P_C)}{(n - k)\, P_C}}} \qquad \text{(Eq. 9)}$$

where $P_{T/C}$ is the observed or conditional probability of the target code (T), given that the criterion code (C) occurred k lags before it; P_T is the expected or unconditional probability of the target code; P_C is the expected or unconditional probability of the criterion code; n is the overall number of the codes in the sequence; and, as noted, k is the number of units lagged.

Using this formula, the z values corresponding to the 24 conditional probabilities in Table 5a can be computed; they are shown in Table 5c. (Similar computations could be made for Table 5b, or any code × lag table where conditional probabilities are available.) When n exceeds 25, the z-statistic approximates a standardized normal distribution and thus z-values exceeding an absolute value of 1.96 are considered to be statistically significant at $p < .05$. A positive significant value indicates that the target code is more likely to occur than is expected at that lag following the criterion, whereas a negative significant value indicates that the target code is less likely to occur than is expected. Returning to Table 5, it can be seen that the z-scores (Table 5c) parallel the conditional probabilities (Table 5a), thus confirming the pattern initially identified in step 4.

However, had any of the z-scores been less than 1.96, a useful rule is to consider the sequence as having ended at that point. The nonsignificant test statistic thus indicates that a return to the unconditional probability or base rate level has occurred. The entire data set can be explored, at either the individual dyad or aggregated dyads level, by repeating steps 1 through 6 with a different criterion for each iteration.

Step 7 (Optional)

Conduct parametric statistical analyses (e.g., multiple regression, multivariate analysis of variance), using as dependent measures the z-scores computed for each dyad at each lag for all designated criterion codes. This step can be considered optional because any parametric analyses that are undertaken should be guided by the hypotheses of the investigation. Nevertheless, the combination of lag sequential analysis with more common forms of analysis can be quite powerful (e.g., Margolin & Wampold, 1981; Phelps & Slater, 1985) and warrants consideration in the design and data reduction phases of social interaction research.

For instance, in the present example, a multivariate analysis of variance might be proposed, with two between-subjects factors of two levels each (distressed, nondistressed × malevolent, benevolent attributional style), and one within-subjects factor of four levels (for lags). For each of the resulting 16 cells, a number of z-scores, each representing a different criterion and its subsequent sequence, could be examined. To determine if the four groups differ in their patterns of negative affect reciprocity, the z-scores for two criterion codes, $H-$ and $W-$ would be used as dependent variables. In many other domains of research, similar analytic strategies could be used to test hypotheses of group differences in sequences of coded behaviors.

Assumptions and Guidelines

Gottman (1979, p. 41) has recommended that a transitional probability less than .07 anywhere in a behavioral chain reflects a data sequence that because it is too infrequent, cannot be reliably reported. Similarly, when second- and higher-order sequential dependencies are examined, adequate estimates of conditional probabilities are needed. One means of obtaining reliable conditional probability estimates is to generate more data by, for example, using data collapsed over subjects or obtaining longer samples of behavior within dyads. When the first of these strategies is adopted, it is important to ensure that the homogeneity assumption is not violated.

In the present context, the homogeneity assumption refers to the fact that lag 1 conditional probabilities for each couples' behavior are considered to be sampled from the same population. This assumption can be tested for any given antecedent code to check whether the probability of consequent or target codes varies across samples. Repeating this procedure across all antecedents thus provides an overall test of homogeneity. Castellan (1979, p. 95) describes a test statistic for this purpose that is asymptotically distributed as chi-square.

An analogous procedure can be used to test the stationarity assumption. According to this assumption, one would expect a stable probability structure throughout the course of the observed interaction. As in the case of log-linear analysis, this assumption can be tested by dividing the data into parts that correspond to segments of the interaction. The lag 1 conditional probabilities for a given antecedent, and overall for all antecedents, can be computed and tested using chi-square in the manner outlined (for an example, see Notarius, 1981).

Finally, it should be noted that the large number of significance tests conducted in the course of lag sequential analysis increases the probability of Type I error. Consequently, it behooves the investigator to demonstrate that the number of significant conditional probabilities is greater than that which would be expected solely on the basis of chance.

Summary

To summarize, lag sequential analysis is a statistical technique for examining dependencies among coded behaviors. Based upon the simple concepts of conditional and unconditional probability, this technique permits the identification of likely patterns or sequences in a behavioral record, which can then be compared across experimental groups. In addition to introducing the major assumptions and guidelines underlying the application of lag sequential analysis, the steps involved in conducting this procedure have been discussed. These steps are summarized in Figure 2.

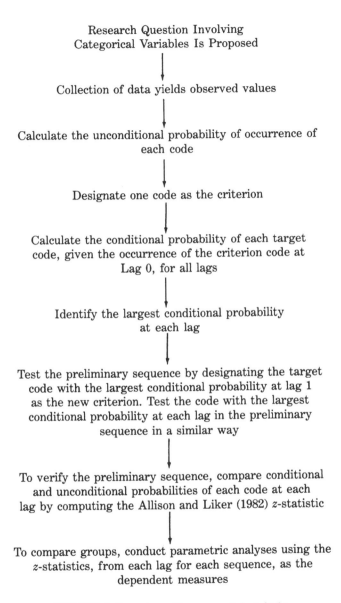

Research Question Involving
Categorical Variables Is Proposed

Collection of data yields observed values

Calculate the unconditional probability of occurrence of
each code

Designate one code as the criterion

Calculate the conditional probability of each target
code, given the occurrence of the criterion code at
Lag 0, for all lags

Identify the largest conditional probability
at each lag

Test the preliminary sequence by designating the target
code with the largest conditional probability at lag 1
as the new criterion. Test the code with the largest
conditional probability at each lag in the preliminary
sequence in a similar way

To verify the preliminary sequence, compare conditional
and unconditional probabilities of each code at each
lag by computing the Allison and Liker (1982) z-statistic

To compare groups, conduct parametric analyses using the
z-statistics, from each lag for each sequence, as the
dependent measures

FIGURE 2. Overview of lag sequential analysis.

OVERVIEW

The purpose of this chapter has been to provide the behavioral scientist with an introduction to two methods for the analysis of sequence in social interaction. These methods are important alternatives to the analysis of rates of behavior, which cannot capture the temporal order of human interaction. In the remainder of this section, log-linear analysis and lag sequential analysis are briefly summarized and contrasted with reference to the example examined throughout this chapter.

In the course of examining the two methods, it was seen that the same raw data set could be analyzed with either procedure. In log-linear analysis, the goal is to identify a model that explains the observed distribution of counts, which are arranged in antecedent code × consequent code subtables (see Table 1). The overall goodness of fit of models is assessed with the likelihood ratio statistic, G^2. The importance of individual elements of the model (i.e., parameters) can be determined by subtracting G^2 values of models including and excluding the parameter of interest. At this stage, the research may be either exploratory or guided by specific hypotheses; in the latter case a model may be predicted on the basis of prior theory. A second goal, suggested by previous research on the association between marital satisfaction and negative affect reciprocity, may be to determine if the fit of certain cells in the contingency table (i.e., W− → H− and H− → W−) covaries with the independent variables of marital satisfaction and attributional style. The fit of individual cells is examined with standardized residuals or Freeman–Tukey deviates. Thus, at the conclusion of the investigation, the log-linear analyst may have an understanding of which variables and which associations among variables are most important in accounting for the observed counts, as well as which cells might be most responsible for the imperfect fit between observed and expected counts.

Lag sequential analysis affords a different perspective on this data set. The goal of this method is to identify the sequence or sequences of codes that are most likely to follow a given code. These conditional probabilities are compared to expected or unconditional probabilities with a modified z-statistic to determine if the sequence they reflect occurs with a probability greater than chance. The marital satisfaction × attributional style groups can then be compared with parametric techniques, treating the z-scores as dependent measures. As with log-linear analysis, lag sequential analysis may proceed in either an exploratory or a hypothesis-driven fashion (or both in a given investigation). Thus with lag sequential analysis, an understanding of the sequences that discriminate between groups can be obtained.

The most obvious distinction to be drawn from this simplified comparison is that lag sequential analysis is more amenable than log-linear analysis to the study of longer sequences of behavior. That is, in log-linear analysis, data of relatively lower order (i.e., comprising sequences of fewer codes, such as antecedent–consequent pairs) will be most common, whereas the sequences identified with lag sequential analysis will typically involve more codes. This implies that only the proximal or immediate effects of coded behaviors on subsequent behaviors can be examined with log-linear analysis, whereas both proximal and distal effects are accessible with lag sequential analysis. A second basic distinction is also apparent. Log-linear analysis is used to discover which parameters are most adequate in accounting for, or modeling, the observed cross-classification of counts. In contrast, lag sequential analysis allows one to discover sequential dependencies among codes. It is these dependencies or patterns that are used to account for differences among groups on some independent measure (e.g., marital satisfaction; attributional style).

In conclusion, both methods of analysis described in this chapter can serve as useful tools to further an understanding of sequence in social interaction. However, log-linear analysis and lag sequential analysis should not be viewed as interchangeable methodologies. Two of the most obvious features that distinguish them have been outlined, and it should be realized that each approach provides unique information. The choice of which method to use will depend upon the purpose of an investigation, and thus it behooves researchers to identify clearly the questions they seek to answer before selecting a means for analyzing temporally ordered data.

ACKNOWLEDGMENTS

Thomas N. Bradbury was supported in the preparation of this chapter by grants from the National Science Foundation (BNS 8813052) and the National Institute of Mental Health (MH09740-01). Frank D. Fincham was supported by a Faculty Scholar Fellowship from the W. T. Grant Foundation and by grants from the National Institute of Child Health and Human Development (R23 HD 20530-01) and the National Institute of Mental Health (MH44078-01).

REFERENCES

Allison, P. D., & Liker, J. K. (1982). Analyzing sequential categorical data on dyadic interaction: A comment on Gottman. *Psychological Bulletin, 91*, 393–403.
Anderson, T. W., & Goodman, L. A. (1957). Statistical inference about Markov chains. *Annals of Mathematical Statistics, 28*, 89–110.
Bradbury, T. N., & Fincham, F. D. (1990). Attributions in marriage: Review and critique. *Psychological Bulletin, 107*, 3–33.
Brown, M. B. (1976). Screening effects in multidimensional contingency tables. *Applied Statistics, 25*, 37–46.
Castellan, N. J., Jr. (1979). The analysis of behavior sequences. In R. B. Cairns (Ed.), *The analysis of social interactions: Methods, issues, and illustrations* (pp. 81–116). Hillsdale, NJ: Erlbaum.

Catalano, R. A., Dooley, D., & Jackson, R. (1983). Selecting a time-series strategy. *Psychological Bulletin, 94*, 506–523.

Chatfield, C. (1980). *The analysis of time series: An introduction* (2nd ed.). London: Chapman and Hall.

Duncan, S., Jr., Kanki, B. G., Mokros, H., & Fiske, D. W. (1984). Pseudounilaterality, simple-rate variables, and other ills to which interaction research is heir. *Journal of Personality and Social Psychology, 46*, 1335–1348.

Fincham, F. D., & O'Leary, K. D. (1983). Causal inferences for spouse behavior in maritally distressed and nondistressed couples. *Journal of Clinical and Social Psychology, 1*, 42–57.

Fincham, F. D., Beach, S. & Nelson, G. (1987). Attributional processes in distressed and nondistressed couples: 3. Causal and responsibility attributions for spouse behavior. *Cognitive Therapy and Research, 11*, 71–86.

Fincham, F. D., & Bradbury, T. N. (1991). Cognition in marriage: A program of research on attributions. In D. Perlman & W. Jones (Eds.), *Advances in personal relationships* (Vol. 2, pp. 159–203). London: Kingsley Publications.

Gottman, J. M. (1979). *Marital interaction: Experimental investigations.* New York: Academic Press.

Gottman, J. M. (1981). *Time-series analysis: A comprehensive introduction for social scientists.* New York: Cambridge University.

Gottman, J. M., & Levenson, R. W. (1985). A valid procedure for obtaining self-report of affect in marital interaction. *Journal of Consulting and Clinical Psychology, 53*, 151–160.

Gottman, J. M., Markman, H., & Notarius, C. (1977). The topography of marital conflict: A sequential analysis of verbal and nonverbal behavior. *Journal of Marriage and the Family, 39*, 461–477.

Heider, F. (1944). Social perception and phenomenal causality. *Psychological Review, 51*, 358–374.

Heider, F. (1958). *The psychology of interpersonal relations.* New York: Wiley.

Holtzworth-Munroe, A., & Jacobson, N. S. (1985). Causal attributions of married couples: When do they search for causes? What do they conclude when they do? *Journal of Personality and Social Psychology, 48*, 1398–1412.

Jones, E. E., & Davis, K. E. (1965). From acts to dispositions: The attribution process in person perception. In L. Berkowitz (Ed.), *Advances in experimental social psychology* (Vol. 2, pp. 220–266). New York: Academic Press.

Kelley, H. H. (1967). Attribution theory in social psychology. In D. Levine (Ed.), *Nebraska Symposium on Motivation* (Vol. 15, pp. 192–238). Lincoln: University of Nebraska Press.

Levenson, R. W., & Gottman, J. M. (1983). Marital interaction: Physiological linkage and affective exchange. *Journal of Personality and Social Psychology, 45*, 587–597.

Levenson, R. W., & Gottman, J. M. (1985). Physiological and affective predictors of change in relationship satisfaction. *Journal of Personality and Social Psychology, 49*, 85–94.

Margolin, G., & Wampold, B. E. (1981). Sequential analysis of conflict and accord in distressed and nondistressed marital partners. *Journal of Consulting and Clinical Psychology, 49*, 554–567.

McCain, L. J., & McCleary, R. (1979). The statistical analysis of the simple interrupted time-series quasi-experiment. In T. D. Cook & D. T. Campbell (Eds.), *Quasi-experimentation: Design & analysis issues for field settings* (pp. 233–293). Boston: Houghton Mifflin.

McCleary, R., & Hay, R. A. (1980). *Applied time series analysis for the social sciences.* Beverly Hills: Sage.

Notarius, C. I. (1981). Assessing sequential dependency in cognitive performance data. In T. V. Merluzzi, C. R. Glass, & M. Genest (Eds.), *Cognitive assessment* (pp. 343–357). New York: Guilford Press.

Phelps, R. E., & Slater, M. A. (1985). Sequential interactions that discriminate high- and low-problem single mother-son dyads. *Journal of Consulting and Clinical Psychology, 53*, 684–692.

Revenstorf, D., Vogel, B., Wegener, C., Hahlweg, K., & Schindler, L. (1980). Escalation phenomena in interaction sequences: An empirical comparison of distressed and non-distressed couples. *Behavior Analysis and Modification, 4*, 97–115.

Sackett, G. P. (1979). The lag sequential analysis of contingency and cyclicity in behavioral interaction research. In J. D. Osofsky (Ed.), *Handbook of infant development* (pp. 623–649). New York: Wiley.

Schaap, C. (1982). *Communication and adjustment in marriage.* The Netherlands: Swets & Zeitlinger B.V.

Ting-Toomey, S. (1983). An analysis of verbal communication patterns in high and low marital adjustment groups. *Human Communication Research, 9*, 306–319.

Wampold, B. E., & Margolin, G. (1982). Nonparametric strategies to test the independence of behavioral states in sequential data. *Psychological Bulletin, 92*, 755–765.

APPENDIX I: FURTHER READINGS ON LOG-LINEAR ANALYSIS AND RELATED TOPICS

Note. For convenience, references are identified as:
[IL] = Introductory level
[AL] = Advanced level
[EA] = Empirical application
[ST] = Specialized topic

Baker, F. B. (1981). Log-linear, logit-linear models: A didactic. *Journal of Educational Statistics, 6*, 75–102. [IL]

Bishop, Y. M. M., Fienberg, S. E., & Holland, P. W. (1975). *Discrete multivariate analysis: Theory and practice.* Cambridge, MA: MIT Press. [AL]

Bonett, D. G., & Bentler, P. M. (1983). Goodness-of-fit procedures for the evaluation and selection of log-linear models. *Psychological Bulletin, 93*, 149–166. [ST]

Brier, S. S. (1982). Analysis of categorical data. In G. Keren (Ed.), *Statistical and methodological issues in psychology and social sciences research* (pp. 347–383). Hillsdale, NJ: Erlbaum. [AL]

Budescu, D. V. (1984). Tests of lagged dominance in sequential dyadic interaction. *Psychological Bulletin, 96*, 402–414. [ST]

Feick, L. F., & Novak, J. A. (1985). Analyzing sequential categorical data on dyadic interaction: Log-linear models exploiting the order in variables. *Psychological Bulletin, 98*, 600–611. [ST]

Fienberg, S. E. (1980). *The analysis of cross-classified categorical data* (2nd ed.). Cambridge, MA: MIT Press. [AL]

Gilbert, G. N. (1981). *Modelling society: An introduction to loglinear analysis for social researchers.* London: George Allen & Unwin. [IL]

Goodman, L. A. (1978). *Analyzing qualitative/categorical data.* Cambridge, MA: Abt Books. [AL]

Gottman, J. M. (1987). The sequential analysis of family interaction. In T. Jacob (Ed.), *Family interaction and psychopathology: Theories, methods, and findings* (pp. 453–478). New York: Plenum Press. [IL]

Gottman, J. M., & Roy, A. K. (1990). *Temporal form: Detecting sequences in social interaction.* New York: Cambridge University Press. [AL]

Green, J. A. (1988). Loglinear analysis of cross-classified ordinal data: Applications in developmental research. *Child Development, 59,* 1–25. [IL]

Haberman, S. J. (1978). *Analysis of qualitative data, Vol. 1: Introductory topics.* New York: Academic Press. [AL]

Haberman, S. J. (1979). *Analysis of qualitative data, Vol. 2: New developments.* New York: Academic Press. [AL]

Hawes, L. C., & Foley, J. M. (1976). Group decisioning: Testing a finite stochastic model. In G. R. Miller (Ed.), *Explorations in interpersonal communication* (pp. 237–254). Beverly Hills: Sage. [EA]

Iacobucci, D., & Wasserman, S. (1988). A general framework for the statistical analysis of sequential dyadic interaction data. *Psychological Bulletin, 103,* 379–390. [AL]

Kennedy, J. J. (1983). *Analyzing qualitative data: Introductory log-linear analysis for behavioral research.* New York: Praeger. [IL]

Knoke, D., & Burke, P. J. (1980). *Log-linear models.* Beverly Hills: Sage. [AL]

Marascuilo, L. A., & Busk, P. L. (1987). Loglinear models: A way to study main effects and interactions for multidimensional contingency tables with categorical data. *Journal of Counseling Psychology, 34,* 443–455. [IL]

Notarius, C. T., Benson, P. R., Sloane, D., Vanzetti, N. A., & Hornyak, L. M. (1989). Exploring the interface between perception and behavior: An analysis of marital interaction in distressed and nondistressed couples. *Behavioral Assessment, 11,* 39–64. [EA]

Shaffer, J. P. (1973). Defining and testing hypotheses in multidimensional contingency tables. *Psychological Bulletin, 79,* 127–141. [AL]

Sillars, A. L., Pike, G. R., Jones, T. S., & Murphy, M. A. (1984). Communication and understanding in marriage. *Human Communication Research, 10,* 317–350. [EA]

Upton, G. J. G. (1978). *The analysis of cross-tabulated data.* New York: Wiley. [AL]

APPENDIX II: FURTHER READINGS ON LAG SEQUENTIAL ANALYSIS AND RELATED TOPICS

Note. For convenience, references are identified as:
[IL] = Introductory level
[AL] = Advanced level
[EA] = Empirical application
[ST] = Specialized topic

Bakeman, R. (1978). Untangling streams of behavior: Sequential analyses of observational data. In G. P. Sackett (Ed.), *Observing behavior, Vol. 2: Data collection and analysis methods* (pp. 63–78). Baltimore: University Park Press. [IL]

Bakeman, R. (1983). Computing lag sequential statistics: The ELAG program. *Behavior Research Methods and Instrumentation, 15,* 530–535. [ST]

Bakeman, R., & Adamson, L. B. (1984). Coordinating attention to people and objects in mother-infant and peer-infant interaction. *Child Development, 55,* 1278–1289. [EA]

Bakeman, R., & Dabbs, J. M., Jr. (1976). Social interaction observed: Some approaches to the analysis of behavior streams. *Personality and Social Psychology Bulletin, 2,* 335–345. [IL]

Bakeman, R., & Gottman, J. M. (1990). Applying observational methods: A systematic view. In J. Osofsky (Ed.), *Handbook of infant development* (2nd ed.; pp. 181–223). New York: Wiley. [IL]

Bakeman, R., & Gottman, J. M. (1986). *Observing interaction: An introduction to sequential analysis.* New York: Cambridge University Press. [IL]

Biglan, A., Hops, H., Sherman, L., Friedman, L. S., Arthur, J., & Osteen, V. (1985). Problem-solving interactions of depressed women and their husbands. *Behavior Therapy, 16*, 431–451. [EA]

Cousins, P. C., & Power, T. G. (1986). Quantifying family process: Issues in the analysis of interaction sequences. *Family Process, 25*, 89–105. [IL]

Gottman, J. M. (1980). Consistency of nonverbal affect and affect reciprocity in marital interaction. *Journal of Consulting and Clinical Psychology, 48*, 711–717. [EA]

Gottman, J. M. (1983). How children become friends. *Monographs of the Society for Research in Child Development, 48*(3, Serial No. 201). [EA]

Gottman, J. M., & Bakeman, R. (1979). The sequential analysis of observational data. In M. E. Lamb, S. J. Suomi, & G. R. Stephenson (Eds.), *Social interaction analysis: Methodological issues* (pp. 185–206). Madison: University of Wisconsin Press. [AL]

Gottman, J. M., & Notarius, C. (1978). Sequential analysis of observational data using Markov chains. In T. Kratochwill (Ed.), *Single subject research: Strategies for evaluating change* (pp. 237–285). New York: Academic Press. [AL]

Hahlweg, K., Goldstein, M. J., Nuechterlein, K. H., Magana, A. B., Mintz, J., Doane, J. A., Miklowitz, D. J., & Snyder, K. S. (1989). Expressed emotion and patient-relative interaction in families of recent onset schizophrenics. *Journal of Consulting and Clinical Psychology, 57*, 11–18. [EA]

Kienapple, K. (1987). The microanalytic data analysis package. *Behavior Research Methods, Instruments, and Computers, 19*, 335–337. [ST]

Lichtenberg, J. W., & Heck, E. J. (1986). Analysis of sequence and pattern in process research. *Journal of Counseling Psychology, 33*, 170–181. [IL]

Lytton, H., & Zwirner, W. (1975). Compliance and its controlling stimuli observed in a natural setting. *Developmental Psychology, 11*, 769–779. [EA]

MacTurk, R. H., McCarthy, M. E., Vietze, P. M., & Yarrow, L. J. (1987). Sequential analysis of mastery behavior in 6- and 12-month-old infants. *Developmental Psychology, 23*, 199–203. [EA]

Maxim, P. E., Bowden, D. M., & Sackett, G. P. (1976). Ultradian rhythms of solitary and social behavior in rhesus monkeys. *Physiology and Behavior, 17*, 337–344. [EA]

Notarius, C. I., Krokoff, L. J., & Markman, H. J. (1981). Analysis of observational data. In E. E. Filsinger & R. A. Lewis (Eds.), *Assessing marriage: New behavioral approaches* (pp. 197–216). Beverly Hills: Sage. [IL]

Sackett, G. P. (1978). Measurement in observational research. In G. P. Sackett (Ed.), *Observing behavior, Vol. 2: Data collection and analysis methods* (pp. 25–43). Baltimore: University Park Press. [IL]

Sackett, G. P. (1980). Lag sequential analysis as a data reduction technique in social interaction research. In D. B. Sawin, R. C. Hawkins, L. O. Walker, & J. H. Penticuff (Eds.), *Exceptional infant, Vol. 4: Psychosocial risks in infant-environment transactions* (pp. 300–340). New York: Brunner/Mazel. [IL]

Sackett, G. P., Holm, R., Crowley, C., & Henkins, A. (1979). A FORTRAN program for lag sequential analysis of contingency and cyclicity in behavioral interaction data. *Behavioral Research Methods and Instrumentation, 11*, 366–378. [ST]

Suen, H. K., & Ary, D. (1989). *Analyzing quantitative behavioral observation data.* Hillsdale, NJ: Erlbaum. [AL]

Wampold, B. E. (1984). Tests of dominance in sequential categorical data. *Psychological Bulletin, 96*, 424–429. [ST]

Wampold, B. E. (1986). State of the art in sequential analysis: Comment on Lichtenberg and Heck. *Journal of Counseling Psychology, 33*, 182–185. [IL]

Williamson, R. N., & Fitzpatrick, M. A. (1985). Two approaches to marital interaction: Relational control patterns in marital types. *Communication Monographs, 52*, 236–252. [EA]

Index

Lightning Source UK Ltd.
Milton Keynes UK
UKHW041545271119
354321UK00002B/131/P